The Politics of Consolation

THE POLITICS OF CONSOLATION

Memory and the Meaning of September 11

Christina Simko

OXFORD
UNIVERSITY PRESS

OXFORD
UNIVERSITY PRESS

Oxford University Press is a department of the University of Oxford.
It furthers the University's objective of excellence in research, scholarship,
and education by publishing worldwide.

Oxford New York
Auckland Cape Town Dar es Salaam Hong Kong Karachi
Kuala Lumpur Madrid Melbourne Mexico City Nairobi
New Delhi Shanghai Taipei Toronto

With offices in
Argentina Austria Brazil Chile Czech Republic France Greece
Guatemala Hungary Italy Japan Poland Portugal Singapore
South Korea Switzerland Thailand Turkey Ukraine Vietnam

Oxford is a registered trade mark of Oxford University Press
in the UK and certain other countries.

Published in the United States of America by
Oxford University Press
198 Madison Avenue, New York, NY 10016

Library of Congress Cataloging-in-Publication Data
Simko, Christina.
 The politics of consolation : memory and the meaning of September 11 / Christina
Simko.
    p.   cm.
 Includes bibliographical references and index.
 ISBN 978-0-19-938178-4 (hardcover : alk. paper) — ISBN 978-0-19-938179-1
(pbk. : alk. paper) 1. Disasters—Political aspects—United States. 2. Collective
memory—Political aspects—United States. 3. Consolation—Political aspects.
4. September 11 Terrorist Attacks, 2001—Political aspects. I. Title.
 E179.S58 2015
 303.48'5—dc23
                        2014026939

CONTENTS

PREFACE

When Hurricane Katrina hit the Gulf Coast in the summer of 2005, U.S. President George W. Bush was at his ranch in Crawford, Texas. En route back to Washington on August 31—two days after the storm made landfall near the city of New Orleans—Air Force One flew low over the devastated area. The president gazed out the window, surveying the damage. He did not touch down.

Back in the capital, Bush delivered remarks from the White House Rose Garden. His speech enumerated the human and material resources that the federal government had devoted to the relief effort: the Federal Emergency Management Agency (FEMA) had "deployed more than 50 disaster medical assistance teams"; the National Guard had "nearly 11,000 guardsmen on State active duty to assist Governors and local officials"; the Department of Transportation had "provided more than 400 trucks to move 1,000 truckloads containing 5.4 million Meals, Ready to Eat or MREs, 13.4 million liters of water, 10,400 tarps, 3.4 million pounds of ice . . . 135,000 blankets, and 11,000 cots."[1] Bush concluded with a pledge that the Gulf Coast region, and indeed the nation as a whole, would emerge stronger from the crisis: "New communities will flourish; the great city of New Orleans will be back on its feet; and America will be a stronger place for it."[2] But the images of the disaster that were ubiquitous in the media seemed to belie Bush's pledge: bloated corpses floating in contaminated floodwaters; refugees—overwhelmingly poor and black, many elderly and sick—in the Superdome without air conditioning, showers, or functioning toilets; children crying for food.

Prominent media outlets swiftly called Bush to account for his failures of leadership. In doing so, however, they not only cited his bureaucratic shortcomings—his failures as the nation's chief administrator. They also condemned the president for his failure to provide moral and symbolic guidance in the face of such profound human suffering. On September 1, the *New York Times* editorialized that the president's speech at the Rose

Garden was "one of the worst speeches of his life," denouncing it as "of a quality more appropriate for an Arbor Day celebration" than a national calamity.[3] More specifically, the *Times* suggested, Bush had neglected to address "the level of national distress and the need for words of consolation and wisdom."[4] Likewise, *Time* magazine reflected that the president "came across as cool to the point of uncaring," that "when it came to enacting the role of Consoler in Chief, he sometimes sounded more like a quartermaster, running through long lists of things the government was sending to the Gulf Coast, rather than empathizing with people."[5]

These critiques of the president, articulated promptly and forcefully, illuminate the core insight that animates this book. Integral to American political leadership is the task of providing existential guidance, addressing not only the symbolic matters surrounding collective identity—"who Americans are" as a people—but also even more fundamental human questions about the meaning of suffering, loss, and finitude. Whatever else Americans expected of Bush in those last days of August 2005—and it is clear that he fell short of the mark as an administrator, too—many looked to the president for consolation, for wisdom and insight that would ameliorate a palpable sense of national crisis, even despair, and forge a path forward. Such moments—when leaders fall short—lay bare these generally unstated expectations in a particularly powerful way.

Indeed, in the face of mounting criticism, Bush would eventually work to embody this consoler role—to address the meaning of the disaster for the nation and its citizenry—with a speech in Jackson Square on September 15.[6] For many, perhaps most, Americans, it was too little and too late. Much more than his speech in Jackson Square, the image of Bush gazing out the window of Air Force One at the wreckage would come to symbolize his response to Katrina, as would the sound bite from a September 2 address in Mobile, Alabama, in which he said to FEMA director Michael Brown: "Brownie, you're doing a heck of a job."[7] Nevertheless, the president eventually found himself accountable to the symbolic dimensions of his office, working to communicate empathy, promote solidarity, and provide consolation.

Accordingly, this book probes the existential dimensions of American politics, examining how U.S. leaders have engaged in what I call "political consolation" through the prism of some of the nation's most gripping crises. At the heart of the book is an investigation of the response to the events of September 11, 2001. How did American political leaders explain the violence that erupted on that sunny Tuesday morning? How, especially, did they describe the meaning of the suffering and death that the day wrought? The speeches I examined reveal an intricate effort to provide consolation and symbolic orientation, and this effort reverberated in the elaborate commemorative rituals headlined by political leaders in the years that followed.

Yet September 11 took on meaning primarily in and through its association with pivotal moments from the American past. In the midst of widespread public mourning, it was memory that provided consolation, orientation, and hope. At times, these meaning-conferring memories took the shape of overt comparisons or analogies—to Pearl Harbor or Iwo Jima, Gettysburg or Valley Forge. But even when political leaders asserted no specific comparisons, the very symbols that once endowed these pivotal moments in the national past with meaning resurfaced more subtly, giving shape and significance to the present as it unfolded. The more I worked to understand the meanings that political leaders attributed to September 11, the more I became convinced that—for all the talk of historical rupture, of unprecedented events that ushered in a new era—doing so would require me to examine a much longer tradition of political consolation discourse.

I therefore found myself not only tracking the historical analogies or comparisons that pervaded interpretations of 9/11, but also tracing the long history of consolation discourse in American politics, to understand how and why the frameworks that provided meaning in the aftermath of September 11 were so readily available from the first. Before delving into the interpretive response to September 11, then, I present this broad history, a history that I argue is an essential precursor to understanding the ways that American leaders confronted the existential matters raised so powerfully by 9/11. In presenting historical texts, I am guided not by the historian's goal of uncovering new material from an archive—indeed, my concern is predominantly with well-known moments in American political life—but the interpretive sociologist's goal of placing them within a common frame that yields fresh theoretical insight.

My commitment to placing my contemporary narrative within a rich historical context has led me to structure this book in a somewhat unconventional fashion. Its two parts—a historical account of watershed moments in political consolation discourse followed by a more detailed analysis of the intricate interpretive work through which the events of September 11 assumed shape and meaning over more than a decade—could be read as stand-alone texts. My hope, however, is that providing the reader with a more sustained immersion in historical texts will enrich his or her encounter with the more contemporary material, illuminating—as Philip Abrams put it—the "struggle to create a future *out of* the past" in a way that simply noting parallels between past and present cannot.[8]

ACKNOWLEDGMENTS

This book would not have been possible without extraordinary support from both individuals and institutions. First, the Department of Sociology at the University of Virginia proved an outstanding place to become a cultural sociologist. I owe an exceptional debt to my mentor, Jeffrey Olick. Jeff's intellectual generosity has been incomparable, and this project emerged in and through our ongoing conversation about the place of suffering in the sociological tradition. I am grateful for the many times he read the manuscript with attentiveness and care, for his incisive commentary, and for his moral support over many years. Most of all, I am grateful that our conversation continues. I am also fortunate to have encountered a number of other dedicated teachers who shaped my intellectual agenda decisively. In particular, James Davison Hunter and Sarah Corse provided thoughtful guidance and encouragement at critical moments throughout this project and commented perceptively on the manuscript. Alon Confino also offered valuable feedback from a historian's perspective.

I completed much of the book as a postdoctoral fellow at the Institute for Advanced Studies in Culture (IASC) at the University of Virginia. In addition to providing generous financial support, the IASC offered an unparalleled intellectual environment that simultaneously challenged and sustained me. Thanks to James Davison Hunter and his colleagues for the scholarly community they have cultivated, and to the fellows for the conversation and camaraderie they offered on a daily basis. I benefited especially from the discussions that took place in the Culture and Catastrophe working group, organized by Joshua Yates and George Thomas, and from the opportunity to present a portion of this book at the IASC's annual fellows' colloquium. The Dietrich School of Arts and Sciences at the University of Pittsburgh also provided generous fellowship support during the final stages of the project.

My editor, James Cook, took an immediate interest in the project, provided valuable feedback, and shepherded the manuscript through the publication process with care. Three anonymous reviewers for Oxford University Press offered exceptionally thoughtful comments that improved the final product significantly. Thanks also to Peter Worger at OUP for his assistance and to Susie Hara for excellent copyediting.

Numerous other colleagues and teachers provided guidance, insight, and support in various ways. They include Claudio Benzecry, Tristan Bridges, Joseph Davis, Jennifer Geddes, David Hsu, Megan Juelfs-Swanson, Krishan Kumar, Claire Maiers, Charles Mathewes, Sarah Mosseri, Daniel Potter, Licheng Qian, Isaac Ariail Reed, Greta Snyder, Hephzibah Strmic-Pawl, Julia Ticona, Stephen Vaisey, Catalina Vallejo, Robin Wagner-Pacifici, and Haiming Yan. I am especially grateful to Benjamin Snyder and Tara Tober for many years of intellectual support and friendship. The students in Jeff Olick's spring 2013 graduate seminar on Evil, Disaster, and Suffering provided a lively context for engaging theoretical issues at the core of this book; I thank them all for their energy and enthusiasm.

Finally, I am deeply grateful to the many friends and family members who have loyally supported me throughout this process. Foremost among them is Matt Martin, whose generosity and partnership have sustained me more than he knows. These words would never have been written without his unyielding encouragement, patience, and confidence.

Introduction

Just before 8:46 a.m. on September 11, 2002—the first anniversary of September 11—New York City Mayor Michael Bloomberg stood on the site where the World Trade Center's Twin Towers once stretched into the sky. "Again, today, we are a nation who mourns," he began. "Again, today, we take into our hearts and minds those who perished on this site one year ago, and those who came to toil in the rubble to bring order out of chaos, and those who throughout these last 12 months have struggled to help us make sense of our despair."[1] As the clock turned to 8:46—the precise moment when American Airlines Flight 11 struck the north tower a year before—Bloomberg invited onlookers in New York to join with President George W. Bush as he led the nation in a moment of silence from the White House lawn. He then introduced New York Governor George Pataki, who delivered a eulogy for the fallen.

Perhaps surprisingly, Pataki's eulogy made no mention of hijacked planes carrying unsuspecting passengers or office workers immersed in quotidian routines. Indeed, it did not even mention the firefighters, police officers, and other first responders so often lauded for the courage they exhibited on September 11, 2001. Pataki turned, instead, to familiar words penned in a bygone era—words that had almost unquestionably become America's most famous eulogy in the intervening years. "One hundred thirty-nine years ago," Bloomberg said as he introduced Pataki, "President Abraham Lincoln looked out at his wounded nation, as he stood on a once beautiful field that had become its saddest and largest burying ground. Then, it was Gettysburg. Today, it is the World Trade Center, where we gather on native soil to share our common grief."[2] The eulogy that followed, of course, was Lincoln's Gettysburg Address:

> Four score and seven years ago our fathers brought forth on this continent, a new nation, conceived in liberty, and dedicated to the proposition that all men are created equal.
>
> Now we are engaged in a great civil war, testing whether that nation, or any nation so conceived and so dedicated, can long endure. We are met on a great battle-field of that war. We have come to dedicate a portion of that field, as a final resting place for those who here gave their lives that that nation might live. It is altogether fitting and proper that we should do this.
>
> But, in a larger sense, we cannot dedicate—we cannot consecrate—we cannot hallow—this ground. The brave men, living and dead, who struggled here, have consecrated it, far above our poor power to add or detract. The world will little note, nor long remember what we say here, but it can never forget what they did here. It is for us the living, rather, to be dedicated here to the unfinished work which they who fought here have thus far so nobly advanced.
>
> It is rather for us to be here dedicated to the great task remaining before us—that from these honored dead we take increased devotion to that cause for which they gave the last full measure of devotion—that we here highly resolve that these dead shall not have died in vain—that this nation, under God, shall have a new birth of freedom—and that this government of the people, by the people, for the people, shall not perish from the earth.[3]

With that, former New York Mayor Rudolph Giuliani, who had been in office on September 11, 2001, began reading the names of "these honored dead"—not, of course, the fallen soldiers Lincoln had eulogized over a century before at Gettysburg, but the people who had perished in the Twin Towers in 2001. "Gordon M. Aamoth Junior. Edelmiro Abad. Maria Rose Abad. Andrew Anthony Abate. Vincent Abate. Laurence Christopher Abel. . . ."[4]

Shortly after 9:00 a.m. on September 11, 2002, President George W. Bush, Defense Secretary Donald Rumsfeld, and other public officials joined mourners at the Pentagon, just outside the nation's capital. In contrast to Pataki's borrowed eulogy, the words these officials offered were ostensibly new—penned with the specific intention of memorializing the 184 people who had perished at the Pentagon in September of 2001. Yet a careful reading reveals curious resonances with the famous words uttered at Gettysburg in 1863 and repeated again that very morning in lower Manhattan. Early in his address, Rumsfeld explained to his listeners that "we meet on a battlefield"—a battlefield whose identity as such was only concealed by "the singular devotion of the men and women who worked day and night to fulfill a solemn vow that not one stone of this building would be out of place on this anniversary."[5] And the individuals who perished on that battlefield, Rumsfeld asserted, died for a larger cause: "We're here today," he explained, "to honor those who died in this place and to rededicate ourselves to the cause for which they gave their lives, the cause of human liberty."[6] Even in the midst of such admirable tenacity and resolve—the "fierceness and resilience" that the workers had displayed in rebuilding the Pentagon—Rumsfeld exhorted: "we must not forget what happened here."[7]

Bush, too, seemed occasionally to echo the bygone era from which Pataki had borrowed more explicitly. Although those who perished on September 11 "died in tragedy," he said, "they"—like those honored dead who fell at Gettysburg—"did not die in vain."[8] For they perished—Bush suggested—in a noble cause. Their deaths "set in motion the first great struggle of a new century," Bush explained.[9] And "[t]he enemies who struck us," he said, "will be stopped," for they are "opposed by freedom-loving people in many lands."[10]

Unlike Bloomberg and Pataki, Rumsfeld and Bush never mentioned Lincoln overtly. Yet the language they employed in memorializing those who died on September 11 rendered these losses explicable as part of the cause that had also claimed so many lives at Gettysburg—the quest to pre-serve freedom, liberty, and democracy. Like Lincoln, Rumsfeld and Bush called upon their audience to take up the cause. Through victory, they as-serted, the living would ensure that the fallen "did not die in vain"—that their deaths were not meaningless losses, but *sacrifices* in a larger quest.

POLITICS AND CONSOLATION

What meaning or purpose can be found in calamity and suffering? This question is perennial, dating back to the book of Job and even further. It is a core subject for theological and philosophical meditation, and addressing it has been central to the pastoral vocation of clergy. Today, however, it is also a significant part of political leadership. In times of uncertainty, shock, or despair, we frequently look to political leaders to provide answers to such questions, to offer comfort and reassurance, and to remind us that we are not alone. Our leaders, in turn, increasingly recognize consolation as a cultural expectation, and they often work hard to fulfill this role. Indeed, many are remembered particularly for how they did so: think not only of Lincoln at Gettysburg, but also of Franklin Delano Roosevelt's D-Day prayer, Robert Kennedy's moving speech following the assassination of

Martin Luther King, Jr., or Ronald Reagan's eulogy for the crew members who died aboard the Challenger.

Nevertheless, the task of consolation presents significant challenges for leaders, bringing them face-to-face with events that threaten cherished collective identities and received national narratives. The events of September 11, 2001, for instance, powerfully threatened the image of the American nation as a "city upon a hill" and a model to the world, an image inspired by the biblical Sermon on the Mount.[11] Why would this "city upon a hill," a bulwark for freedom and democracy, be assaulted with such violence? In such moments, politicians are generally expected to shore up familiar collective narratives, to restore the self-images at the heart of national identity.

Yet calamitous events also raise even deeper and more fundamental questions—questions we might categorize as existential. What is the meaning of human suffering? What is the place of evil in the world? How can we come to terms with the finality of death and loss? Indeed, this book's central claim is that American political leaders frequently assume responsibility for addressing such existential dilemmas, and that they face a powerful cultural expectation to perform this role. In the pages that follow, I delve into the official speechmaking that has followed national crises from the founding moment of the Republic to the dawn of the twenty-first century, developing a historical account of American political consolation. What terms and tropes, ideas and images, have American political leaders deployed in their efforts to come to terms with collective crises and the suffering they unleash? How has consolation discourse changed over time? How do earlier moments in this trajectory bear on subsequent speechmaking? I then present a detailed interpretation of the discourse surrounding September 11, attending to the interplay between past and present and examining the specific challenges of political consolation in the contemporary moment.

Before undertaking the historical narrative, the remainder of the introduction provides an orientation to the basic theoretical commitments that animate this book. The effort to understand and explain suffering is a basic human task, and part of my purpose is to illuminate continuities between political speechmaking and the meditations of theologians, philosophers, and clergy. I begin, then, by outlining the history of this task in broad strokes, examining how it took on new force in the Enlightenment and how the rise of the nation-state provided fresh vocabularies for addressing age-old dilemmas. More recently, however, the nation-state's status as a, if not *the*, central purveyor of collective meanings has eroded,[12] a development that I suggest is bound up with the emergence of "trauma" as an increasingly pervasive frame for collective suffering. More and more, calamitous events are understood through a traumatic lens—as leaving indelible wounds on the body politic—and I consider how the recent discourse on cultural trauma[13] can help us understand the challenges of political consolation in the contemporary moment. Following this broad framing account, I describe the task of political consolation in more detail and outline the organization of the book.

SUFFERING AND THE NATION

Though the effort to interpret suffering is a basic human task, numerous commentators suggest that it seems to have taken on special force in modernity.[14] Enlightenment thought unsettled theistic views of the world, and the great philosophers—among them Hume and Leibniz, Rousseau and Voltaire—vigorously engaged the question of how a just, benevolent, and omnipotent God could allow the evil and suffering they so plainly observed.[15] Hume formulated the problem memorably: "Is he willing to prevent evil, but not able? then he is impotent. Is he able, but not willing? then he is malevolent. Is he both able and willing? Whence then is evil?"[16] As he grappled with these questions, Leibniz penned his famous 1710 treatise *Theodicy*, which mounted an elaborate defense of God by advancing the thesis that we live in "the best of all possible worlds."[17] Yet for many, such justificatory vocabularies failed to satisfy. The earthquake that devastated the city of Lisbon in 1755 has come, in retrospect, to represent a watershed moment, after which defenses of God—the vocabularies Leibniz termed "theodicy"—seemed to crumble with unprecedented finality.[18] Voltaire's *Candide*, with its withering satire of Leibnizian optimism, is emblematic.[19]

Yet the existential matters underlying Enlightenment theodicy—the meaning of suffering, the nature of evil, the quest for transcendence in the face of finitude—only became more pressing. Modern narratives promised to extend the human capacity for prediction and control. And alongside this progressive teleology emerged a distinctively modern conviction that suffering is not inevitable but, on the contrary, surmountable, reshaping basic cultural expectations concerning the role of suffering in human life and rendering confrontations with calamity increasingly problematic.[20]

Two centuries after Leibniz, Max Weber offered a sociological perspective on these historical transformations.[21] Weber appropriated the language of "theodicy" for social theory, using the term in a general analytic sense to capture interpretive vocabularies across religious traditions that endowed evil, suffering, and inequity with meaning.[22] As the prevailing image of the world became increasingly rationalized, Weber argued, explanations or interpretations that rendered apparent injustices comprehensible became ever more imperative: "The need for an ethical interpretation of the 'meaning' of the distribution of fortunes among men increased with the growing rationality of conceptions of the world," Weber wrote.[23] By the standards of a rational worldview, "[i]ndividually 'undeserved' woe was all too frequent; not 'good' but 'bad' men succeeded."[24] The chasm between cultural expectations and concrete experiences with hardship and suffering opened wider, and theodicy—in Weber's broad, sociological sense—emerged to address that gap.

The existential strand powerfully evident in these passages from Weber reverberates in an ongoing, though not self-consciously integrated, line of sociological theory. Peter Berger, Colin Campbell, Eva Illouz, and others have powerfully argued that the basic questions of meaning that Weber captured under the rubric of theodicy are not merely the province of theology and philosophy or even religion broadly conceived.[25] They are, instead, core human questions that permeate secular culture as well. As Berger and his colleagues put it: "Modern society has threatened the plausibility of religious theodicies, but it has not removed the experiences that call for them."[26] The fundamental questions that plagued Job, Leibniz, and Voltaire clearly resonate within our own cultural and historical moment, even if the terms in which they are articulated have profoundly changed.[27]

Perhaps more than any other modern institution, the nation-state provides collective meaning—interpretive frames that offer moral and symbolic orientation in an uncertain, and often perilous, world.[28] Drawing the comparison between nations and religions as forms of collective life, Benedict Anderson argues that the "imagined community" of the nation provides collective narratives within which discrete events, and indeed individual lives, take on transcendent meaning and significance.[29] Just as theology "responds to obscure intimations of immortality . . . by transforming fatality into continuity (karma, original sin, etc.)," so, too, does the imagined community of the nation affect "a secular transformation of fatality into continuity, contingency into meaning."[30] National narratives, then, not only offer a source of collective identity and solidarity, but also address abiding existential questions of the sort that Weber associated with theodicy—fundamental human insecurities concerning suffering and mortality. Even more, nations—as forms of collective life—took shape as part of the continual human quest to come to terms with suffering and finitude.[31]

National narratives confer such existential meaning largely through shared memories, the prevailing sense of a common past that underwrites powerful bonds in the present. The nation-state's "transformation of fatality into continuity," that is, takes place through stories that integrate individuals into communities whose roots are understood as deep, even perennial, and whose bonds are perceived as indissoluble.[32] These links create what Robert Bellah and his colleagues term a "community of memory" that is continuously engaged in retelling its meaning-conferring constitutive narrative.[33] Understanding the existential power of national narratives, then—their ability to provide consolation in times of uncertainty or anguish—requires attention to collective memory, to the special role that images of the past play in imbuing subsequent challenges with meaning.[34]

Memory scholar Astrid Erll captures this interplay between past and present with the twin concepts of *remediation* and *premediation*; I adopt this conceptual apparatus in the pages that follow to illuminate how, specifically, symbolism inherited from the past comes to serve as a source of orientation and solace in the present. First, *remediation* captures how the past is re-presented, and thus in some sense refashioned or reinterpreted, in new and often disparate contexts.[35] When politicians turned to Lincoln on the first anniversary of September 11—whether explicitly, like Bloomberg and Pataki, or implicitly, like Bush and Rumsfeld—they remediated this iconic moment, endowing it with new significance. Second, *premediation* captures how symbolic frameworks inherited from the past impinge upon our understanding of the present even as it unfolds; "existent media which circulate in a given society," Erll explains, "provide schemata for new experience and its representation."[36] Indeed, Lincoln's powerful interpretation of national suffering also premediated September 11, providing some of the very symbolism through which the day's chaos and uncertainty were understood from the first. At times, the meaning-conferring power of the past is quite overt or obvious, but premediation also reveals how the past infuses and structures the present "inconspicuously," even unconsciously, as we reflexively turn to familiar frames to impose order upon new and unsettling events.[37]

The nation-state, of course, is neither monolithic nor unchanging, and its centrality as a source of collective meaning has waxed and waned over time. Most importantly in the context of this study, a number of authors have argued that the nation-state's authority and legitimacy—and thus its centrality as a meaning-conferring "community of memory"—have declined significantly over the past several decades.[38] Though there are certainly debates about timing, the Second World War is frequently cited as a decisive crisis point for the nation-state and its constitutive narratives.[39] Even more, World War II—and especially the atrocities associated with the Holocaust—is often understood as a crisis point for representation and meaning in general. Jean-François Lyotard famously argued that the

Holocaust marked the dawn of the "postmodern condition," defined by its "incredulity" toward grand narrative.[40] In a similar vein, Emmanuel Levinas theorized that the Holocaust undermined any possibility for theodicy, revealing "the disproportion between suffering and every theodicy . . . with a glaring, obvious clarity."[41] And the philosopher Susan Neiman identifies the Holocaust as a watershed moment on the order of the Lisbon earthquake, suggesting that these events mark "the beginning and the end of the modern."[42]

Accounts identifying a postwar crisis of representation frequently emanate from Western Europe, and the United States has, of course, followed a trajectory distinct from—though very much intertwined with—the European context. The social and cultural upheavals of the 1960s and 1970s brought a pivotal "time of trial" for the American nation, chipping away at triumphalist, even messianic, narratives as their darker implications were manifest—both abroad in Vietnam and at home in the form of political violence.[43] The 1980s and 1990s brought deepening political polarization and the rancorous debates that James Davison Hunter characterized as "culture wars"—debates that revealed profound dissensus on the meaning of America and archetypal national values such as freedom and liberty, equality and justice, tolerance and pluralism.[44] More recent research suggests that these political-cultural rifts have continued to deepen.[45]

In the United States and beyond, then, the postwar era has called into question national narratives as a particular source of collective meaning, as well as the very possibility of collective meaning in the first place. Amidst these challenges has arisen a growing sense that history is traumatic—that collective suffering cannot be adequately explained or interpreted, but instead leaves enduring, even indelible, wounds. Just as the older language of theodicy once compelled Enlightenment philosophers, the language of cultural trauma has become a central prism for understanding collective suffering in our own time.

CULTURAL TRAUMA

Originally, trauma referred to a physical wound, a bodily injury, and indeed the term still carries that meaning—as in the "trauma center" of a hospital. The contemporary sense of trauma as a psychic wound originated in the curious effects of "railway spine": victims of railway accidents exhibited symptoms whose origins could not be traced to physical causes.[46] Eventually, trauma took on a strictly psychological meaning, codified in the psychiatric diagnosis of post-traumatic stress disorder.[47] Unable to fully process or assimilate a catastrophic event, the sufferer experiences intrusive recollection: memories of the traumatic moment return, seemingly of their own volition, against the sufferer's will.[48] Today, however, trauma is not only a diagnostic category; it has also "infiltrate[d] social discourse" and become a moral and cultural category, a ubiquitous frame for filtering painful experiences whose effects are understood to be ineradicable.[49]

Discussions of "cultural,"[50] "collective,"[51] or "national"[52] trauma extend the metaphor to the level of the community. In recent years, Jeffrey Alexander, Ron Eyerman, and their associates have pioneered an influential approach to cultural trauma, which has now been applied across a wide range of cases spanning disparate geographical locations and historical periods.[53] Cultural traumas, they theorize, are crises that produce a breach in collective narratives, creating "wounds to social identity"[54] and setting off "a deep-going public discourse" that questions and interrogates the very foundation of that identity.[55] Ultimately, such events leave "indelible marks upon . . . group consciousness, marking [the collectivity's] memories forever and changing [its] future identity in fundamental and irrevocable ways."[56]

Arguably, cultural traumas become increasingly common in response to the pervasive challenges to collective meaning discussed above. Indeed, numerous scholars have suggested that trauma and atrocity have now supplanted heroism and triumph as the linchpins of collective identity.[57] Shared suffering has perhaps always played a role in generating social solidarity and underwriting group identity,[58] but over the past several decades, the work of mourning traumas has in many ways become more central to collective life than that of celebrating triumphs.[59] In Bernhard Giesen's apt phrase, "victims assume the place that was, before, the place of heroes."[60] Similarly, while state leaders once called forth images of a glorious past in order to legitimate their authority,[61] today, legitimacy is increasingly contingent upon public confrontations with shameful aspects of the past and public atonement for misdeeds, a shift Jeffrey Olick refers to as the rise of a "politics of regret."[62] The constitutive narratives that define nations as "communities of memory" are thus increasingly preoccupied with the darker aspects of the past, including both suffering inflicted *upon* the collectivity and suffering perpetrated *by* it.

In this vein, historian Frank Ankersmit argues that a "traumatic experience of history" is a distinctive feature of contemporary Western historical consciousness.[63] Borrowing terminology from Pierre Janet, Ankersmit explains: "whereas 'normal' history is the result of association, of a narrative integration or concatenation of experiences so that they can be 'appropriated' or 'owned' by us, 'traumatic' history is the result of a process of dissociation, of presenting our faculty of historical and narrative association with a challenge that it is, as yet, unable to meet."[64] Collective traumas, then, interrupt the constitutive narratives that provide cultural foundations for "imagined communities," posing representational challenges that these narratives—or rather, their purveyors—struggle to meet. The unfolding present cannot be unproblematically reconciled with the received narrative of the past and the future it envisions. "Collective suffering" then takes on "the features of a reality that is continuously most painfully present to us, but that we are, at the same time, unable to assimilate in ourselves."[65] And this inability to assimilate calamitous experiences leaves the collectivity unable to move forward in time beyond the moment of injury.[66] Collective traumas may even remain "unassimilable" across generations, creating breaches in collective narratives that endure well after individuals who experienced the events first-hand are gone.[67]

Alexander and his colleagues rightly underscore the role of "carrier groups" in actively constructing cultural traumas. As Alexander puts it, "cultural traumas are for the most part historically made, not born," and they come into being when "[c]ollective actors 'decide' to represent social pain as a fundamental threat to their sense of who they are, where they came from, and where they want to go."[68] Crucial as the cultural work of carrier groups may be, however, the core of the trauma concept is a sense of "what the past does *to* us," the interpretive and representational struggles that ensue when we cannot forge a place for an event in existing narratives.[69] Ankersmit's conception of traumatic history captures this interpretive struggle, in which collective actors grapple with painful histories that they cannot quite assimilate. In this sense, trauma does not inhere strictly in the event itself, nor is it determined solely by its representation. It emerges, instead, in the interplay between them, structured powerfully by cultural and historical context.[70] And our own, again, is a context in which the work of assimilating suffering seems to have become especially challenging. As Weber argued, in a world envisioned as orderly and rational, suffering and misfortune come to seem ever more random and senseless. Trauma represents an inability to bridge the gap between cultural expectations and concrete experiences, instances when we are unable to forget our suffering or fully move beyond it. It is these interpretive struggles—the interaction between anomalous events and extant narrative frames—that concern me here.

What happens, then, when history is unassimilable and a catastrophic event becomes a cultural trauma? Eyerman suggests that cultural traumas result in the disorientation and meaninglessness that Émile Durkheim captured with the concept of "anomie."[71] Cultural trauma, he writes, is "a form of identity crisis in which a collectivity loses the secure sense of itself and seems to be adrift, existing in that liminal space Durkheim called anomie."[72] Even more, Olick theorizes that this liminality—the inability to bridge the gap between expectation and experience that is the hallmark of trauma—can produce what Friedrich Nietzsche and Max Scheler referred to as *ressentiment*: a deep-seated and incurable hatred that arises when a situation is perceived as unjust but remains beyond the suffering party's control.[73] Building on Nietzsche's discussion, Weber theorized the connection between *ressentiment* and theodicy in his work on ancient Judaism, arguing that *ressentiment* arose out of a disjuncture between Jewish theodicy—specifically, the conception of Jews as "chosen people"—and the experience of subordination, which left an unbridgeable gap between expectation and experience.[74] Accordingly, Olick identifies *ressentiment* as the "outer-directed manifestation" of trauma, the visible response to such unbridgeable gaps.[75] Indeed, the case of September 11 illuminates the contemporary struggle to assimilate collective suffering within canonical national narratives—to bridge the gulf between expectation and experience. The conceptual connection to *ressentiment*, in turn, provides a fresh window onto the vociferous public debates that have unfolded in the process of reconstructing the World Trade Center site, the sacred center for September 11 memory.[76]

WHAT IS POLITICAL CONSOLATION?

Political leaders, then, are the collective actors who perform the interpretive work of bridging—or, at least, attempting to bridge—the gulfs created by calamitous events. In the face of suffering, atrocity, and loss, it is now incumbent upon political leaders to forge a place for calamity in national narratives—narratives that offer not only a sense of identity and solidarity, but also existential orientation and meaning. Within this historical context, consolation discourse has become an important *genre* of political speechmaking.[77] Genre, in the sense that I employ the term here, signals not only a distinctive type of address structured in accordance with common conventions, but also a temporal and historical dimension. Shared memories provide the basis for collective meaning-making in the present, and as such, speech genres are not unchanging structures but— as Olick puts it, drawing on the literary critic Mikhail Bakhtin—"historical accretions" that unfold dialogically.[78] Each moment is structured by, and responds to, earlier moments in the same trajectory. The concepts of premediation and remediation, introduced above, provide analytic leverage on this historical dimension of speech, illuminating how symbolic frameworks inherited from the past structure what can be said in the present. In the illustration I have been developing, the Gettysburg Address—and its subsequent remediations—powerfully shapes the meanings that can be attributed to national suffering, even a century and a half after it was uttered. Political consolation discourse in the United States almost invariably takes shape in dialogue with this seminal text in the genre.

Much as the search for existential meaning is bound up with the emergence of the nation itself, the expectation that political leaders address these matters has intensified over time, and it has become especially powerful in our own mass-mediated age. Calamities now unfold before the public in real time: for instance, Americans in Chicago and Los Angeles awoke, on September 11, 2001, to images of crashing planes and burning buildings that brought the catastrophe vividly to life. The reaction to such events, then, "[can] be both immediate and simultaneous, in other words, shared as a collective."[79] Photographs and video footage, replayed continuously, compress geographic distance[80] and "[heighten] the public's sense of catastrophe and insecurity in the face of death-dealing events."[81] The desire for meaning and consolation following such events thus extends well beyond those immediately or personally affected to a much wider community of sufferers. And in the context of this mediatized milieu, the performative, theatrical, and rhetorical dimensions of politics have become increasingly central, leaving political leaders with both the opportunity and the obligation to address the widespread desire for symbolic guidance.[82]

This book is about American politics specifically, and some of its implications are particular to the case at hand. Arguably, the existential dimension of politics is particularly prominent in the U.S. context: as Philip Gorski puts it, "America remains, for better or worse, a highly religious country in the conventional sense of that term and a deeply metaphysical country over and above that."[83] The relationship between politics and religion in the United States is a unique and complex one, and even today, religion is intertwined with U.S. politics in a way that it is not in most other secular democracies. The enduring salience of religion in American public life has perhaps encouraged U.S. politicians to embrace the symbolic, even priestly, dimensions of their role with special enthusiasm.[84] Indeed, theistic language is pervasive in American political consolation discourse, which frequently places the nation and its suffering within a cosmic frame of reference.

Political consolation in the U.S. context is also shaped in distinctive ways by the presidential system: symbolic and bureaucratic leadership are united in the single office of the president rather than divided between a monarch and a prime minister, or a mostly ceremonial head of state and a head of government. As politics has become increasingly performative, the symbolic dimension of the American presidency has been elevated in importance, often overshadowing the institution's bureaucratic side: "rhetorical leadership," as Jeffrey Tulis argues, has become "the heart of the presidency—its essential task."[85] The president has become "the nation's chief storyteller, its interpreter-in-chief";[86] as "chief ceremonialist," presidents "preside, award, debate, interrogate, announce, proclaim, respond, evade, challenge, reflect, instruct, and celebrate"[87]—and in a similar vein, they also comfort and console. Political consolation is not a strictly presidential task, but the words of American presidents are central to the genre, and these transformations in the presidency as an institution are emblematic of shifts in the political landscape more generally.

Nevertheless, this book also works to shed light on the symbolic and existential dimensions of politics in ways that transcend the American case. First, it reinforces the argument—articulated powerfully in recent works by leading cultural sociologists—that meaning-making practices play a constitutive role in political processes. As Robin Wagner-Pacifici puts it, "the business of event framing is part and parcel of the continuing effect flow of events."[88] Consolation discourse intersects with and informs other genres of political speechmaking, and this interplay illuminates its constitutive, event-shaping power: after September 11, for instance, terms and tropes from consolation discourse figured prominently in speeches that sought to define and legitimate the "war on terror" and its expansion. Politicians' symbolic and existential meditations are no artifact or epiphenomenon, but an integral part of the struggle for power, influence, and legitimacy.

At the same time, consolation discourse demonstrates—perhaps more clearly than any other genre of political speechmaking—that political symbols and meanings are "the ends of power itself."[89] Whatever other interests it serves, political consolation should also be understood as part of the human quest for moral and symbolic orientation in problematic times.[90] Calamitous events unsettle our basic assumptions about how the world *ought* to operate, creating moments of cultural and political liminality when even our most cherished collective narratives might be scrutinized, questioned, and—perhaps—restructured. The consolation genre is thus a crucial venue for reflecting upon, rethinking, and, in rare but significant moments, reorganizing extant political meaning systems. Consolation discourse has wide-ranging implications and consequences, but it is most centrally "about" identity and meaning—narrating the nation in light of its confrontation with suffering and paving the way forward.

Understanding the consolation genre requires a firm grasp of its historical foundations. In order to trace the continuities and transformations in American political consolation discourse from the nation's founding moment to the present, I examined several types of texts: the canonical political texts that Bellah described as "civil scriptures,"[91] speeches delivered by American presidents and other key public officials in response to collective crises throughout the nation's history, speeches from subsequent ceremonies memorializing and commemorating these crises, and speeches from ceremonies held to dedicate memorials that recognize the events and/or honor those affected. Although my historical account focuses predominantly on these sources—texts that address specific experiences with collective suffering in a direct fashion—it also reflects an engagement with a wider body of empirical material. Specifically, I examined remarks delivered by federal officials on national holidays that invite consolation discourse (Memorial Day, Veterans Day, and Independence Day) and during the nation's most prominent and symbolically freighted political rituals (State of the Union addresses and presidential inaugurals).

To understand the discursive response to September 11, I analyzed public remarks by federal, state, and local officials—including presidents and vice presidents, members of the cabinet, members of Congress, and governors and mayors from the states and localities where the events of 9/11 unfolded—that made reference to the event, covering the period from September 11, 2001, through June 2014.[92] In presenting the findings, I pay particular attention to remarks delivered during rituals with the highest symbolic significance. These include speeches from memorial services, anniversary speeches, State of the Union addresses and other presidential speeches to Congress, and presidential addresses to the nation concerning the issue of terrorism and the wars in Afghanistan and Iraq. I also devote special attention to the remarks delivered during official commemorative ceremonies at each of the three 9/11 crash sites—lower Manhattan, the Pentagon, and Shanksville, Pennsylvania—from 2002 to 2013. Finally, I examined newspaper articles and op-eds, transcripts from television interviews, official documents such as the *9/11 Commission Report*, and other public accounts such as memoirs to grasp the "discursive surround"[93] of these ceremonial rituals. In particular, I delved into both local and national media sources in order to understand high-profile public debates over the future of the World Trade Center site in lower Manhattan. These debates expose the struggle to come to terms with 9/11 in American civil society and shed light on the interplay between official discourse and public understandings of this landmark event.[94]

In analyzing these materials, I sought to identify the terms and tropes, ideas and images, that speakers deployed in order to interpret and explain collective suffering. Throughout the process, I worked to uncover thematic continuities across speeches and symbolic resonances between past and present, while also attending as faithfully as possible to the nuances and complexities of each specific text. In the pages that follow, I present substantial excerpts alongside my own interpretations, inviting readers to evaluate my conclusions along the way. While my focus is on decoding official symbolism—which, in the end, has a unique role in defining collective identities and constituting the effect flow of events—I take seriously the critiques advanced in reception theory.[95] Symbols are polysemic; audiences are not passive recipients, but active interpreters who often reconstruct official symbols in ways that differ from or challenge their creators' intentions. Accordingly, the meanings politicians attribute to calamity are not simply received, but struggled over, debated, and at times reformulated. I therefore work to situate official symbols within their broader discursive contexts, especially by highlighting moments when popular dissent has been significant enough to unsettle and even reorient official narratives.[96]

I present my findings in two parts. Part I provides a history of American political consolation, tracing pivotal moments in the development of the genre from the American Revolution to the end of the twentieth century. These chapters constitute a broad historical account in their own right, but they are also intended as a backdrop for understanding September 11, which was premediated by memories of past suffering in decisive ways. Part II, in turn, examines the response to September 11, detailing the complexities of rendering collective suffering in the contemporary United States, and examining the interplay between past and present in giving shape to this unsettling event.

Chapter 1 examines how the "civil scriptures"—canonical political texts that provided narrative foundations for the American nation— address the meaning of suffering. As the ensuing chapters reveal, texts from defining moments of crisis in the eighteenth and nineteenth centuries—especially the American Revolution and the Civil War— continue to reverberate in consolation discourse even today. In chapter 2, I trace the ascendancy of a *dualistic* mode of political consolation in the twentieth century.[97] During the Second World War, President Franklin Delano Roosevelt incorporated familiar tropes from the civil scriptures into a broad interpretive framework that conceptualized the conflict as a monumental struggle between good and evil, civilization and savagery;

this struggle moved teleologically—if painfully—toward the triumph of the good. Dualistic discourse echoed powerfully during the Cold War and again in World War II commemorations, especially the 50th anniversary observances during the 1990s. This frame was thus readily available when the nation confronted crisis in 2001.

Yet the political-cultural context within which September 11 unfolded was marked indelibly by the challenges of the postwar era. Chapter 3 provides the conclusion to my historical narrative, tracing the emergence of an alternate, *tragic* mode of political consolation. With roots in Lincoln's second inaugural, the tragic mode became much more prominent and politically viable in the 1960s, especially in response to the interpretive and existential challenges posed by political assassinations and the war in Vietnam.

With this historical backdrop in mind, part II presents the interpretive response to September 11. In chapter 4, I examine high-profile speeches and public mourning rituals that took place on September 11 and in the weeks that followed. Here, I work to capture the intricate process through which American political leaders gave shape and meaning to this unsettling event, narrating overwhelmingly in the dualistic mode. Chapter 5, in turn, examines the legacies of consolation discourse in American foreign policy, showing how the dualistic interpretation of 9/11 shaped its "effect flow"[98] in the years that followed.

Chapters 6 and 7 grapple with 9/11 memory, identifying fissures in the dualistic discourse that so rapidly coalesced in the fall of 2001. Chapter 6 examines commemorative ceremonies at the three crash sites, illuminating how these annual rituals extend the work of political consolation beyond the immediate aftermath of calamity. In this chapter, I pay particular attention to the ways that speakers have departed—whether intentionally or inadvertently—from the dualistic mode. Finally, chapter 7 continues to probe the challenges of memory in lower Manhattan, examining public debates that have unfolded in the process of reconstructing the World Trade Center site. These debates, I argue, reveal that September 11 remains an enduring cultural trauma, an event that continues to present Americans' "faculty of historical and narrative association with a challenge that it is, as yet, unable to meet."[99] More broadly, these conflicts surrounding the sacred center of September 11 expose deep disagreements concerning the meaning of basic national ideals—freedom and liberty, tolerance and pluralism—that help explain the particular challenges of coming to terms with collective suffering in the present moment.

My foremost task in these pages is an empirical and interpretive one. How have American political leaders worked to console the public in the face of crisis? How has consolation discourse changed over time and why? How does the past infuse and structure interpretations of the present? Standing at the crossroads between the humanities and the social sciences, sociology is defined by both an interpretive project—whose central goal is to understand the stories we tell as we seek to impose order and meaning on raw experience—and a scientific project that aims primarily to explain and predict. These projects are neither mutually exclusive nor inherently opposed.[100] But this book is guided first and foremost by the interpretive impulse. In the pages that follow, then, I work to capture collective storytelling on its own terms. And indeed, I argue that consolation discourse sheds light on the task of meaning-making in a particularly powerful way: these speeches represent attempts to articulate meaning under the most difficult conditions, when our expectations about how the world *ought* to operate are deeply threatened.

As I identify and disentangle the trajectories that bear heavily on our understanding of the present, I also contribute to the historical and sociological project that William Sewell terms "the de-reification of social life"—unsettling taken-for-granted narratives, revealing that interpretations ordinarily taken to be self-evident are, in the last analysis, contingent human products.[101] Such analysis evokes a sense of historical responsibility—we are very much the co-creators of the worlds we inhabit[102]—and in the process, normative questions inevitably arise alongside the theoretical questions I have elaborated here. Such concerns are perhaps especially pressing in the context of a study that grapples with a relatively recent and morally freighted event such as September 11, whose legacies are still unfolding as I write. How *should* Americans have understood and interpreted the events of September 11? What *did* these events, and the cultural and political response to them, reveal about "who Americans are" as a people? In the conclusion, then, I venture briefly onto normative terrain, considering how a more robust engagement with the alternate, tragic mode of political consolation might have altered the effect flow of 9/11. The careful interpretive analysis I present in the intervening pages is the core focus and contribution of this book. At its best, however, social science that attends to collective storytelling as a human task sui generis can help us to become more reflective about the symbolic and existential projects in which we are continually engaged.

PART I

Political Consolation in American History

CHAPTER 1

Revisiting the Civil Scriptures

Even before they arrived on the shores of the New World, Puritan colonists understood themselves as a chosen people, a new Israel embarking on a journey toward their own promised land.[1] Images of the Exodus have long since endowed American collective life with meaning, even cosmic significance, providing the powerful sense of transcendence that Benedict Anderson identified at the heart of national narratives.[2] During the American Revolution, this Exodus symbolism, and the larger Puritan covenant theology within which it was embedded, would come together with classical republicanism to form the basis for what Robert Bellah termed "American civil religion."[3] In this chapter, I revisit the "civil scriptures"—core texts from this tradition—that most decisively shaped the consolation genre, providing a sort of sociological exegesis of the interpretive vocabularies they contain. I then examine more recent moments when these texts from the distant past have figured centrally in political consolation, illuminating their continued importance as well as highlighting the multivocal qualities that have helped enable their endurance.

American civil religion, Bellah argued, draws heavily upon Judeo-Christian symbolism—archetypes such as "Exodus, Chosen People, Promised Land, New Jerusalem, Sacrificial Death and Rebirth."[4] Yet it is also, as Bellah put it, "genuinely American and genuinely new," with "its own prophets and its own martyrs, its own sacred events and sacred places," and its own canonical texts or scriptures.[5] Though the term "civil religion" has largely fallen out of favor in contemporary sociology,[6] I find it is a valuable analytic tool for grasping a foundational symbolic structure whose core themes and texts continue to reverberate in disparate contexts.[7] In revisiting the civil scriptures, I cover well-worn ground. My goal, then, is not to uncover heretofore unknown history, but to place familiar texts within a new frame that yields fresh theoretical insight. What interpretive resources do the civil scriptures offer for grappling with the fundamental matters of suffering and finitude, and how have they reverberated in the consolation genre?

ORIGINS AND PRECURSORS

The Puritan colonial experience is a crucial backdrop for American civil religion; John Winthrop's 1630 sermon "A Model of Christian Charity," delivered on board the *Arbella*, represents a sort of ur-text for the tradition.[8] This text remains an emblematic and enduring testament to the longstanding image of the colonies—and subsequently, the American nation—as a new Israel. "We shall find that the God of Israel is among us," Winthrop declared, "when ten of us shall be able to resist a thousand of our enemies; when he shall make us a praise and glory that men shall say of succeeding plantations, 'the Lord make it like that of New England.' For we must consider that we shall be as a city upon a hill. The eyes of all people are upon us."

The providential promises that the colonists enjoyed came with significant obligations, however. The chosen people had a covenant to uphold, and Winthrop warned that the penalty for waywardness was severe: "if we shall deal falsely with our God in this work we have undertaken, and so cause him to withdraw his present help from us, we shall be made a story and a by-word through the world." Winthrop thus urged his fellow colonists to uphold the covenant, invoking "that exhortation of Moses . . . in his last farewell to Israel" described in Deuteronomy 30:

> Beloved, there is now set before us life and good, death and evil, in that we are commanded this day to love the Lord our God, and to love one another, to walk in his ways and to keep his commandments and his ordinance and his laws, and the articles of our covenant with him, that we may live and be multiplied, and that the Lord our God may bless us in the land whither we go to possess it.

Warning once again that God's favor was contingent upon the colonists' faithfulness, Winthrop insisted: "Therefore let us choose life."[9]

Winthrop's Hebraic rhetoric transformed the colonists' journey into an Exodus narrative: the ocean crossing became "a crossing of the Red Sea and the Jordan River," and the Massachusetts Bay became "a promised land."[10] His words stood in the tradition of the jeremiad, a political sermon named for the lamentations of the prophet Jeremiah, who interpreted the calamities that befell Israel as products of the people's failure to uphold the Mosaic covenant.[11] "As the European Reformers adapted the jeremiad from the medieval pulpit," Sacvan Bercovitch explains, "it was a dirge over fallen humanity."[12] Indeed, even during the first decade of settlement, Puritan clergy "were already thundering denunciations of a backsliding people" who had fallen short in the covenant they were bound to uphold.[13] Calamities and misfortunes could be understood as a product of moral and spiritual failings.

Yet the Puritans would subtly transform the jeremiad in their new milieu. And the contrast between the European form of the jeremiad and its American variant—a distinction already evident in Winthrop's words— reveals one of the core impulses of the American consolation genre. In both Europe and America, jeremiads castigated a people gone astray, interpreting collective misfortunes as a punishment for sin and a sign of God's judgment. The Puritan colonists, however, mitigated their lamentations with a deep-seated optimism.[14] Even as they accepted "the threat of divine retribution," the Puritans "qualified it in a way that turned threat into celebration."[15] In the American jeremiad, Bercovitch argues, "God's punishments were *corrective*, not destructive"; God's "vengeance was a sign of love," and in the end, the "punishments" that the chosen people suffered "confirmed their promise."[16] The American jeremiad thus posited a progressive teleology, portraying struggles and misfortunes as setbacks in a story that nonetheless culminates in success and prosperity for the chosen people—people who will, in turn, serve as a guiding lamp to all others, the "city upon a hill" that Winthrop envisioned. Within this tradition, calamities became "instruments of progress," enabling adherents to respond to collective suffering with resilience and hope.[17] During the Revolutionary era, the Puritans' Exodus symbolism and the progressive teleology within which it was embedded became the bedrock for an American civil religion, and the core narrative for its "Old Testament."[18]

FOUNDING MOMENTS

Periodization is a social and cultural process: "the flow of history," as Eviatar Zerubavel points out, "is continuous," and thus "the selection of those historical events which constitute the 'beginnings' of chronological eras" is in a certain sense "arbitrary."[19] Yet events that are understood to demarcate the onset of a new era have a special sociological significance. Invested with "profound collective meaning," such moments generally become wellsprings for symbolism far into the future.[20] The American founding moment—including the Declaration of Independence, the Revolution, and the frontier mythology that proved central in knitting the colonies together as a nation—is no exception,[21] and even today underpins much American political consolation.

The Declaration and the Revolution

The particular circumstances surrounding America's founding moment only augment its symbolic significance. The American nation began on an identifiable date—July 4, 1776—and "as a result of a series of conscious decisions," acts of "conscious meaning-creation" that were "redolent of the sacred."[22] The Declaration of Independence, of course, provided the language that literally gave life to the nation. In doing so, it also provided terminology that both the founding generation and their descendents deployed to come to grips with national struggle and the suffering it wrought.

The Declaration articulated the nation's founding ideals, set them in opposition to the values that King George III purportedly embodied, and imbued the revolutionaries' values with a sacred, and indeed transcendent, significance. At the limit, the Declaration's signatories proclaimed that establishing these values was a task more meaningful than life itself. "We hold these truths to be self-evident," the Declaration states, "that all men are created equal, that they are endowed by their Creator with certain unalienable Rights, that among these are Life, Liberty, and the pursuit of Happiness."[23] Describing "the history of the present King of Great Britain" as "a history of repeated injuries and usurpations, all having in direct object the establishment of an absolute Tyranny over these States," the Declaration proclaimed that the colonists had not only the right, but also the "duty, to throw off such Government."[24] The document concluded with a pledge that leaders would echo in trials to come: "And for the support of this Declaration, with a firm reliance on the protection of divine Providence, we mutually pledge to each other our Lives, our Fortunes and our sacred Honor."[25]

This first text in the scriptural canon has played innumerable roles in American political culture since 1776. Among them, it provided an early source of political consolation and a foundation for this genre. Framing the nation's founding struggle as a struggle for "liberty" against "tyranny," the Declaration expressed confidence that the American cause enjoyed providential favor, signaling the enduring salience of the New Israel image—the conviction that Americans represented a chosen people.[26] But it also portrayed the "unalienable rights" that the Declaration identified as worthy of great sacrifice, thereby bringing national meaning to losses endured in the struggle.[27]

While the Declaration addressed the meaning of suffering in an oblique way, the violent revolution called for meditations from political and religious leaders that tackled the issue more overtly. According to Bercovitch, the Jeremiahs of the day—who now included emerging political leaders as well as clergy—understood the Revolution as "the often-prophecied, long-expected apocalyptic moment" for the chosen people.[28] The trials associated with this episode could thus be cast as blessings even from the outset: "It may be the Will of Heaven that America shall suffer Calamities still more wasting and Distresses yet more dreadfull," John Adams wrote to his wife, Abigail Adams, on July 3, 1776. "If this is to be the Case, it will have this good Effect, at least: it will inspire Us with many Virtues, which We have not, and correct many Errors, Follies, and Vices, which threaten to disturb, dishonour, and destroy Us. The Furnace of Affliction produces Refinement, in States as well as Individuals." As such, Adams expressed abiding optimism for the outcome: "I am well aware of the Toil and Blood and Treasure, that it will cost Us to maintain this Declaration, and support and defend these States," he wrote. "Yet through all the Gloom I can see the Rays of ravishing Light and Glory."[29]

During the Revolution, historian Sarah Purcell argues, Americans created a national mythology that "transformed the bloodshed, division, and violence of war into beautiful symbols of unity and national cohesion."[30] Patriot rhetoric drew upon a Christian tradition of martyrological imagery to create "a new kind of martyr, one who sacrificed himself purely for the cause of liberty and sanctified the American nation with his death."[31] For instance, in his sermon on the first anniversary of the April 19, 1775, encounters at Lexington and Concord, the Reverend Jonas Clarke— Lexington's Congregational minister—sanctified patriot losses in terms at once religious and nationalistic, employing language that would continue to figure centrally in American political consolation. The men who perished, Clarke declared, "bleed, they die, not in their own cause only; but in the cause of this whole people—in the cause of God, their country, and posterity.—And they have not bled, they shall not bleed, in vain."[32] Clarke also articulated the encounter's historical significance in stark binary terms that would echo well into the future: "And from the nineteenth of April, 1775, we may venture to predict, will be dated, in future history, THE LIBERTY or SLAVERY of the AMERICAN WORLD."[33]

Similarly, memorable passages from Thomas Paine's The American Crisis offered consolation while urging soldiers onward. Written at a moment of grave uncertainty and diminishing morale, the words from Paine's first essay spoke so powerfully to General George Washington that he ordered his officers to read them aloud to the Continental Army on December 23, 1776. Paine's opening lines have proven especially influential:

> These are the times that try men's souls. The summer-soldier and the sunshine patriot will, in this crisis, shrink from the service of their country; but he that stands by it now, deserves the love and thanks of man and woman. Tyranny, like hell, is not easily conquered; yet we have this consolation with us, that the harder the conflict, the more glorious the triumph.[34]

The promise of future glory offered justification and reassurance amidst profound insecurity. And Paine offered the further consolation that triumph was providentially assured: "my secret opinion," he wrote, "has ever been, and still is, that God will not give up a people to military destruction, or leave them unsupportedly to perish, who had so earnestly and so repeatedly sought to avoid the calamities of war, by every decent method which wisdom could invent."[35] Americans, he suggested, were innocent and morally righteous—they had not provoked the conflict, and were thus entitled to divine protection. In the struggle between liberty and tyranny, liberty could not but prevail: "though the flame of liberty may sometimes cease to shine," Paine reflected, "the coal never can expire."[36] The assumptions Paine expressed in this oft-remediated essay—that an innocent and morally righteous nation would emerge victorious; that liberty was destined to triumph over tyranny—would reverberate powerfully in generations to come.

In memory—and in accordance with well-established symbolism—the Revolution came to represent "the final act of the Exodus from the old lands across the waters,"[37] "a national *rite de passage*" that supplied an increasingly heterogeneous collectivity "with a common source of political culture."[38] Within the overarching Exodus narrative, George Washington was cast in the role of "the divinely appointed Moses who led his people out of the hands of tyranny."[39] Likewise, pivotal moments from the Revolution became emblems of American fortitude in the face of trial, and thus central images in subsequent consolation discourse that sought to foster resilience amidst suffering and loss. As Edward Linenthal argues, the encounters at Lexington and Concord—understood as the Revolution's inaugural moments—came to signify the courage of minutemen, "instinctive warriors" who fought bravely against a powerful enemy in order to secure liberty. Debates over the nature of the encounter on Lexington Green reveal the meaning-conferring power of the predominant image: "If the encounter . . . was not a battle but a massacre, were the martyred minutemen really the first models of how Americans die in war or just further examples of colonial victims?" Patriotic sacrifices, deaths in defense of a cause, are meaningful, purposeful, and thus in some sense comprehensible in a way that straightforward victimhood is not. Lexington, then, is officially commemorated as a battle in which valiant patriots fought nobly in response to British aggression. As Linenthal puts it, the minuteman is portrayed as a "humane warrior" who "killed not out of hate but out of the forceful inspiration of the love of liberty."[40] In offering their lives, the canonical narrative has it, the minutemen gave birth to the nation. On the April 19, 1875, centennial, for instance, an inscription on the triumphal arch at the entrance to Lexington Green read: "Welcome to the Birthplace of American Liberty."[41] In Concord, George William Curtis drew an analogy to the birth of Christ: "Just as angels sang 'Glory to God in the highest, for Christ is born,' on April 19, Curtis said, they 'whispered . . . Good-will to men: America is born.'"[42] The colonial army's defeats and struggles—most centrally the 1775 battle of Bunker Hill and the winter of 1777–1778 at Valley Forge—also came to anchor the narrative of the Revolution when they were recast as "momentary episodes in a longer, transcendent narrative" that culminated in victory.[43]

Running throughout these key texts and iconic images from the Revolution is an assumption in keeping with the broad vision Winthrop articulated aboard the *Arbella*. Namely, American leaders in the Revolutionary era frequently understood their experiment in encompassing terms, as having global significance and indeed implications for all humanity. This New Israel thus faced "the twin tasks of being an example of democratic equality"—a moral and political city upon a hill—"and fulfilling a mission to bring that democracy to others."[44] George Washington's 1789 inaugural—which marked the denouement of the Revolutionary era[45]— gave voice to this sense of stewardship and mission in an official ceremonial setting: "the preservation of the sacred fire of liberty and the destiny of the republican model of government," Washington reflected, "are justly considered, perhaps, as *deeply*, as *finally*, staked on the experiment entrusted to the hands of the American people."[46] The chosen people were to play a millennial role, to act as a "redeemer nation."[47] The ways in which this sense of destiny has influenced American national identity and foreign policy, fostering a deep-seated sense of "American exceptionalism,"[48] are well documented.[49] And the words and events that gave way to this sense of national destiny have been remediated time and again to bring meaning to collective suffering.

Frontier Mythology

This overriding sense of mission informed a frontier mythology that pre-dated the Revolution, but played a particularly important role in constituting a genuinely national imagination afterward.[50] At the core of American frontier mythology is the belief in "regeneration through violence."[51] As Richard Slotkin puts it: "The first colonists saw in America an opportunity to regenerate their fortunes, their spirits, and the power of their church and nation; but the means to that regeneration ultimately became the means of violence, and the myth of regeneration through violence became the structuring metaphor of the American experience."[52] In the seventeenth century, Slotkin argues, the Puritans understood the Native Americans as "a darkened and inverted mirror image of their own culture," but believed that they could perhaps "capture" this "devil's city and turn his demons to good men."[53] Later, following the Revolution, Americans needed "unique cultural traditions to stand beside" their "newfound political unity," and, as Barry Schwartz suggests, the frontier experience was a wellspring for such symbolism,[54] providing an "Other" against which this heterogeneous collectivity could define itself. "As long as the frontier was expanding," Schwartz explains, "the dualism of civilization and savagery was essential to Americans' self-conception. Americans defined their civility in terms of its opposite, savagery."[55] This foundational dualism and the frontier mythology it supported not only underwrote collective identity, but also provided crucial resources for political consolation—not necessarily in the form of "scriptural" texts, but a narrative template that would be deployed time and again as a source of orientation in crisis moments.[56]

The protagonist in this myth—the frontiersman or pioneer, subsequently reimagined as the cowboy[57]—came to be understood as a "conqueror-hero engaged in a violent struggle against the infinite frontier environment."[58] Guided by his "infallible natural authority,"[59] equipped with "rugged individualis[m]"[60] and exceptional "martial prowess,"[61] the frontier hero battled "the forces of evil," including "the savagery" of both "the wilderness itself" and its inhabitants, the "Indian or outlaw."[62] On the frontier, violence became an instrument for good, "the means to a higher end."[63] In most versions of the frontier narrative, the hero's sacrifice is "one of alienation [rather] than death": he does not perish, but rides off into the sunset, as the very individualism that enabled his conquests undermines his ability to become integrated into a community.[64] Inevitably, however, violent struggles involve some degree of death and destruction, even among the eventual victors. Defeats and fatalities from the frontier would become touchstones for political consolation, and they were interpreted as losses that not simply preceded, but indeed *enabled*, subsequent triumphs. Remediations of pivotal struggles in the American West, then, underscore how suffering and defeat paved the way for "progress." Most frequently remediated in consolation discourse is the 1836 battle at the Alamo mission, located in present-day San Antonio, in which all of the Alamo's defenders—including the frontiersman-turned-Congressman Davy Crockett—perished. In memory, the losses at the Alamo became an emblem for the notion of regeneration through violence: they were understood as sacrifices that not only secured victory over "the tyrannous forces of Santa Anna," but also enabled national rebirth in a more general sense.[65] Within such retellings, the suffering and death that took place at the boundary between "civilization" and "savagery" thus assumed meaning as part of an ultimate battle between good and evil, light and darkness, as they propelled the frontier forward.

In fact, this American mythology transformed the very meanings theretofore associated with the idea of a "frontier." Traditionally, a frontier was an unbridgeable division that separated "one people from another."[66] In the American context, it came to represent instead "a *figural* outpost, the outskirts of the advancing kingdom of God" and indeed "a summons to territorial expansion."[67] In the 1840s, frontier mythology fused with the nation's overriding sense of mission in the concept of "manifest destiny." The phrase "manifest destiny" gained currency after the New York *Morning News* published an editorial in 1845 positing that Americans had a right "to overspread and to possess the whole of the continent which Providence has given us for the development of the great experiment of liberty and federated self-government entrusted to us."[68] It thus distilled and perpetuated the image of the United States as trustee for liberty, expressed in Washington's 1789 inaugural, and synthesized it with an expansionist project.

Frontier mythology received perhaps its fullest, or at least its most explicit, articulation in 1893, three years after the Census Bureau declared the frontier closed. Its source was the historian Frederick Jackson Turner's essay "The Significance of the Frontier in American History." Originally delivered at a meeting of the American Historical Association, then published later in the year, Turner's essay was simultaneously an academic reinterpretation of American history that placed the frontier at the center of the national experience and an effort to bring more definitive shape to the longstanding mythology of the American West.[69] As he sketched the archetype of the frontiersman and described this character's distinctive impact on American national identity, Turner repeatedly invoked a set of interrelated binaries that underscored the sharp boundary between "'savagery' and 'civilization'"—including "'good' and 'evil'; 'dangers' and 'benefits';

'primitive' and 'developed'; 'bonds of custom' and 'unrestraint.'"[70] In doing so, Turner provided a portrait that would continue to compel the nation and its leaders in the years to come.[71] Frontier mythology would, for instance, give shape to space exploration,[72] American wars abroad,[73] and even the activities of the Peace Corps;[74] presidents from Theodore Roosevelt to Lyndon Johnson, Ronald Reagan, and George W. Bush would work to embody the characteristics of the archetypal frontiersman or the cowboy. Most importantly for present purposes, this mythology—and especially that fundamental binary between civilization and savagery that provided an "Other" against which the fledgling nation defined itself—would premediate collective crises throughout the twentieth century and beyond, providing a powerful source of consolation.

THE SECOND "TIME OF TRIAL"

The Revolutionary era brought significant trials for the newfound American nation and gave birth to vocabularies for coming to terms with collective suffering that reverberate today. Nearly a century later, however—when civil war threatened to tear the young republic apart—questions of meaning resounded with exceptional force. For one, Americans grappled with the profound contradiction between the practice of slavery and the conception of liberty at the heart of national identity. Moreover, the war's unprecedented carnage made the existential matters of suffering, loss, and finitude an urgent priority.[75] For what purpose were so many young and vibrant lives extinguished? During this second "time of trial," the "theme of death, sacrifice, and rebirth" anticipated in Revolution era rhetoric and frontier mythology was "indelibly written into the civil religion."[76] As he guided the nation politically, militarily, and existentially through the crisis of the Civil War, President Abraham Lincoln became a symbolic Christ figure, and his most celebrated oratory provided the core for a "New Testament" in the American civil scriptures.[77] Foremost among these "scriptures" was the Gettysburg Address. As I noted in the introduction, even today, the Gettysburg Address remains perhaps *the* defining text in the consolation genre.

Gettysburg and the Discourse of National Sacrifice

Lincoln traveled to Gettysburg, Pennsylvania, in November 1863 to dedicate a cemetery where Union soldiers had been laid to rest. Though the battle of Gettysburg came in retrospect to represent a crucial turning point in the war, the dedication ceremony took place at a time of grave uncertainty for the Union. As such, Lincoln simultaneously sought to offer consolation and to urge the Union forward even as it mourned its dead.[78]

In Lincoln's address, the deaths at Gettysburg are premediated through the language of the Declaration, and assume meaning in reference to its fundamental "proposition that all men are created equal."[79] The Declaration, Lincoln's words implied, generated "not only . . . an entity, but also . . . a mission," and Lincoln suggested that the battle of Gettysburg must be understood as part of the effort to fulfill this mission.[80] The Union soldiers' deaths thus became acts of blood sacrifice that secured new life for the nation and, more broadly, for the democratic ideals it represented. The fallen, Lincoln reflected, "gave their lives that that nation might live."[81] In doing so, they compelled their comrades and survivors to complete their "unfinished work"—to ensure that the fallen "shall not have died in vain." In this narrative, the violence that unfolded at Gettysburg would be regenerative, and would come to represent a moment on the road to "a new birth of freedom," helping to secure the promise that "government of the people, by the people, for the people, shall not perish from the earth."[82] Fusing an image of sacrifice that drew on both the Bible and the Greek funeral oration with the Declaration's commitment to liberty and equality, Lincoln suggested that death on the battlefield represented a soldier's ultimate gift to his nation and to the democratic project writ large.[83]

It would be quite some time before the Gettysburg Address took its place among the canonical civil scriptures.[84] Schwartz points out that "most newspapers did not report, let alone reprint it"; the Democratic newspapers that did cover the speech "refused to take it seriously," while "[t]he Republican press, responding positively to all Lincoln speeches, found nothing special about the one at Gettysburg."[85] Over time, however, Lincoln's words—which were eventually remediated in a wide array of disparate settings—came increasingly to define the consolation genre, and, again, have maintained an overwhelming influence on subsequent efforts to come to terms with national suffering.[86] Transforming fallen soldiers into Christ figures who, as Drew Gilpin Faust puts it, serve as "the vehicle for salvation, the means for a terrestrial political redemption,"[87] Lincoln's words offered the ultimate consolation for bloodshed.

Lincoln's 1864 "Bixby letter" echoed these themes in more intimate language, and it, too, would subsequently assume a prominent place in the consolation genre.[88] The letter was sent from the Lincoln White House to Lydia Bixby—a widow living in Boston whom Lincoln believed had lost five sons in the Union cause—in November 1864.[89] Acknowledging the futility of any effort at consolation in the face of such great loss, Lincoln nonetheless sought to render death meaningful with the language of national sacrifice:

Dear Madam,

I have been shown in the files of the War Department a statement of the Adjutant General of Massachusetts that you are the mother of five sons who have died gloriously on the field of battle.

I feel how weak and fruitless must be any word of mine which should attempt to beguile you from the grief of a loss so overwhelming. But I cannot refrain from tendering you the consolation that may be found in the thanks of the Republic they died to save.

I pray that our Heavenly Father may assuage the anguish of your bereavement, and leave you only the cherished memory of the loved and lost, and the solemn pride that must be yours to have laid so costly a sacrifice upon the altar of freedom.

Yours, very sincerely and respectfully,

A. Lincoln[90]

Here, Lincoln not only honored the five young men who perished in battle, expressing "the thanks of the Republic they died to save." He also honored Lydia Bixby's own gift to her nation, giving her grief a meaningful place in the struggle by highlighting "the solemn pride" she must feel at having "laid so costly a sacrifice on the altar of freedom."[91] The notion of national sacrifice thus subtly expands in this text—a text that, according to John Channing Briggs, was likely understood by its author from the beginning as "a private message available to be overheard."[92] Paradoxically, the letter's power as a source of consolation derives at least in part from Lincoln's explicit recognition of his own powerlessness: "In 'tendering' comfort, the letter's gesture gives consolation without giving it. Consolation, if it is there, is passed from a source beyond the recipient, who is invited to accept it."[93] Even the president can only deliver the message, and articulate his own prayer that the mother's grief would diminish.

Lincoln was not alone in articulating this discourse of national sacrifice, which also found expression in enduring texts such as Julia Ward Howe's "Battle Hymn of the Republic." Originally published in the *Atlantic Monthly* in 1862, the "Battle Hymn" made explicit the comparison between the Union dead and Christ, portraying soldiers' deaths as redemptive sacrifices: "As he died to make men holy, let us die to make men free."[94] And the circumstances surrounding Lincoln's own death—in April 1865, just after Robert E. Lee's surrender, and with peace on the horizon—imbued his conception of national sacrifice with even greater power in the American imagination. In the end, the canonical narrative has it, Lincoln too gave his life that his nation might live. Following his assassination, Lincoln was swiftly cast as a martyr, the Christ figure in the American civil scriptures.[95] That he was shot on Good Friday only bolstered the analogy.[96]

This imagery was immediately evident in eulogies honoring the fallen president. In his sermon at the White House funeral for Lincoln, Phineas D. Gurley—pastor of the New York Avenue Presbyterian Church that Lincoln attended while in office—drew a vivid portrait of Lincoln as a Christ figure. Assuring mourners that Americans remained God's chosen people despite the trials they had recently endured—"He has chosen us as He did his people of old in the furnace of affliction"—Gurley foreshadowed better days on the horizon: "despite of this great and sudden and temporary darkness, the morning has begun to dawn—the morning of a bright and glorious day, such as our country has never seen."[97] The most significant worldly agent in this progressive narrative was Abraham Lincoln. God, Gurley claimed, had "raised [Lincoln] up for a great and glorious mission, furnished him for his work, and aided him in its accomplishment."[98] Although Lincoln had perished, Gurley pledged that the president's message would reverberate across the ages: "he *will* speak through the ages and to all rulers and peoples in every land, and his message to them will be, 'Cling to Liberty and right; battle for them; bleed for them; die for them, if need be; and have confidence in God.'"[99] The "cause of freedom and humanity," Gurley said, had become "dearer to us now than ever before, because consecrated by the blood of its most conspicuous defender, its wisest and most fondly-trusted friend."[100] The language Lincoln had employed to console his fellow citizens powerfully infused the meanings they later attributed to his death.

In an address at Lincoln's burial in Springfield, Illinois, Matthew Simpson—a bishop in the Methodist Episcopal church—echoed and elaborated these themes, explicitly describing Lincoln as a national martyr. "Mr. Lincoln was no ordinary man," Simpson reflected. "I believe the conviction has been growing on the nation's mind, as it certainly has been on my own . . . that by the hand of God he was especially singled out to guide our government in these troublesome times, and it seems to me that the hand of God may be traced in many of the events connected with his history." Simpson compared Lincoln to Moses rather than to Christ himself. But his praise for the fallen president was no less soaring. Indeed,

Simpson suggested that because of his act of emancipation, Lincoln compared favorably with the biblical Moses:

> We have all been taught to revere the sacred characters. Among them Moses stands pre-eminently high. He received the law from God, and his name is honored among the hosts of heaven. Was not his greatest act the delivering of three millions of his kindred out of bondage? Yet we may assert that Abraham Lincoln, by his proclamation, liberated more enslaved people than ever Moses set free, and those not of his kindred or his race. Such a power, such an opportunity, God has seldom given to man.

Lincoln, then, was to be understood and remembered as "the nation's great martyr for liberty." As he closed his oration, Simpson addressed his words to Lincoln: "Thou didst not fall for thyself. The assassin had no hate for thee. Our hearts were aimed at, our national life was sought. We crown thee as our martyr, and humanity enthrones thee as her triumphant son. Hero, Martyr, Friend, FAREWELL!"[101] In memory, Lincoln thus became the ultimate icon for the concept of national sacrifice he himself had articulated so movingly at Gettysburg.

The Second Inaugural

Lincoln's legacy in American civil religion is more complex and multiple than these texts indicate, however. In March 1865, just before Lincoln's untimely death, and with a Union victory on the horizon, Lincoln delivered his second inaugural address in the nation's capital. Once again, his central concern was to define the war's meaning. Yet the interpretation he offered differed substantially from the discourse of national sacrifice underpinning the Gettysburg Address and his letter to Lydia Bixby.

Reviving the theme of covenant and judgment that permeated Winthrop's sermon aboard the *Arbella*—as well as many Puritan jeremiads that followed—Lincoln cast the war as providential punishment for the national sin of slavery.[102] As Faust argues, in this address, the deaths on both sides were understood not as sacrifices, but as atonement.[103] Here, the war was not a fight to preserve freedom and democracy, undertaken consciously by morally motivated actors with a clear sense of their cause. Instead, Lincoln's second inaugural constructed a complicated portrait of two sides tragically plunged into a war that neither truly wanted.[104] "On the occasion corresponding to this four years ago all thoughts were anxiously directed to an impending civil war," Lincoln recalled. "All dreaded it, all sought to avert it. . . . Both parties deprecated war, but one of them would *make* war rather than let the nation survive, and the other would *accept* war rather than let it perish, and the war came."[105] The war thus became a historical subject in its own right; despite vigorous efforts to enact their intentions, the parties to the conflict were left at the mercy of forces beyond their control.

Though chastened by this sense of the limitations on human action, and indeed a sense of the limitations on human understanding of historical events, Lincoln nonetheless ventured an interpretation of the war's cause. "One-eighth of the whole population were colored slaves, not distributed generally over the Union, but localized in the southern part of it," Lincoln continued. "These slaves constituted a peculiar and powerful interest. All knew that this interest was somehow the cause of the war."[106] Slavery, then—an institution localized in the south—was "somehow" the fundamental cause of this tragic conflict. Yet even at a moment when his onlookers likely expected triumphant self-congratulation—affirmation that God had always been on the Union side—Lincoln asked instead for careful reflection.[107] The two sides, he pointed out, had a great deal in common: "Neither party expected for the war the magnitude or duration which it has already attained," Lincoln said. "Neither anticipated that the *cause* of the conflict might cease with or even before the conflict itself should cease. Each looked for an easier triumph, and a result less fundamental and astounding. Both read the same Bible and pray to the same God, and each invokes His aid against the other."[108]

Invoking these basic commonalities between enemies, Lincoln not only cautioned northerners against judgment, but also, in the end, portrayed slavery as a *national*, not regional, sin. "It may seem strange that any men should dare ask a just God's assistance in wringing their bread from the sweat of other men's faces, but let us judge not, that we be not judged," Lincoln said. "The prayers of both could not be answered. That of neither has been answered fully. The Almighty has His own purposes."[109] Lincoln's reflections once again evoked the tragic impasse that plunged the states into the war. As he came to his own interpretation of the war's ultimate meaning, Lincoln quoted from the gospel of Matthew (18:7):

"Woe unto the world because of offenses; for it must needs be that offenses come, but woe to that man by whom the offense cometh." If we shall suppose that American slavery is one of those offenses which, in the providence of God, must needs come, but which, having continued through His appointed time, He now wills to remove, and that He gives to both North and South this terrible war as the woe due to those by whom the offense came, shall we discern therein any departure from those divine attributes which the believers in a living God always ascribe to Him?[110]

Lincoln thus cautioned the north against self-righteousness without ever exculpating the south.[111] The war was a punishment for slavery, but it was a punishment for *American* slavery, not *southern* slavery.[112] The judgment issued was a judgment against the entire national collectivity; northerners as well as southerners were culpable. As Reinhold Niebuhr suggests, Lincoln resisted any temptation to "identify providence with the cause to which he was committed," a remarkable move for the president of a nation that understood its role in messianic terms from the first.[113] Instead, Lincoln placed "the enemy into the same category of ambiguity as the nation to which his life was committed."[114] In this light, then, the suffering and loss of both sides became atonement for a joint offense.[115]

Much as he underscored the limits of human action and intention,[116] Lincoln famously called upon his audience to work toward reconstituting the nation torn asunder in this tragic drama: "With malice toward none, with charity for all, with firmness in the right as God gives us to see the right, let us strive on to finish the work we are in, to bind up the nation's wounds, to care for him who shall have borne the battle and for his widow and his orphan, to do all which may achieve and cherish a just and lasting peace among ourselves and with all nations."[117] Speaking in circumstances that differed considerably from the uncertainty he faced in November of 1863 at Gettysburg, Lincoln took a vastly different approach to political consolation. Without declaring victory, Lincoln offered an interpretation of the war that both explained the devastating losses experienced on both sides and provided a basis for a renewed sense of collective identity, of nationhood.[118]

Even today, Lincoln's second inaugural remains an exceptional moment in the consolation genre, and in American political speechmaking more generally. Despite his firm belief in the nation's special mission, articulated forcefully in his Gettysburg Address, Lincoln's second inaugural publicly confronted the nation's shortcomings—in Lincoln's language, the nation's sins. Rejecting the notion that God was on his side, Lincoln gave voice to shared culpability and shared humanity, refusing, as John Burt puts it, to see his enemies "as a different moral kind from himself."[119] He grappled mightily with the meaning of historical events, the existential matters at the core of the consolation genre. Yet he also acknowledged that actors always make their way "among various half-understood alternatives," and that none can grasp history's direction *en medias res*.[120] Lincoln's tragic interpretation of national suffering would provide a thematic basis for the consolation genre in a "minor key," a tragic mode that would have considerably greater influence much later, beginning in the latter half of the twentieth century.

THE CIVIL SCRIPTURES IN TWENTIETH-CENTURY CRISES

The texts that form the basis for this chapter come from distant moments in the American past, and were intended as interpretations of specific episodes that posed their own anomalous challenges, both politically and existentially. Yet time and again, these texts—the terms and tropes, ideas and images, at the heart of the civil scriptures—have premediated subsequent national crises, giving shape and meaning to new realities even as they came into being. In the next two chapters, I consider how the civil scriptures provided the basis for the two basic modes of consolation I identify in twentieth-century political speechmaking: the dualistic and the tragic. And in the second half of the book, I describe how these texts continued to provide symbolic and existential orientation at the dawn of the twenty-first century—on September 11, 2001, and in the years that followed. First, however—to underscore the importance of these civil scriptures on their own terms—I conclude this chapter by considering their role in premediating the discursive responses to three national calamities from the twentieth century: the John F. Kennedy assassination, the Challenger disaster, and the Oklahoma City bombing. These events illuminate in especially striking ways the enduring influence of the civil scriptures and, in more general terms, the power of the past as a source of consolation in the present.

John F. Kennedy as National Martyr

In November 1963—100 years after Lincoln dedicated the national cemetery at Gettysburg—President John F. Kennedy was assassinated as he rode in a motorcade through Dealey Plaza in downtown Dallas, Texas. Symbolic associations with Lincoln quickly endowed his death with the aura of patriotic national sacrifice. During the official mourning rituals that followed Kennedy's assassination, politicians and clergy invited the nation to remember the fallen president as a national martyr who perished in a cause continuous with Lincoln's. In a eulogy at the Capitol, Chief Justice Earl Warren lamented the "martyrdom of our beloved president."[121] During a funeral mass held in Boston and broadcast on national television, Richard Cardinal Cushing suggested that the only consolation he could offer the bereaved family was the connection between Kennedy and his martyred predecessor: "What comfort can I extend to their heavy hearts today—what beyond the knowledge that they have given history a youthful Lincoln, who in his time and in his sacrifice, had made more sturdy the hopes of this nation and its people."[122]

One month after the assassination, on December 22, President Lyndon Johnson spoke at a candlelight service honoring Kennedy, held at the Lincoln Memorial. Both the setting for the ceremony and the words uttered therein richly evoked the image of Lincoln. Johnson's eulogy incorporated several of the most memorable tropes from the Gettysburg Address:

> One hundred years, thirty-three days, and several hours ago, the 16th President of the United States made a few appropriate remarks at Gettysburg. The world has long remembered what he said there. He lives on in this memorial, which is his tabernacle. As it was 100 years ago, so it is now. We have been bent in sorrow, but not in purpose. We buried Abraham Lincoln and John Kennedy, but we did not bury their dreams or their visions.[123]

The coincidence in timing that Johnson underscored reinforced the turn toward Gettysburg for consolation, and contributed to the perception that the parallel between Lincoln and Kennedy was self-evident. Using words originally intended to memorialize fallen soldiers, Johnson portrayed Kennedy's death as the highest form of sacrifice. And, like Lincoln, Johnson exhorted the living to imbue Kennedy's blood sacrifice with retrospective meaning, to ensure that it motivated the nation's enduring quest for freedom: "So let us here on this Christmas night determine that John Kennedy did not live or die in vain, that this Nation under God shall have a new birth of freedom."[124] In this interpretation, Kennedy, like the Union soldiers Lincoln memorialized and indeed like Lincoln himself, died so that that nation might live.

The Challenger Disaster and the Contemporary Frontier

Seventy-three seconds into the space shuttle Challenger's flight on January 28, 1986, a giant fireball erupted. The shuttle broke apart amidst a cloud of smoke, and its fragments descended into the Atlantic Ocean. All seven of the shuttle's crew members perished, becoming the first American astronauts lost in flight.[125] In the aftermath of this highly visible disaster—major news networks continually replayed footage from the launch—President Ronald Reagan postponed his State of the Union address, which had been scheduled for that evening. He instead addressed the American public with brief remarks from the Oval Office, putting aside his bureaucratic role to fully embody the symbolic and existential expectations of his office. "Today is a day for mourning and remembering," he said, expressing his own sorrow and that of his wife, Nancy Reagan. "Nancy and I are pained to the core by the tragedy of the shuttle Challenger. We know we share this pain with all of the people of our country. This is truly a national loss."

In his effort to offer consolation, Reagan turned to tropes from frontier mythology. The seven members of the Challenger crew, he suggested, were pioneers. Space represented the contemporary frontier:

> For the families of the seven, we cannot bear, as you do, the full impact of this tragedy. But we feel the loss, and we're thinking about you so very much. Your loved ones were daring and brave, and they had that special grace, that special spirit that says, "Give me a challenge, and I'll meet it with joy." . . . We've grown used to wonders in this century. It's hard to dazzle us. But for 25 years the United States space program has been doing just that. We've grown used to the idea of space, and perhaps we forget that we've only just begun. We're still pioneers. They, the members of the Challenger crew, were pioneers.

The expectation that Reagan provide reassurance and consolation was heightened by the fact that many children had been watching television coverage of the Challenger launch in school—and, furthermore, by the fact that one among the seven who perished was a high school teacher, Christa McAuliffe, selected for the voyage through NASA's Teacher in Space program. Reagan addressed children directly in his remarks, explaining: "sometimes painful things like this happen. It's all part of the process of exploration and discovery. It's all part of taking a chance and expanding man's horizons." Reagan noted that the Challenger disaster occurred precisely 390 years after Sir Francis Drake perished aboard ship off the coast of Panama. "In [Drake's] lifetime the great frontiers were the oceans," Reagan said,[126] implying that the "pioneers" in the Challenger crew, like Drake before them, sought to transcend the frontier of their own epoch. Frontier mythology thus provided powerful symbolic resources for political consolation, and Reagan asserted that the Challenger deaths took on meaning as part of a far longer and more encompassing quest.[127]

The Oklahoma City Bombing and the Legacy of the Civil Scriptures

Following the bombing of the Alfred P. Murrah Federal Building in Oklahoma City on April 19, 1995, public officials once again drew from the distant past as a source of symbolic orientation. The incident—which left 168 dead and several hundred more wounded—undermined the assumption that the American heartland was safe and secure and occasioned widespread shock and mourning. Most heart-wrenching were the deaths of numerous infants and toddlers; the explosion occurred less than 30 feet from a day care center located in the Murrah Building, and 19 children under the age of six perished in the blast.[128]

As they worked to make sense of the event, political leaders frequently drew analogies between the Oklahoma City dead and fallen soldiers, suggesting that those who died in the Murrah Building had perished in a quest for freedom. In 1998, when Vice President Al Gore traveled to the groundbreaking ceremony for the national memorial that would be constructed at the site, he said: "The people who died here were victims of one of the cruelest visitations of evil this nation has ever seen. But we offer them today not pity, but *honor*—for as much as any soldier who ever fought in any war—they paid the price of our freedom."[129] At the dedication ceremony for the memorial in 2000, Oklahoma Governor Frank Keating offered a more specific analogy:

> One hundred thirty-six years ago, Abraham Lincoln spoke at the dedication of another American shrine, the battlefield at Gettysburg. He said, "the world will little note nor long remember what we say here, but it can never forget what . . . they did here." Make no mistake—the names inscribed on those chairs on a smooth, grassy slope where a building once stood are the names of heroes and heroines all.[130]

For Keating, the memory of Lincoln at Gettysburg served to imbue the dead with agency, to assert that people who might otherwise be perceived as hapless victims were in fact heroes who perished in a cause.

During this same ceremony, President Bill Clinton reached back to the founding moment for consolation. Central to the interpretation he offered was a parallel in timing that evoked continuity between past and present, linking Oklahoma City to the nation's earliest history:

> As the Governor said in alluding to Gettysburg, there are places in our national landscape so scarred by freedom's sacrifice that they shape forever the soul of America—Valley Forge, Gettysburg, Selma. This place is such sacred ground. . . . I think you should all know that it was on this exact day 225 years ago that the American Revolution began. What a 225 years it has been. The brave Americans we lost here 220 years later were not fighting a war, but they were patriots in service to their fellow citizens, just as much as the police and

fire and other public servants are here among us today. And they were children whose promise keeps our old democracy forever young.[131]

Even as Clinton acknowledged the differences between the Oklahoma City dead and fallen soldiers, he asserted that the losses he memorialized took on meaning in a narrative that began on April 19, 1775. They, too, were "patriots" whose deaths represented "freedom's sacrifice." The legacy of the Revolution thus provided a meaningful interpretation of terrorist violence that took place over two hundred years later, at the close of the twentieth century.

THE AMBIGUITIES OF THE CIVIL SCRIPTURES

The more contemporary speeches described above clearly illustrate the enduring power of the civil scriptures in premediating emerging realities and imbuing disruptive events with meaning. These symbols link discrete moments in the context of a common narrative, provide interpretations of collective suffering, and offer a sense of continuity in the face of mortality. Yet it is worth noting that these symbols have been so enduring at least in part because of their interpretive ambiguity. Ideals such as "freedom," "liberty," "equality," and "democracy" that elicit widespread consensus also permit widely divergent, even contradictory, understandings. Indeed, national symbols are most enduring when they accommodate a wide range of interpretations.[132]

In her study of centennial and bicentennial celebrations, Lyn Spillman finds that the American founding moment "offers multivalent symbols" that frequently "bridge gulfs between mainstream cultural producers and their critics."[133] In 1876, for instance, disaffected southerners grounded their critiques of official commemorations using symbols derived from the Revolution. But recent interpretive conflicts in American political culture suggest that while these symbols at times "bridge gulfs," they may also expose cultural chasms.[134] The Oklahoma City bombing offers one such example.

As Clinton indicated in his address at the dedication of the memorial, the Oklahoma City bombing occurred on the 220th anniversary of Lexington and Concord. Clinton invoked this parallel in order to forge a connection between past and present that would imbue mourners' losses with the ultimate national significance. The bombing's perpetrator, Timothy McVeigh, also employed images and tropes from the Revolution to account for the violence and destruction that unfolded on April 19, 1995;

the timing of the bombing was intentional, not coincidental. McVeigh, however, understood *himself*—not those who perished in the bombing—as the "patriot and freedom fighter, defending his country against the alleged forces of tyranny and treason." McVeigh and his co-conspirators were members of the Patriot movement, and their act of violence was motivated centrally by the memory of the events that unfolded two years prior—on April 19, 1993—at the Branch Davidian settlement outside Waco, Texas. Citing Waco and the deadly 1992 confrontation in Ruby Ridge, McVeigh and others involved with the Patriot movement identified "a growing pattern of government tyranny." Arguing that the U.S. government was "waging war against its own citizens," they located themselves within the nation's revolutionary legacy, believing that the time had once again come for citizen-soldiers to rebel against government tyrants. When he was executed in June 2001, McVeigh understood himself to be a "martyred patriot," and actively cultivated an image that he believed would encourage others to view him in the same light.[135] In McVeigh's mind, *he* was the freedom fighter.

McVeigh and Clinton thus employed the same language, the same symbols, to articulate interpretations of the Oklahoma City bombing that were diametrically opposed. Who were the freedom fighters, and who were the tyrants? Who were the citizen-soldiers defending American liberty on April 19, 1995? The multivalence of these symbols—illustrated so powerfully in the discourse surrounding Oklahoma City—can at times bring diverse constituencies together in public mourning rituals or commemorative ceremonies.[136] Yet their ambiguities can also fuel polarizing cultural conflicts, as actors invoke the same symbols to support widely divergent interpretations of historical events. Such struggles over the meaning of quintessential American ideals have become especially vociferous in the effort to interpret September 11 and to forge a place for it in American collective memory; I take up the ambiguities of ideals espoused in the civil scriptures at greater length in chapter 7.

Critical as these civil scriptures would be in premediating September 11, post-9/11 political consolation discourse must also be understood in light of comparatively more recent speechmaking. During the twentieth century, especially with the rise of mass media, the symbolic dimension of politics took on ever-greater significance, elevating the importance of the consolation genre. While this chapter has offered a sociological exegesis of the civil scriptures and their import for consolation discourse, the next two chapters continue the historical narrative, tracing how these canonical texts gave way to two distinct modes of consolation in the twentieth century. I turn first to the dualistic mode, which built upon dominant themes from the civil scriptures to place collective suffering within a Manichean framework that moves inexorably toward the triumph of good over evil. I then describe the minor key in the consolation genre, the tragic mode that has its roots in Lincoln's second inaugural.

CHAPTER 2

The War of Good and Evil

During the Second World War, symbols from the civil scriptures played a central role in underwriting a broad interpretive framework that American political leaders articulated to make sense of the global struggle and to bring meaning to the massive losses that the United States sustained throughout. In this chapter, I trace the development of the *dualistic* mode of political consolation—which drew sharp binary distinctions between good and evil, freedom and tyranny—during the World War II era and show how it reverberated in American memory. Dualism is an ideal type in the Weberian sense, and although official representations of World War II have been extraordinarily consistent, I also attend to occasional departures from the dominant discourse. But by the 50th anniversary of World War II, the dualistic interpretation generated remarkable consensus. Several years later, this framework would powerfully premediate the events of September 11, as political leaders recalled the 1941 attack on Pearl Harbor and vigorously offered consolation in the dualistic mode.

ANTICIPATING THE CRISIS

Like Lincoln before him, Franklin Delano Roosevelt would become a seminal figure for the consolation genre. For Roosevelt, the presidency was "not merely an administrative office" or an "engineering job, efficient or inefficient."[1] Quite the contrary, it was "predominantly a place of moral leadership."[2] He thus envisioned himself as a "preaching president" in the tradition of his cousin, Theodore Roosevelt.[3] Indeed, Franklin Roosevelt's particular rhetorical gifts intersected with the advent of radio in ways that reshaped the presidency as an institution, heightening the expectation that incumbents fulfill the role of what Mary Stuckey calls the nation's "chief storyteller, its interpreter-in-chief."[4] Addressing the mass public through the radio, Roosevelt managed to cultivate a sense of intimacy with his listeners, and to create "the feeling that he understood them as individuals."[5] No doubt this sense of intimacy derived at least in part from Roosevelt's attention to human emotion, especially in times of crisis; Roosevelt embraced the task of consolation as an obligation of his office. In doing so, he laid the groundwork for those to follow, both by routinely addressing existential matters and by elaborating a mode of consolation that seamlessly incorporated images of Washington at Valley Forge and Lincoln at Gettysburg while also attending to the larger global context.

Japan's attack on Pearl Harbor on December 7, 1941—the event that drew the United States into the war—called for interpretation and consolation as the nation coped with shock, mourned the dead, and prepared for the fight ahead. Yet even before Pearl Harbor, Roosevelt's public rhetoric—which laid the groundwork for the United States to enter the conflict—offered a kind of anticipatory consolation. Recognizing that the years ahead would almost inevitably demand sacrifice in various forms, Roosevelt provided a framework for finding meaning in national suffering. When he accepted the Democratic nomination for the presidency in 1940, Roosevelt portrayed world affairs in stark binary language, suggesting that the survival of civilization itself was at stake:

> We face one of the great choices of history.
>
> It is not alone a choice of Government by the people versus dictatorship.
>
> It is not alone a choice of freedom versus slavery.
>
> It is not alone a choice between moving forward or falling back. It is all of these rolled into one.
>
> It is the continuance of civilization as we know it versus the ultimate destruction of all that we have held dear—religion against godlessness; the ideal of justice against the practice of force; moral decency versus the firing squad; courage to speak out, and to act, versus the false lullaby of appeasement.[6]

With the world sharply divided, Roosevelt argued, it was not only specific values or a system of governance, but also good itself that hung in the balance.

Roosevelt expanded this framework in high-profile speeches as he concluded his second term as president and began his third. His January 6, 1941, State of the Union address—now better known as the "four freedoms" speech—outlined the threat that "tyranny" posed for "the democratic way of life." In a speech that would not only prove influential in its own moment, but also reappear as a prominent symbolic framework in the 9/11 era, Roosevelt argued that people "everywhere in the world" ought to enjoy "four essential human freedoms": "freedom of speech and expression," the "freedom of every person to worship God in his own way," "freedom from want," and "freedom from fear." These ideals, he argued, were "no vision of a distant millennium," but instead "a definite basis for a kind of world attainable in our own time and generation." And they stood in direct opposition to the Axis vision for the world: "That kind of world is the very antithesis of the so-called new order of tyranny which the dictators seek to create with the crash of a bomb. To that new order we oppose the greater conception—the moral order." The American people, Roosevelt argued—channeling the antitheses that had long underwritten frontier mythology—faced a fundamental choice between competing ways of life: civilization and barbarism, freedom and tyranny, morality and immorality, good and evil. Even as he sought to persuade Americans that their "manner of life" was worth defending—and indeed extending across the globe—Roosevelt pledged that victory was assured: "the justice of morality must and will win in the end."[7]

Two weeks later, in his January 20, 1941, inaugural address, Roosevelt explicitly forged a place for present challenges in the American constitutive narrative. In terms befitting the ceremonial occasion, Roosevelt invoked pivotal trials from the nation's past to provide meaning for the present:

> In Washington's day the task of the people was to create and weld together a Nation.
>
> In Lincoln's day the task of the people was to preserve that Nation from disruption from within.
>
> In this day the task of the people is to save that Nation and its institutions from disruption from without.
>
> To us there has come a time, in the midst of swift happenings, to pause for a moment and take stock—to recall what our place in history has been, and to rediscover what we are and what we may be. . . .
>
> The democratic aspiration is no mere recent phase in human history. It is human history. . . .
>
> In the Americas its impact has been irresistible. . . .

Its vitality was written into our own Mayflower Compact, into the Declaration of Independence, into the Constitution of the United States, into the Gettysburg Address. . . .

In the face of great perils never before encountered, our strong purpose is to protect and to perpetuate the integrity of democracy.[8]

Recalling both the nation's founding moment and the image of Lincoln at Gettysburg, Roosevelt asserted that the nation had an obligation—even a sacred one—to intervene on democracy's behalf. Stewardship of democracy, Roosevelt argued, is "our place in history," "what we are"—an essential component of national identity and a legacy that the present generation was compelled to carry forward.

As the sense of crisis mounted, Roosevelt continually borrowed language from the American past to interpret the present, working to render the unfolding crisis comprehensible within a narrative that began with the Revolution. In his 1941 Independence Day address, Roosevelt argued that the "cause of human freedom" that had "swept across the world" over the past century and a half faced "a new resistance, in the form of several new practices of tyranny."[9] Echoing the closing pledge of the Declaration, Roosevelt preemptively articulated an interpretation for the death and suffering that was likely on the horizon: "It must be our deep conviction that we pledge as well our work, our will and, if it be necessary, our very lives."[10] Throughout the war years, remediations of the past would figure centrally in official discourse, bolstering the dualistic interpretation of the conflict at hand.

THE DUALISTIC MODE

As the crisis of Pearl Harbor claimed American lives and drew the United States into the war, the task of consolation—which Roosevelt had so clearly anticipated—became pressing. In response, Roosevelt elaborated the dualistic narrative that would come to define the era in national memory. Incorporating the language Roosevelt had already deployed to characterize the global struggle, the dualistic mode explained suffering and loss as part of an encompassing battle between good and evil. Though this ongoing conflict inevitably leaves loss and suffering in its wake, dualistic discourse posits that the struggle drives inexorably toward the triumph of the good. I borrow and adapt the term "dualistic" from Weber's writings on theodicy; as Weber put it, in the dualistic view, "[t]he world process, although full of inevitable suffering, is a continuous purification of the light from the contamination of darkness."[11] Suffering takes on meaning within this progressive teleology. Integrating the longstanding notion of national sacrifice into this encompassing worldview, dualistic discourse interprets deaths on the battlefield as glorious sacrifices that help ensure future triumph.

The dualistic narrative that coalesced during World War II made sense of a chaotic world by using a number of binary oppositions, contrasting "good" and "evil," "freedom" and "tyranny," and—drawing inspiration from the frontier mythology described in chapter 1—"civilization" and "savagery" or "barbarism."[12] The dualistic mode of political consolation might thus be understood as an extreme variant of the binary contrasts that Jeffrey Alexander and Philip Smith have identified at the core of American civil society discourse.[13] The contrast between "liberty" and "repression" that Alexander and Smith underscore comes, in the dualistic mode, to signal an even more fundamental contrast between humanity and inhumanity. In the case of World War II, the United States and its allies were understood as benevolent and humane—stewards of "civilization"—while their enemies were cast as not only malevolent and repressive, but also somehow less than human. Dualism, then, asserted rigid, even impermeable, symbolic boundaries[14] between rivals.

At the limit, these binary contrasts take on transcendent meaning; the dualistic mode of political consolation conceptualizes earthly events as manifestations of a cosmic struggle between light and darkness, good and evil, truth and falsehood. The assurance of victory, then—the triumph of liberty and humanity over repression and inhumanity—is providential. Though the dualistic view of the world long predates the establishment of the American nation, it has a particular affinity with canonical American narratives and the images of the nation reified in the civil scriptures. The language of American exceptionalism and the triumphant images of the American past that continually reappear in public discourse reinforce dualism's progressive teleology: the "chosen" nation, enjoying "special providence," is presumed to be morally righteous, ever on the side of light and right; in times of conflict or trial, it can do nothing but prevail.

INTERPRETING PEARL HARBOR

In his now iconic December 8, 1941, radio address—memorable especially for its declaration that December 7, 1941, was "a date which will live in infamy"—Roosevelt began to account for Pearl Harbor in dualistic language.[15] Describing Japan's "treachery" in launching an "unprovoked and dastardly attack," Roosevelt pledged that the struggle would culminate in victory: "No matter how long it may take us to overcome this premeditated invasion, the American people in their righteous might will win through to absolute victory."[16] He bolstered his claim with reference to divine providence: "With confidence in our armed forces—with the unbounding determination of our people—we will gain the inevitable triumph—so help us God."[17]

Three days later, in his message to Congress requesting war declarations against Italy and Germany, Roosevelt interpreted the conflict in encompassing language that exemplified the dualistic frame: "The forces endeavoring to enslave the entire world now are moving toward this hemisphere. Never before has there been a greater challenge to life, liberty, and civilization. . . . Rapid and united effort by all of the peoples of the world who are determined to remain free will insure a world victory of the forces of justice and of righteousness over the forces of savagery and of barbarism."[18] Civilization faced a formidable challenge, but dualistic teleology—the promise that civilization would inevitably prevail—offered hope and meaning in the face of this threat. Just as the United States had overcome the barbarism beyond the frontier on its own continent, Roosevelt implied, so too would it push beyond new frontiers across the oceans. The power of the past in premediating the present, giving symbolic shape to chaos and uncertainty, is clear.

The task of consolation was particularly central in Roosevelt's 1941 Christmas Eve address. That the crisis had descended in the midst of a season sacred to most Americans only increased the expectation that the president provide a meaningful account. Roosevelt delivered his address alongside British Prime Minister Winston Churchill, who visited Washington in the aftermath of Pearl Harbor. In his remarks, Roosevelt acknowledged that many citizens must find it difficult to rejoice in the midst of "resisting the evil thing." Yet he suggested that observing the Christmas holiday would provide the moral and spiritual preparation that the oncoming struggle would require:

> There is another preparation demanded of this Nation beyond and beside the preparation of weapons and materials of war. There is demanded also of us the preparation of our hearts; the arming of our hearts. And when we make ready our hearts for the labor and the suffering and the ultimate victory which lie ahead, then we observe Christmas Day—with all of its memories and all of its meanings—as we should.

Roosevelt framed the national struggle in language that called forth Christian ideals, counterposing these ideals with the image of a malevolent enemy: "Against enemies who preach the principles of hate and practice them, we set our faith in human love and in God's care for us and all men everywhere." And as he introduced Churchill, Roosevelt reinforced the interpretation of the war as a Manichean struggle, lauding those who had "been engaged in the task of defending good with their life-blood for months and for years."[19]

The day after Christmas—December 26, 1941—Churchill delivered a stirring address before a joint session of the U.S. Congress, invoking American civil scriptures as ably as any U.S. politician and bolstering Roosevelt's dualistic narrative. Churchill reflected that throughout his own life, he had "steered confidently towards the Gettysburg ideal of government of the people, by the people, for the people." He offered consolation for the suffering ahead with the exhortation that "we are doing the noblest work in the world, not only defending our hearths and homes, but the cause of freedom in every land." And while he underscored the Allies' agency, their power to ensure a victorious outcome—"we are the masters of our fate," Churchill proclaimed, and the "pangs and toils" of the task ahead "are not beyond our endurance"—he also invoked divine design. Churchill's address concluded with a firm and confident assurance that the Allies enjoyed providential favor: "he must indeed have a blind soul who cannot see that some great purpose and design is being worked out here below of which we have the honor to be the faithful servants."[20]

When he delivered his State of the Union address on January 6, 1942, Roosevelt warned of "a hard war, a long war, a bloody war, a costly war."[21] Untold suffering, he acknowledged, was clearly on the horizon. But this suffering would be anything but senseless, because the war, and all the losses it would entail, held transcendent significance:

We are fighting to cleanse the world of ancient evils, ancient ills.

Our enemies are guided by brutal cynicism, by unholy contempt for the human race. We are inspired by a faith that goes back through all the years to the first chapter of the Book of Genesis: "God created man in His own image."

We on our side are striving to be true to that divine heritage. We are fighting, as our fathers have fought, to uphold the doctrine that all men are equal in the sight of God. Those on the other side are striving to destroy this deep belief and to create a world in their own image—a world of tyranny and cruelty and serfdom.

That is the conflict that day and night now pervades our lives. . . . There never has been—there never can be—successful compromise between good and evil. Only total victory can reward the champions of tolerance, and decency, and freedom, and faith.[22]

Good versus evil; cynicism versus faith; tyranny versus freedom—the struggle left no room for ambivalence or ambiguity. There could be no "successful compromise," only "total victory." The American cause was also the cause of providence. Understood in this light, hardships and losses took on meaning and purpose.

THE WAR YEARS

Throughout the war, Roosevelt continued to narrate unfolding events in the dualistic mode, amplifying this interpretation with vivid imagery from the civil scriptures. In a February 1942 fireside chat, he reminded Americans of the hardships George Washington had faced during the eight years of the Revolution: "In a sense, every winter was a Valley Forge," Roosevelt reflected, recalling that the nation owed its very existence to patriots who engaged in a long, bloody struggle.[23] Indeed, Roosevelt suggested, "Washington's conduct in those hard times has provided the model for all Americans ever since—a model of moral stamina. He held to his course, as it had been charted in the Declaration of Independence."[24] Roosevelt called upon his contemporaries to renew Washington's commitment, quoting from Paine's *The American Crisis* and reminding his listeners that these same words were also read to the Continental Army in a moment of grave uncertainty:

> "The summer soldier and the sunshine patriot will, in this crisis, shrink from the service of their country; but he that stands it now, deserves the love and thanks of man and woman. Tyranny, like hell, is not easily conquered; yet we have this consolation with us, that the harder the sacrifice, the more glorious the triumph."

> So spoke Americans in the year 1776.

> So speak Americans today![25]

When Roosevelt spoke at ceremonies memorializing the American dead, he rendered losses meaningful as sacrifices in this storied lineage. In a 1944 address in Philadelphia, Roosevelt said: "I want to express the conviction that the greatest of our past American heroes—the heroes of Bunker Hill and Gettysburg—and San Juan Hill and Manila Bay and the Argonne—would consider themselves honored to be associated with our fighting men of today."[26] Like their predecessors, the soldiers who fell in World War II would live on in their nation, and would also attain a prized place in its collective memory. War propaganda reinforced this narrative. For instance, a U.S. Office of War Information poster encouraging Americans to purchase war bonds featured an image of the Lincoln Memorial. In it, Lincoln gazed down upon a fallen soldier, and alongside the scene was a phrase from the Gettysburg Address: "that we here highly resolve that these dead shall not have died in vain."[27]

Themes from Roosevelt's speeches also echoed in General Dwight D. Eisenhower's message to the troops just prior to the invasion of Normandy on June 6, 1944—"D-Day." "The hopes and prayers of liberty-loving people everywhere march with you," Eisenhower wrote. "In company with our brave Allies and brothers-in-arms on other Fronts, you will bring about the destruction of the German war machine, the elimination of Nazi tyranny over the oppressed peoples of Europe, and security for ourselves in a free world."[28] Although the Allies faced a "well trained" and "battle-hardened" enemy that would "fight savagely," Eisenhower declared that the tide had turned, and the Allies would move inexorably forward toward triumph: "The free men of the world are marching together to Victory!"[29] The task at hand was nothing less than to secure victory for civilization against a savage enemy, and to liberate the oppressed in the name of freedom.

Ever attuned to the human desire for consolation, Roosevelt offered a public prayer on June 6, 1944, broadcast to the American people as the invasion unfolded. "Almighty God," Roosevelt appealed, "[o]ur sons, pride of our Nation, this day have set upon a mighty endeavor, a struggle to preserve our Republic, our religion, and our civilization, and to set free a suffering humanity."[30] Acknowledging that some of these American sons would never return from their mission, Roosevelt prayed that God would recognize their cause as his own: "Embrace these, Father, and receive them, Thy heroic servants, into Thy kingdom." Even as he directed his words toward the divine, Roosevelt expressed confidence that victory was on the horizon: "With Thy blessing, we shall prevail over the unholy forces of our enemy."[31] With this public prayer, Roosevelt sought to articulate the purpose of loss and suffering to citizens who listened not knowing whether their sons and brothers had already fallen on the Normandy beaches. Even amidst the invasion, the commander-in-chief also embraced the role of consoler-in-chief.

As the war drew to a close, Roosevelt's successor, Harry Truman, continued to narrate world events in the dualistic mode. In his address on May 8, 1945—the day that Germany surrendered, known in the United States as "V-E Day," and only a few short weeks after Roosevelt's death—Truman announced: "The flags of freedom fly over all Europe."[32] While Truman expressed sorrow at "the terrible price we have paid to rid the world of Hitler and his evil band," he also asserted that each life lost should be understood as "a sacrifice to redeem our liberty."[33] The victory in Europe thus affirmed the interpretation that Roosevelt had begun to articulate even before the first American soldiers perished on the battlefield. And once again, this pivotal event was premediated through previous moments in the consolation genre. Truman's May 8 address clearly bore the influence of the Lincolnian conception of sacrifice; soldiers' deaths were redemptive and secured new life for liberty.

Truman portrayed the war in dualistic terms to the last. When the United States dropped atomic bombs on the Japanese cities of Hiroshima and Nagasaki in August 1945, Truman depicted the new technology as a God-given mechanism for ensuring that good triumphed over evil. Although he briefly acknowledged "the tragic significance of the atomic bomb," Truman argued forcefully that its development and use were imperative to prevent further suffering at the hands of a malevolent enemy:

> Having found the bomb we have used it. We have used it against those who attacked us without warning at Pearl Harbor, against those who have starved and beaten and executed American prisoners of war, against those who have abandoned all pretense of obeying international laws of warfare. We have used it in order to shorten the agony of war, in order to save the lives of thousands and thousands of young Americans.[34]

Pledging to continue using the bomb "until we completely destroy Japan's power to make war" or until Japan surrendered, Truman said: "We must constitute ourselves trustees of this new force—to prevent its misuse, and to turn it into the channels of service to mankind. It is an awful responsibility which has come to us. We thank God that it has come to us, instead of to our enemies; and we pray that He may guide us to use it in His ways and for His purposes."[35] According to Truman's interpretation, then, Americans' very possession of the bomb provided further evidence of the longstanding conviction that the United States was a chosen nation, morally righteous and destined for victory. In this way, the nation's oldest tropes premediated official representations of technology its founders could scarcely have imagined.

On September 1, 1945, when Japan announced its surrender, Truman proclaimed a final victory of good over evil, civilization over tyranny, once again invoking providential design. According to Truman, the crisis at Pearl Harbor—a crisis that had occasioned fear, mourning, and anxiety about the future—had at long last culminated in the triumph of civilization:

> Four years ago, the thoughts and fears of the whole civilized world were centered on another piece of American soil—Pearl Harbor. The mighty threat to civilization which began there is now laid at rest. It was a long road to Tokyo—and a bloody one.
>
> We shall not forget Pearl Harbor.
>
> The Japanese militants will not forget the U.S.S. *Missouri*.
>
> The evil done by the Japanese war lords can never be repaired or forgotten. But their power to destroy and kill has been taken from them. . . .
>
> To all of us there comes first a sense of gratitude to Almighty God who sustained us and our Allies in the dark days of grave danger, who made us to grow from weakness into the strongest fighting force in history, and who has now seen us overcome the forces of tyranny that sought to destroy His civilization.[36]

Lauding the sacrifices of those who perished, Truman described "our responsibility—ours, the living—to see to it that this victory shall be a monument worthy of the dead who died to win it," subtly echoing Lincoln's exhortation at Gettysburg.[37] And as he proclaimed September 2, 1945—the day that Japan would formally sign the terms of surrender—"V-J Day," Truman once again invoked the memory of Pearl Harbor. V-J Day, Truman declared, brought the retribution his predecessor had promised nearly four years prior: "it [V-J Day] is a day which we Americans shall always remember as a day of retribution—as we remember that other day, the day of infamy. . . . God's help has brought us to this day of victory. With His help we will attain . . . peace and prosperity for ourselves and all the world in the years ahead."[38] God had ever been, and would continue to be, on America's side.

Throughout the war years, there were often gaps between official discourse and popular sentiment. The historian John Bodnar describes "a vast public argument over how to understand what was going on and how to frame the unprecedented turbulence in the world that the war brought."[39] As Ernest Renan famously argued, however, forgetting such episodes of dissent and disagreement is critical in binding nations together.[40] As the years passed, the dualistic interpretation that public officials had articulated during the war generated remarkable consensus, and World War II came to be understood as "the good war"—a noble fight for an unquestionably just and worthy cause, befitting such substantial American sacrifice.[41] This Manichean frame would also reverberate powerfully in other genres of political speechmaking during crises to come. During the Cold War, American political officials repeatedly posited that—though the contours had shifted—the world was once again divided between good and evil, freedom and tyranny. Perhaps most famously, in the 1980s, President Ronald Reagan described the Soviet Union as an "evil empire,"[42] and predicted that "the march of freedom and democracy . . . will leave Marxism-Leninism on the ashheap of history as it has left other tyrannies which stifle the freedom and muzzle the self-expression of the people."[43]

Most important for present purposes is how dualistic discourse reverberated in the consolation genre, especially in official World War II commemorations toward the end of the century. In the 1990s, a series of elaborate and high-profile 50th anniversary observances firmly solidified the Manichean image of the conflict that U.S. leaders had long articulated. Subjected to a treacherous surprise attack in 1941, the innocent nation had risen to the occasion, fighting bravely and sacrificing nobly to liberate Europe and indeed to preserve liberty itself. In the remainder of this chapter, I examine how World War II commemorations revisited the meaning of suffering and death. Later, in part II, I will show how political leaders drew upon these interpretive materials, both implicitly and explicitly, in order to give shape to the shock of September 11.

REMEMBERING WORLD WAR II: COMMEMORATION AS PREMEDIATION

Pearl Harbor Anniversaries

Perhaps surprisingly—at least from the vantage point of our own historical moment, which is saturated with commemoration—it took quite some time before the anniversary of Pearl Harbor attracted significant attention on the national stage. Presidential speeches acknowledging the anniversary, for instance, were few and far between in the decades immediately following World War II.[44] Furthermore, anniversary commemorations at Pearl Harbor and other major events held at the site—including the dedication of the U.S.S. *Arizona* Memorial on Memorial Day in 1962 and the opening of the Visitors' Center there in 1980—attracted relatively little notice in the national media and among the general public.[45] It was not until the 50th anniversary, in 1991, that the Pearl Harbor anniversary garnered widespread national attention, and featured a series of addresses in Hawaii by the sitting president, George H. W. Bush.

The 50th anniversary of Pearl Harbor occasioned a complex commemorative dilemma. For one, the U.S.-Japan relationship was in flux. With the end of the Cold War, the United States and Japan were no longer united against a common threat, and the two nations found themselves debating their respective roles as well as their financial responsibilities for the Persian Gulf War.[46] In addition, the date called forth not only the memory of Japan's surprise attack, but also the memory of moments from the war years that threatened the stark binary terms within which American officials generally portrayed World War II: the internment of Japanese Americans and the atomic bombings of Hiroshima and Nagasaki.

Early in the planning process, controversy centered on the scope of the commemoration and its significance for U.S.-Japan relations. Who should participate in an official capacity? Should the commemoration serve as a symbolic vehicle for reconciliation with Japan, or as a strictly national event honoring Americans who fought and died at Pearl Harbor? For instance, one National Park Service proposal for the ceremony envisioned American children joining hands with Japanese children in a ritual of reconciliation.[47] During the summer, however, the U.S. State Department set the tone for a strictly national event with a statement barring foreign guests from participating in any official capacity:

> In our commemoration of the anniversary of Pearl Harbor, we will honor the memory of the service men who lost their lives and reflect upon this historic turning point in American history. It would be wrong to interpret this commemoration as directed against Japan in any way. It is not and will not be an anti-Japanese event.
>
> We envision no participation by foreign guests in Pearl Harbor commemorative events. These events mark a solemn national occasion. At the same time, we want to make clear that it is not our intention to exclude anyone from events commemorating Pearl Harbor's Fiftieth anniversary, and foreign visitors are of course free to attend any of the commemorative events [in an unofficial capacity].[48]

A subsequent suggestion to invite Japanese American children from Hawaii to participate in the ritual "was also dismissed as contrary to the central focus of the ceremonies."[49]

The statement did not, however, mark the end of the controversy. In fact, as the anniversary of the August 6, 1945, bombing of Hiroshima came and went, the debate took on trans-national dimensions. Honolulu Mayor Frank Fasi sparked the controversy when he "rejected the Bush administration's 'Americans only' approach to the anniversary and suggested that Japanese [representatives] be invited—after they had apologized for the attack."[50] His suggestion reached Tokyo, where "the chief cabinet secretary retorted that America ought to apologize for its bombing of Japan as well."[51]

In the week leading up to the Pearl Harbor anniversary, President Bush weighed in on the issue during an interview with ABC News. The interview—which aired on *This Week with David Brinkley* on Sunday, December 1—featured Bush's reflections on his personal memory of Pearl Harbor: he had enlisted in the U.S. Navy shortly after the attack, and in the interview he considered how his own combat experience shaped his attitude toward Japan as president. Toward the end of the segment, Brinkley said: "Mr. President, some of the Japanese leadership—I don't know how much—believes we owe them an apology."[52] The exchange that ensued foreshadowed the tone Bush would adopt in the commemoration several days later:

BUSH: For what?

BRINKLEY: I think for Hiroshima, the atomic bomb and so on.

BUSH: Yeah—not from this President. I was fighting over there. I had my orders to go back there when the war ended and American lives were saved. Now, do we mourn the loss of innocent civilians? Yes. Can I empathize with a family whose child was victimized by these attacks? Absolutely. But I can also empathize with my roommate's mother, my roommate having been killed in action. . . . And so, war is hell and it's a terrible thing, but there should be no apology requested and that, in my view, is rank revisionism. Truman faced a terrible decision. He had just come in and taken over from a popular Commander-in-Chief, Franklin D. Roosevelt, and they handed him this dilemma, this decision. "We're at war. Are you going to go all-out to win this war?" . . . He made a tough, calculating decision and it was right because it spared the lives of millions of American citizens and we were at war, having been attacked. So what we have tried to do and what we should continue to try to do is heal any wounds and express our proper concern and sympathy for the victims of war wherever they may be.

BRINKLEY: But no apology?

BUSH: No apology is required and it will not be asked of this President, I can guarantee you because I think—I've spoken, I think, before on this—but I feel so strongly about it. You see, I was there, in a tiny little way and I think what we have done with Japan—helping restore that country—is appreciated by Japan and so I don't think there's anybody looking for apologies one way or another.[53]

For Bush, the notion that the U.S. bombing of Hiroshima required an apology was apparently so unimaginable that he sought clarification: "For what?" Allowing that Americans should mourn the loss of "innocent civilians," he nonetheless implied that the United States need not shoulder guilt for their deaths. Emphasizing that Japan struck first—"we were at war, having been attacked"—Bush invoked a familiar justification for Truman's decision: it saved American lives.[54] Moreover, he depicted the United States as benevolent in victory, arguing that Japan's current stature was a byproduct of generous U.S. policy that helped "restore that country" in the postwar era. While Bush emphasized that there was no need for enduring animosity, his position on an apology for Hiroshima was stark and clear: the issue was a simple matter of right and wrong. (It is worth noting that the subsequent U.S. bombing of Nagasaki went unmentioned in the interview.)

In keeping with this exchange, Bush's commemorative speechmaking largely echoed the dualistic narrative that Roosevelt had articulated 50 years prior, a narrative carried forward in Cold War rhetoric that continued to apprehend global politics in stark binary terms. Not surprisingly, Bush made no mention of Hiroshima or Nagasaki. He did, however, complicate the dualistic narrative in another way, grappling explicitly with the difficult legacies of U.S. internment policy. In doing so, Bush subtly chipped away at the sharp symbolic boundary between an innocent nation caught by surprise and a savage attacker that defines the dualistic interpretation.

On December 7, 1991, Bush delivered a series of addresses in Hawaii. The first took place during a sunrise ceremony at the National Memorial Cemetery of the Pacific—also known as the Punchbowl—in Honolulu. Here, Bush began with a familiar narrative:

From this sacred ground near the waters of Pearl Harbor, we remember the moment when the Pacific Ocean erupted in a storm of fire and blood. We remember a morning when America, where some thought isolation meant security, awoke wounded, and reeling, plunged into a desperate fight for world freedom. I remember the crackle of the radio and the voice of our President.

"We are going to win the war," FDR told us, "and we are going to win the peace that follows." We won the war and secured the peace because American men and women responded bravely and instinctively to their Nation's call.[55]

The cruelty of the attackers, the American instinct to respond with valor, the cause of freedom, the pledge that victory was inevitable—Bush articulated key elements of an interpretation that originated with Roosevelt and drew upon some of the founding tropes in American political culture. As he told stories of individual valor exhibited on December 7, 1941, Bush evoked an image of sacrifice at once biblical and national: "The Bible says, 'Love is as strong as death.' To die for country, for family: that is the truth whispered by these rows of markers."[56]

Yet Bush went on to complicate his portrayal of the victors: heroic they were, but the Americans, too, committed misdeeds in the course of the conflict. Bush's first speech of the day acknowledged one such transgression:

Americans did not wage war against nations or races. We fought for freedom and human dignity against the nightmare of totalitarianism. The world must never forget that the dictatorships we fought, the Hitler and Tojo regimes, committed war crimes and atrocities. Our servicemen struggled and sacrificed not only in defense of our free way of life, but also in the hope that the blessings of liberty some day might extend to all peoples.

Our cause was just and honorable, but not every American action was fully fair. This ground embraces many American veterans whose love of country was put to the test unfairly by our own authorities. . . . They were sent to internment camps simply because their ancestors were Japanese. Other Asian-Americans suffered discrimination, and even violence, because they were mistaken for Japanese. And they, too, were innocent victims, who committed no offense.[57]

With these words, Bush injected a reflective recognition of American injustices into the familiar dualistic narrative, subtly unsettling its hallmark binary oppositions. At the same time, however, Bush also invoked what Olick terms a "grammar of exculpation"—that is, a way of "framing the problems of the . . . past so that they appear less burdening."[58] In this particular case, Bush mitigated the burdens of the past by juxtaposing the memory of American injustice with the memory of Axis "war crimes and atrocities," and by issuing a reminder that Americans fought not only to protect their own freedom, but also to provide deliverance for others—to expand "the blessings of liberty" across the globe.[59] On the one hand, then, Bush's words at the Punchbowl allowed for a more complex rendering of the Second World War than the ideal-typical dualistic narrative. On the other hand, his words excused, or at least minimized, injustice even as they acknowledged it.

Following these reflections, Bush turned back to more familiar language, heralding the "war generation" that helped Japan, Germany, and Italy "grow strong in the exercise of democracy and free enterprise," and asserting that their descendants had continued this legacy in Korea, Vietnam, and the Cold War, as well as more recently in the Persian Gulf.[60] The world for which American soldiers fought in World War II, Bush claimed, had begun to come into view. And the progress that had occurred in the decades since Pearl Harbor affirmed the meaning and purpose of the losses he commemorated: "Every soldier and sailor and airman buried here offered his life so that others might be free," Bush said. "Not one of them died in vain."[61]

When he spoke at the U.S.S. *Arizona*—the "sacred center" for Pearl Harbor commemoration,[62] both a memorial and a burial ground—Bush was more circumspect, adhering closely to the dualistic narrative. Reflecting on the symbolic meaning of the oil that rises continually from the *Arizona*, Bush suggested that God joined the righteous victors in mourning their losses: "With each drop, it is as though God Himself were crying," he said.[63] Bush did underscore Japanese American contributions to the war effort in specific terms, noting that in the past soldiers of Japanese descent had wrongly been excluded from the standard heroic narrative: "One of Pearl Harbor's lessons is that together we could 'summon lightness against dark'; that was Dwight Eisenhower," Bush reflected.[64] And he pledged that vigilance in the present would bring continued meaning to the sacrifices that allowed the righteous to prevail in the 1940s: gazing down "at *Arizona*'s sunken hull," he said, "reminds us of the might of ideals that inspire boys to die as men. Everyone who aches at their sacrifice knows America must be forever vigilant. And Americans must always remember the brave and the innocent who gave their lives to keep us free."[65]

Bush delivered his final address of the day before an assemblage of World War II veterans and families at a shoreside pier. In these remarks, Bush quoted Roosevelt as he re-asserted an encompassing dualistic image of the conflict: "On that day of infamy, Pearl Harbor propelled each of us into a titanic contest for mankind's future. It galvanized the American spirit as never, ever before into a single-minded resolve that could produce only one thing: victory." The day after Pearl Harbor, Bush recalled, "President Roosevelt proclaimed the singular American objective: 'With confidence in our Armed Forces, with the unbounding determination of our people, we will gain the inevitable triumph, so help us, God.'" The victory in World War II laid the foundation for the future, and the next generation prevailed in its own Manichean struggle: "And now," Bush declared, "we stand triumphant, for the third time this century, this time in the wake of the Cold War."

Yet once again, triumphalism did not go unmitigated in this final address. In fact, Bush addressed the difficult aspects of America's World War II past even more overtly and extensively than he had in his remarks at the Punchbowl. Here, he largely abandoned the exculpatory tropes he had invoked earlier, discussing American injustices on their own terms without mentioning atrocities on the other side:

> In remembering, it is important to come to grips with the past. No nation can fully understand itself or find its place in the world if it does not look with clear eyes at all the glories and disgraces, too, of the past. We in the United States acknowledge such an injustice in our own history: The internment of Americans of Japanese ancestry was a great injustice, and it will never be repeated. Today, all Americans should acknowledge Japan's Prime Minister Miyazawa's national statement of deep remorse concerning the attack on Pearl Harbor. It was a thoughtful, it was a difficult expression much appreciated by the people of the United States of America.

Bush's expression of regret neglected the most difficult elements of World War II memory in America: the bombings of Hiroshima and Nagasaki, for which he had so resolutely refused to apologize. Nevertheless, the president's words acknowledging this difficult aspect of the American past on an anniversary with profound symbolic significance for the nation should not go unnoticed.

With that acknowledgment, however, Bush turned to the positive legacies of the Allied victory:

> The values we hold dear as a Nation—equality of opportunity, freedom of religion and speech and assembly, free and vigorous elections—are now revered by many nations. Our greatest victory in World War II took place not on the field of battle, but in nations we once counted as foes. The ideals of democracy and liberty have triumphed in a world once threatened with conquest by tyranny and despotism.

Crucially, the triumph that came to pass provided a sort of retrospective consolation for combat losses:

> Today as we celebrate the world's evolution toward freedom, we commemorate democracy's fallen heroes, the defenders of freedom as well as the victims

of dictatorship who never saw the light of liberty. . . . The friends I lost, that all of us lost, upheld a great and noble cause. Because of their sacrifice, the world now lives in greater freedom and peace than ever before.

Not only did the United States triumph—"We won. We crushed totalitarianism," Bush proclaimed—but Americans also exhibited exemplary moral virtue as they spread freedom to their former enemies: "And when that was done, we helped our enemies give birth to democracies." Inviting his fellow veterans and their family members to recall those who perished, Bush once again offered reflections on the existential questions that reverberated five decades hence. As the president articulated the meaning and purpose of the losses he commemorated, he subtly remediated Lincoln: "Don't you think each one is saying, 'I did not die in vain'?"[66]

Commemorating Victory in the 1980s and 1990s

From the U.S. perspective, the other watershed moments in World War II, suitable for commemoration, were June 6 (D-Day), May 8 (V-E Day), and September 2 (V-J Day). Though the 50th anniversary ceremonies would be even more extensive, the 40th anniversary of D-Day attracted significant attention among Americans. On June 6, 1984, President Ronald Reagan delivered a stirring address in Normandy, France, paving the way for the ascendancy of "the myth of the 'good war'" that would become a fixture in American public culture in years to come.[67]

Reagan began with an image of helpless victims desperate for deliverance. "We're here to mark that day in history when the Allied armies joined in battle to reclaim this continent to liberty," he said.

> For four long years, much of Europe had been under a terrible shadow. Free nations had fallen, Jews cried out in the camps, millions cried out for liberation. Europe was enslaved, and the world prayed for its rescue. Here in Normandy the rescue began. Here the Allies stood and fought against tyranny in a giant undertaking unparalleled in human history.

Central in rescuing these victims were the 225 American Rangers—the so-called "boys of Pointe du Hoc"—for whom Reagan offered special praise. The Rangers—Reagan recounted—climbed "sheer and desolate cliffs" to "take out the enemy guns" that were trained on the Allied forces as they approached. And according to Reagan, these liberators fought with the confidence that they served a just cause: "The men of Normandy had faith that what they were doing was right, faith that they fought for all humanity, faith that a just God would grant them mercy on this beachhead or on the next." Reagan then addressed veterans directly: "You all knew that some things are worth dying for. One's country is worth dying for, and democracy is worth dying for, because it's the most deeply honorable form of government ever devised by man."[68] Like the prayer Roosevelt uttered over the radio in 1944, Reagan's words offered consolation for the losses sustained at Normandy. They did so by reiterating the core claim of Lincoln's Gettysburg Address: that the men who died were martyrs for both their nation and for democracy itself.[69]

A decade later, when the 50th anniversaries of D-Day and the Allied victory arrived, broad themes in American public culture bolstered the dualistic frame that state officials continued to articulate.[70] As veterans aged and passed away, prominent "moral entrepreneurs"[71] launched vigorous efforts to publicly remember and celebrate the Allies' triumph—and in doing so, to cement an image of the era that cast veterans' achievements in a heroic light. News anchor Tom Brokaw's bestseller *The Greatest Generation* evinced a nostalgic view of a generation whose "individualism, discipline, and self-sacrifice" won the "prosperity and freedom" that Americans enjoyed in the 1990s,[72] and lauded them for exhibiting exceptional personal virtue.[73] Similarly, the historian Stephen Ambrose's *Band of Brothers* offered a heroic image of the 101st Airborne, blending personal recollections with a morality tale that chronicled the men's struggle to victory in Germany.[74]

On the 50th anniversary of D-Day, President Bill Clinton traveled to Normandy, where he delivered a series of addresses before dignitaries, veterans, and families. During a sunrise ceremony off the coast of Normandy, Clinton described "that fateful morning" of D-Day as "the pivot point of the war, perhaps the pivot point of the 20th century."[75] He concluded this brief address with words Eisenhower had uttered 50 years prior: "'Let us all beseech the blessing of almighty God upon this great and noble undertaking.'"[76]

In a subsequent ceremony at Utah Beach, Defense Secretary William Perry described the American soldiers' fight for "freedom," their willingness to risk their lives "so that others may live in peace and without fear," as "the greatest work that God can have us do."[77] In his own remarks at this site, Clinton exhorted his audience "never" to "forget that thousands of people gave everything they were, or what they might have become, so that freedom might live."[78] His words once again remediated Lincolnian themes: the soldiers' deaths secured life for freedom itself. Calling on the present generation to "turn the pain of loss into the power of redemption so that 50 or 100 or 1,000 years from now, those who bought our liberty with their lives will never be forgotten," Clinton concluded: "To those of you who have survived and come back to this hallowed ground, let me say that the rest of us know that the most difficult days of your lives bought us 50 years of freedom."[79] Similarly, in yet another address at Pointe du Hoc, Clinton called upon subsequent generations—"the children of your sacrifice"—to "carry on the work you began here."[80] Lincoln's influence is once again clear. Clinton reassured the aging veterans that they had played a vital role in a community of memory that would endure beyond them: "We commit ourselves, as you did, to keep [freedom's] lamp burning for those who will follow. You completed your mission here. But the mission of freedom goes on; the battle continues."[81] The president's words thus offered consolation by assimilating "the most difficult days" of veterans' lives into a triumphant national narrative.

The anniversaries of the Allied victory called forth yet another round of soaring speeches. On May 8, 1995, Clinton reflected that no generation can fully eradicate evil: "You could not banish the forces of darkness from the future," he said, addressing the World War II generation.[82] Yet the triumph the Allies achieved "taught us the most important lesson: that we can prevail over the forces of darkness, that we must prevail."[83] Four months later, on September 2, Clinton "commemorate[d] the triumph of freedom over tyranny" at the National Cemetery of the Pacific in Honolulu. "The seeds of democracy you [the World War II generation] planted and nurtured flower today in every corner of the globe," Clinton observed,[84] once again reminding veterans of their place in a story that would outlive them—their symbolic immortality in the ongoing vitality of their nation.

WORLD WAR II MEMORY AND THE RESISTANCE TO REGRET

In the preceding pages, I have traced the development of a dualistic mode of political consolation. Drawing on ideas and images from the civil scriptures, this dualistic discourse interpreted the Second World War as an episode in a cosmic battle between good and evil. Death and suffering took on meaning as part of this unfolding teleology, and political leaders pledged that light and right, liberty and democracy, would triumph in the end. Fifty years later, the dualistic mode overwhelmingly prevailed in high-profile commemorations, at which point romantic images of the "good war" generated remarkable consensus among Americans generally.[85] The dualistic symbolism that reverberated so powerfully in the final decade of the twentieth century was thus readily available when the

United States confronted a shocking assault under very different circumstances on September 11, 2001, and indeed—as I will illustrate in part II—World War II would premediate this distant event in decisive ways.

The continued flourishing of dualistic discourse runs counter to the tendencies identified in many scholarly accounts of postwar political culture, which frequently point to the Second World War as the last gasp of a heroic or triumphalist era. George Mosse argues that World War II brought the demise of the "Myth of the War Experience," which had—through the First World War—compellingly transformed the horrors of death on the battlefield into glorious images of martyrdom.[86] Tom Engelhardt argues that the bombings of Hiroshima and Nagasaki signaled "the end of victory culture" in the United States, ushering in an era where "victory and defeat, enemy and self, threatened to merge."[87] Schwartz identifies World War II as the watershed moment after which the United States entered its present "post-heroic era," in which "the very notion of greatness has eroded."[88] And, as I noted in the introduction, taking stock of these shifts, Olick theorizes the rise of a "politics of regret." No longer able to ground legitimation claims with reference to untainted images of a glorious past, states increasingly face pressure to acknowledge their own atrocities and misdeeds —to openly confront the difficult and shameful aspects of their histories—in order to maintain legitimacy.[89]

On the one hand, even if dualistic discourse overwhelmingly predominated, commemorative speechmaking during the 50th anniversary of the war evinced subtle gestures toward a politics of regret. The expectations of an apologetic age clearly weighed on Bush at Pearl Harbor in 1991, where he complicated the sharp symbolic boundary that had once divided villains and victors when he discussed the internment of Americans with Japanese ancestry, conceding that "not every American action was fully fair." On the other hand, however, such gestures have been both understated and fleeting, at least in the case of World War II; perhaps most revealingly, they have, as yet, evaded the difficult legacies of the decision to use nuclear weapons in the cities of Hiroshima and Nagasaki.

The ways in which American political leaders have dealt with—or rather, avoided dealing with—these events illustrates the resilience of the dualistic mode as an interpretation of the Second World War and as an element of American political culture more generally. Bush's incredulity at the very suggestion that an apology for Hiroshima might be merited reflects broad tendencies in official discourse. Hiroshima and Nagasaki have overwhelmingly been met with silence among U.S. presidents: since 1945, "Hiroshima" has been mentioned only 21 times in a public address by a sitting president; "Nagasaki" has been mentioned only seven times.[90] On those rare occasions when presidents have addressed these events, they have assiduously relied upon a grammar of exculpation, most commonly deflecting responsibility by referring to the bombings in the passive voice. Reagan's address on the 40th anniversary of Hiroshima—the only presidential address commemorating the anniversary of either event in U.S. history to date—is emblematic. "We must never forget what nuclear weapons wrought upon Hiroshima and Nagasaki," he said, as though the bombs themselves—and not the people who developed or deployed them—were the agents at work.[91]

The public controversy that erupted in the mid-1990s over the proposed exhibition at the National Air and Space Museum featuring the *Enola Gay*—the B-29 bomber from which U.S. forces dropped the bomb on Hiroshima—revealed the enduring taboo on any robust effort to reevaluate Truman's decision at the level of official memory.[92] Indeed, even a plan to engage with the tremendous suffering that the bombings unleashed on the ground proved controversial. Among the proposals that generated dissent from veterans' organizations were artifacts and photographs from a section titled "Ground Zero" that depicted the atomic blast and scenes from its aftermath.[93] When Clinton stepped in to arbitrate, he sided with the dissenting veterans. Citing his own conviction that "President Truman did the right thing," Clinton explained: "I do not believe on the celebration of the end of the war and the service and the sacrifice of our people, that that is the appropriate time to be asking about or launching a major reexamination of that issue."[94]

Clinton thus worked to preserve the longstanding image of the United States as a redeemer nation, a beacon of civilization that stands over and against the darkness of the savage or barbaric forces that threaten human freedom.[95] And in fact, before nightfall on September 11, 2001, the very nomenclature that originally referred to those sites of U.S. perpetration in Hiroshima and Nagasaki—"ground zero"—had been appropriated as an emblem for *American* innocence and victimhood. After 9/11, the term quickly came to refer to the site in lower Manhattan where the Twin Towers once stood. Now commonly rendered as a proper noun—"Ground Zero"—this usage further obscures the difficult memory of American perpetration, and reinscribes the symbolic boundaries established in official interpretations of World War II.[96]

Resistance toward the politics of regret, then, has been striking in the U.S. case, no doubt aided by American economic and military power. Yet as Engelhardt, Schwartz, and others have observed, more ambiguous images of the American collectivity did indeed emerge in the postwar era. Amidst the social and cultural upheavals of the 1960s and 1970s, public officials—prodded by the civil rights movement, incidents of racial and political violence, and vigorous public debates concerning the American military involvement in Vietnam—grappled with injustices perpetrated by the so-called redeemer nation, complicating the sharp symbolic binaries through which political leaders had long interpreted the nation's history. Within this context, an alternate, tragic mode of political consolation—which has roots in Lincoln's second inaugural address—became an increasingly resonant frame for coming to terms with collective suffering in American political discourse.

CHAPTER 3

American Tragedies

Both popular and scholarly wisdom holds that Americans lack a sense of the tragic.[1] An optimistic, and indeed even triumphalist, sense of history runs deep among the people who transformed the European jeremiad into a hopeful genre; in the American political imagination, suffering has habitually been understood as a harbinger of future triumph. Yet as I noted in chapter 2, the social, cultural, and intellectual conditions of our own epoch—the declining legitimacy of the nation-state and the increasing salience of narratives highlighting injustice and oppression perpetrated by its elites, as well as growing skepticism toward the very possibility for collective meaning in and of itself—have made such heroic narratives considerably more difficult to sustain. The regretful undercurrent that destabilized the sharp symbolic boundaries between barbaric villains and beneficent victors during the 50th anniversary of Pearl Harbor is but one small window onto these developments. During the 1960s and 1970s, the American military involvement in Vietnam and the series of high-profile political assassinations that left the nation reeling would raise powerful challenges to the dualistic mode of political consolation.

In the face of these challenges, engagement with the tragic has become a considerably more common response to collective suffering. This chapter considers such engagements and their impact on the consolation genre, identifying the threads that constitute an alternate, tragic mode of political consolation. My intention is not to identify a single watershed moment that divides a dualistic epoch from a tragic one. The tragic mode has a long history, with roots in Lincoln, especially his second inaugural.[2] Moreover, these competing modes continue to exist in tension, overlapping and at times intertwining in official interpretations of collective suffering even today; despite its relative ascendancy in the postwar era, the tragic mode remains the minor key in the consolation genre. Nonetheless, this chapter provides a window onto a broad historical shift in the conditions of meaning-making that has influenced American political consolation in significant ways. Before delving into the empirical material that illustrates this shift, however, it is worth a brief look at the meaning of the tragic and its connection to the existential matters at the heart of this book.

THE TRAGIC MODE

The history of tragedy begins with the Greeks, for whom it represented a dramatic genre. Aeschylus's plays provide the earliest surviving window onto the tragic form, while Aristotle's *Poetics* offers the foundation for theorizing the tragic. Greek tragedy inspired subsequent variants of tragic drama—Elizabethan tragedy is a familiar example—but it also gave way to philosophical reflection on the *idea* of the tragic in more general terms.[3] Originating in German Romanticism, as Rita Felski explains, this philosophical approach gave the notion of the tragic "general theoretical salience and metaphorical power as a prism through which to grasp the antinomies of the human condition."[4] Tragedy, then, is not only a literary category that describes a particular plot structure. It is also a broader philosophical category that captures a distinctive orientation to existential questions, and provides a lens for contemplating the causes of human suffering as well as the meaning of that suffering for both individual biography and collective life. "The central problem of tragedy," literary critic T. R. Henn writes, "has always been the moral or religious problem of the place of evil and suffering in the world."[5]

While the disappearance of the tragic *form*—the plot structure underpinning dramas penned by Aeschylus and Euripides, Seneca and Shakespeare—prompted theorists such as George Steiner to declare "the death of tragedy," others have pointed to the enduring relevance of tragic themes and sensibilities in the modern world.[6] As Felski points out, "traditional tragedies are no longer being written," yet "they are still being read, watched, performed, revised, and invoked"; she thus identifies "the persistence of a tragic mode in modernity" that bears the influence of its long genealogy yet also responds to the contemporary context.[7] A mode, Felski explains, denotes "a selective group of features rather than a text's overall defining structure," transcending the "prescriptive taxonomies" that define tragic dramas while also retaining more specificity than colloquial uses of the tragic to refer to something "very sad."[8] Indeed, scholars across disciplines—including literary theory,[9] political theory,[10] anthropology,[11] and sociology[12]—have recently revivified a robust discourse on the tragic, working to retheorize the concept in terms faithful to its history, yet also meaningful and useful in the modern moment. Many such efforts aim to identify not a transcendent and unchanging form or a strictly delimited plot structure, but "a *combinatoire* of overlapping features" or Wittgensteinian "family resemblances"[13]—in sociological terms, ideal-typical features—and thus provide the basis for outlining the tragic mode of political consolation.

The tragic mode offers a lens for contemplating human suffering that resonates powerfully with the broad cultural climate of the postwar era—increasingly regretful, apologetic, and open to contemplating the complex legacies of the past. At its core, the tragic mode rejects the progressive teleology and the sharp symbolic binaries that give life to dualism. Rather than projecting a triumphant future that will emerge inexorably out of past turmoil, David Scott suggests, the tragic mode offers instead "an agonic confrontation that holds out no necessary promise of rescue or reconciliation or redemption"[14]—only reflection, introspection, and questioning.[15] Rejecting "modern dreams of progress and perfectibility," Felski argues that the tragic mode confronts "the role of the incalculable and unforeseeable in human affairs," recognizing "that individuals may act against their own interests and that the consequences of their actions may deviate disastrously from what they expected and hoped for."[16]

In doing so, it unsettles the fundamental moral contrasts through which dualistic discourse gives shape and meaning to human suffering. Within the tragic universe—where "reason and unreason, blindness and insight, innocence and guilt, are deeply interconnected"[17]—even the best-intentioned actors may find themselves complicit in causing or exacerbating human suffering. Moral ambiguity, not moral absolutism, is the order of the day. Binary distinctions between good and evil crumble; the boundaries between civilization and savagery collapse, too, as heroes confront their own flaws and missteps and villains are recognized as human; clear ethical prescriptions and moral judgments give way to protracted contemplation on the causes of human misfortune and the wisdom that might be derived from calamity and suffering. As Terry Eagleton puts it, tragedy "matters to modernity" precisely "as a theodicy, a metaphysical humanism, a critique of Enlightenment, a displaced form of religion or political nostalgia."[18] The tragic mode, then, provides a vehicle for contemplating existential questions outside progressive teleologies, whether they are animated by providence, modernity, or both.

Because it unsettles the binary oppositions that are so often the life-blood of democratic culture,[19] tragedy has long been a wellspring for political critique.[20] In ancient Athens, performances of tragic dramas followed immediately on the heels of civic ceremonies that reaffirmed the values of the state and, remarkably, proceeded to expose the "flaws and contradictions" in state ideology.[21] Tragic dramas, that is, "again and again [took] key terms of the normative and evaluative vocabulary of civic discourse, and depict[ed] conflicts and ambiguities in their meanings and use."[22] Today, the tragic mode—with its openness to self-examination and self-reflection—similarly serves as a source of internal critique. What factors *within* the collectivity might have contributed to calamity? What wisdom can be derived from the confrontation with human suffering and loss? Such questions were the driving force behind Lincoln's second inaugural, and the tragic mode of political consolation continues to engage them publicly.

INTERPRETING POLITICAL ASSASSINATION

In the 1860s, the disparity between the foundational American principle that "all men are created equal" and the institution of slavery eventually gave way to Lincoln's tragic interpretation of the Civil War. Slavery was a national sin; death and suffering on both sides became atonement rather than noble sacrifice. Into the twentieth century, the institution that Lincoln had described as a national sin cast a long shadow. In the 1960s, a full century after Lincoln, violence and turmoil within the United States once again drew attention to the vast disparity between the nation's ideals and its practices. On April 4, 1968, the assassination of Martin Luther King, Jr.—the civil rights leader immersed in the continuing struggle for racial justice—would once again call forth public reflections from the nation's leaders on the tragic dimensions of American life.

The response to the King assassination, of course, can only be understood in the context of the tumultuous period now captured under the rubric of "the sixties."[23] King's death was not the first violent incident of the decade that commanded national attention and called for consolation. In 1963, the assassination of President John F. Kennedy shocked Americans and occasioned widespread grief and mourning. Unsettling as it was, however, this violent event quickly assumed a place in familiar collective narratives: Kennedy, as I explained in chapter 1, became a "youthful Lincoln,"[24] a national martyr who gave his life for a cause greater than himself. The nation had suffered, but its identity remained intact.[25] Its pain was real, but citizens could find consolation in a familiar narrative. As Eyerman argues, five turbulent years later, King's assassination at the

Lorraine Motel in Memphis called forth far deeper reflections on the meaning of these violent acts emerging from within the American body politic.[26]

When the news of King's assassination broke, Senator Robert Kennedy—the younger brother of the martyred president—was on the road, campaigning for the Democratic presidential nomination. Among many Americans, Robert Kennedy's candidacy had come to represent the nation's finest hope for healing the wounds of a violent and polarizing decade: for devising a way out of the war in Vietnam and restoring America's moral stature in the international community, for engaging disaffected youth, and for bridging the enduring racial divides manifest in three summers of inner-city riots.[27] On the evening of April 4, Kennedy was scheduled to speak in a predominantly black neighborhood in Indianapolis. His remarks in Indianapolis would only augment the mythology surrounding his candidacy.[28] Having confirmed with aides that his audience had not yet heard the news of King's assassination, Kennedy asked that they lower their campaign signs and delivered it himself.

"I have some very sad news for all of you," he said, "and, I think, sad news for all of our fellow citizens, and people who love peace all over the world; and that is that Martin Luther King was shot and was killed tonight in Memphis, Tennessee."[29] Screams erupted, but eventually, the crowd allowed Kennedy to continue. "Martin Luther King dedicated his life to love and to justice between fellow human beings," Kennedy reflected. "He died in the cause of that effort."[30] Only the night before, King had spoken publicly of his willingness to give his life in the struggle for racial justice, expressing hope that such a sacrifice, if rendered, would be redemptive.[31] Kennedy offered reassurance that King's life and death had meaning as part of this struggle, appealing to a longstanding discourse of national sacrifice.

But Kennedy did not stop there. Instead, he went on to complicate the progressive national narrative that his opening lines had evoked. King's assassination, he said, was an occasion for intensive reflection, for reexamining the basic vision guiding the nation forward into the future: "in this difficult time for the United States, it's perhaps well to ask what kind of a nation we are and what direction we want to move in." Kennedy acknowledged the human impulse to seek revenge in the face of such violence: "For those of you who are black—considering the evidence evidently is that there were white people who were responsible [for the assassination]—you can be filled with bitterness, and with hatred, and a desire for revenge." Yet to indulge this impulse, meeting violence with intensified hatred or with further violence, would be contrary to King's vision and his legacy:

> We can move in that direction as a country, in greater polarization—black people amongst blacks, and white amongst whites, filled with hatred toward one another. Or we can make an effort, as Martin Luther King did, to understand, and to comprehend, and replace that violence, that stain of bloodshed that has spread across our land, with an effort to understand, compassion, and love.

And thus Kennedy, who empathized with the pain and outrage of his on-lookers at the most intimate level, called for understanding:

> For those of you who are black and are tempted to . . . be filled with hatred and mistrust of the injustice of such an act, against all white people, I would only say that I can also feel in my own heart the same kind of feeling. I had a member of my family killed, but he was killed by a white man. But we have to make an effort in the United States. We have to make an effort to understand, to . . . go beyond these rather difficult times.[32]

This rare public glimpse into Kennedy's private pain lent exceptional moral gravity to his words.

Indeed, Kennedy had struggled mightily to come to terms with his brother's death, and to reconcile the pain of the loss with his own religious faith.[33] Through his grief, he found solace in Greek tragedy.[34] As he spoke in Indianapolis, he directed his audience toward words that had brought meaning to his own inward struggle: "my favorite poet was Aeschylus," he said. "And he once wrote:

> 'Even in our sleep, pain which cannot forget
> falls drop by drop upon the heart,
> until, in our own despair,
> against our will,
> comes wisdom
> through the awful grace of God.'"[35]

Suffering, these words suggest, yields wisdom, yet that wisdom can only be grasped in retrospect. In the earliest moments of despair, meaning cannot yet be discerned, only contemplated.

King's death, then, was an occasion for contemplation, and for beginning or renewing the work of mutual comprehension. It was a time to break down binaries and boundaries, symbolic or otherwise, rather than to reinforce them. "What we need in the United States is not division," Kennedy said, "what we need in the United States is not hatred; what we need in the United States is not violence and lawlessness, but is love, and wisdom, and compassion toward one another, and a feeling of justice toward those who still suffer within our country, whether they be white or whether they be black."[36] Kennedy acknowledged the struggle that remained on the horizon, noting that present events did not mark the end of "violence," "lawlessness," or "disorder."[37] This struggle, however, would not be a confrontation between opposing and irreconcilable forces of civilization and savagery. Instead, Kennedy called for an effort to tame humanity's savage impulses—to diminish the darkness that existed *within* the nation and its citizens—in order to secure a future more peaceful than the past: "And let's dedicate ourselves to what the Greeks wrote so many years ago: to tame the savageness of man and make gentle the life of this world."[38] Fallible humans would continue to struggle with savagery, but it would be their own, not that of some dehumanized enemy or "other." Consolation and critique came together as one. The crowd cheered. Riots broke out in urban landscapes across America, but not in Indianapolis.[39]

In accounting for Kennedy's remarkable ability to connect with his predominantly African American audience at such a moment, political theorist Robert Pirro points to a shared tragic sensibility, springing from disparate sources but nonetheless converging in a common understanding of this violent event.[40] As Cornel West argues, among the major "intellectual and existential sources" shaping King's own rhetoric and worldview were the American civil religion, the Gandhian approach to nonviolent social change, and the black church tradition.[41] The latter, according to West, "was a communal response to an existential and political situation in which no penultimate reasons suffice to make any kind of sense or give any type of meaning to the personal circumstances and collective condition of Afro-Americans," and thus "put the pressing and urgent problem of evil—the utterly and undeniably *tragic* character of life and history—at its center."[42] A master at hybridization, King emplotted his struggle using metaphors from American civil religion—the struggle for racial justice became an Exodus; violent deaths became (potentially) redemptive sacrifices—while also rejecting its penchant for collective self-celebration.[43] Filtered through this more tragic lens, "King's America"—as Jonathan Rieder explains—"was less a redeemer nation than a nation in need of redemption."[44] Kennedy's confrontation with the violence and inhumanity that sprung from *within* the American nation, his openness in publicly grappling with the ways that the self-proclaimed city upon a hill fell short of its moral and political ideals, thus resonated with themes from King's own speechmaking.

The day after King's death, Kennedy continued to interpret the event—and the escalating violence across the nation more generally—in the tragic mode. Speaking at the Cleveland City Club, Kennedy began: "This is a time of shame and sorrow."[45] He would offer consolation and hope, but not before taking a hard look at the complex causes of what he called the "mindless menace of violence in America."[46] Invoking Lincoln, Kennedy depicted a nation gone astray. "'Among free men,' said Abraham Lincoln, 'there can be no successful appeal from the ballot to the bullet; and those who take such appeal are sure to lose their cause and pay the costs.' Yet we seemingly tolerate a rising level of violence that ignores our common humanity and our claims to civilization alike," he said.[47] Again, in contrast to the dualistic image of a struggle between civilization and savagery, humanity and inhumanity, Kennedy portrayed a people struggling with, and indeed in many ways succumbing to, its own violent and destructive impulses—impulses that undermined its most cherished ideals, the oft-repeated claim that America represented the pinnacle of civilization. Exhorting that "violence breeds violence," Kennedy described the process by which Americans had come "to look at our brothers as aliens."

> When you teach a man to hate and fear his brother, when you teach that he is a lesser man because of his color or his beliefs or the policies he pursues, when you teach that those who differ from you threaten your freedom or your job or your family, then you also learn to confront others not as fellow citizens but as enemies—to be met not with cooperation but with conquest, to be subjugated and mastered.[48]

Overcoming the "mindless menace of violence" would require Americans to dismantle the boundaries that separated erstwhile "enemies" and "others," to "admit the vanity of our false distinctions among men," and to remember "that those who live with us are our brothers."[49]

Kennedy concluded with consoling words, again channeling Lincoln. But the Lincoln text he chose was not the Gettysburg Address, the text so often invoked to imbue his brother's death with the sacred aura of redemptive national sacrifice. He turned, instead, to the ur-text for the tragic mode of political consolation, the second inaugural, expressing hope for reconciliation in a nation once again torn asunder by internal violence: "Surely we can learn, at least, to look at those around us as fellow men," Kennedy said, "and surely we can begin to work a little harder to bind up the wounds among us and to become in our hearts brothers and countrymen once again."[50]

President Lyndon Johnson also addressed King's death, first in a brief statement on the evening of April 4, then at greater length in an address to the nation the following day. Johnson's credibility had eroded considerably, especially in light of the mounting controversy over the Vietnam War, and he had bowed out of the race for the Democratic presidential nomination just days before. His voice was therefore less powerful than it had once been. But he, too, incorporated tragic themes. On the night of the assassination, Johnson called for contemplation: "I hope that all Americans tonight will search their hearts as they ponder this most tragic incident," he said.[51] The next day, he spoke of a nation in mourning—weeping, he explained, "for a tragedy that denies the very meaning of our land."[52] In Johnson's interpretation, violence was more a disembodied force than a dark impulse emanating from within the collectivity: "If we are to have the America that we mean to have," he said, "all men—of all races, all regions, all religions—must stand their ground to deny violence its victory."[53] This is an important difference, inviting unity against a common (albeit abstracted) foe rather than an examination of collective shortcomings. Johnson projected hope for King's cause—"the quest for freedom" and "the vision of brotherhood" that King espoused. But actualizing King's vision would require continued struggle against these abstract forces. Johnson, too, borrowed from Lincoln: "Men who are white—men who are black—must and will now join together as never in the past to let all the forces of divisiveness know that America shall not be ruled by the bullet, but only by the ballot of free and of just men."[54]

Following his powerful performance in Indianapolis, Kennedy secured primary victories in Indiana, Nebraska, South Dakota, and California. On the night of June 4, 1968—the day that he secured victories in both South Dakota and California—Kennedy addressed supporters at the Ambassador Hotel in Los Angeles. His remarks built upon "the myth . . . that his campaign was uniting every opposite," that he was the one who could heal the nation's wounds.[55] "The vote in South Dakota—the most rural state—and in California—the most urban state—indicates we can end the division within the United States," Kennedy declared.[56] As he exited the hotel through a narrow kitchen corridor, shortly after midnight on June 5, the shots rang out. One day later, in the early morning hours of June 6, Kennedy's spokesman, Frank Mankiewicz, announced the senator's death.[57] The vibrant hopes surrounding his candidacy were extinguished.

Less than five years after his brother's violent death and only two short months after Martin Luther King's death, Robert Kennedy's assassination seemed to defy any effort at meaning-making.[58] These crimes had no place in narratives of a morally righteous redeemer nation, city upon a hill and beacon to the world; the image of the fallen candidate, supported by 17-year-old busboy Juan Romero, was not the image of freedom and democracy. On the morning of June 5, Johnson's press secretary, George Christian, issued a statement in the president's name: "There are no words equal to the horror of this tragedy," it said.[59]

Nevertheless, words were required. Even as doctors worked to spare Kennedy's life, Johnson addressed the nation, speaking "not only as your President, but as a fellow American who is shocked and dismayed, as you are, by the attempt on Senator Kennedy's life, deeply disturbed, as I know you are, by lawlessness and violence in our country, of which this tragedy is the latest spectacular example."[60] Though he cautioned against the view "that our country itself is sick"—countering one of the media narratives that coalesced after King's death and intensified after Kennedy was shot—he nonetheless raised questions that suggested otherwise: "What in the nature of our people and the environment of our society makes possible such murder and such violence?"[61] He announced the appointment of a commission to address such questions, to examine the "tragic phenomenon" of "violence and assassination" in the United States.[62] Through this effort, Johnson explained, "we hope to learn why we inflict such suffering on ourselves."[63] The time had come for an officially sanctioned form of self-examination.

During Kennedy's funeral, themes from the senator's own most memorable speechmaking reverberated, as did Lincoln's meditations on the tragedy of the Civil War. In a eulogy for his brother, Senator Edward Kennedy read from Robert Kennedy's speech delivered during the 1966 Day of Affirmation in South Africa. Like the words of consolation Robert Kennedy had offered his fellow citizens two months before his death, this earlier speech reflected on the sources of human misery in the tragic mode. Robert Kennedy portrayed human beings as complex composites of good and evil, virtue and vice, while also calling upon his listeners to strive, as much as possible, to "bind up the wounds" inflicted by oppression and inequality in its various forms.

> There is discrimination in this world and slavery and slaughter and starvation. Governments repress their people. Millions are trapped in poverty, while the nation grows rich and wealth is lavished on armaments everywhere.
>
> These are differing evils, but they are the common works of man. They reflect the imperfection of human justice, the inadequacy of human compassion, our lack of sensibility towards the suffering of our fellows.
>
> But we can perhaps remember, even if only for a time, that those who live with us are our brothers, that they share with us the same short moment of life,

that they seek as we do nothing but the chance to live out their lives in purpose and happiness, winning what satisfaction and fulfillment they can.

Surely this bond of common faith, this bond of common goals, can begin to teach us something. Surely we can learn at least to look at those around us as fellow men. And surely we can begin to work a little harder to bind up the wounds among us and to become in our own hearts brothers and countrymen once again.[64]

Here, too, Robert Kennedy's words poignantly juxtaposed a keen awareness of human fallibility with a potent sense of hope. We may remember our common humanity only for a time, but in doing so, we might heal the wounds inflicted by the preceding violence, and learn to live better together.

CONSOLATION AND DEFEAT: THE VIETNAM WAR

Much as these assassinations threatened American collective identity and unleashed profound existential struggles, the U.S. military involvement in Vietnam posed even more powerful challenges for political consolation. As American soldiers fought and died, and as veterans returned home bearing horrific physical and psychological wounds, the citizenry engaged in divisive debates over the war's meaning and purpose. After the fall of Saigon in 1975, Americans remained unable to agree on the cause for which they had been fighting, let alone whether it was noble and just. How were Americans to come to terms with over 58,000 lives lost, and countless more forever scarred, in the face of a lost war whose meaning remained elusive? In the beginning, John Hellman argues, "Americans generally saw themselves entering yet another frontier, once again 'western pilgrims' on a mission of protection and progress."[65] But ultimately, as Engelhardt aptly summarizes: "There was no American narrative form that could long have contained the story of a slow-motion defeat inflicted by a nonwhite people in a frontier war in which the statistics of American victory seemed everywhere evident."[66]

Even at the level of official politics, the interpretive response to Vietnam has been complex, varied, and at times internally contradictory. John F. Kennedy's "new frontier" rhetoric opened the way for the United States to "regenerate its traditional virtues while serving future progress," and the Green Berets—the Special Forces in which JFK demonstrated particular interest—"symbolized the rededication to the American errand."[67]

As the U.S. involvement in Vietnam escalated throughout the 1960s, President Johnson invoked Thomas Paine, Abraham Lincoln, and Franklin Roosevelt, and generally offered consolation in the dualistic mode. This time, the confrontation between "liberty" and "tyranny" took shape as a struggle against communism; not only Vietnam, but also all of Southeast Asia, was at stake, posing another grave threat to freedom and demanding another valiant struggle to protect it. Yet as a steady stream of public critique unsettled this soaring narrative, politicians increasingly grappled with questions of meaning, and the task of consolation, in the tragic mode. Eventually, the tension between these competing modes of consolation would be set in stone, articulated in the Vietnam Veterans Memorial on the national mall.

The War Years

Johnson's early efforts to give shape to the conflict, and to justify the losses it would bring, resonated clearly with Roosevelt's World War II speechmaking. In a Christmas message to Americans in Vietnam, issued on December 23, 1964, Johnson articulated the familiar claim that the nation's good fortune entailed profound global responsibilities: "You are in Viet-Nam, far from the places and people you love, because the forces that have given our Nation strength and wealth have also placed upon it the burden of defending freedom."[68] In shouldering this burden, American soldiers joined a storied lineage: "We Americans celebrate this holy season in liberty because our forebears had the courage, the determination, the will to sacrifice, that was equal to the challenges before them. Future generations in many lands will spend Christmas days in freedom because there are men everywhere who are equal to this grim challenge in our time."[69] With deaths to mourn and more losses on the horizon, Johnson offered reassurance that, painful as it might be, the soldiers' suffering stood firmly within the cause of freedom.

Johnson would reiterate this narrative as he sought to offer consolation to an increasingly divided national public in the years to come. In his January 1966 State of the Union address, he acknowledged that "tonight, as so many nights before, young Americans struggle and young Americans die in a distant land." But he once again identified their cause as worthy: "We fight for the principle of self-determination—that the people of South Vietnam should be able to choose their own course, choose it in free elections without violence, without terror, and without fear."[70] The basic binary between freedom and fear, liberty and repression that was so pervasive in Roosevelt's speechmaking also gave shape to this new struggle and brought meaning to the American lives lost in it. Johnson expressed sadness at "young men dying in the fullness of their promise," and reflected on the gravity of his responsibility as commander-in-chief, sending them into the line of fire.[71] Yet his commitment to the cause, and his conviction that the nation's current course of action was the right one, was unwavering: "as long as others will challenge America's security and test the clearness of our beliefs with fire and steel, then we must stand or see the promise of two centuries tremble."[72]

Indeed, according to Johnson, faltering in the cause would not only undermine the sacrifices already rendered in Vietnam, but also the sacrifices rendered in the confrontations between freedom and tyranny that preceded it. "Americans will be fighting and dying in Vietnam this Memorial Day," Johnson acknowledged in a 1966 Memorial Day proclamation. "Their sacrifice is part of an ancient legacy that begins with man's first act of transcendent courage, and that contains all that is noble and selfless in human character. Our own liberty was won in a struggle against tyranny. In two world wars and in Korea, brave Americans and their allies gave their lives that men might live and prosper in freedom. We shall not forsake their sacrifice."[73] To surrender would be to betray the trust of the "brave Americans" whose sacrifices in wars past had earned them a cherished place in the community of memory, dating all the way back to the original "struggle against tyranny" that gave birth to the American nation.

Like Roosevelt before him, Johnson turned regularly to the civil scriptures. In his 1967 State of the Union, Johnson recovered words from the founding moment to make sense of the present, quoting Thomas Paine:

> We . . . know that this Nation was not forged and did not survive and grow and prosper without a great deal of sacrifice from a great many men.
>
> For all the disorders that we must deal with, and all the frustrations that concern us, and all the anxieties that we are called upon to resolve, for all the issues we must face with the agony that attends them, let us remember that "those who expect to reap the blessings of freedom must, like men, undergo the fatigues of supporting it." . . .
>
> Let us remember that we have been tested before and America has never been found wanting.[74]

This trial, like those that preceded it, would culminate in victory.

At the Presidential Prayer Breakfast in February 1968, Johnson remediated Roosevelt explicitly. Quoting from Roosevelt's June 14, 1942, radio address, Johnson sought to bind together events separated by a quarter of a century:

> It was in 1942—when we were challenged in both oceans—at a season when the winds of the world blew harsh and the dawn of a brighter day seemed very far away, Franklin Delano Roosevelt offered to this Nation these words and I repeat them in these times now: "God of the free, we pledge our hearts and lives today to the cause of all free mankind. . . . Grant us a common faith that man shall know bread and peace, that he shall know justice and righteousness, freedom and security, and an equal chance to do his best, not only in our own lands, but throughout the world."[75]

Even as he expressed humility, Johnson suggested that righteousness would give way to triumph in the end: "What we pray for with all our hearts is an end to war and tyranny. . . . We are fighting now—as we fought 25 years ago—to prevent any further expansion of totalitarian coercion over the souls of men," he said. "We do all of this with a very deep sense of humility—recognizing our own fallibilities and errors—but with an equally strong belief that the cause of humanity cannot be permitted to lose by default. We can never be so arrogant as to claim God's special blessing for America, but we can express the hope that in His eyes we have at least tried to help make possible a new vitality of the human conscience . . . throughout all the world."[76]

Johnson's expression of humility came in the midst of vigorous public criticism that had, by 1968, reached a fever pitch. As early as 1963, Bob Dylan's "With God on Our Side" had portrayed the assumption that American causes enjoyed providential favor as self-righteous and naïve, though at the time it made no explicit mention of Vietnam.[77] As the sixties wore on, ironic and tragic renderings of the war became increasingly pervasive in popular culture. At Woodstock in August 1969, Jimi Hendrix's ironic reinterpretation of "The Star-Spangled Banner" offered a wordless but eviscerating critique of the nation celebrated in the anthem; Country Joe McDonald—himself a Navy veteran—performed his "I-Feel-Like-I'm-Fixin'-To-Die Rag," which undercut the very possibility for political consolation.[78] Indeed, in the cultural climate of the sixties, protesters and critics reversed the very binaries that Johnson invoked to give shape to the war. Engaging in what Philip Smith terms "inversion"—"retaining institutionalized discourses but switching their empirical referents"[79]—these critics effectively flipped the dualistic script, placing the United States on the opposite site of the ledger. *America* was evil, violent, and tyrannous; *America* was inhumane.

Among the most memorable critiques came from Martin Luther King. In an April 4, 1967, sermon at Riverside Church in New York City, King fused his critique of racial injustice at home with a critique of the violence and domination that the United States perpetrated abroad. U.S. leaders claimed to be protecting and extending the nation's abiding commitment to freedom, yet in doing so, the nation sent young black men "eight thousand miles away to guarantee liberties in Southeast Asia which they had not found in southwest Georgia and East Harlem." In truth, however, America had not really brought freedom at all. The Vietnamese people, King reflected, "must see Americans as strange liberators." In King's interpretation, the Americans who claimed to be torchbearers for freedom and democracy had instead become violent oppressors and indeed the worst kind of villains:

> What do the peasants think as we ally ourselves with the landlords and as we refuse to put any action into our many words concerning land reform? What do they think as we test out our latest weapons on them, just as the Germans tested out new medicine and new tortures in the concentration camps of Europe? Where are the roots of the independent Vietnam we claim to be building?

Far from continuing the quest for freedom that the Allies pursued during World War II, according to King, the United States had done the opposite—it had become like the Nazis. He quoted an unnamed Vietnamese Buddhist leader as suggesting that the longstanding American script had been inverted irreversibly: "The image of America will never again be the image of revolution, freedom, and democracy, but the image of violence and militarism." King himself still harbored hope, though tentative, for a better outcome. "The world now demands a maturity of America that we may not be able to achieve," he said, calling on Americans to "see the enemy's point of view, to hear his questions, to know his assessment of ourselves." For King, the war was a national sin that required atonement: "In order to atone for our sins and errors in Vietnam, we should take the initiative in bringing a halt to this tragic war." Quoting the poet James Russell Lowell, King depicted an America that had come to embody the evil it claimed to oppose, while also suggesting there was still time to shift course:

> Once to every man and nation comes a moment to decide,
> In the strife of Truth and Falsehood, for the good or evil side;
> Some great cause, God's new Messiah offering each the bloom or blight,
> And the choice goes by forever 'twixt that darkness and that light.[80]

Among the many factors that create obstacles for state leaders to admit mistakes at war is the very task that is the core subject of this book: the task of consolation. Soldiers enter battle with the promise of symbolic immortality in a triumphant nation, a nation that—thanks to their sacrifice—will continue to flourish, and to move progressively forward, coming ever more to embody the ideals for which they might be called upon to give their lives. Johnson's words on Memorial Day in 1966 laid bare this assumption, suggesting that an admission of error would pose not just a political threat, but an existential threat, undermining the meanings ascribed to the events that had come before.

In the 1968 presidential primary, however, Johnson's challengers offered new narratives. On the very first stop of his campaign, Robert Kennedy reinterpreted the Vietnam War in the tragic mode, calling for a change of course while at the same time addressing the existential questions that such a change would so powerfully raise. The speech took place on March 18 at Kansas State University, as part of the Alfred M. Landon Lectures on Public Issues. Kennedy argued that the moment of national crisis—of "questioning and uncertainty at home, divisive war abroad"—was a time for engaging in reflections that cut to the heart of national identity.[81] The year 1968 was "a year when we choose not simply who will lead us, but where we wish to be led," by taking stock of both the present, "the country we want for ourselves," as well as the future that would be built upon it—"the kind [of country] we want for our children."[82]

Kennedy's divergence with Johnson on the issue of Vietnam was the motivating force behind his campaign, and his speech criticized the Johnson administration for steadily escalating the American military presence in Vietnam. Time and again, Kennedy said, the administration had assured the public "that this one last step would bring victory."[83] Before he criticized the president's policies, however, he acknowledged his own culpability, casting his past decisions in a tragic light.

> I was involved in many of the early decisions on Vietnam, decisions that helped set us on our present path. It may be that the effort was doomed from the start. . . . If that is the case, as it well may be, then I am willing to bear my share of the responsibility, before history and before my fellow citizens. But past error is no excuse for its own perpetuation. Tragedy is a tool for the living to gain wisdom, not a guide by which to live. Now as ever, we do ourselves best justice when we measure ourselves against ancient tests, as in the *Antigone* of Sophocles: "All men make mistakes, but a good man yields when he knows his course is wrong, and repairs the evil. The only sin is pride."[84]

Interpreting Vietnam in the tragic mode gave Kennedy a frame for justifying a change of course while still giving past events a meaningful place in a collective narrative. Kennedy argued that human events yield wisdom only in retrospect, and in the tragic view, some measure of human error is perhaps unavoidable: we choose with imperfect understanding, and often among irreconcilable goods. In fact, the course we believed to be good and right may turn out to generate its own unanticipated evils. While tragic dramas generally culminate in the hero's demise, social actors—who may become aware of their own hubris in a way that fictional protagonists are not—have the capacity to redirect the flow of events, to avert the final catastrophe. Kennedy thus suggested that they may interrupt the unfolding of an archetypal tragic plot by engaging in the kind of self-examination that tragic dramatists sought to facilitate among their audiences.[85]

Kennedy's tragic interpretation of Vietnam was not a full-fledged inversion of the dualistic script. He acknowledged American errors and even atrocities, complicating the "redeemer nation" image, but he also spoke of the nation's virtues. And he spoke openly of the enemy's cruelty: "The Viet Cong are a brutal enemy indeed. Time and time again, they have shown their willingness to sacrifice innocent civilians, to engage in torture and murder and despicable terror to achieve their ends. . . . There can be no easy moral answer to this war, no one-sided condemnation of American actions." As such, Kennedy prepared for an ambiguous outcome: "at a real negotiating table," he said, "there can be no 'victory' for either side; only a painful and difficult compromise." But—recalling Lincoln's depiction of the Civil War as a tragedy that neither side truly wanted—Kennedy argued that Vietnam "can be ended, in a peace of brave men who have fought each other with a terrible fury, each believing he and he alone was in the right. We have prayed to different gods, and the prayers of neither have been answered fully. Now, while there is still time for some of them to be partly answered, now is the time to stop." There would be no total victory, but some of America's hopes might still be brought to fruition. Yet only an admission of error, followed by a change of course, would restore the nation as the moral exemplar it had long aspired to be. "Our country is in danger," Kennedy said, and "not just from foreign enemies; but above all, from our own misguided policies—and what they can do to the nation that Thomas Jefferson once told us was the last, best, hope of man."[86]

Of course, an RFK presidency—and the tragic mode of interpretation and consolation that might have accompanied it—was not to be. Johnson's eventual successor, Richard Nixon, also promised change in Vietnam, pledging to secure an "honorable peace" by withdrawing American combat troops and training the South Vietnamese to assume their responsibilities.

In his first inaugural, Nixon spoke of "the title of peacemaker" as "[t]he greatest honor history can bestow," and suggested that this very honor "now beckons America."[87] Citing a national "crisis of the spirit," Nixon summoned Lincoln's image, inviting Americans to embrace "the better angels of our nature."[88] Yet through the news of the My Lai massacre and the controversial bombings of Cambodia, the "slow-motion defeat"[89]—and the widespread disillusionment that accompanied it—only continued. On January 23, 1973, Nixon announced "an agreement to end the war and," as he had promised, "bring peace with honor."[90] He called for pride in the young Americans who served "in one of the most selfless enterprises in the history of nations," and for "those who sacrificed, who gave their lives so that the people of South Vietnam might live in freedom and so that the world might live in peace."[91] After the withdrawal of U.S. troops, however, the ceasefire was fleeting, and for many Americans, the events that followed brought continued shame. When the last U.S. personnel were evacuated from Saigon in April 1975, Nixon's successor, Gerald Ford, simply called on Americans "to close ranks, to avoid recrimination about the past, to look ahead to the many goals we share."[92]

Commemorating Vietnam

Of course, 58,000 deaths, and the long years of national discord that accompanied them, could not simply be consigned to the past. The "collective amnesia"[93] of the postwar period ultimately gave way as the narrative contradictions pressed in. How could Americans sustain that cherished myth of "regeneration through violence"—and the conviction that their heroic warriors, no matter the obstacles in their path, would inevitably emerge victorious—in the aftermath of Vietnam?[94] If Americans had always achieved victory because they took up arms only when their cause was morally righteous—with God on their side—what did it mean that the nation had now met with defeat on the field of battle? Such questions not only threatened the nation's self-image, but also the very ability to provide existential meaning that Anderson identified at the core of nationhood.

Ultimately, Vietnam veterans—whose individual biographies were now inextricably bound up with national narratives—brought about a reckoning with the war and its meaning at the level of official memory. In May 1979, Jan Scruggs—himself a wounded veteran—initiated the process that culminated in the Vietnam Veterans Memorial on the national mall.[95] Officially, the Vietnam Veterans Memorial Fund stipulated that the memorial would remain silent on the political significance of the war: "The Memorial will make no political statement regarding the war or its conduct. It will transcend those issues."[96] Indeed, this commitment is embodied in the very nomenclature that identifies the memorial: as Patrick Hagopian points out, it is the Vietnam *Veterans* Memorial, not the Vietnam *War* Memorial.[97] From its inception, then, the memorial was understood as a venue for paying tribute to the individual soldier while remaining silent on larger questions of the war's meaning and purpose: "Honor the soldier, not the cause" was the memorial's "original framing rule."[98] Yet questions concerning the meaning of the losses commemorated would inevitably reverberate throughout the process of designing, constructing, and dedicating the memorial.

How could a memorial honor the fallen without glorifying the cause they served? Maya Lin's winning design addressed this powerful commemorative dilemma by inscribing the names of the American soldiers who perished in Vietnam on black granite walls, representing massive loss without identifying its meaning. The names, listed in the order in which the soldiers died and making no reference to rank, take the place of the heroic symbolism that typically defines war memorials.[99] Its intention, as Lin explained, was to foster introspection: "What people see or don't see is their own projection."[100] The V-shaped design cuts into the landscape, carving out a space for visitors to contemplate what they encounter therein.

In the very act of acknowledging the fallen, listing row after row of names, the memorial opens the questions that define the consolation genre. How are visitors to make sense of these names, the long list of lives extinguished? But it opts, as Peter Ehrenhaus puts it, for "silence," and thus "places both the burden and the freedom upon us to discover what these past events mean, whether these deaths do have meaning, what virtue is to be found in sacrifice, and what our own relationship should be to our political institutions."[101] It is, in other words, a place that acknowledges the human impulse to seek meaning, to engage the existential matters that the war so clearly raised, without offering specific answers to the questions raised by its representation of overwhelming national loss. Even in the face of the memorial's ambiguity, however, the events surrounding its dedication prompted public figures to give narrative shape to Vietnam memory—or, at the very least, to reflect aloud on the difficulties surrounding this task. As they confronted the memory of the 58,000 dead, the task of consolation was pivotal.

Like the Vietnam Veterans Memorial itself, the official speechmaking surrounding the dedication embodied the contradictions, ambivalence, and deep disagreement surrounding the conflict it commemorated.

So, too, did the rituals that filled the weeklong salute to Vietnam veterans preceding the dedication. These rituals included, for instance, a parade dotted with American flags as well as a somber 56-hour candlelight vigil at the National Cathedral in which each fallen soldier's name was read aloud.[102] During his remarks at the dedication ceremony on November 13, 1982, Everett Alvarez, Jr.—the deputy director of the Veterans Administration, and also a Vietnam veteran who had spent over eight years in captivity as a prisoner of war—reflected openly on the challenge of memorializing Vietnam. "Many Americans today still have a difficult time in dealing with that war—with its effect on our society and with the legacy of those of us sent to fight it," he said. "But no one can debate the service and sacrifice of those who fell while serving."[103] Alvarez thus reiterated the charge to honor the soldier even amidst the controversies surrounding his or her cause. The memorial, Alvarez suggested, would be a place that fostered reflection on matters of conscience and on the questions surrounding Americans' collective responsibilities:

No one can doubt that the Vietnam Veterans Memorial will be an eternal touchstone for the conscience of this nation. It will tell us as no words can of the awesome responsibility that we have as members of a free and a dedicated society. This memorial is a tribute to all who served in Southeast Asia. It vividly enshrines the memory of those who did not return, and it symbolizes the heroic, unselfish acceptance of duty by the millions of Americans who went there. The words that we speak today are a vivid contrast to the eternal silence of this memorial. That silence, inspired by the reverence and the respect for those who died and those who served, is in and of itself a tribute. There was a time long ago when words would have mattered more. But at this place, for all time, it is our hearts that speak.[104]

Even as Alvarez hailed soldiers' heroism, the vocabulary he deployed to describe their service underscored a certain passivity: they were "sent to fight," and in doing so they exhibited "unselfish acceptance of duty." This language allows a separation between a soldier's sense of duty and his or her other moral and political convictions—a notable contrast to the agentic images of soldiers fighting for freedom that typically pervade American political speechmaking.

Senator John Warner, a Virginia Republican who delivered the keynote address, stayed closer to canonical vocabularies of political consolation, gesturing toward the national symbolism contained on the mall in an effort to connect Vietnam with more glorious moments in the national past:

> these names shall forever be embraced—to our right, by our first president, George Washington, and to our left, by Abraham Lincoln. Indeed, this will always be one of the most hallowed pieces of ground in America. Some may realize that just beyond that hill, there is nearing completion a monument to the 56 signers of the Declaration of Independence. They, too, made sacrifices. But let us also remember that the Vietnam veterans made sacrifices no less in the cause of freedom.[105]

At the same time, however, Warner subtly engaged the moral quandaries that the memory of Vietnam inevitably called forth. Warner described the memorial as:[106]

> a symbol of everlasting hope—hope that the human sacrifice of the service men and women and their families will serve as a check and a balance far greater than any laws passed by Congress . . . and impress on future and present leaders of America to pursue every possible solution before committing Americans to battle. The hope that if this nation ever again must respond to the call to defend freedom, that those at home will realize that victory can only be achieved if we support and follow those we send to fight.[107]

Even Warner's more heroic discourse, then—discourse that overtly asserted the cause of freedom—laid bare the symbolic and existential challenges Vietnam posed.

The week's events concluded with a service at the National Cathedral in Washington, D.C., where the Reverend Theodore H. Evans, Jr.—a Vietnam veteran—provided remarks. Evans grappled centrally with the meaning of suffering and loss, the existential questions and anxieties that the war's carnage raised. In the process, he thematized his own ambivalence vis-à-vis traditional war narratives, approaching Vietnam in the tragic mode.

Evans began by recalling a service he attended about 20 years prior, on Remembrance Sunday, in a church used by the Anglican-Episcopal Congregation of Saigon.

> I remember feeling in that service a sense of terrible ambivalence: the ambivalence of remembering the dead (especially on the anniversary of the war that was supposed to be the war to end war) at a time and in a place where another war was beginning. I remember the feeling of ambivalence in honoring people

who had made sacrifices for their countries, their convictions, and their friends while wondering how it could have happened that such terrible sacrifices became necessary. And I remember wondering who it was we were supposed to be remembering. Was it only soldiers? Was it only those on "our side"? Was it everyone whose life was lost or broken or disrupted by a century of wars?

Now it is twenty years later and those questions and feelings of ambivalence remain for me and they are harder to bear because there are so many thousands more to remember; all those thousands named and thousands more unnamed and the families that go with each one.

Evans overtly questioned, and thereby unsettled, received tropes central to the consolation genre. As the canonical narrative has it, war deaths take on distinctive, indeed even transcendent, meaning because they are sacrifices in a cause: they are motivated by conviction, by love of one's nation and the ideals for which it stands. But what—Evans asked at the climactic conclusion of a week honoring veterans—made those sacrifices necessary? He did not provide an answer, at least not an explicit one. Moreover, Evans called attention to the far wider carnage and devastation that wars leave in their wake: it was not only soldiers whose lives were ended or damaged, sometimes irreparably; it was not only Americans and their allies who suffered and died. For Evans—and presumably for many of those in his audience—Vietnam made these questions even more difficult, occurring, as it did, in an era well beyond the "war to end war" originally commemorated on Remembrance Sunday.

After giving voice to his ambivalence, and articulating his struggle to come to terms with war's loss and suffering, Evans encouraged his audience to remember Vietnam in all its complexity. It was in doing so, he suggested, that Americans might tackle the difficult task of narrativizing a tragic moment in the national past.

Remembering is hard work. It means reliving the pain, the alienation, the debate. It means recalling the dehumanization that is always, tragically, a part of war; when enemies turn each other into something less than human so that they can be treated as less than human. Remembering Vietnam means something similar to what it may mean for a person who has had some terrible childhood experience that restricts his or her growth. It has to be remembered if she or he is to be whole. For us at this time in our history it means that we have to pull a painful memory from the recesses of our collective memories, look at it, understand it, and begin to reconcile it as an important and tragic part of our national life, but one with power to heal and make us whole again.

In line with his broadly tragic view of the conflict, Evans suggested that assimilating Vietnam into a national narrative would require dismantling the very binaries that enable enemies to transform one another into something less than human.

Evans ultimately turned to religious language as a source for guidance and meaning. But his words diverged sharply from more familiar uses of biblical imagery in official national ceremonies. Biblical stories, he argued, unsettle the binaries of good and evil that enable war while at the same time offering a transcendent source of hope:

> That is why we read the Bible, to remember the old stories, to relive them in our own ways, to recognize ourselves in them, and to discover in ourselves that mixture of good and evil, that we know ourselves to be; people with moments of glory and heroism, and people with moments of horrendous cruelty and stupidity. But in all the stories there is an affirmation that while we remember, there is also a God who remembers us, who loves us, who takes and judges our worst and brings it to life.

Though it drew from the familiar repertoire of Christian symbolism, then, Evans' religious imagery departed from the portrait of America as a redeemer nation. Instead, he suggested that the Bible offers a tragic view of humanity—a humanity that is a complex mélange of good and evil. Recalling war deaths through this tragic lens, he suggested, might yield peace in the long term: "Isn't it also possible in our remembering of so many sacrifices and so many losses of our most precious resources, the youth of our nation, that we will find other ways of solving problems and resolving differences instead of war?"[108]

Though compelling to many, the memorial dedicated in 1982 also generated significant criticism from veterans who agitated for heroic symbolism of the sort that typically defines war memorials.[109] Their outcry culminated in the addition of an American flag and a realist statue of three male soldiers—one white, one black, and one Hispanic—which was unveiled two years later.[110] With this addition, the memorial came to represent "a kind of *coincidentia oppositorum*" that "brings . . . opposed meanings together without resolving them."[111] President Reagan delivered remarks at the dedication of the statue on Veterans Day in 1984. Like the statue itself, Reagan's words embodied a more traditional approach to political consolation. "The men and women of Vietnam fought for freedom in a place where liberty was in danger," Reagan said. "They put their lives in danger to help a people in a land far away from their own. Many sacrificed their lives in the name of duty, honor, and country. All were patriots who lit the world with their fidelity and courage."[112] Yet he, too, acknowledged the "great moral and philosophical disagreements about the rightness of the war," and indeed suggested that "we cannot forget them because there is no wisdom to be gained in forgetting."[113]

In the end, however, it is not the more traditional statue, but Maya Lin's engraved granite walls that seem to compel the memorial's visitors most powerfully. It is the walls that overwhelmingly elicit visible emotional responses; it is almost invariably along the walls that visitors leave tokens— flags, flowers, letters, poems, and the like.[114] Thus the Vietnam memorial, and much Vietnam memory, juxtaposes dualistic and tragic, pride and regret, heroism and defeat, articulating the conflict between them without resolving it. But the tragic dimension has had a remarkable salience, perhaps even predominance, and Vietnam remains a painful episode in American collective memory—an episode that continues to evoke reflection, contemplation, and dissent.

In this context, it is worth considering one comparatively recent effort to engage the meaning of the Vietnam War in the tragic mode. This effort came from former Defense Secretary Robert McNamara, who held the post from 1961 to 1968 and played a central role in escalating U.S. involvement in Vietnam. McNamara's 1995 memoir *In Retrospect* chronicled his gradual shift "from concern to skepticism to frustration to anguish" over the war, culminating in his departure from the Pentagon at the height of the Tet Offensive in 1968.[115] In a largely apologetic and regretful tone, McNamara offered a detailed account of both the internal decision-making process as it unfolded during the Kennedy and Johnson administrations and of his own growing personal torment concerning the war. Like Robert Kennedy before him, McNamara invoked Greek tragedy as a frame for his effort to reexamine the past and excavate the lessons it might hold for foreign policy challenges in the present, especially the threat of nuclear disaster. "I want Americans to understand why we made the mistakes we did, and to learn from them," he wrote. "I hope to say, 'Here is something we can take away from Vietnam that is constructive and applicable to the world of today and tomorrow.' That is the only way our nation can ever hope to leave the past behind."[116] Even in the 1990s, McNamara recognized, the United States was still haunted by the difficult legacy of Vietnam, and he sought to transform that legacy to one of wisdom and insight: "The ancient Greek dramatist Aeschylus wrote, 'The reward of suffering is experience.' Let this be the lasting legacy of Vietnam."[117]

In the final lines of his memoir, McNamara addressed the task of consolation—the meaning of the lives lost in Vietnam—in light of his admission that American political leaders had acted unwisely. "In the end, we must confront the fate of those Americans who served in Vietnam and never returned," he reflected. "Does the unwisdom of our intervention nullify their effort and their loss?"[118] Recall once again Johnson's argument, as the United States escalated its involvement, that admitting error would do just that—and even more, that it would represent an affront to all soldiers who had fallen in the cause of freedom since the Revolution. McNamara answered differently: "I think not."[119] By then, the distinction between soldier and cause was an institutionalized feature of Vietnam memory, and McNamara argued that the soldier's responsibilities differed from those of public officials: "They did not make the decisions. They answered their nation's call to service. They went in harm's way on its behalf. And they gave their lives for their country and its ideals. That our effort in Vietnam proved unwise does not make their sacrifice less noble." The way to ensure that their deaths have enduring meaning to the nation is thus not to celebrate their cause, but to reflect on what can be learned from the misguided effort that their leaders set before them—the errors in judgment that might, in light of honest and sustained reflection on the past, be avoided in the future. "Let us learn from their sacrifice," McNamara wrote, "and, by doing so, validate and honor it."[120]

Today, a kind of regret for the war is now etched in stone on the national mall, in the form of a quotation on the Martin Luther King, Jr. Memorial that was dedicated in 2011. Inscribed on the memorial's south wall are the following words: "I oppose the war in Vietnam because I love America. I speak out against it not in anger but with anxiety and sorrow in my heart, and above all with a passionate desire to see our beloved country stand as a moral example of the world."[121] These words clearly express patriotic devotion and indeed even suggest a sense of American exceptionalism, a desire to serve "a moral example" on an international stage. They thus offer a considerably more benign statement of King's critique than his inversion of the dualistic script. But they also point to the Vietnam era as a moment when the nation fell short of its most cherished ideals and of its image as a "city upon a hill."

The violence that occurred both at home and abroad throughout the 1960s, then, brought to the surface an alternate, tragic mode of political consolation. Complicating the moral contrasts that form the basis for dualistic discourse, the tragic mode suggests that coming to terms with suffering requires introspection and self-questioning, even critique. Indeed, the very meaning of suffering resides in the wisdom gained throughout such processes. This tragic discourse, and the ways in which it chipped away at the progressive teleology that had long animated canonical national narratives, provides a crucial backdrop for understanding American political consolation in the twenty-first century. Though soaring dualistic narratives would quickly give shape to the events of September 11, 2001, at the level of official politics, this is not the whole story. The struggle to memorialize September 11, especially at the event's sacred center in lower Manhattan, would reveal deep interpretive difficulties, an ongoing battle to identify the event's symbolic and existential meaning and forge a place for it in a common national narrative.

PART II

Politics and Consolation after September 11

CHAPTER 4

September Mourning

While the story and materials I have presented in the first half of this book are important in their own right, their main purpose has been to set the stage for understanding the interpretive response to September 11. The dualistic mode of political consolation that coalesced during the World War II era and reverberated so forcefully in commemorative ceremonies during the 1990s powerfully premediated the state response to 9/11, impinging on official interpretations of the day's events even as they unfolded. In the pages that follow, I trace the process through which this dualistic interpretation solidified in official discourse, working to recapture the sense of solidarity, even collective effervescence, that emerged in the immediate aftermath of September 11 while also identifying early cracks in the façade.

I begin by considering the fundamental questions that political leaders faced in light of September 11, demonstrating that the basic task of defining the event itself—was it a horrible crime or an act of war?—was bound up with more encompassing existential matters. Why was America, that shining city upon a hill, assaulted with such brutality? How was the nation to understand the shocking act of violence that seemed to unfold so suddenly, without warning, and come to terms with suffering and loss that confronted most observers as random, senseless, and unmerited? I then examine how elected officials and other public figures responded to these questions in the collective mourning rituals that took place in the weeks immediately following September 11. The terms and tropes, ideas and images, invoked in these early moments after 9/11 provided a foundation for the war rhetoric and commemorative speechmaking that I examine in subsequent chapters. Even more, they illuminate the centrality of political consolation discourse in contemporary American collective life.

By now, the story is all too familiar. It was a Tuesday. The skies were blue and nearly cloudless. It was election day in New York City—and thus some residents altered their routines to cast their votes in the mayoral primary—but otherwise, it was an ordinary morning on the east coast. Or at least it appeared to be until 8:46 a.m., the moment when a commercial flight soared through the clear sky over Manhattan and into the north tower of the World Trade Center. Even then, onlookers in New York, around the nation, and across the globe generally assumed that they were witnessing a horrible accident. On NBC's *Today* show, Katie Couric reported information that the aircraft was "a small commuter plane," and Al Roker recalled the crash at the Empire State Building in the 1940s in an effort to provide historical context.[1] For his part, President George W. Bush continued with his scheduled visit at Emma Booker Elementary School in Sarasota, Florida. Indeed, he was reading with second graders when another plane crashed into the World Trade Center, striking the south tower at 9:03. Only then did he alter his plans, recognizing that a national crisis was unfolding.

Before leaving the school, Bush delivered brief remarks. In this 9:30 a.m. address, his speech was halting. The United States, he explained, had experienced "a national tragedy," "an apparent terrorist attack."[2] He promised a swift response in the form of a federal investigation "to hunt down and to find those folks who committed this act."[3] The demonstrative pronoun "this" ("this act") took the place of a clear definition of the event, and Bush alluded to a bureaucratic—rather than military—response.

In retrospect, it is all too easy to forget the uncertainty and confusion that surrounded the events of September 11 as they unfolded. Yet in these earliest moments, observers the world over—including the American head of state—grasped for an interpretive frame. Even when it became clear that these crashes were no accident, the day's events nonetheless remained difficult to categorize, existing somewhere in the liminal space between crime and war.[4] No contemporary writing can fully depict the ambiguity of those moments. Yet there is analytic value in the effort to recapture the uncertainty that prevailed, for it exposes the indeterminacy of interpretations that later came to be taken for granted.

The president addressed the nation once again in the early hours of the afternoon, this time from Barksdale Air Force Base in Louisiana. By the time he spoke, a third hijacked plane had crashed into the Pentagon—the headquarters of the U.S. Department of Defense, located in Arlington, Virginia, just outside the nation's capital—and a fourth had crashed in rural

Somerset County, Pennsylvania, near a town called Shanksville. In this address, Bush's interpretation was more decisive: "Freedom itself was attacked this morning by a faceless coward, and freedom will be defended," he declared as he opened his remarks. "Make no mistake; the United States will hunt down and punish those responsible for these cowardly acts."[5] Even in the course of these few short hours, Bush's frame of reference became substantially more encompassing. Events Bush had defined as an attack on the *nation* at 9:30 a.m. were recast, a few hours later, as an attack on *freedom* writ large.

When Bush delivered his final address on September 11—speaking from the Oval Office at 8:30 p.m.—he addressed the challenge of interpretation, and the task of consolation, in more definitive terms. In rhetoric no longer halting, Bush offered the following account of the day's events:

> Today our fellow citizens, our way of life, our very freedom came under attack in a series of deliberate and deadly terrorist attacks. . . . Thousands of lives were suddenly ended by evil, despicable acts of terror.
>
> The pictures of airplanes flying into buildings, fires burning, huge structures collapsing, have filled us with disbelief, terrible sadness, and a quiet, unyielding anger. These acts of mass murder were intended to frighten our nation into chaos and retreat, but they have failed. Our country is strong. A great people has been moved to defend a great nation. Terrorist attacks can shake the foundations of our biggest buildings, but they cannot touch the foundation of America. These acts shattered steel, but they cannot dent the steel of American resolve.
>
> America was targeted for attack because we're the brightest beacon for freedom and opportunity in the world. And no one will keep that light from shining.
>
> Today our nation saw evil, the very worst of human nature. And we responded with the best of America, with the daring of our rescue workers, with the caring for strangers and neighbors who came to give blood and help in any way they could.[6]

At 9:30 a.m. on September 11, Bush had grasped for words, clearly struggling to categorize this rapidly unfolding but profoundly ambiguous event. By 8:30 p.m., however, he began to offer an explanation. In these remarks from the Oval Office, Bush reiterated the claim—initially articulated in his afternoon address—that not only the nation, but also *freedom* writ large had been attacked that morning. In this view, he suggested, the nation had been targeted precisely *for* its goodness, *because* it is an emblem of freedom and opportunity on a global stage. He juxtaposed the "evil" of the perpetrators, who exhibited "the very worst of human nature," with "the best of America," the "daring" and "caring" and "help" that citizens exhibited. And he juxtaposed the perpetrators' nefarious vision—they intended, Bush claimed, to shake the very foundations of the nation and its "way of life"—with the resilience and the quintessentially "American resolve" that citizens had exhibited in the face of crisis. No longer searching for a definition of the event, Bush pledged: "America and our friends and allies join with all those who want peace and security in the world, and we stand together to win the war against terrorism."[7] The day's events, this statement implied, were acts of war, and marked the beginning of a longer struggle—a confrontation not just with the specific perpetrators of the day's violence, but with "terrorism" itself.

Bush did not draw explicit historical analogies in this series of addresses on September 11. But reading his words alongside the World War II discourse described in chapter 2 reveals the subtle yet powerful workings of premediation. During his evening remarks, Bush asserted that the day's events would, in memory, fit neatly into triumphant national narratives: "America has stood down enemies before, and we will do so this time," he pledged. "None of us will ever forget this day, yet we go forward to defend freedom and all that is good and just in our world."[8] In the war that had begun, then, the cause at stake was once again freedom, and indeed goodness itself—"all that is good and just in our world." It is worth noting that Bush was not the first U.S. president to argue that America had been the target of terrorist violence because of its exceptional qualities, its commitment to freedom, and its role as steward for democracy. In a radio address the day after the bombings at American embassies in Kenya and Tanzania in August 1998, Bill Clinton explained: "Americans are targets of terrorism, in part, because we have unique leadership responsibilities in the world, because we act to advance peace and democracy."[9] Even more, he said: "The bombs that kill innocent Americans are aimed not only at them but at the very spirit of our country and the spirit of freedom."[10] For Bush, however, the distinction between American freedom and terrorist repression would take on more encompassing, even apocalyptic, proportions whose contours began to take shape in these early addresses.

Bush's remarks on September 11 were, of course, crucial in the collective struggle to find symbolic and existential orientation in this disruptive moment. Yet the president was out of sight for much of the day—flying first to Barksdale Air Force Base and then to Offutt Air Force Base near Omaha, Nebraska, before returning to Washington. For many, New York

Mayor Rudolph Giuliani became a powerful symbol of collective strength, and an immediate source of comfort and inspiration. Giuliani was physically present at the epicenter of the disaster—he arrived at the Fire Department's command post moments after United Airlines Flight 175 struck the south tower—and he stepped rapidly into a symbolic as well as bureaucratic leadership role. When he took to the airwaves, Giuliani not only provided information, but also worked to convey sympathy and inspire resilience—to offer consolation to both New Yorkers in particular and the American public more generally. During a press conference on the afternoon of September 11, Giuliani offered assurance that a vigorous rescue effort was underway and portrayed a city—indeed a nation—unbowed by the morning's violence: "we will strive now very hard to save as many people as possible and to send a message that the city of New York and the United States of America is much stronger than any group of barbaric terrorists, that our democracy, that our rule of law, that our strength and our willingness to defend ourselves will ultimately prevail."[11] Even as he reasserted his city's and his nation's agency, however, the mayor's own raw emotion was palpable. Asked during the same press conference whether he knew the number of casualties, Giuliani declined to speculate: "The number of casualties will be more than any of us can bear ultimately," he said, communicating empathy and humanity.[12]

Like many others who addressed the public as the events of September 11 unfolded, Giuliani oscillated between the language of crime and the language of war, struggling to pinpoint the very nature of the event. When reporters asked if the day's events constituted an act of war, he deferred to the president: "I don't know that I want to use those words. I think the president is the one that has to respond."[13] Yet he deployed vivid war imagery as he described the scene, and he projected an assertive national response: "we will . . . send a message that the city of New York and the United States of America is much stronger than any . . . barbaric terrorists . . . that our strength and our willingness to defend ourselves will . . . prevail."[14] The "vicious, unprovoked, horrible attack on innocent men, women and children," he claimed, was "one of the most heinous acts . . . in world history."[15] He offered assurance "that all of us in New York" would support the president "in the efforts that he's going to have to make . . . to make a point that people can't do this. You can't attack innocent men, women, and children."[16] In these initial statements, Giuliani's language—perhaps even more clearly than the president's—evoked the encompassing dualistic themes associated with World War II, defining the event as an attack on democracy and the American "way of life" even if he stopped short of declaring it an act of war. Later, Giuliani would reflect that, from the earliest moments of the crisis, he had channeled Winston Churchill, and indeed he would refer to Churchill explicitly in his remarks during the coming days.[17]

The connection political leaders evoked between World War II and the conflict that would come to be known as the "war on terror" grew ever stronger as they expanded upon the interpretive frames articulated in these initial moments. At times, the connection took the shape of specific analogies—to Pearl Harbor, the Battle of Britain, or the Blitz—as officials linked the present to the past. More generally, officials adopted the sharp symbolic boundaries that define the dualistic mode. Political leaders continually reinforced the fundamental moral oppositions between "good" and "evil," juxtaposing American "innocence," "courage," "bravery," "sacrifice," and "selflessness" with the perpetrators' "barbarism," "cowardice," "villainy," and "hate." They portrayed these diametrically opposed forces as engaged in a "battle" that pits "freedom" or "liberty" against "fear" or "tyranny"—a battle "for civilization," as Bush often put it, recalling frontier mythology. Occasionally, this rhetoric featured gender binaries, casting the United States and its allies in masculine terms—as protectors of "innocent" civilians, especially women and children in Afghanistan (and later, Iraq)—and portraying the enemy as weak and effeminate.[18] More fundamentally, however, it evoked the fundamental contrast between humanity and inhumanity described in chapter 2.

Once again, the sharp distinctions that characterize the dualistic mode of political consolation erected rigid, seemingly unbridgeable, symbolic boundaries between good and evil, ally and enemy. Implicit and explicit references to World War II reinforced dualism's progressive teleology, bolstering the claim that good would ultimately triumph over evil. As in World War II, familiar texts and images from the civil scriptures were integral to this interpretation—they, too, offered consolation and bolstered the claim that victory was assured. As I document in chapters 6 and 7, cracks would soon begin to appear in the façade of the dualistic interpretation and undermine the national unity it inspired. Yet the dualistic frame did much to foster solidarity and underwrite consensus in the immediate aftermath of September 11, and it was remarkably resilient in state discourse even as time wore on.

Bush's public remarks on September 12 asserted the dualistic narrative more decisively than his addresses the day before. Just before 11 a.m., following a meeting with his national security team, Bush unambiguously categorized the previous day's events as acts of war: "The deliberate and deadly attacks which were carried out yesterday against our country were more than acts of terror; they were acts of war. . . . Freedom and democracy are under attack. . . . This enemy attacked not just our people, but all freedom-loving people everywhere in the world."[19] At the time, Bush was not yet able to identify the enemy in specific terms. But he nonetheless vowed that victory was assured: "This battle will take time and resolve. But make no mistake about it, we will win."[20] To support this pledge, Bush placed the events within an encompassing frame: "America is united. The freedom-loving nations of the world stand by our side. This will be a monumental struggle of good versus evil, but good will prevail."[21]

NATIONAL MOURNING

As these speeches reveal, political leaders addressed the task of consolation almost immediately, beginning in the hours after American Airlines Flight 11 struck the north tower on the morning of September 11. On September 14, organized rituals of national mourning foregrounded the task of consolation, and the existential questions raised so powerfully by the loss and suffering of September 11. Early in the afternoon, public officials and other dignitaries gathered for a memorial service at Washington National Cathedral. Here, the voices of prominent American clergy—representing Protestant, Catholic, Muslim, and Jewish traditions—joined with President Bush to offer consolation before a national audience. The consolation discourse deployed in this ritual proved a pivotal moment in politicians' larger effort to construct an interpretation that accounted for the shock and horror of 9/11—that clearly and compellingly addressed the meaning of suffering—and restored the nation's exceptionalist narrative.

In keeping with the expectations for the occasion, the memorial service more overtly addressed themes of grief, loss, and sorrow than Bush or Giuliani's early speeches.[22] The service was, after all, a time set aside for mourning, in a space fitting for such a purpose.[23] In this setting, speakers occasionally gestured toward the tragic mode of consolation. Yet tragic themes were rapidly overshadowed by the dualistic narrative. In general, speakers pivoted quickly from meditations on grief and mourning to expressions of hope and even pledges of triumph—acknowledging suffering, but never lingering on it, and thus encouraging onlookers not to linger in sorrow, either.

In her invocation, Reverend Jane Holmes Dixon, a bishop serving the Episcopal Diocese of Washington, set the tone for the proceedings. She quickly countered references to grief and mourning, tragedy and suffering with optimistic projections for the future. She spoke of "those who lost their lives" in "unspeakable tragedy," then immediately pledged that "love is stronger than hate, and . . . love lived out in justice will in the end prevail." She suggested that the National Cathedral was an appropriate "container for your grief. But in addition to that, we want you to know that the light that burns here—the light of love, the light of justice, the light of hope—shines brighter than any light in the world." In keeping with the dualistic mode, light would overcome darkness; "love" would triumph over "hate"; "justice" would "prevail" over cruelty.

Reverend Nathan Baxter, the dean of the National Cathedral, veered furthest from the emerging dualistic narrative. Baxter prayed "for divine wisdom, as our leaders consider the necessary actions for national security—wisdom of the grace of God that as we act, we not become the evil we deplore." His acknowledgment that America, too, had the potential to perpetrate evil—and that this was a time to reflect upon and guard against that potential—represents a significant gesture toward the tragic mode. While evoking strong binary contrasts between evil and innocence, he subtly countered the assertion, already evident in Giuliani's public remarks, that 9/11 was a singular event in world history: "The evil hand of hate and cowardly aggression, which has devastated the innocent in many other lands, has visited America this week, and too many of her children are no more." Baxter thus affirmed the claim that the events of 9/11 were a manifestation of "evil" while also suggesting that Americans' suffering placed them in solidarity with many others across the globe who found themselves grappling with the ramifications of "cowardly aggression." His prayer for healing also reflected an awareness of his own nation's capacity for violence or prejudice, and expressed hope that Americans would resist any darker impulses that might emerge in the days to come: "Heal our grief, soothe our suffering hearts, save us from blind vengeance, from random prejudice and from crippling fear."

Dualistic discourse, however, was far more pervasive in this service. Muzammil H. Siddiqi, president of the Islamic Society of North America, reflected: "Lord, you said . . . if any do seek for glory and power, to God belong all glory and power. To him mount up all works of purity. He exalts all righteous deeds. But those that lay . . . the plots of evil, for them is the penalty terrible. And the plotting of such shall not abide. Goodness and evil are not equal. Repel the evil with the good." Drawing sharp, clear distinctions between "goodness" and "evil," Siddiqi affirmed dualism's progressive teleology with the assurance that "the plotting" of evil "shall not abide."

Reverend Billy Graham's more extensive remarks imbued the rapidly solidifying dualistic narrative with the stamp of his own considerable religious authority. Like previous speakers, he suggested that "tragedy" and "suffering" would quickly be eclipsed. In doing so, Graham drew an analogy with the Christian narrative of resurrection:

> For the Christian . . . the cross tells us that God understands our sin and our suffering, for he took upon himself, in the person of Jesus Christ, our sins and our suffering. And from the cross God declares, "I love you. I know the heartaches and the sorrows and the pains that you feel, but I love you."

> The story does not end with the cross, for Easter points us beyond the tragedy of the cross to the empty tomb. It tells us that there is hope for eternal life, for Christ has conquered evil and death and hell.

In this narrative, tragedy and suffering are a fleeting moment on a journey toward resurrection and redemption. According to Graham, so, too, were the events of September 11. Graham predicted that 9/11 would give way to "a spiritual renewal in this country." And this spiritual renewal, he suggested, would be intertwined with triumph in worldly affairs: "Today we say to those who masterminded this cruel plot and to those who carried it out that the spirit of this nation will not be defeated by their twisted and diabolical schemes. Someday, those responsible will be brought to justice." As he closed his remarks, Graham predicted: "this is going to be a day that we will remember as a day of victory."[24]

The mourning ritual at the cathedral culminated with an address from President Bush. Like several of the clergy who preceded him, Bush opened on a somber note, giving voice to the suffering that the events of 9/11 had unleashed and engaging the matters of grief and sorrow more extensively than he had in the preceding days:

> We are here in the middle hour of our grief. So many have suffered so great a loss, and today we express our nation's sorrow. We come before God to pray for the missing and the dead, and for those who loved them.

> On Tuesday, our country was attacked with deliberate and massive cruelty. We have seen the images of fire and ashes and bent steel. Now come the names, the list of casualties we are only beginning to read. . . . We will read all these names, we will linger over them and learn their stories, and many Americans will weep.

In the reflective and contemplative tone of a national priest, Bush articulated sadness and empathy on behalf of the nation, highlighting the significance of each life lost and legitimizing expressions of grief. Again, the occasion invited, perhaps even required, such reflections.

Yet Bush did not dwell on such matters at length. Indeed, all the while, he underscored the "cruelty" of the attackers, alluding to the argument he would make for a swift and violent response. After expressing "the deepest sympathy of the nation" to those suffering personal losses, he shifted decisively away from this contemplative, mournful language, and concentrated instead on how the United States would react to the cruelty visited upon it. The nation, he said, could not linger in sadness because it faced an imperative to act: "Just three days removed from these events, Americans do not yet have the distance of history, but our responsibility to history is already clear: to answer these attacks and rid the world of evil." The pain and suffering that many Americans felt so powerfully in the moment were sure to be fleeting, and Bush placed them within a cosmic frame: "This world He created is of moral design," Bush declared, in language that recalled Churchill's 1941 address to Congress. "Grief and tragedy and hatred are only for a time. Goodness, remembrance and love have no end."[25]

Within God's "moral design," Bush asserted, America enjoyed special providence. Here, the president explicitly forged a place for 9/11 in the nation's exceptionalist narrative:

> Today we feel what Franklin Roosevelt called the warm courage of national unity. . . . Our unity is a kinship of grief and a steadfast resolve to prevail against our enemies. And this unity against terror is now extending across the world. America is a nation full of good fortune, with so much to be grateful for; but we are not spared from suffering. In every generation, the world has produced enemies of human freedom. They have attacked America because we are freedom's home and defender. And the commitment of our fathers is now the calling of our time.[26]

America's unique "good fortune," Bush suggested—echoing a longstanding refrain—confers unique responsibilities. Reiterating the claim he had articulated on the evening of September 11, Bush asserted that America was attacked *because* of the ideals it represents, *because* the nation is "freedom's home and defender." In this eulogy at the National Cathedral, standing alongside prominent clergy and amidst religious symbolism, Bush argued that protecting these ideals is a *calling*, imbuing the nation's responsibilities with sacred significance. Sorrow, he acknowledged, is real and warranted "for a time." Yet the events of September 11 would find their meaning not in quiet contemplation, but in a fight for freedom—extending "the commitment of our fathers" that had become "the calling of our time."

Bush's remarks were immediately followed with a rendition of the "Battle Hymn of the Republic." The audience joined with the Navy Sea

Chanters, singing lyrics penned by Julia Ward Howe during the Civil War.[27] The hymn, as I noted in chapter 1, draws an analogy between Christ's sacrifice and that of fallen Union soldiers:

> As he died to make men holy, let us die to make men free,
> While God is marching on.[28]

THE CALL TO ARMS

Closing the national memorial service with the Battle Hymn suggested a connection between the 9/11 dead and fallen soldiers, and, in some sense, symbolically signaled the end of national mourning with a call to arms. In the subsequent days, Bush would continue to offer consolation in dualistic language while also vigorously articulating this call to arms, seeking to energize the American nation and its allies for a war between "good" and "evil," "civilization" and "barbarism," "freedom" and "fear." Efforts at consolation, then, were bound up with efforts to articulate the imperative — indeed the "calling"—to act.

Following the service at the National Cathedral, Bush traveled to lower Manhattan for the first time since September 11. At the World Trade Center, Bush delivered impromptu remarks to the rescue workers laboring at the site. He began with an expression of gratitude, speaking in the mournful tone he had adopted in the early lines of his address at the National Cathedral. The nation, he said, "is on bended knee in prayer for the people whose lives were lost here, for the workers who work here, for the families who mourn."[29] But as he spoke, a rescue worker yelled: "I can't hear you!" In response, Bush shifted his tone dramatically. Bellowing into a bullhorn he had borrowed to amplify his words, he declared: "I can hear you! I can hear you! The rest of the world hears you! And the people—and the people who knocked these buildings down will hear all of us soon!"[30] His words inspired an effervescent reaction, as rescue workers chanted fervently: "U.S.A.! U.S.A.! U.S.A.!"[31] In memory, the image of Bush standing atop the rubble, bullhorn in hand, became a crucial emblem for the American response to 9/11. And indeed, it seemed to mark a turning point for Bush himself, as he fully abandoned any of the uncertainty that initially seemed to overtake him on the morning of September 11 and assumed the more strident posture he embodied memorably during that first visit to lower Manhattan.

In the coming days, elected officials from across the political spectrum followed Bush's lead—echoing his interpretation, reinforcing his resolve, and offering comfort and reassurance with the pledge that good would inevitably triumph over evil. When New York Senators Chuck Schumer and Hillary Clinton—both Democrats—delivered their party's response to the president's weekly radio address on September 15, Schumer referred to "[t]he terrorist attack that occurred Tuesday" as "the 21st century Pearl Harbor," an attack on the nation that required unwavering resolve. "Like after Pearl Harbor," he said, "we need to be resolute in the months and years to come, until we secure the unconditional surrender of the terrorists and those that harbor them." Similarly, Clinton described September 11 as "an attack on America and our values," and pledged to "show the world that though buildings can crumble and innocent people sacrifice their lives, America and New York remain strong, our democracy is intact, and our faith in God and in each other secure." As ever, suffering and sacrifice would be regenerative, and would give way to a more vital, resilient nation: "The events of September 11, 2001, form a crucible out of which an even stronger nation can be forged," Clinton declared.[32] In remarks from the White House on Sunday, September 16, Bush firmly stated that the grieving period had come to a close: "Today, millions of Americans mourned and prayed, and tomorrow we go back to work," he said. "[M]y administration has a job to do. And we're going to do it. We will rid the world of the evildoers."[33]

In the days after 9/11, Bush stepped ever more fully into the role of consoler-in-chief: he offered an explanation and interpretation for the devastation and suffering that had unfolded on September 11; he expressed sorrow and sympathy while evoking national resolve and seeking to inspire moral renewal. The dualistic mode of political consolation addressed the meaning of suffering head-on, promising redemption for anguish and loss. At the same time, Mayor Giuliani's consolation discourse also continued to influence emerging narratives of 9/11 in significant ways. The mayor readily adopted and reinforced the president's war frame and his Manichean understanding of the emerging conflict, with its references—both explicit and implicit—to the Second World War. He did so as he continued to enact the role of both local and national consoler, politician-cum-priest: attending nearly 200 funerals, eulogizing fallen rescuers, expressing his own pain and the anguish of his city while also working to inspire a defiant return to ordinary life—accompanied by a renewed spirit of solidarity.[34] In tandem with Bush, Giuliani worked to affect a symbolic and emotional shift from grief and mourning to resilience and recovery.

For instance, on September 15, Giuliani reflected on the loss of three prominent officials from the city's fire department—Pete Ganci, the fire chief; Bill Feehan, the first deputy fire commissioner and the New York City Fire Department's (FDNY's) second-highest official; and Mychal Judge, a Franciscan friar who served as an FDNY chaplain. Funerals for all three men were held that day, and in his public remarks, Giuliani memorialized them as fallen soldiers, analogous to those who perished at Pearl Harbor: "to each of their families we give our support, our love and condolences, and look upon this as three people who have lost their lives as casualties of war," he said. "They are heroes. They're like the heroes that we had at Pearl Harbor." His words echoed themes from Bush's eulogy at the National Cathedral within a local, even personal, frame of reference. Acknowledging that the day of these memorials was "a very difficult day and a very emotional one and only the beginning of what we're going to have to go through," and empathizing with New Yorkers' grief and suffering, he also evoked newfound reserves of strength. "I think we realize that we have the strength to deal with this, to overcome it," he said. "And I think people should be mournful and sorrowful, but they should also be very encouraged that we have tremendous courage in New York, we have tremendous courage in America, and the courage will be there in our generation as it was in prior generations."[35]

On Sunday the 16th, Giuliani—like Bush—worked to guide New Yorkers and the nation in a return to ordinary life. Sunday, Giuliani said, was "an appropriate day for people to reflect on what happened last week." But he observed that "the life of the city is going on, and the prediction that I made on the first day is proving to be true: the city is stronger than it was last week at this time."[36] Throughout this difficult period, Giuliani reflected, he had found meaning in Winston Churchill's World War II speeches, and he encouraged New Yorkers to remember that "civilizations have been attacked, democracies have been attacked, and they've had the strength and the will and the courage to deal with it."[37] He suggested one specific point of comparison, arguing New Yorkers had "conducted themselves as brave [sic] as the people of Britain during the Battle of Britain."[38] When the New York Stock Exchange reopened on Monday, September 17, Giuliani reflected: "This is another remarkable indication of the very, very strong and indomitable spirit of the people of New York City, the people of this region . . . and the people of the United States."[39] The nation's economic resilience symbolized broader spiritual resilience: Giuliani argued that the 9/11 perpetrators had "failed in their endeavor to break the spirit of the people of New York and the people of America. That spirit today is 10 times stronger than it was last Monday."[40]

These early addresses offered meaningful orientation amidst uncertainty and shock, addressing existential and interpretive questions that reverberated powerfully across the nation. The terms and tropes articulated during this period—themselves a product of a much longer tradition of American political consolation—have had a remarkable afterlife, as I illustrate in the pages that follow. However, perhaps the signal moment for the development of the official state interpretation of September 11—the moment when its full contours became clear—was Bush's address to Joint Congress on September 20, 2001. Blending the encompassing and at times overtly theistic language of consolation with an effort to articulate a foreign policy for a new era, Bush's speech commanded attention around the country and across the globe. It also suggested that the ultimate meaning of September 11 would be defined retrospectively, in light of the nation's—and even the world's—response to the "calling" issued that fateful day.

The address Bush delivered on September 20 was a special event, but the setting evoked ritual associations with the State of the Union. Bush called forth these associations overtly as he began his remarks: "[I]n the normal course of events, presidents come to this chamber to report on the state of the Union," he said. "Tonight, no such report is needed. It has already been delivered by the American people."[41] From the beginning, then, Bush reasserted American agency in the face of this assault, transforming the wounded superpower from unsuspecting victim to resilient hero. Bush lauded "the courage of passengers who rushed terrorists to save others on the ground"—referring to the people aboard United Flight 93 whose assault on the hijackers apparently caused the plane to crash in rural Pennsylvania before it could reach its intended target.[42] He praised "the endurance of rescuers working past exhaustion."[43] He heralded public expressions of patriotism, generosity, and faith: "We've seen the unfurling of flags, the lighting of candles, the giving of blood, the saying of prayers in English, Hebrew and Arabic. We've seen the decency of a loving and giving people who have made the grief of strangers their own."[44] Americans, he suggested, possess a deep and essential goodness, and in the aftermath of 9/11 this goodness was vividly on display. Praising the moral regeneration that had transpired in the days following September 11—and in doing so, working to talk such regeneration into life—Bush addressed the citizenry with optimism and confidence: "My fellow citizens, for the last nine days, the entire world has seen for itself the state of our Union, and it is strong."[45]

Once again, Bush underscored the claim that the mourning period had concluded—and once again, he pledged that suffering was but the harbinger of future triumph. "Tonight we are a country awakened to danger and called to defend freedom," Bush said.[46] With these words, he implicitly recalled Pearl Harbor and reminded the nation of its mission, reiterating the language of a collective "calling" and invoking the values Americans were bound to protect. He also sought to provide the emotional underpinning for the oncoming struggle, suggesting that the passing days had produced an important affective transformation and elaborating "emotion codes" along with his interpretation.[47] "Our grief has turned to anger and anger to resolution," he declared. "Whether we bring our enemies to justice or bring justice to our enemies, justice will be done."[48]

Bush thus opened his address with words for the nation, seeking to inspire solidarity and patriotism, and to underwrite not only resilience, but also retaliation. Subsequently, however, he turned to his global audience, addressing "the world" on behalf of his nation. He expressed gratitude for the "outpouring of support" that followed 9/11 and acknowledged "the citizens of 80 other nations who died with our own." He concluded with a reference to the "hundreds of British citizens" who had perished. "America has no truer friend than Great Britain," Bush said. "Once again we are joined together in a great cause. I'm so honored the British Prime Minister has crossed an ocean to show his unity with America." The chamber erupted into applause, and the television cameras focused on Prime Minister Tony Blair. In drawing attention to Blair's presence, Bush not only honored a current alliance, but also called forth powerful images from the past. Churchill, too, "crossed an ocean" in the weeks following the surprise attack on Pearl Harbor that had prompted the United States to take up arms in the cause of freedom 60 years prior.

As he continued his remarks, Bush reinforced the symbolic link between World War II and 9/11 while also evoking a sense of historical rupture. The events of 9/11, Bush asserted, were unambiguously acts of war, and their closest analog was Pearl Harbor. However, they represented an even more egregious offense than anything that had come before:

On September the 11th, enemies of freedom committed an act of war against our country. Americans have known wars, but for the past 136 years they have been wars on foreign soil, except for one Sunday in 1941. Americans have known the casualties of war, but not at the center of a great city on a peaceful morning. Americans have known surprise attacks, but never before on thousands of civilians. All of this was brought upon us in a single day, and night fell on a different world; a world where freedom itself is under attack.

In this interpretation, September 11 broadened the American experience of war: the day's events were comprehensible within this familiar cultural category and yet more painful and distressing than their predecessors, including the "Sunday in 1941" when Japanese forces struck Pearl Harbor. Once again, Bush described the target of the assault in abstract and encompassing terms—the perpetrators attacked not just the American nation, but also the ideals for which it stands. He thus reinforced his claim that the events of 9/11 represented not only an "act of war against our country" specifically, but also the dawn of an era in which "freedom itself"—and not just a single nation—"is under attack."

By September 20, Bush was able to identify the perpetrator in more specific terms, and he explained that the evidence pointed to al Qaeda. Phrasing the question in stark us-and-them language—"why do they hate us?"—Bush presented an expansive view of al Qaeda's motivations and aims. "Its goal is remaking the world and imposing its radical beliefs on people everywhere," he said. Al Qaeda's members, Bush asserted, "hate what they see right here in this chamber, a democratically elected government. Their leaders are self-appointed. They hate our freedoms: Our freedom of religion, our freedom of speech, our freedom to vote and assemble and disagree with each other." It was thus not only human lives but cherished values that were at stake: "These terrorists kill not merely to end lives but to disrupt and end a way of life." Al Qaeda's "vision for the world," Bush argued, could be seen in Afghanistan, where their leadership "has great influence . . . and supports the Taliban regime in controlling most of that country." "Afghanistan's people have been brutalized," Bush said. "Many are starving and many have fled. Women are not allowed to attend school. You can be jailed for owning a television. Religion can be practiced only as their leaders dictate. A man can be jailed in Afghanistan if his beard is not long enough." As these passages illustrate, Bush cast the 9/11 perpetrators as the diametric opposite of the generous and patriotic Americans he had described in his opening remarks, and indeed argued that these "ways of life" were, in the end, irreconcilable. Al Qaeda became the epitome of evil, standing in sharp contrast to the beacon of goodness and freedom that they had struck.

Though Bush ostensibly offered an opportunity to avert an invasion of Afghanistan—he addressed the Taliban directly, issuing a series of demands that were, he said, "not open to negotiation or discussion"—the words that followed suggested that the U.S. president viewed war as inevitable. He foreshadowed an expansive and protracted engagement, "a long struggle." "Americans should not expect one battle, but a lengthy campaign unlike any other we have ever seen," Bush said. "It may include dramatic strikes visible on TV and covert operations, secret even in success." Announcing that he had "called the armed forces to alert," he addressed members of the U.S. military directly: "The hour is coming when America will act, and you will make us proud."

Ultimately, Bush explained, the struggle on the horizon would divide the world unambiguously into good and evil, allies and enemies. Turning once again to his global audience, Bush declared: "Every nation in every region now has a decision to make: either you are with us or you are with the terrorists." The struggle left no room for neutrality, no middle ground. In the process, Bush underscored the fundamental values that were at stake: "This is not . . . just America's fight. And what is at stake is not just America's freedom. This is the world's fight. This is civilization's fight. This is the fight of all who believe in progress and pluralism, tolerance and freedom." Despite the threat at hand, however, past triumphs foreshadowed a glorious future. Terrorists, Bush said, "are the heirs of the murderous ideologies of the 20th century. By sacrificing human life to serve their radical visions, by abandoning every value except the will to power, they follow in the path of fascism, Nazism and totalitarianism. And they will follow that path all the way to where it ends, in history's unmarked grave of discarded lies." The resonance with Reagan's "ashheap of history" is clear.

Even as he portrayed the struggle in ever more expansive terms, seeking to shore up support across the world, Bush maintained that America's special role within it was consonant with its longstanding task of preserving and protecting freedom on the global stage. Echoing his remarks at the National Cathedral, he argued that the suffering of 9/11 had awakened the present generation to their role in fulfilling the nation's enduring mission:

Great harm has been done to us. We have suffered great loss. In our grief and anger, we have found our mission and our moment. Freedom and fear are at war. The advance of human freedom, the great achievement of our time and the great hope of every time now depends on us. Our nation, this generation will lift the dark threat of violence from our people and our future. We will rally the world to this cause by our efforts, by our courage. We will not tire, we will not falter, and we will not fail.

The imperative to preserve freedom would require Americans to continually summon resolve as their grief faded: "Even grief recedes with time and grace. But our resolve must not pass. Each of us will remember what happened that day and to whom it happened." As he drew his remarks to a close, Bush unambiguously articulated the full cosmic contours of the dualistic narrative. "The course of this conflict is not yet known, yet its outcome is certain," Bush declared. "Freedom and fear, justice and cruelty, have always been at war, and we know that God is not neutral between them. Fellow citizens, we'll meet violence with patient justice, assured of the rightness of our cause and confident of the victories to come." America's success in its mission, then, was not only foreshadowed by its triumphant history—by its signal role in securing victory over "fascism, Nazism and totalitarianism." Even more, it was ordained by God.

MOURNING IN NEW YORK

Public mourning rituals continued in the weeks that followed, even after the nation "went back to work." Like the September 14 service at the National Cathedral, such rituals drew politicians together with prominent clergy in events that continued to foreground the task of consolation. Perhaps the most visible such ritual was the prayer service held on September 23, 2001, at Yankee Stadium—formally called "A Prayer for America"—which was also broadcast live on television. Over the course of two and a half hours, speakers—including clergy from a wide range of traditions, American celebrities, and politicians representing both New York City and New York state—offered prayers and reflections. In this venue, speakers continually invoked the moral oppositions that form the backbone for dualistic discourse. Contrasting "evil" perpetrators with "innocent" victims and "heroic" Americans who responded to "cruelty" with valor—and in some cases sacrificed their own lives—speakers at Yankee Stadium echoed and elaborated the official mode of consolation.

Cardinal Edward Egan, the Archbishop of New York, underscored these moral contrasts in his invocation, drawing a distinction between "your [God's] noble people, your virtuous people—yes, Lord, your holy people" and "the evildoers, who have harmed us so fiercely," echoing the president's characterization of the perpetrators as "evildoers." In his "Prayer for the Country," Rabbi Arthur Schneier used similar language, contrasting "barbarism" and "terrorist evil" with "victims" and "their heroic rescuers." Prayers from participating clergy thus reinforced Bush's claim that the outcome of the present struggle was divinely ordained—and that God was on America's side. Schneier asked for God's blessing on President Bush, "who sounded the clarion call to battle the terrorists at home and abroad and unify the nation to defend freedom, democracy and, yes, the civilized world." Similarly, Rabbi Marc Gellman invoked the belief—a belief that he claimed is common among the Abrahamic faiths—"that a good God will not allow evil to win forever over goodness, hate to win over hope, or death to win over life." Not only do the Abrahamic faiths promise that good will triumph over evil, but—Gellman claimed, as Bush had done three days before—"[h]istory proves this" as well. Among clergy, too, the past provided a foundation for projecting a triumphant future.

These fundamental moral oppositions served as a backdrop for speeches that reflected on canonical national narratives at length, forging connections between past and present in richer detail. During the presentation of the colors, Admiral Robert Natter, Commander and Chief of the Atlantic Fleet, drew a line from Valley Forge to the World Trade Center. In doing so, he invoked an image that had rapidly become iconic in the days following September 11: a photograph of three New York City firefighters raising an American flag over the rubble at the World Trade Center. The photograph—officially titled "Ground Zero Spirit"—originally appeared on the front page of the Bergen County, New Jersey newspaper *The Record* on September 12. Distributed through the Associated Press wire, it was also published in newspapers throughout the world. At Yankee Stadium, Natter said:

> For the past 13 days, the citizens of our great nation have drawn strength from our flag. It is truly a remarkable image, it is the same stars and stripes that flew over George Washington's continental army at Valley Forge in December, 1777, that stood guard over regular army and militia forces defending Fort McHenry during the War of 1812, gave strength to soldiers fighting in the bloody trenches of Ardenne in 1917. The same flag whose raising atop Mt. Suribachi inspired our Marines at Iwo Jima, and led the charge ashore of our forces at Inchon. It is the same colors that stood fast during the siege at Khe Sanh in 1968.

> And just within this past year it was the battle ensign that flew over the U.S.S. Cole and rallied her crew to heroism. These images of our history are now joined for eternity with the actions of three New York City firemen. Determined to erect a flagstaff and hoist our colors over the rubble that was the World Trade Center, each of these images clearly illustrates that our flag is much, much more than a symbol, it is a living testimony of our American spirit.

> It has brought us together in the past, it brings us together today, and it will lead us to victory in the future.

In this narrative, the firefighters who hoisted the American flag above the rubble become like soldiers, joining the celebrated national cause inaugurated in the 1770s. By extension, the World Trade Center becomes a battlefield. Though Natter invoked a long list of historical associations in these remarks (and it is worth noting that this heroic trajectory now included Vietnam, with a reference to Khe Sanh), the image he described—"Ground Zero Spirit"—most clearly evokes the association with Iwo Jima. From the time it was published, numerous commentators pointed to the resemblance between this photograph and Joe Rosenthal's February 23, 1945, photograph "Raising the Flag on Iwo Jima." The implied association with World War II thus took center stage once more, and anticipated a victorious future.

In his "Prayer for the Families," Rabbi Alvin Kass—a chaplain with the New York Police Department—also reached deep into the American past in order to imbue recent losses with sense and meaning. He prayed:

> may we all be buoyed up by the realization that these victims have, through their heroism, self-sacrificed courage and bravery inspired a renewed appreciation throughout this entire nation and the world in the American spirit at its very best.
>
> And may all of us forever understand that what the victims want more than anything else is that the survivors should continue to live for what they died for, a society founded on justice and equity, democracy and right, a place where government by the people, for the people and of the people will not perish from the earth.

Kass's prayer imbued the 9/11 deaths with the highest national significance, deploying Lincolnian language to portray these losses as patriotic sacrifices. Those who perished, he claimed, *died for* democracy: in the hope that "government by the people, for the people and of the people will not perish from the earth." Gettysburg powerfully premediated 9/11 as Kass imputed Lincoln's vision to the dead, boldly suggesting that the preservation of democracy is "what the victims want more than anything else."

Politicians, too, invoked the notion of patriotic sacrifice in their efforts to provide meaning and consolation. For instance, Giuliani asserted: "All of the victims of this tragedy were innocent. All of them were heroes." He lauded the specific sacrifices of the rescue workers using biblical language: "The Bible says 'greater love hath no man than this: that a man lay down his life for his friends.'" Yet Giuliani also claimed that *all* those who died—not just rescue workers—should be remembered in heroic terms: "The people they [rescue workers] were trying to rescue . . . were each engaged in the quiet heroism of supporting their families, pursuing their dreams, and playing their own meaningful part in a diverse, dynamic, and free society."

Like Natter, Giuliani worked to forge a place for September 11 in the collective narrative that begins with the American Revolution. In his remarks, Giuliani remediated pivotal moments from the American past in light of 9/11. He described the long history of St. Paul's Chapel, which "stood directly in the shadow of the World Trade Center towers" prior to September 11 and survived the towers' collapse. Invoking the civil religion's Moses figure, Giuliani explained that George Washington knelt down in prayer in that very chapel after his inauguration on April 30, 1789. The chapel, Giuliani said, "survived our War of Independence, including seven years of wartime occupation" and then, through "a small miracle," survived September 11 as well. Giuliani interpreted St. Paul's survival in language consonant with broad dualistic themes: "the presence of that chapel standing defiant and serene amid the ruins of war sends an eloquent message about the strength and resilience of the people of New York City and the people of America." Here, the World Trade Center was once again represented as a battlefield. And accordingly, Giuliani argued that, in light of 9/11, it fell to the present generation to carry forward the American story of resilience and triumph:

> Like our founding fathers who fought and died for freedom, like our ancestors who fought and died to preserve our Union and to end the sin of slavery, like our fathers and grandfathers who fought and died to liberate the world from Nazism and fascism and communism, the cluster of arrows to defend our freedom and the olive branch of peace have now been handed to us. We will hold them firmly in our hands, honor their memory and lift them up to Heaven to light the world.

> In the days since this attack, we have met the worst of humanity with the best of humanity.

Giuliani's speech thus echoed Bush's sharp symbolic contrasts as well as his claim that the events of 9/11 awakened the present generation to its role in the American drama, their specific calling within an enduring national mission.

Reverend Calvin Butts, of the historic Abyssinian Baptist Church in Harlem, provided the most extensive remarks at Yankee Stadium. His sermonic address once again juxtaposed the particular American story with an encompassing cosmic narrative, reinforcing Bush's claim that in the emerging struggle, God was squarely on America's side:

> even though now we're facing cowards who hide behind the terror of secrecy, I want you to know that as a nation, even though the president said this will be

a hard fight, there was a great poet who said, "Harder yet may be the fight and right may often yield to might. Wickedness a while may reign and Satan's cause may seem to gain. Oh, but there is a God who rules above and He's got a hand of power and a heart of love. And if I've right that God will fight my battles." We'll get through it. . . .

We will get through it because we are the United States of America. And I will say this, we have died on every battlefield. We died in Normandy. . . . We've died on every battlefield that the world has ever known and our beloved sisters and brothers lost their lives on the battlefield of the World Trade Center. But listen, they are patriots of America.

Ultimately, Butts asserted, divine providence was at work: God will ensure that good prevails, and indeed "will fight my battles." But—like Bush on September 20 and Gellman earlier in the same service—he also claimed that American history testifies to this teleology. The blood sacrifices offered by American "patriots" on battlefields across the globe had secured victory in the past. Likewise, Butts implied, the "patriots" who perished "on the battlefield of the World Trade Center" would help to secure victory in the present struggle.[49]

Several weeks later, on October 28, politicians and clergy—including some of the same figures who gathered at Yankee Stadium—would come together once again for a memorial in New York. This time, the service was held at the event's sacred center: the World Trade Center crash site, which was by then commonly known as "ground zero." The ruins still smoldered. Though the service was primarily intended for a smaller audience—those personally affected by the death and destruction that was still so visible at the site—it was also broadcast on cable news networks. Politicians—including Mayor Giuliani, Senator Clinton, and Governor Pataki—were in attendance. But here, they did not speak. Instead, the service featured four prayers—delivered by clergy representing Catholic, Jewish, Muslim, and Protestant faiths—which were interspersed with music, including a rendition of the national anthem by a New York City police officer, Daniel Rodriguez, and a rendition of "Ave Maria" by opera singer Andrea Bocelli.

During this service—the first major collective mourning ritual on the ground where the Twin Towers once stood—there emerged a considerably more subdued approach. The sobriety and solemnity that prevailed in this ritual set the tone for a very different way of grappling with the meaning of September 11 in the ceremonies held at its sacred center. As I illustrate in chapter 6, this divergence would continue in commemorations over the coming decade and beyond. For one, the politicians' silence is notable.

Moreover, the words uttered by clergy also featured subtle departures from the dualistic narrative that suffused political rhetoric. Egan, the cardinal who had also spoken at Yankee Stadium, invoked familiar binaries when he reflected on the "innocent" lives that "were brutally, viciously, unjustly taken from us," and contrasted the "good and wholesome sons and daughters of God" who perished on 9/11 with the "villains filled with violence and hate" who took their lives. Yet the prayers also reflected more self-consciously on the difficulties of providing consolation, and one overtly expressed ambivalence about waging war in response to September 11. Imam Izak-El Mu'eed Pasha, a chaplain with the New York Police Department, prayed: "We ask you, God, to bless us with words that will be comforting to the families gathered here today. And let them know that what we say, we mean only good by it." Consolation, he suggested, does not come easily. While portraying war as necessary and just, he expressed sorrow and regret at the prospect—a contrast with the strident position most speakers had assumed in official public mourning rituals to date: "War is not something that any human being wants. But in defense of ourselves, we must fight. But God, let us fight for peace. Let us not deviate from establishing peace."[50]

It was not long before mourning rituals gave way to ritualized retrospection, and, as I argue in chapter 6, commemorations of 9/11 are settings where politicians continue to address a powerful cultural expectation to provide consolation. Here, however, it is worth considering one final text that encompasses the terms and tropes, ideas and images, crucial in shaping official interpretations of September 11 and providing a framework for its remembrance: Giuliani's December 2001 farewell address.

In this speech—delivered at St. Paul's Chapel just before his term as mayor expired—Giuliani extended the narrative he had articulated at Yankee Stadium. The chapel, he said, was "thrice-hallowed ground"— "hallowed," he explained, by its consecration as a "house of God" and "by the presence of George Washington and all of our brave heroes that gave their lives."[51] The World Trade Center and the surrounding area "is going to be a place that is remembered 100 and 1,000 years from now, like the great battlefields of Europe and of the United States"—among them "Normandy or Valley Forge or Bunker Hill or Gettysburg."[52] And it is "the sacrifice of our patriots and their heroism that is going to be what this place is remembered for."[53] As he concluded his farewell, Giuliani incorporated the 9/11 dead into the very cause Lincoln evoked at Gettysburg:

> I'm going to conclude not with my words but with somebody else's. On a battlefield in Pennsylvania where a similar number of Americans died for the very

same reason, to preserve our Union, a president whose hero when he was growing up was George Washington, gave a speech, a poem and a prayer. And it
really says it so much better than I can say it. I'd like to read and conclude with
the last part of it.[54]

With that, Giuliani delivered an excerpt from the Gettysburg Address,
ending with Lincoln's final lines: "we here highly resolve that the dead
shall not have died in vain, that the nation shall under God [sic] have a
new birth of freedom and that government of the people, by the people
and [sic] for the people shall not perish from this earth."[55] The 9/11 dead,
Giuliani asserted, "died for the very same reason" as the Union soldiers.

For a time, at least, Giuliani exemplified for many the amalgamation of
emotion and authority, empathy and action that contemporary Americans
have come to expect of their political leaders in crisis moments. When
Oprah Winfrey introduced him during the Yankee Stadium service, she
cited his "extraordinary grace under pressure" and noted that he had come
to be called "America's Mayor."[56] As Giuliani left office, *Time* magazine
named him its "Person of the Year" for 2001, referring to him as "Mayor of
the World" and "consoler in chief" and describing how he "became the
voice of America" on September 11: speaking "words full of grief and iron"
and "inspiring New York to inspire the nation," remaining "strong enough
to let his voice brim with pain, compassion and love."[57]

Indeed, the foregoing pages reveal how extensively Giuliani, Bush, and
other political leaders addressed the existential alongside the pragmatic
as they navigated the crisis. This is because the task of consolation is a far
more important one than sociological accounts of politics generally
recognize. Yet it is not, of course, a politician's only role, and it intersects
with other expectations of public office—and other genres of political
speechmaking—in complex ways.[58] In the next chapter, I examine how
consolation discourse informs and legitimates policymaking, tracing how
the dualistic framing helped to constitute the "effect flow"[59] of 9/11. The
terms and tropes deployed in public mourning rituals, I show, played a
central role in the legitimation discourse that sought to define and justify
the "war on terror" in the years that followed. If September 11 was an assault on freedom, and if the 9/11 dead perished in a mission to preserve
democracy, the proper response was to retaliate with military force.
Indeed, victory in this struggle would imbue the lives lost on September
11 with retrospective meaning, securing symbolic immortality for those
who perished.

Dualistic discourse, however, suggested that the conflict at hand was
not just a war against a specific, delimited enemy. It was, instead, a struggle

against "terror," and even "evil," writ large. As Bush put it on September 14, America's task was not simply to defeat al Qaeda or even the Taliban regime in Afghanistan, but to "rid the world of evil."[60] The effort to fulfill this pledge would leave an indelible mark on both national and global politics in the years to come. As the next three chapters reveal, though, the stark dualistic narrative—and the pride and anger it conjured—would erode over time. The meaning of September 11, and its place in larger collective narratives, would continue to be the object of vigorous struggle in foreign policy debates, commemorative ceremonies, and public controversies concerning the future of lower Manhattan.

CHAPTER 5
From Consolation to Legitimation

The existential dimensions of political speechmaking, so vividly evident in the immediate response to the events of September 11, deserve analytic attention on their own terms. National narratives are a crucial source of moral and symbolic orientation, especially in times of uncertainty or anguish, and they should be understood as such. After September 11, references to earlier moments of national struggle, including Gettysburg, Pearl Harbor, and Normandy—at both implicit and explicit levels—rendered the shocking violence comprehensible in familiar terms. Indeed, the memory of these decisive moments in the national story impinged on the events of 9/11 even as they unfolded, giving shape and significance to suffering from its beginnings. Placing the 9/11 dead within this heroic legacy affected the "secular transformation of fatality into continuity, contingency into meaning" that Anderson identified at the heart of national narratives.[1]

At the same time, however, consolation discourse is also bound up with broader political agendas—with the struggles for power and resources that are generally understood to be the substance of political life.[2] In this chapter, I take up the relationship between consolation and legitimation. Meaning, I show, plays a constitutive role in ongoing political processes; the dualistic mode of consolation very clearly helped to constitute the "effect flow" of September 11. It is not just that memories of collective suffering aided political leaders in justifying prefabricated agendas, though there is compelling evidence that this was part of the story. Even more, the dualistic interpretation of 9/11 helped to define political interests and agendas in the first place; these agendas take shape alongside, and indeed as part of, the symbolic and existential searching that becomes so pressing in the face of adversity. As Olick puts it: "Political meanings and symbols are . . . always simultaneously tools for achieving a purpose, expressions of existing identities, and defining frameworks for future interests and identities."[3] In the case of September 11, the symbolism articulated in consolation speeches not only reconstituted national narratives, but also gave way to an encompassing effort known as the "war on terror," which began in Afghanistan and continued in Iraq.

THE BUSH YEARS

As I argued in the last chapter, the effort to define American interests and articulate a policy agenda in response to September 11 was bound up with the task of consolation even in the earliest mourning rituals. When President Bush interpreted the present in light of the American past, he also worked to figure the future, and indeed promises of eventual triumph—for instance, his pledge that America would "rid the world of evil"—were a central part of his consolation narrative. Moving forward, political leaders continued to conceptualize 9/11 in dualistic terms as they sought to define and legitimate the "war on terror" before both national and international audiences. Moreover, the very image of 9/11—the harrowing memory of planes crashing into iconic buildings on a bright Tuesday morning—played a central role in official narratives justifying war, and its human costs, at times when public support declined.

The first strikes in the "war on terror" took place in October 2001. Political speechmaking in the period leading up to these strikes incorporated central themes from consolation discourse to define the nature of the conflict at hand and to imbue it with legitimacy. As early as September 17, Bush addressed military officials at the Pentagon, establishing the groundwork for the "war on terror" and for its legitimating narrative.

In this address, the frontier mythology that was implicit in the president's claims that the struggle ahead was a struggle "for civilization" played a more overt role in justifying a violent response to September 11. Here, a president who had embraced a "cowboy" image well before 9/11 redefined the frontier in global terms.[4] Civilization, he suggested, now faced a threat from a "barbaric people" who had "no rules" and knew "no borders."[5] In past wars, there had been "beaches to storm and islands to conquer."[6] But this time, the United States faced "an enemy that . . . likes to hide and burrow in," to "hit and [then] hide in some cave somewhere."[7] Bush thus constructed the enemy not only as barbaric, but also as less than human, akin to an animal that will "hide" or "burrow."[8] The fight ahead would be analogous to a hunt: "we're going to smoke 'em out," he said.[9]

Even as he insisted that this was a new kind of war, Bush nonetheless defined it using the nation's oldest mythology: "The American people are going to have to be more patient than ever with . . . our combined efforts—not just ourselves, but the efforts of our allies—to get 'em running and to find 'em, and to hunt 'em down."[10]

Asked by a reporter whether he wanted Osama bin Laden dead, Bush called forth the image of vigilante justice in unambiguous terms: "I want justice. And there's an old poster out West, as I recall, that said 'Wanted: Dead or Alive.'"[11] Again, although he emphasized the unique challenges of combating terrorism, Bush suggested that this undertaking would require an old-fashioned kind of violence, alluding to the cowboy's extralegal pursuit of justice and the moral authority long vested in this mythic figure to distinguish right from wrong. Such efforts, he underscored, would far transcend the hunt for bin Laden: "this is a long-term battle—war," he said. "Our mission is to battle terrorism, and to join with freedom-loving people."[12]

In the weeks that followed September 11, American leaders worked to legitimate a military response before global as well as domestic audiences. On October 1, the United Nations General Assembly convened in New York City for a special session on terrorism. Among the speakers was Mayor Giuliani, whose moral credibility as a representative for New Yorkers personally affected by September 11 was significant. In this appeal to a broad international community, Giuliani echoed Bush's claim that the events of September 11 left no room for neutrality, that the struggle inaugurated on 9/11 was indeed a struggle to preserve civilization itself:

> The evidence of terrorism's brutality and inhumanity, of its contempt for life and the concept of peace is lying beneath the rubble of the World Trade Center, less than two miles from where we meet today. Look at that destruction, that massive, senseless, cruel loss of human life, and then, I ask you to look in your hearts and recognize that there is no room for neutrality on the issue of terrorism. You're either with civilization or with terrorists.

Indeed, Giuliani claimed that the issue is so clear-cut—"We're right and they're wrong," he said. "It's as simple as that"—that the perpetrators' rationale did not merit contemplation or an effort at understanding. "Those who practice terrorism," Giuliani argued, "lose any right to have their cause understood by decent people and lawful nations." To support his stance, Giuliani once again drew an analogy with the Second World War:

> Love does eventually conquer hate. I believe that; I'm sure you do.

But it also needs our help. Good intentions alone are not enough to conquer evil. Remember British Prime Minister Neville Chamberlain who, armed only with good intentions, negotiated with the Nazis and emerged hopeful that he had achieved peace in his time.

Hitler's wave of terror was only encouraged by these attempts at appeasement. At the cost of millions of lives, we've learned that words alone, although important, are not enough to guarantee peace. It is action alone that counts.[13]

Not only did Giuliani explicitly invoke parallels with World War II, but he also intermingled the language of past and present in his effort to underscore their similarities (i.e., "Hitler's wave of terror"). Forging the comparison between the 9/11 perpetrators and Adolf Hitler—understood across much of the globe as the ultimate emblem of evil[14]—Giuliani sought to undermine calls for dialogue or negotiation, or even reflection on the motives that drove the 9/11 perpetrators. They had, he claimed, lost "any right to have their cause understood." In his final lines, Giuliani suggested that the 9/11 perpetrators were in some sense less than human: "we know this is not a clash of civilizations. It's a conflict between murderers and humanity."[15]

Less than a week later, on October 7, Bush announced the first strikes in Afghanistan, invoking the dualistic narrative to define the contours of the conflict in encompassing terms. "Today we focus on Afghanistan," Bush explained, "but the battle is broader. Every nation has a choice to make. In this conflict, there is no neutral ground."[16] The operation, he announced, was called "Enduring Freedom": "We defend not only our precious freedoms, but also the freedom of people everywhere to live and raise their children free from fear."[17] At this point, then, the dualistic discourse that suffused rituals of public mourning also underwrote state violence.

These early addresses laid the groundwork for a more expansive "war on terror" in which defeating the Taliban would only be the first step. In keeping with the dualistic interpretation that Bush and others had articulated from the outset, the state's definition of its enemy continually expanded in the months and years that followed. Again, the "mission" was not simply to retaliate against specific perpetrators or even those who aided and abetted their efforts, but to "rid the world of evil" itself. It was with this expansive mission in view that the Bush administration began to establish a narrative association between September 11 and Iraqi dictator Saddam Hussein, and to make the case that Iraq represented the next logical front in the war on terror. This argument unfolded in a series of public statements in 2002 and early 2003.

Consider first the ways in which the dualistic worldview animated Bush's remarks on the so-called "axis of evil" during his January 2002 State of the Union address. In this speech, Bush asserted that the war in Afghanistan had revealed "the depth of our enemies' hatred"—for instance, "in videos where they laugh about the loss of innocent life." In Afghanistan, he said, the United States had found that "far from ending there, our war against terror is only beginning." He explained: "These enemies view the entire world as a battlefield." Thus—Bush implied—so, too, should the United States and its allies. Bush named North Korea, Iran, and Iraq, and declared: "States like these and their terrorist allies constitute an axis of evil, arming to threaten the peace of the world."[18] The 9/11 perpetrators, he suggested, had awakened the nation to much larger forces of "evil" at work in the world. The phrase evoked the memory of World War II—especially through the use of the term "axis"[19]—as well as Reagan's "evil empire," and suggested that a global struggle of epic proportions was once again underway.

In this address, Bush also celebrated the successes of the war on terror to date, portraying American soldiers as liberators of the innocent and oppressed. He emphasized especially the impact that the U.S. invasion had on Afghan women: "The last time we met in this chamber [on September 20, 2001], the mothers and daughters of Afghanistan were captives in their own homes, forbidden from working or going to school. Today women are free and are part of Afghanistan's new government."[20] This gendered discourse continued the effort to reassert American agency by "remasculinizing" the nation after the wound inflicted on 9/11.[21] It did so by placing the United States in an agentic and indeed heroic (masculine) role in liberating passive (female) victims. And the achievements Bush highlighted in the process endowed the larger struggle with meaning and legitimacy.

Even if Americans generally accepted that Hussein's regime was "evil," however, the argument for taking action to topple the Iraqi dictator required a new doctrine, a justification for waging preemptive war. Bush articulated this justification in a June 2002 commencement address at West Point, arguing that the events of September 11 ushered in an era when national security—and indeed the preservation of liberty itself—would at times require the nation to strike first. The president situated his argument for preemption within a larger Manichean frame, and defended his absolutist language—the sharp moral contrasts associated with the dualistic mode—in explicit terms.

Early in the speech, Bush recalled General George C. Marshall's words to the class of 1942: "We're determined that before the sun sets on this terrible struggle, our flag will be recognized throughout the world as a symbol of freedom on the one hand, and of overwhelming power on the other." Bush elaborated the link between past and present: "History has also issued its call to your generation," he said, suggesting that the class of 2002 was not only "commissioned to the Armed Forces" but "also commissioned by history, to take part in a great new calling for their country." Even for all the ways that the present resembled the past, however, its differences—the sense of historical rupture Bush had evoked on September 20, 2001—required transformations in outlook and in foreign policy. In this new era, Bush argued, "we face a threat with no precedent." While waging war against America once required "great armies and great industrial capabilities," the "chaos and suffering" of September 11 required only "a few hundred thousand dollars in the hands of a few dozen evil and deluded men." Positing that "[t]he gravest danger to freedom lies at the perilous crossroads of radicalism and technology," Bush argued: "If we wait for threats to fully materialize, we will have waited too long." In such a world, "our security will require all Americans to be forward-looking and resolute, to be ready for preemptive action when necessary to defend our liberty and to defend our lives."[22] There was no explicit cowboy imagery here, but the assumption that the United States possessed the moral insight and authority to discern when violence was justified—bound by no external strictures—certainly gestured toward a much older notion of vigilante justice.[23]

Moreover, Bush said, Americans must also face the mounting threats with "firm moral purpose," a willingness to "speak the language of right and wrong."[24] Here, the president defended the stark, absolutist terms within which he apprehended the world: "Different circumstances require different methods, but not different moralities," he said. "Moral truth is the same in every culture, in every time, and in every place."[25] He offered examples of such transcendent moral truths: "Targeting innocent civilians for murder is always and everywhere wrong. Brutality against women is always and everywhere wrong. There can be no neutrality between justice and cruelty, between the innocent and the guilty. We are in a conflict between good and evil, and America will call evil by its name."[26] The president's convictions concerning the nature of good and evil—his position on questions of broad existential import—were, he suggested, the primary impetus behind his political decision-making. One need not take his words at face value in order to affirm the theoretical point that meaning and interest are bound up together, and in the end inextricable.[27]

In September of 2002, just days before the first anniversary of 9/11, members of the Bush administration launched a more forceful effort to articulate their case for a preemptive strike in Iraq.[28] The use of the term "ground zero" to describe the site in lower Manhattan where the Twin Towers once stood already evoked nuclear imagery at an implicit level, and indeed the prospect of an actual nuclear attack became a focal point in the administration's case for war. Claiming that Iraq had attempted to acquire aluminum tubes designed to enrich uranium, administration officials suggested that inaction could bring Americans' most apocalyptic fears to fruition. During an interview on *Meet the Press* on September 8, Vice President Dick Cheney said: "we do know, with absolute certainty, that he [Hussein] is using his procurement system to acquire the equipment he needs in order to enrich uranium to build a nuclear weapon."[29] Appearing on CNN's *Late Edition* the same day, National Security Adviser Condoleezza Rice sought to awaken Americans' nuclear fears in no uncertain terms with words that became a famous sound bite: "we don't want the smoking gun to be a mushroom cloud."[30] Bush echoed the phrase a month later, on October 7, in a speech outlining the threat Iraq allegedly posed: "Facing clear evidence of peril," he said, "we cannot wait for the final proof—the smoking gun—that could come in the form of a mushroom cloud."[31]

In the midst of this intensifying rhetoric—and the public debate it generated—the president marked the first anniversary of September 11 with a national address from Ellis Island. The Statue of Liberty lit the night sky behind him during a carefully choreographed performance.[32] Against this symbolic backdrop, Bush reiterated the argument that the war on terror was a national mission undertaken on behalf of humanity writ large; in this commemorative context, he did not mention Iraq specifically, but his words were unmistakably intended to bolster his case for expanding the war on terror. At the limit, his address evoked the fundamental contrast between light and darkness.

> Tomorrow is September the 12th. A milestone has passed, and a mission goes on. Be confident. Our country is strong. And our cause is even larger than our country. Ours is the cause of human dignity, freedom guided by conscience and guarded by peace. This ideal of America is the hope of all mankind. That hope drew millions to this harbor. That hope still lights our way, and the light shines in the darkness, and the darkness will not overcome it.[33]

The bright symbol of freedom behind the president bolstered his pledge. The next day, Bush spoke to the United Nations, recalling "the innocent lives taken that terrible morning," and suggesting the grim possibility that the suffering 9/11 wrought could be multiplied.[34] "With every step the Iraqi regime takes toward gaining and deploying the most terrible weapons, our own options to confront that regime will narrow," he said. "And if an emboldened regime were to supply these weapons to terrorist allies, then the attacks of September the 11th would be a prelude to far greater horrors."[35]

Bush continued to build his administration's case for an Iraq war during his January 2003 State of the Union. The argument took shape within the absolutist framework he had defended at West Point, and it relied on overtly establishing a narrative link between Hussein and the memory of September 11. In this address, Bush urged Americans to remember that "our calling, as a blessed country, is to make this world better."[36] Integral in fulfilling this calling was "leading the world in confronting and defeating the . . . evil of international terrorism."[37] And, in this ongoing struggle, "the gravest danger" was at that point "outlaw regimes that seek and possess nuclear, chemical and biological weapons."[38] Foremost among these threats, Bush claimed, was Saddam Hussein.

Imagine those 19 hijackers with other weapons and other plans, this time armed by Saddam Hussein. It would take one vial, one canister, one crate slipped into this country to bring a day of horror like none we have ever known. . . .

The dictator who is assembling the world's most dangerous weapons has already used them on whole villages, leaving thousands of his own citizens dead, blind, or disfigured.

Iraqi refugees tell us how forced confessions are obtained: by torturing children while their parents are made to watch. International human rights groups have catalogued other methods used in the torture chambers of Iraq: electric shock, burning with hot irons, dripping acid on the skin, mutilation with electric drills, cutting out tongues, and rape.

If this is not evil, then evil has no meaning.[39]

Juxtaposing the 9/11 hijackers and Saddam Hussein in an imagined nightmare scenario, Bush assigned Hussein a clear place in a bifurcated world. Hussein became, along with bin Laden, a quintessential emblem of the "evil" that the war on terror sought to eradicate. Once again, Bush's conclusion placed the present moment within a cosmic frame that afforded Americans special privileges while also assigning them unique responsibilities: "The liberty we prize is not America's gift to the world; it is God's gift to humanity. We Americans have faith in ourselves, but not in ourselves alone. We do not . . . claim to know all the ways of providence, yet we can trust in them, placing our confidence in the loving God behind all of life and all of history."[40] American forces became agents of a higher power, stewards of the "liberty" that is "God's gift to humanity." This claim is a familiar one in American history—recall, for instance, Truman's assertion after the U.S. dropped a nuclear weapon on Hiroshima that the United States was a providentially appointed "trustee" of the atomic bomb.

Shortly after Bush's State of the Union—on February 5, 2003—U.S. Secretary of State Colin Powell addressed the United Nations, delivering a speech that would subsequently be understood as a pivotal moment in the buildup to the Iraq War. At the time, Powell's speech added substantial legitimacy to the case for deposing Hussein. This legitimacy stemmed not only from the substantive claims Powell articulated, but perhaps even more from the person articulating them: Powell was a well-established and well-respected moderate voice who garnered trust from across the political spectrum, both within the United States and abroad. In his remarks, Powell confidently asserted that Hussein's regime was "concealing their efforts to produce more weapons of mass destruction," a crucial component in the Bush administration's case for war.[41] Moreover, he described a link between Iraq and al Qaeda, reinforcing Bush's claim that— without military intervention—Hussein was likely to aid terrorist groups in gaining access to these weapons. "Iraq and terrorism go back decades," Powell said. "But what I want to bring to your attention today is the potentially much more sinister nexus between Iraq and the al Qaeda terrorist network, a nexus that combines classic terrorist organizations and modern methods of murder."[42] Countering arguments that the contacts between Hussein and al Qaeda "do not amount to much," or that "Hussein's secular tyranny and al Qaeda's religious tyranny do not mix," Powell put his own credibility on the line: "I am not comforted by this thought. Ambition and hatred are enough to bring Iraq and al Qaeda together, enough so al Qaeda could learn how to build more sophisticated bombs and learn how to forge documents; and enough so that al Qaeda could turn to Iraq for help in acquiring expertise on weapons of mass destruction."[43]

Powell focused primarily on relating intelligence information; here, symbolism and meaning were clearly secondary. Yet Powell clearly categorized Hussein in dualistic language, claiming that his "inhumanity has no limits" and citing his "utter contempt for human life."[44] Ultimately, he echoed the sense of historical rupture underlying Bush's doctrine of preemption. The events of 9/11 ushered in a new era, and in this new era, it became imperative to take a preemptive approach to Iraq: "Leaving Saddam Hussein in possession of weapons of mass destruction for a few more months or years is not an option, not in a post–September 11th world," Powell said.[45]

Powell would later express regret for his words, acknowledging that the claims he had so forcefully articulated before a global audience were based on faulty intelligence. In 2005, after leaving office, he referred to the speech as "blot" on his record, adding: "It was painful. It's painful now."[46] At the time, however, the speech was central to the Bush administration's narrative linking Hussein with September 11 and underwriting the 2003 invasion of Iraq, which began several weeks later. In an address to the nation on March 19, Bush announced that "American and coalition forces are in the early stages of military operations to disarm Iraq, to free its people and to defend the world from grave danger."[47] He termed the effort "Operation Iraqi Freedom," and—in its earliest hours—reiterated familiar assurances: "My fellow citizens, the dangers to our country and the world will be overcome. We will pass through this time of peril and carry on the work of peace. We will defend our freedom. We will bring freedom to others. And we will prevail."[48]

It is now well established that top officials within the Bush administration—including Vice President Dick Cheney, Defense Secretary Donald Rumsfeld, and Deputy Defense Secretary Paul Wolfowitz— had an explicit interest in toppling Hussein's regime before the events of September 11.[49] On this basis, it would perhaps be easy to assume that the symbolic politics I have been tracing here were merely epiphenomenal—a tool to achieve longstanding, predefined interests: removing Hussein, securing control over Iraqi oil, establishing the precedent for preemptive or "preventive" war in order to further unshackle American power and solidify the nation's hegemony in the post–Cold War world.

Yet we should not dismiss the constitutive power of symbolism too quickly. The effect flow of September 11 represents the complex interplay of concrete events, preexisting instrumental interests, and the symbolic structures that—after all—help to constitute interests in the first place. Even before September 11, would war in Iraq have been conceivable without the longstanding and deeply entrenched sense of national mission—of the United States as a redeemer nation, responsible for liberating the oppressed and serving as democracy's steward on behalf of all humanity? Perhaps the Bush administration capitalized cynically on the pain and suffering associated with 9/11 in order to achieve a long-established political goal. But the goal itself—not to mention the administration's ability to carry it forward— is incomprehensible outside of the national narratives that brought meaning to these specific historical challenges. As Smith argues, analysts "should not confuse the fact that they find the justifications for the war incredible or manufactured with the theoretical claim that culture is irrelevant."[50] Quite the contrary, "the very effort that went into constructing a meaningful groundwork" for the Iraq War "confirms the centrality of storytelling to legitimacy."[51] The profound and encompassing meaning attached to September 11—the place that 9/11 assumed in a teleological dualistic narrative, and the ways in which this narrative continued to offer consolation amidst an enduring sense of collective suffering and national loss—played a substantial role in constituting the sequence of events that followed.

There is, of course, an important distinction between *legitimation*—the efforts to build support for an agenda—and its reception, the popular perception of *legitimacy*.[52] The decision to invade Afghanistan in October 2001 generated widespread support across the nation, and indeed from allies around the globe. British forces joined the campaign from the beginning, and when the strikes began, Bush announced that Canada, Australia, Germany, and France had also pledged to commit forces as the operation continued. Domestically, an ABC News/*Washington Post* poll immediately after Bush's September 20 address to Joint Congress found that 90 percent of respondents supported taking military action against "the groups or nations responsible" for the September 11 attacks.[53] Eighty-three percent said they supported military action even "if that meant getting into a war."[54] And 63 percent supported "a broader war against terrorist groups and the nations that support them," not only those directly responsible for September 11.[55] Asked whether the United States had made a mistake in sending troops to Afghanistan in a November 2001 Gallup poll, 89 percent said the decision was *not* a mistake; by January 2002, the percentage had risen to 93.[56] Members of Congress expressed overwhelming support for military action when they passed the September 14, 2001, Authorization for Use of Military Force, a joint resolution authorizing the President to "use all necessary and appropriate force against those nations, organizations, or persons he determines planned, authorized, committed, or aided the terrorist attacks that occurred on September 11, 2001, or harbored such organizations or persons." Only one member of Congress—Barbara Lee, a Democrat from California serving in the House—voted against the resolution. Popular support waned as the conflict wore on: by July 2004, 25 percent of respondents to the Gallup poll said the United States had made a mistake, while 72 percent voiced continued support for the war in Afghanistan; by March 2013, 44 percent said the decision was a mistake, while 51 percent voiced support.[57] Among politicians, too, the war in Afghanistan became a more divisive issue over time. But initially, the decision to take military action was overwhelmingly perceived as legitimate.

The decision to invade Iraq—and the Bush administration's argument that Iraq was the next front in the "war on terror"—was far more controversial from the outset. As I have shown, the claim that Saddam Hussein possessed weapons of mass destruction (WMD) provided the basis for the narrative association that the administration forged between Iraq and 9/11: Bush, Powell, and others argued that Hussein would supply WMD to al Qaeda or other terrorist organizations, leading to death and destruction far greater than that which occurred on September 11. Revelations that the weapons programs the administration had described did not, in fact, exist thus powerfully undermined subsequent efforts to legitimate the ongoing campaign. So, too, did an ongoing insurgency, sectarian violence, and reports of U.S. atrocities at the Abu Ghraib prison. The latter brought legal memoranda justifying so-called "enhanced interrogation techniques" such as sleep deprivation and waterboarding to public attention, unsettling the binaries within which the Bush administration portrayed the conflict. The United States, too, perpetrated cruelty, even exhibited inhumanity. Recalling the Vietnam era, some commentators on the left even inverted the dualistic script, transforming America into "the world's biggest villain," guided by leaders who abandoned the very democratic values they espoused in their quest for power.[58] As Michael Rogin argues, engaging in "demonology"—creating "monsters . . . by the inflation, stigmatization, and dehumanization of political foes"—provides justification "in the name of battling the subversive, to imitate [one's] enemy."[59] Public commentary underscored these parallels ever more frequently as time wore on.

Although domestic debates over the Iraq War were heated from the outset, and the invasion was not sanctioned by the U.N. Security Council, popular support within the United States was initially fairly high. A January 2003 Pew Research Center poll found that 68 percent of respondents—asked whether they would "favor or oppose taking military action in Iraq to end Saddam Hussein's rule"—said they were in favor. Twenty-five percent expressed opposition.[60] In a Gallup poll conducted from March 24 to 25, 2003—just after the invasion—23 percent of respondents reported that the United States had made a mistake in sending troops to Iraq; 75 percent said the decision was *not* a mistake.[61] Both the House and the Senate passed the Iraq War Resolution—formally known as the Authorization for the Use of Military Force Against Iraq Resolution of 2002—in October 2002, though over notable opposition.[62]

In retrospect, Bush's May 1, 2003, speech aboard the aircraft carrier U.S.S. *Abraham Lincoln*—now better known as the "mission accomplished" speech—came to represent a watershed moment in Iraq War discourse.

Prior to the speech, Bush landed on the aircraft carrier in a jet and posed while clad in a flight suit for photographs with pilots and crew members. The address itself did not contain the words "mission accomplished," but a banner emblazoned with the declaration provided a backdrop for Bush's remarks. In his address, he announced: "Major combat operations in Iraq have ended. In the battle of Iraq, the United States and our allies have prevailed."[63] This victory, Bush argued, marked a decisive moment in the war that began on 9/11:

> The battle of Iraq is one victory in a war on terror that began on September the 11th, 2001, and still goes on. That terrible morning, 19 evil men, the shock troops of a hateful ideology, gave America and the civilized world a glimpse of their ambitions. They imagined, in the words of one terrorist, that September the 11th would be the "beginning of the end of America." By seeking to turn our cities into killing fields, terrorists and their allies believed they could destroy this nation's resolve and force our retreat from the world. They have failed.[64]

To be sure, the president's performance was compelling to some, especially at the time. But as organized resistance began to coalesce in Iraq, Bush's declaration of victory—and the triumphant posture he adopted as he delivered the news—quickly came to appear premature. Many commentators portrayed the event as misguided and overly theatrical: a boyish president playing "G.I. Joe," or emulating Tom Cruise's character from *Top Gun* in a carefully choreographed moment of "presidential theater."[65] On October 6, 2003, the cover of *Time* magazine featured a photograph of a grinning Bush donning his flying gear with the headline: "Mission Not Accomplished."[66]

The narrative association between Hussein and 9/11 remained ubiquitous in Bush's speechmaking as he sought to shore up the war's legitimacy—and his own—in the face of steadily declining support. Winning the war, he claimed, was essential in preventing another violent nightmare at home. In a September 2003 address to the nation, Bush reported that "[w]e are rolling back the terrorist threat to civilization," and that Iraq had become "the central front" in "the war on terror."[67] Bush again underscored America's special role in the battle between "tyranny" and "liberty," and in leading "the cause of the civilized world." In closing, he recalled the events of two years prior and urged the nation onward: "Fellow citizens, we have been tested these past 24 months, and the dangers have not yet passed. Yet Americans are responding with courage and confidence. We accept the duties of our generation. We are active and resolute in our own defense. We are serving in freedom's cause, and that is the cause of all mankind."[68] By October 2003, however, public support for the war had declined substantially: the percentage of Gallup poll respondents who reported that sending troops to Iraq was a mistake had risen to 40.[69]

In December 2005, Bush publicly acknowledged that the intelligence indicating that Hussein possessed weapons of mass destruction "turned out to be wrong."[70] But in an address from the Woodrow Wilson Center in Washington, he maintained that Iraq was a crucial front in the war on terror, and he did so by continuing to link the memory of 9/11 with that of Saddam Hussein. Citing "the lessons of September the 11th," Bush asserted that— even though the invasion of Iraq was predicated on faulty intelligence— "my decision to remove Saddam Hussein was the right decision."[71] Toppling Hussein's regime, he indicated, could still be understood within an American quest to liberate, to spread democracy and foster progress, which took on new urgency after September 11. Bush argued: "a liberated Iraq can show the power of freedom to transform the Middle East by bringing hope and progress to the lives of millions."[72] By this point, over half of Americans—52 percent, according to a December 2005 Gallup poll—viewed the invasion as a mistake.[73] Bush, however, maintained the narrative association with September 11 to the last. In March 2008, on the fifth anniversary of combat operations, Bush claimed that to allow "an American failure in Iraq" would require the United States "to ignore the lessons of September the 11th and make it more likely that America will suffer another attack like the one we experienced that day, a day in which 19 armed men with box cutters killed nearly 3,000 people . . . on our soil."[74]

Assimilating the Iraq War into the dualistic 9/11 narrative, then, certainly did not imbue it with unquestioned legitimacy, and the connection Bush invoked between Iraq and 9/11 was the subject of vigorous public criticism and growing dissent. At the same time, however, it is important to recall that the assumption of a link was remarkably widespread in the American population leading up to the invasion and beyond. In January 2003, 68 percent of respondents to a poll conducted by the Program on International Policy Attitudes (PIPA) and Knowledge Networks reported a belief that Iraq played an important role in September 11.[75] In February 2003, they followed up with a more nuanced question. While only 20 percent of respondents asserted that Iraq was *directly* involved in carrying out the September 11 attacks, an additional 36 percent believed that Iraq gave substantial support to al Qaeda. Only 7 percent reported the belief that there was no connection between Iraq and 9/11 at all.[76] The presumed connection between Hussein and 9/11 thus played a crucial role in building public support for the invasion, and it continued to influence voters during the 2004 presidential election.[77]

A comprehensive assessment of the relationship between political discourse and popular beliefs—between legitimation and legitimacy—is beyond the scope of my analysis here.[78] It seems clear, however, that the dualistic interpretation of September 11 was critical in both defining and justifying the "war on terror"—conceived, at the limit, as a battle against "evil" writ large. Namely, it provided a plotline within which the decision to invade Iraq came to seem—among a sufficient number of political elites and a considerable proportion of the American population—a logical and indeed even necessary step in a struggle inaugurated on September 11, 2001. Bush administration goals converged with extant perceptions of Saddam Hussein in the population at large, and Hussein's regime became part of the "evil" enemy in a world that left no room for ambiguity or neutrality. Dualistic symbolism and political interests thus reciprocally shaped one another, illustrating how moral and symbolic "maps of problematic social reality"[79] help to constitute interest and condition action, thereby shaping the effect flow of events.

THE OBAMA YEARS

During his second term, Bush was dogged not only by public outcries over the Iraq War, but also a series of subsequent crises—especially Hurricane Katrina in 2005 and the financial crisis in 2008—that placed his entire presidency in question, even among many erstwhile supporters. His successor, Barack Obama, assumed office amidst soaring promises of "hope" and "change." In many ways, the Democratic candidate—widely perceived as charismatic, eloquent, and thoughtful, though he was also deeply polarizing even from the outset—established an image of himself as Bush's foil.[80]

Obama was indeed an outsider in the Washington political scene, having ascended to national prominence after a stirring address at the Democratic National Convention in 2004. At the time, he was a state senator in Illinois; he arrived in Washington to serve in the U.S. Senate only in January 2005. Notably, he had publicly opposed the Iraq War from the beginning; he pledged throughout his presidential campaign to close the U.S. detention camp at Guantánamo Bay, Cuba; and he stated explicitly that an Obama administration would "reject torture—without exception or equivocation."[81] In an interview with the journalist David Brooks in April 2007, candidate Obama revealed his admiration for the theologian Reinhold Niebuhr, and in doing so suggested a striking attentiveness to the ironic and tragic dimensions of American history. Brooks reflected that the candidate "hates, as Niebuhr certainly would have, the grand Bushian rhetoric about ridding the world of evil and tyranny"—yet "he also dislikes liberal muddle-headedness on power politics."[82] Obama announced his candidacy from the steps of the Old State Capitol in Springfield, Illinois, recalling Lincoln; his youth and vigor frequently generated comparisons with John F. Kennedy; his March 2008 speech on race elicited comparisons with Martin Luther King, Jr. For many on the left and even at the center, it appeared that a President Obama could "reinvent American political culture" at a critical juncture.[83]

Over time, however—as the charismatic candidate became governing official and the collective effervescence of the campaign gave way to the everyday challenges of democratic politics—Democrats identified profound continuities between the president's counterterrorism policies and his predecessor's.[84] Obama ended the so-called "enhanced interrogation techniques" employed during the Bush administration, but urged Americans to look ahead to the future rather than reckoning in any formal way with the legacies of this policy. In a January 2009 interview on the ABC News program *This Week*, president-elect Obama expressed "a belief that we need to look forward as opposed to looking backwards."[85] His pledge to close Guantánamo quickly crumbled in the face of political realities. And his use of unmanned aircraft, or drones, to carry out targeted killings in the war on terror proved especially controversial on the left, prompting many supporters to question how much had truly changed since Obama assumed office.

Here, I consider how Obama's public speechmaking has grappled with the two wars he inherited, examining continuities and contrasts between his legitimation discourse and that of his predecessor. Obama has clearly drawn upon the memory of 9/11 and key tropes from dualistic discourse in his efforts to shore up support for the increasingly unpopular war in Afghanistan. The ways in which he has grappled with the legacies of Bush's justifications for the Iraq War, however, are more complex. As president, Obama has faced the challenge of honoring war sacrifice—and providing consolation in the face of continued losses—while also maintaining continuity in his own position on Iraq, especially because this position figured centrally in his 2008 campaign. In a more general sense, these speeches provide a particularly revealing prism onto the interplay between the president's agency and the structure of the institutionalized discourses he inherited, revealing the dialogical quality of speech genres. Obama may transform the materials he inherited—the narrative link between Hussein and September 11; the understanding of the Iraq War as another chapter in a monumental struggle that began the moment that the first plane hit the north tower—but he must do so in dialogue with these earlier claims and frames.[86]

Consider first Obama's speechmaking on the war in Afghanistan. In a December 1, 2009, speech at West Point explaining the rationale for a troop increase in Afghanistan, Obama invoked the memory of 9/11 to legitimate the sacrifices that the surge would require:

> it's important to recall why America and our allies were compelled to fight a war in Afghanistan in the first place. We did not ask for this fight. On September 11th, 2001, 19 men hijacked four airplanes and used them to murder nearly 3,000 people. They struck at our military and economic nerve centers. They took the lives of innocent men, women and children, without regard to their faith or race or station. Were it not for the heroic actions of passengers on board one of those flights, they could have also struck at one of the great symbols of our democracy in Washington and killed many more.[87]

The justifications Obama called forth here are familiar. The United States was compelled to respond militarily to an attack on innocent civilians, the implication being that the nation itself is blameless for the events and their aftermath in Afghanistan—"We did not ask for this fight." But the fight must be carried through to victory: "I do not make this decision lightly," Obama said. "I make this decision because I am convinced that our security is at stake in Afghanistan and Pakistan. This is the epicenter of violent extremism practiced by al Qaeda. It is from here that we were attacked on 9/11, and it is from here that new attacks are being plotted as I speak."[88]

In this fight, Obama claimed—echoing his predecessor—present-day Americans continued the legacy of the World War II generation. "Since the days of Franklin Roosevelt and the service and sacrifice of our grandparents and great grandparents, our country has borne a special burden in global affairs," he said. "As a country, we're not as young, and perhaps not as innocent, as we were when Roosevelt was president. Yet we are still heirs to a noble struggle for freedom. And now we must summon all of our might and moral suasion to meet the challenges of a new age."[89] Obama's acknowledgment that the American nation may have lost some of its innocence is rare for 9/11 discourse—and indeed for American political speechmaking in general. But by now it is clear that the larger connection he drew between the Second World War and the fight against terrorism is an institutionalized feature of the discourse.

In general, Obama's rhetoric has been considerably less strident than his predecessor's—he speaks less frequently of "evil," and at times works quite overtly to complicate the stark binaries through which Bush filtered the world. Yet his speeches on Afghanistan remained consonant with Bush's in important ways, apprehending the conflict as a struggle to preserve freedoms that were assaulted on 9/11 and offering assurance that victory was inevitable. "As Americans, we've endured and we've grown stronger, and we remain the land of the free only because we are also home of the brave," Obama said in an address at Bagram Air Base in Afghanistan in December 2010. "And because of you, I know that once more, we will prevail."[90]

As he brought the Iraq War to its close—combat operations officially concluded on August 31, 2010—Obama's speeches evinced a more complicated position. Fully understanding the dilemmas Obama faced requires revisiting a 2002 speech that he delivered in Chicago, while serving in the Illinois Senate. In the speech—which was widely publicized during his presidential campaign—Obama unambiguously voiced his support for the war in Afghanistan while sharply criticizing the administration's argument for military action in Iraq.[91]

> After September 11, after witnessing the carnage and destruction, the dust and the tears, I supported this administration's pledge to hunt down and root out those who would slaughter innocents in the name of intolerance, and I would willingly take up arms myself to prevent such tragedy from happening again. I don't oppose all wars. . . . What I am opposed to is a dumb war. What I am opposed to is a rash war. What I am opposed to is the cynical attempt by Richard Perle and Paul Wolfowitz and other armchair, weekend warriors in this administration to shove their own ideological agendas down our throats, irrespective of the costs in lives lost and in hardships borne.[92]

Obama concluded his speech with an assertion that the lives lost at war in Iraq would be senseless, useless—devoid of the profound meaning associated with national sacrifice:

> We may have occasion in our lifetime to once again rise up in defense of our freedom, and pay the wages of war. But we ought not—we will not—travel down that hellish path blindly. Nor should we allow those who would march off and pay the ultimate sacrifice, who would prove the full measure of devotion with their blood, to make such an awful sacrifice in vain.[93]

Here, Obama remediated Lincoln in a different way, in an effort to halt a violent confrontation whose bloodshed he believed would be for naught.

In an Iraq war, Obama suggested, there would be no consolation for combat losses. Death would be meaningless, "in vain."

Several years later, as head of state—and as a commander-in-chief who continued to send American troops to Iraq in order to bring combat operations to a close—Obama faced pressure to both maintain consistency in the position he had so unmistakably articulated and to honor the soldiers who fought and died on the field of battle. Indeed, his task was precisely to offer assurance that fallen soldiers did not die "in vain," as he had asserted they would in 2002. But maintaining his own position required that he imbue these losses with meaning without invoking the narrative association Bush asserted between the Iraq War and September 11.

In a February 2009 speech articulating a strategy for ending the war in Iraq, then, Obama overtly acknowledged the controversy the war had generated while praising American soldiers for their service: "As a nation, we've had our share of debates about the war in Iraq. It has, at times, divided us as a people. To this very day, there are some Americans who want to stay in Iraq longer, and some who want to leave faster. But there should be no disagreement on what the men and women of our military have achieved." In order to honor service members, Obama faced an imperative to identify in specific terms the cause for which they fought—and in some cases, died. Here, he underscored their achievements in toppling Saddam Hussein's regime and laying the groundwork for a sovereign Iraqi democracy: "I want to be very clear. We sent our troops to Iraq to do away with Saddam Hussein's regime—and you got the job done. We kept our troops in Iraq to help establish a sovereign government—and you got the job done. And we will leave the Iraqi people with a hard-earned opportunity to live a better life. That is your achievement. That is the prospect that you have made possible."[94]

This achievement, Obama asserted, reflected and embodied the values for which Americans have long fought. But he evoked no overt connection to "the lessons of September 11." In his address to the nation marking the end of "Operation Iraqi Freedom," Obama praised the troops, who "have served with courage and resolve." Those who fell in battle "gave their lives for the values that have lived in the hearts of our people for over two centuries," and "paid a huge price to put the future of Iraq in the hands of its people." In serving, they joined "an unbroken line of heroes that stretches from Lexington to Gettysburg, from Iwo Jima to Inchon, from Khe Sanh to Kandahar—Americans who have fought to see that the lives of our children are better than our own." With that, Obama shifted the focus back to the ongoing war in Afghanistan. Seeking to shore up support using a familiar narrative before a national public that had grown weary of war, Obama reminded his listeners:

> Americans across the political spectrum supported the use of force against those who attacked us on 9/11. Now, as we approach our 10th year of combat in Afghanistan, there are those who are understandably asking tough questions about our mission there. But we must never lose sight of what's at stake. As we speak, al Qaeda continues to plot against us, and its leadership remains anchored in the border regions of Afghanistan and Pakistan. We will disrupt, dismantle and defeat al Qaeda while preventing Afghanistan from again serving as a base for terrorists.[95]

In Obama's speechmaking, then, Iraq became part of a more generic American tradition of fighting to extend democracy.[96] The fight in Afghanistan—nine years after it began, and beyond—remained an essential response to September 11.

The evening of May 1, 2011, marked a pivotal moment in the 9/11 narrative and an occasion for Obama to grapple with the event's legacies before a wide audience, both within the United States and beyond. In an address to the nation from the White House, Obama announced that a U.S. operation had killed Osama bin Laden—"a terrorist," Obama said, "who is responsible for the murder of thousands of innocent men, women and children."[97] After recalling the haunting images of that September morning, the generosity and compassion Americans exhibited in the aftermath, and the nation's resolve "to bring those who committed this vicious attack to justice," Obama continued:

> The American people did not choose this fight. It came to our shores and started with the senseless slaughter of our citizens. . . .
>
> So Americans understand the costs of war. Yet, as a country, we will never tolerate our security being threatened, nor stand idly by when our people have been killed. We will be relentless in defense of our citizens and our friends and allies. We will be true to the values that make us who we are. And on nights like this one, we can say to those families who have lost loved ones to al Qaeda's terror: Justice has been done.[98]

With these words, Obama underscored the theme of American innocence—the war "came to our shores." He also echoed one of the central assertions underlying Bush's September 20, 2001, address, in which Bush had pledged: "justice will be done." Yet Obama presented a more circumscribed image of the struggle at hand, and he did little to evoke the grand Manichean terms within which Bush apprehended it: even as he condemned "senseless slaughter" and pledged to remain vigilant, in this speech, Obama said nothing of "evil" or "evildoers"—a notable absence.

The role of national identity claims—as Obama put it, "the values that make us who we are"—was especially powerful in this address: most of all, Obama sought to inspire a renewed sense of solidarity and pride in light of the operation's success. In doing so, he recalled the moral unity that emerged in the days following September 11:

> tonight, let us think back to the sense of unity that prevailed on 9/11. I know that it has, at times, frayed. Yet today's achievement is a testament to the greatness of our country and the determination of the American people.
>
> The cause of securing our country is not complete, but tonight we are once again reminded that America can do whatever we set our mind to. That is the story of our history, whether it's the pursuit of prosperity for our people, or the struggle for equality for all our citizens, our commitment to stand up for our values abroad, and our sacrifices to make the world a safer place.
>
> Let us remember that we can do these things, not just because of wealth or power, but because of who we are: One nation, under God, indivisible, with liberty and justice for all.[99]

The version of the nation's constitutive narrative that Obama articulated had a different inflection from that which his predecessor regularly told; Obama's speech underscored the quest for "equality" alongside the quest for liberty. But he also portrayed current military engagements—especially the operation that led to the capture and death of bin Laden—as an expression of enduring American values and as a chapter in the nation's progressive narrative. Reactions to Obama's announcement across the nation certainly varied. But spontaneous public celebrations—replete with patriotic symbolism—that quickly coalesced in American cities to celebrate the news suggest that for many, the operation that killed bin Laden was indeed an expression of "who Americans are" and a triumph worth affirming.

Occurring on the heels of bin Laden's death, the 10th anniversary of September 11 would once again bring interpretive dilemmas. Obama faced a presidential obligation to tie together the complex legacies of September 11, to reflect on the day's meaning a decade hence and, presumably, to articulate its relationship to the two wars that followed. On September 11, 2011, Obama delivered remarks during an evening ceremony at the Kennedy Center in Washington, D.C. (The ceremony was originally scheduled for the National Cathedral, echoing the September 14, 2001, national memorial service, but was relocated because the cathedral had sustained serious damage during an August 2011 earthquake.) The events of September 11, Obama suggested, ushered in "a world in which evil was closer at hand." The "strength and resilience" Americans exhibited, he said, was "the ultimate rebuke to the hateful killers" who struck 10 years before, and he praised the nation's "resolve to defend its citizens, and our way of life." Obama spoke, that is, in familiar binaries: on this commemorative occasion, he contrasted the perpetrators' "evil" and "hate" with American "strength" and "resolve," and claimed that the events of 9/11 were an attack on cherished values—"our way of life." And he honored the sacrifices of American soldiers in the two wars that followed, asserting their place in the ever-unfolding national narrative: "This land pulses with the optimism of those who set out for distant shores, and the courage of those who died for human freedom," Obama said. "Decades from now, Americans will visit the memorials to those who were lost on 9/11. They will run their fingers over the places where the names of those we loved are carved into marble and stone, and wonder at the lives they led. Standing before the white headstones in Arlington, and in peaceful cemeteries and small-town squares in every corner of our country, they will pay respects to those lost in Afghanistan and Iraq." Obama gestured toward, but never explicitly asserted, a connection between Iraq and September 11. "And they will know that nothing can break the will of a truly United States of America."

Even as he projected triumph, however, Obama concluded with reflections that evinced humility as well as pride. "They will be reminded that we are not perfect, but our democracy is durable, and that democracy—reflecting, as it does, the imperfections of man—also gives us the opportunity to perfect our union," Obama said. "That is what we honor on days of national commemoration—those aspects of the American experience that are enduring, and the determination to move forward as one people."[100] While he contrasted American goodness with the evil that had erupted on September 11, then, Obama also called upon his fellow citizens to strive for better, suggesting that perfecting the union remained an unfinished task.

As the war in Afghanistan—and the "war on terror" more broadly conceived—went on, public pressure would lead the president to reflect in more detail on the nation's shortcomings and imperfections. Drone strikes, and the civilian casualties they inflicted, became an increasingly salient source of controversy, and Obama's failure to close Guantánamo haunted his administration. In May 2013, Congress revisited the Authorization for the Use of Military Force that had—for nearly 12 years—served as the justification for U.S. counterterrorism efforts abroad. What were the boundaries around this enduring conflict, and when would it end?

Shortly after, Obama addressed these issues in a speech at National Defense University that signaled a change of course at both pragmatic and symbolic levels. Obama's speech, like so much American political discourse since 2001, included in its introductory lines a harrowing depiction of September 11, recalling the devastation that had, according to this narrative, shattered hopes for peace in a post–Cold War world:

> with the collapse of the Berlin Wall, a new dawn of democracy took hold abroad and a decade of peace and prosperity arrived here at home. And for a moment it seemed the 21st century would be a tranquil time. And then on September 11th, 2001, we were shaken out of complacency. Thousands were taken from us as clouds of fire and metal and ash descended upon a sun-filled morning. This was a different kind of war. No armies came to our shores, and our military was not the principal target. Instead, a group of terrorists came to kill as many civilians as they could.

Yet Obama continued not with a call to renew or intensify the war effort, but instead with reflections on the consequences of the U.S. response to that traumatic scene. "We have now been at war for well over a decade," he said. "What is clear is that we quickly drove al Qaeda out of Afghanistan, but then shifted our focus and began a new war in Iraq. And this carried significant consequences for our fight against al Qaeda, our standing in the world, and, to this day, our interests in a vital region." In the effort to "prevent terror" after 9/11, Obama acknowledged, there were cases where "I believe we compromised our basic values—by using torture to interrogate our enemies, and detaining individuals in a way that ran counter to the rule of law." The time had come "to ask ourselves hard questions about the nature of today's threats and how we should confront them."

In addressing these "hard questions," Obama proposed a profound shift in orientation, invoking the familiar language of evil yet beginning to dismantle the encompassing teleological narrative that originally gave shape to the "war on terror." "We must define the nature and scope of this struggle, or else it will define us," Obama said, citing "James Madison's warning that 'no nation could preserve its freedom in the midst of continual warfare.'"[101] While Bush had declared on September 14, 2001, that America's "responsibility to history" was to "answer these attacks and rid the world of evil,"[102] Obama suggested, 12 years later, that such a pledge would be impossible to fulfill.

"Neither I nor any president can promise the total defeat of terror. We will never erase the evil that lies in the hearts of some human beings nor stamp out every danger to our open society," he said. "But what we can do, what we must do, is dismantle networks that pose a direct danger to us and make it less likely for new groups to gain a foothold, all the while maintaining the freedoms and ideals that we defend." Adopting such a strategy would require making "decisions based not on fear, but on hard-earned wisdom."

Addressing the contentious issue of drone policy, Obama acknowledged the civilian casualties that had resulted from U.S. strikes, stating plainly that "no words or legal construct can justify" such losses for families, though maintaining his stance that these strikes were, at times, the best way to avoid "far more civilian casualties." When he addressed the detention of terrorist suspects, however, Obama called for a more significant shift in policy, and he did so on symbolic grounds. History, he said, "will cast a harsh judgment on this aspect of our fight against terrorism and those of us who fail to end it." Citing the ongoing hunger strike at Guantánamo Bay, where detainees involved in the protest were force-fed, Obama asked: "Is this who we are? Is that something our founders foresaw? Is that the America we want to leave our children?" He answered: "Our sense of justice is stronger than that." While "freedom" had long been the core American value at the heart of 9/11 discourse, here, Obama reflected on its relationship to that other foundational ideal of justice. In doing so, he quoted the judge who sentenced Richard Reid, the so-called "shoe bomber" who unsuccessfully attempted to detonate explosives packed into his shoes on a December 22, 2001, American Airlines flight from Paris to Miami. "In sentencing Reid, Judge William Young told him, 'the way we treat you is the measure of our own liberty.' . . . [H]e went on to point to the American flag that flew in the courtroom. 'That flag,' he said, 'will fly there long after this is all forgotten. That flag still stands for freedom.'"

It was time, Obama suggested, to move beyond the pain inflicted on that bright September morning. "America, we have faced down dangers far greater than al Qaeda," he said, citing "slavery and Civil War, and fascism, and communism." More recently, Americans had exhibited resilience in the face of the "painful recession, mass shootings, [and] natural disasters" that had punctuated his own years in office. Though these events "shook our communities to the core," they "could not come close to breaking us." Obama recalled the words of Lauren Manning, who escaped the World Trade Center on September 11 but suffered severe burns over about 80 percent of her body: "That's my reality. I put a Band-Aid on it, literally, and I move on." And he declared that America needs "a strategy and a politics that reflects this resilient spirit."[103]

Obama's call to "put a Band-Aid on it" and "move on" contrasts sharply with the exhortations—pervasive within political discourse but also ubiquitous in popular representations of 9/11—to "always remember" or "never forget."[104] Indeed, even as Bush sought to transform the nation's grief and sorrow into anger and resolve, and even as collective mourning rituals gave way to retaliation, an ongoing sense of trauma and loss—a conviction that the wound left by 9/11 was indelible—continued to permeate political speechmaking. The collective suffering associated with September 11 thus remained "painfully present,"[105] and—despite vigorous efforts to reconcile the events of 9/11 with canonical American narratives—the collectivity remained, in many ways, unable to move forward in time beyond that harrowing moment. Bush encapsulated this sense of collective trauma in a speech to the United Nations General Assembly in November 2001, when he explained: "for the United States of America, there will be no forgetting September the 11th. . . . We will remember the fire and ash, the last phone calls, the funerals of the children."[106] Again, even Obama's May 2013 speech referred to the "clouds of fire and metal and ash" that "descended upon a sun-filled morning" and ushered in a new era. In chapter 7, I take up the issue of cultural trauma in more detail. For now, though, it is worth noting that an enduring and widespread sense that September 11 left an indelible wound on the American body politic figured centrally within legitimation discourse; Obama's call to "move on" thus marked a significant departure from previous political speechmaking.

A year later, in a May 2014 commencement address at West Point, the president continued the call for a more measured—and arguably less traumatized—response to the challenge of terrorism. "[T]o say that we have an interest in pursuing peace and freedom beyond our borders is not to say that every problem has a military solution," Obama said. "Since World War II, some of our most costly mistakes came not from our restraint but from our willingness to rush into military adventures without thinking through the consequences, without building international support and legitimacy for our action, without leveling with the American people about the sacrifices required."[107] He identified no specific examples, but this rendering makes possible an understanding of Iraq as another Vietnam: a memory that calls forth reflection and, often, regret rather than satisfaction and pride. "As General Eisenhower, someone with hard-earned knowledge on this subject, said at this ceremony in 1947, 'War is mankind's most tragic and stupid folly; to seek or advise its deliberate provocation is a black crime against all men,'" Obama said.[108] Just a few weeks later, the news of a violent offensive by a group known as the

Islamic State of Iraq and Syria (ISIS)—which captured the city of Mosul in Iraq on June 10—raised the specter of Vietnam more powerfully, and made clear that the legacies of September 11 were still unfolding. On the eve of the 13th anniversary of 9/11, Obama delivered an address to the nation reiterating the claim that "[w]e can't erase every trace of evil from the world" while also authorizing a major expansion of the campaign against ISIS. "This is a core principle of my presidency: If you threaten America, you will find no safe haven," he said.[109]

It thus remains to be seen to what extent, and in what ways, these symbolic shifts will reorient the effect flow of 9/11. The speechmaking I examined in this chapter, however, makes clear that consolation discourse—the effort to interpret calamity, to articulate the moral and existential significance of collective suffering—plays a considerable role in shaping the trajectories of historical events. In the next chapter, I return to consolation discourse in a more delimited sense. The commemorative rituals that have become so ubiquitous in our current cultural and historical moment, I show, are oriented centrally toward the interpretive and existential matters that define the consolation genre. Here, too, dualistic themes reverberated powerfully. Yet the effort to memorialize the 9/11 dead would also give way to alternate interpretations, reconstructions of the event that unsettled dualism's binary structure and chipped away at its progressive teleology.

CHAPTER 6

Consolation and Commemoration

In the years that follow national crises, political consolation not only reverberates in other genres of political speechmaking, but also continues in commemorative rituals. In this chapter, I examine discourse from the annual ceremonies held at the three September 11 crash sites: the Pentagon, Shanksville, and the World Trade Center. These rituals, I argue, extend the effort to provide symbolic and existential orientation in light of disruptive events that continued to evoke a sense of national suffering as time wore on. The cultural expectation that political leaders offer consolation, then, helps to explain the special salience of commemorations focused on trauma and atrocity in our current moment. The quest for consolation, and for interpretations that anchor recent episodes of national suffering within a much longer collective narrative, is the very impulse behind such rituals.

In addition to illuminating these broad theoretical matters, 9/11 commemorations also complicate the dualistic account of an epic confrontation between freedom and fear, good and evil that emerged in the immediate aftermath of the event. At the Pentagon and in Shanksville, speakers have largely echoed the dualistic mode of political consolation. Yet the confrontation with the specific events that transpired in these sites has also given way to subtle but significant moments of "contamination" or "hybridization"—when speakers break with the dominant discourse.[1] Even more, in lower Manhattan, local officials have orchestrated commemorative rituals that depart decisively from the dualistic mode. Eschewing political speechmaking altogether, officials have relied on existing texts, primarily poetry and literature, as focal points for anniversary ceremonies that embrace a more tragic orientation to September 11.

Together, these departures from the dualistic mode enable what the literary critic Michael André Bernstein terms "sideshadowing." Sideshadowing,

Bernstein explains, devotes explicit "attention to the unfulfilled or unrealized possibilities of the past," thus serving as "a way of disrupting the affirmations of a triumphalist, unidirectional view of history."[2] Bernstein contrasts sideshadowing with the more familiar technique of *foreshadowing*: "Against foreshadowing, sideshadowing champions the incommensurability of the concrete moment and refuses the tyranny of all synthetic master-schemes; it rejects the conviction that a particular code, law, or pattern exists, waiting to be uncovered beneath the heterogeneity of human existence."[3] Sideshadowing recognizes that history, and its interpretation, is indeterminate. As such, it lingers over unrealized—or not-yet-realized—possibilities rather than projecting teleologies. In this spirit, the commemorative discourses I examine in this chapter reveal alternate ways of constructing and interpreting the events that transpired on September 11, 2001, and provide a foundation for contemplating how these alternate interpretations might have altered the effect flow of these events.

REMEMBERING 9/11 AT THE PENTAGON AND SHANKSVILLE

During anniversary observances at the crash sites, politicians continue the effort that began almost as soon as the news broke, working to offer consolation to both the nation as a whole and the individuals who experienced personal losses on 9/11. But they generally do so with reference to the more specific and delimited events that transpired at each site: their task is to memorialize the people who died in that very place on September 11, 2001. At the Pentagon and in Shanksville, speakers have relied on two distinct rhetorical approaches to assimilate the particular events that occurred at these sites into the dualistic frame. The first is to cast the events of 9/11 as early battles in a war; the 9/11 dead are thus understood as analogous to fallen soldiers. The second is to draw a sharp moral contrast between "evil" perpetrators and their "innocent" victims; the 9/11 losses take on meaning in the ensuing struggle to overcome the evil manifest on 9/11, on behalf of the innocent dead. Speakers' efforts to fit the events they memorialize into the dualistic discourse have not, however, been seamless.

The 9/11 Dead as Fallen Soldiers

The effort to construct the 9/11 dead as fallen soldiers began almost immediately, in Giuliani's speeches memorializing rescue workers who perished at the World Trade Center. Within this narrative, the dead become combatants who played an agentic role in an ongoing struggle. Accordingly, in Shanksville commemorations, the passengers and crew of Flight 93 become "America's first defenders," "heroes who made the ultimate sacrifice," as Pennsylvania Governor Mark Schweiker put it in 2002.[4] They are understood as citizen-soldiers, "minutemen and women," as Colin Powell asserted in 2009.[5] Similarly, at the Pentagon in 2003, Chairman of the Joint Chiefs of Staff Richard Myers characterized the dead as "heroes" who "gave their lives."[6] When he dedicated the Pentagon memorial in 2008, Bush celebrated "the heroes of 9/11," and pledged—in "this hallowed place"—to "never forget their sacrifice."[7]

The interpretation of 9/11 as an inaugural battle (or battles) in the war on terror attributes distinctively nationalistic motives to the dead. Not only did they offer their lives in an act of sacrifice, but they also did so in order to preserve the nation and—especially—its commitment to human liberty. Speaking at Shanksville in 2002, Homeland Security Advisor Tom Ridge referred to the Flight 93 passengers and crew as "America's 21st century patriots," and claimed that they "were armed with . . . a big idea. Freedom is something worth defending."[8] Their actions, Ridge declared in 2004, constituted "their last loving embrace to their nation."[9] At the Pentagon in 2003, Defense Secretary Rumsfeld suggested that the nation had been fortunate to have "a long, unbroken line of patriotic defenders who rise up from this land we call America and take their place on freedom's walls."[10] The 9/11 dead joined that lineage: "And so today," Rumsfeld said, "let us remember all those who died in New York, in Pennsylvania, here at the Pentagon, in the mountains of Afghanistan, in the deserts of Iraq. And let us recommit ourselves to their cause and to our mission: the triumph of freedom over tyranny."[11]

It is, of course, true that some of those who perished, particularly at the Pentagon, were service members. But a majority—129 of the 184 who died at the Pentagon—were not. Even those who were members of the armed forces had not self-consciously entered battle as they made their way to the Pentagon that Tuesday morning. And Flight 93—whose passengers and crew have overwhelmingly been memorialized in language that is typically reserved for fallen soldiers—was no military target, but an ordinary commercial flight. The interpretation of these events as early battles in a war thus requires considerable interpretive work—and analogical or metaphorical reasoning—to articulate.

Rumsfeld's remarks during a September 12, 2002, memorial at the Tomb of the Unknown Soldier illustrate this interpretive labor. The ceremony honored all the Pentagon dead, but it focused especially on memorializing five individuals for whom no remains had been identified. Though the dead were not "unknown," their families had been denied a traditional burial because their physical remains had not been recovered.

In his address, Rumsfeld reflected at length on the parallels between the individuals he memorialized and those traditionally memorialized by the Tomb of the Unknown Soldier.

> Those we honor today died here at home, not on a faraway battlefield. Indeed, they died within view of this cemetery.
>
> Yet they did die on a battlefield, and that battlefield tells us a good deal about the war we are in, this first war of the 21st century. Their attackers said they died because they were Americans. Put another way, they died because they were part of a nation that believes in freedom. They died because they lived according to a generous creed as is written of life, liberty and the pursuit of happiness. . . .
>
> We also know that those we honor today died because of an institution that is a symbol of this generous creed and way of life —a symbol of military power, to be sure, but of power used to right wrong, to do good, to help achieve a more perfect day, when nations might live in peace. But until that time comes, the events of September 11th remind us that the forces of freedom are locked in a new type of struggle with those who oppose all that our freedom represents. . . .
>
> While there's nothing one of us can do to bring back these loved ones, we can celebrate who they were, how they lived their lives, and remember how their lives were lost in a struggle dedicated to the eternal truth of freedom and the human spirit.[12]

Despite the differences between the 9/11 dead and the unknown soldiers with whom they were honored, Rumsfeld posited that the cause in which they perished was continuous; he located its origins in the Declaration, referring to "life, liberty and the pursuit of happiness." Rumsfeld made the linkage with unknown soldiers explicit as he concluded his remarks:

> This day these five join the unknown of past wars, even as we pursue the war that is still unfolding. Known and unknown, those resting here were bound in a brotherhood by their heritage. Soldier and civilian alike, they were dedicated to the cause of freedom. Young and old, their lives and their deaths gave birth to a new pride and patriotism that has rekindled the flame of freedom across this land.[13]

Anderson argues that "tombs of Unknown Soldiers" are the most "arresting emblems of the modern culture of nationalism."[14] More than any other symbols, he suggests, they represent the "secular transformation of fatality into continuity, contingency into meaning" that the imagined community of the nation provides.[15] These "arresting emblems," in other words, are among the most powerful sources of consolation in the face of loss, offering the transcendent meaning within which seemingly senseless deaths take on purpose and significance. In this September 12, 2002, ceremony, Rumsfeld argued resolutely that the 9/11 deaths share the national meaning associated with the deaths of the unknown soldiers honored in such places, that they exhibited a common dedication to "the cause of freedom."[16]

In Shanksville, there is no such symbolism to bolster speakers' claims. The site is a rural field that, prior to 9/11, had no particular national significance. Here, the pervasive comparison with another rural Pennsylvania landscape has been central in constructing the crash site as a battlefield. As Pennsylvania Senator Arlen Specter put it on the fifth anniversary: "One hundred and forty-three years ago, about a hundred miles to the east, President Lincoln on the Gettysburg battlefield said: 'The world will little note, nor long remember what we say here, but could [sic] never forget what they did here.' These words are especially applicable here today."[17] Time and again, commemorative speakers have constructed Shanksville as a contemporary Gettysburg. In 2009, Powell wove quotations from Lincoln's address into a speech that evoked a lineage of patriotic sacrifice stretching from Lexington and Concord to Shanksville. "We must never forget what they did here as they struck the first blow in this battle against terrorism," Powell said.[18] To honor the dead, he suggested, the living must take up the cause for which they sacrificed—a cause continuous with Lincoln's.

> Let us never forget Lincoln's closing sentence: "that from these honored dead we take increased devotion to the cause for which they gave the last full measure of devotion—that we here highly resolve that these dead shall not have died in vain; that this nation under God shall have a new birth of freedom; and that government of the people, by the people, for the people shall not perish from the earth."[19]

Powell concluded with a pledge that embodies the dualistic spirit: "We will prevail over the forces of darkness and remain faithful to all that Abraham Lincoln said this nation stood for."[20] Once again, Lincoln's words, remediated in a distant context, transformed the dead into fallen soldiers whose deaths would give new life to their nation and its cherished ideals.

The 9/11 Dead as Innocent Victims

The second rhetorical approach emphasizes instead the fundamental opposition between "evil" perpetrators and "innocents" murdered. Speakers acknowledge the pain that mourners feel, but pledge that the sacrifices of American service members in the aftermath of September 11 will ensure that those who perished "did not die in vain," as Bush put it at the Pentagon in 2002.[21] This strategy is more pervasive at the Pentagon than in Shanksville. Unlike Flight 93, those aboard American Airlines Flight 77, which crashed into the Pentagon, had no news of other hijackings to guide their response. Any heroic narratives from the day's events were confined to the aftermath, the effort to preserve as much human life as possible.

In this interpretation, the 9/11 dead may not have made conscious sacrifices, but—as Bush explained in his 2002 address—their loss "moved a nation to action in a cause to defend other innocent lives across the world" and "set in motion the first great struggle of a new century."[22] Winning the war on terror, then, becomes the only way to adequately honor the 9/11 dead. Defense Secretary Robert Gates sounded this theme clearly at the Pentagon in 2007: "We ... will stop at nothing to defend this nation, its citizens and our values. ... It is a duty to those who perished here six years ago."[23] Indeed, in this interpretation, giving up the fight would result in the loss of *more* innocent life: "the fight for freedom continues," Rumsfeld said at the Pentagon in 2003, "because we know that if we do not fight the terrorists over there in Iraq, in Afghanistan and across the world, then we will have to face them here, and many more innocent men, women and children, as well as the patriots defending them, will perish."[24]

The opposition between "evil" and "innocence" in these commemorative speeches, then, dovetails with Bush's assertion—common in his legitimation discourse—that U.S. military operations abroad serve to protect innocent citizens (especially women and children) victimized by ruling regimes. It also reinforces the fundamental moral opposition between an innocent nation and violent perpetrators who appear even more malevolent for having struck the blameless. At the same time, the commitment to strike back in memory of the dead restores agency to the United States as defender of those who were powerless to protect themselves.

SLIPPAGE, CONTAMINATION, AND HYBRIDIZATION

Speakers occasionally stumble as they work to interpret the complex events of September 11, to render a disorienting set of occurrences comprehensible by placing them within recognizable cultural codes and familiar collective narratives. As Wagner-Pacifici argues, the memorialization process involves an ongoing "dialectic . . . between socially consequential events and cultural codes."[25] Events are only encoded through the efforts of entrepreneurs, "but the event/code fit is existentially, if not chronologically prior."[26] The fit between event and code is thus "not a once-and-for-all kind of thing"; it is subject to "constant adjustments as events and codes undergo internal elaborations and/or external pressures."[27] Much as the dualistic mode has predominated at the Pentagon and in Shanksville, this discourse is occasionally punctuated by theoretically significant departures. These departures, along with the very different commemorative mode that took shape in Manhattan, complicate my portrait of September 11 memory; in the process, they offer crucial theoretical and historical insight, providing a foundation for sideshadowing.

Slippage and Contamination

At times, a speaker's struggle to place events within intelligible cultural codes results in *discourse contamination*.[28] No single discourse, Wagner-Pacifici explains, is capacious enough to encompass the complexities of real-world events: "Thus an analyst will inevitably find alien images, stylistic flourishes, unanticipated lexical features, and so forth embedded within a given discourse that promises an intact, whole-cloth worldview."[29] This insight is especially relevant in the case of an ambiguous and multifaceted event such as September 11. Indeed, while September 11 is generally understood as a single event, in reality, it encompassed a number of distinct, though certainly interconnected, occurrences spanning several sites. Attention to discourse contamination illuminates complexity and multiplicity that official narratives often obscure.

At a most basic level, speakers' words sometimes evince confusion over how to categorize and portray the dead. That is, images of the dead as brave combatants are occasionally juxtaposed with images of the dead as innocent victims, raising questions about the appropriateness of cultural codes that are often taken for granted. As a small but telling example, consider Admiral Michael Mullen's statement during the 2008 commemoration at the Pentagon, which combines the image of innocent (passive) victims and the notion of (active) sacrifice: "Today we honor the sacrifice of innocent civilians who perished here."[30]

Such confusion or contradiction is also apparent in grammatical shifts—namely, when speakers oscillate between active and passive verbs as they describe the 9/11 deaths. At times, speakers move subtly, perhaps even inadvertently, between the image of the dead as combatants willingly sacrificing in a cause and the image of the dead as innocent victims whose lives were extinguished suddenly and unjustly. Again, speakers' apparent uncertainty sheds light on complexities that these officials rarely acknowledge in explicit terms. For instance, during a December 11, 2001, ceremony at the Pentagon, Richard Myers said: "Those who *lost* their lives in this building and the innocent passengers and crew members on the aircraft were among the first to *give* their life in this . . . global war on terrorism, but certainly not the last."[31] This same slippage was once again evident in Myers's remarks on the second anniversary, in 2003:

> The Nobel Prize–winning American author, William Faulkner, said, "I believe that man will not merely endure; he will prevail. He is immortal because he has a soul, a spirit capable of compassion and sacrifice and endurance."
>
> The patriots who *lost* their lives in the Pentagon on 11 September embody that spirit. They are all heroes, not just because they *gave* their lives, but because they lived their lives as free Americans, and many in service to their country. . . .
>
> Those who *lost* their lives in the Pentagon two years ago were aircrew members, innocent passengers, inside the Pentagon, officers and enlisted, active duty and reserve, civil servants, contractors. . . . But they were all dedicated to serving our nation and defending our freedoms. . . .
>
> And in memory of all those killed at the Pentagon two years ago, we will not merely endure; we will prevail.[32]

Did the people who perished in the Pentagon *lose* their lives, or *give* their lives? Myers explicitly claimed that the 9/11 deaths were *sacrifices*. Yet in shifting from active to passive constructions (e.g., "lost," "killed"), he subtly implied that those who perished had little agency. Attending to these subtle shifts illuminates the complexity of the event (events?) he memorialized, the difficulty of comprehending it (them?) within extant cultural codes.

Similarly, during the 2005 commemoration in Shanksville, Attorney General Alberto Gonzales articulated the claim that the Flight 93 deaths were "innocent lives *taken* by incredible evil" and then—merely a few lines later—heralded the passengers and crew who "*sacrificed* their lives for others."[33] Later in his address, he acknowledged—though only fleetingly—that claims about the values motivating the uprising aboard Flight 93 remain speculative: "it's comforting to remember those terrifying moments in the context of the things that make America such a wonderful place to live. After all, it's the protection of those cherished ideals—*I imagine*—that provided the courage necessary to overtake that cockpit."[34] Like the categorical and grammatical shifts I have just described, Gonzales's brief moment of overt speculation complicates the standard war frame that so powerfully underwrites dualistic vocabularies of consolation.

Hybridization

While moments of discourse contamination generally occur "only in so-called marginal moments, in socially unconscious leaks in texts and speeches," discourse *hybridization* is more conscious. Hybridization refers to "a practical acknowledgment of the incompleteness, the partiality of a given discursive formation" that "involves discursive self-critique and an openness to other discourses." Ultimately, it aims toward "the deinstitutionalization of discourse." Hybridization, with its reflective and indeed even subversive qualities, is more rare than the discourse contamination that occurs "behind the backs of the very speakers."[35] Yet its relative rarity belies its theoretical significance.

Consider, for instance, former president Bill Clinton's address on September 10, 2011, during the dedication ceremony for the Flight 93 National Memorial. In his remarks, Clinton reflected at length on the distinction between willing combatants and the passengers and crew of Flight 93 who fought to overtake their hijackers. "There has always been a special place in the common memory for people who deliberately, knowingly, certainly laid down their lives for other people to live," Clinton said. One such example, he noted, is the Alamo: "those people knew they were going to die. But the time they bought and the casualties they inflicted in the cause of freedom allowed the whole idea of Texas to survive."[36] He then delved deeper into history:

> The first such great story I have been able to find that reminds me of all your loved ones, however, occurred almost 2,500 years ago. When the Greek king of Sparta facing a massive, massive Persian army took 300 of his finest soldiers to a narrow pass called Thermopylae. There were thousands upon thousands upon thousands of people. They all knew they were going to die. He told them that when they went. And the enemy said we're going to fill the air with so many arrows that it will be dark. And the Spartans said, fine, we will fight in the shade. And they all died.

But the casualties they took and the time they bought saved the people they loved. *This is something different.* For at the Alamo and at Thermopylae, they were soldiers, they knew what they had to do. Your loved ones just happen[ed] to be on a plane.

With almost no time to decide, they gave the entire country an incalculable gift. They saved the capitol from attack. They saved god knows how many lives. They saved the terrorists from claiming the symbolic victory of smashing the center of American government. And they did it as citizens.[37]

Clinton grappled overtly with the complexity of the events that occurred aboard Flight 93, and the challenges they pose for commemoration. On the one hand, he compared the Flight 93 passengers and crew with combatants—the soldiers at the Alamo and at Thermopylae, he said, "[remind] me of all your loved ones." On the other hand, however, he also drew a distinction between the actions that the passengers and crew took on Flight 93 and the willing sacrifices of soldiers: "This is something different. . . . Your loved ones just happen[ed] to be on a plane."

In Clinton's remarks, the gift tendered by Flight 93 is still portrayed in nationalistic terms. The actions of those aboard protected a national symbol, and Clinton claimed that "they did it as citizens"—failing, in line with the prevailing commemorative mode, to acknowledge that two of the passengers were not, in fact, citizens at all, that understanding their deaths surely required a vocabulary other than nationalism. But there was genuine discourse hybridization in Clinton's remarks. Rather than appropriating the symbolic frameworks found, for instance, in the Gettysburg Address, and deployed so frequently in Shanksville, Clinton juxtaposed familiar historical comparisons with more particularistic meditations on the specific event he memorialized, reflecting aloud on the relationship between events and culturally available codes.

Discourse hybridization most often occurs among agents who occupy complex or contradictory social locations, and this example is illustrative.[38] Clinton, as a former president, is associated symbolically with the state. But his political career has come to a close: as he himself reflected in his remarks, "since I am no longer in office, I can do unpopular things."[39] His words elicited a moment of laughter rare for such solemn proceedings. (Clinton was not referring to the interpretation he offered as potentially unpopular, though perhaps his conscious awareness of the liberties he enjoyed influenced his remarks.)[40] Having left office—and indeed, having left office prior to September 11, 2001—Clinton occupies a unique position. He is able to speak with authority, yet he also has the license to engage in public reflections that unsettle the dominant discourse. This separates him from current state officials—such as Vice President Joe Biden, who spoke during this same ceremony—and even former President Bush, for whose legacy 9/11 is central. Indeed, Bush's remarks during the September 10, 2011, ceremony were emblematic of the established commemorative mode, drawing centrally on the Gettysburg Address to glorify the Flight 93 dead and sacralize the Shanksville site.[41]

The theoretical significance of discourse hybridization resides in its potential to shed light on alternatives to the dominant discourse. In doing so, it opens the possibility for understanding events outside the boundaries of entrenched cultural codes, for interrupting and even displacing institutionalized interpretations. In this way, moments of discourse contamination and hybridization represent opportunities for sideshadowing—again, for lingering over unrealized possibilities and thus disrupting unilinear teleologies, including those that were so pervasive in post-9/11 political discourse.

Similarly, it is perhaps useful to think of the very different commemorative mode that has solidified in Manhattan as a kind of organically occurring sideshadowing. For alongside the dualistic mode of political consolation emerged a commemorative mode that draws on some of the symbolic resources discussed in chapter 3 in order to grapple with questions of meaning in a vastly different manner, evincing a tragic orientation to September 11.

SEARCHING FOR MEANING AT AMERICA'S "GROUND ZERO"

While speakers at the Pentagon and in Shanksville have forcefully articulated the meaning of the 9/11 attacks and their place within national narratives, politicians in Manhattan have been considerably more circumspect. In New York, open-ended commemorative rituals have provided a shared space for engaging and contemplating questions of meaning without themselves providing clear solutions. Following the practice established at the first memorial service, on October 28, 2001, politicians have uttered no original speeches in anniversary observances at the World Trade Center site, which is still commonly known as "ground zero." From the first year through the 10th anniversary in 2011, politicians relied on existing texts—including canonical political texts and occasionally biblical texts, but primarily poetry and literature—that gave voice to suffering. These multivocal texts directed interpretation in subtle ways, but—drawn from a wide array of times and places—never incorporated

September 11 into a narrative framework.[42] On the 11th anniversary, even these multivocal texts disappeared from the ceremony, which focused strictly on the annual ritual of reading the names of those who perished. This approach to commemoration, I suggest, is broadly consonant with the tragic mode of political consolation and borrows in significant ways from efforts to officially memorialize the divisive war in Vietnam. Yet the extent of politicians' silence is striking, and indeed has generated calls for a more robust effort toward political consolation at this sacred center for 9/11 memory.

SEPTEMBER 11, 2002

The first anniversary commemoration stood somewhere between the familiar dualistic mode and the tragic orientation that would coalesce in lower Manhattan in the coming years. Notably, the observance was organized through New York City Mayor Michael Bloomberg's office, in consultation with family members and Governor Pataki. Bloomberg's vision shaped this commemoration, as well as those that followed in the coming decade, indelibly. He articulated his intentions publicly from the outset. Leading up to the September 11, 2002, event, Bloomberg explained that the "most important" element of the ceremony was that there be "[n]o political speeches."[43] He elaborated: "The families said that a lot, but I think independently I couldn't agree more."[44] In the effort to orchestrate a commemoration free from politics, officials settled upon readings from the civil scriptures—the Gettysburg Address and the Declaration of Independence—and a more recent text that carried forward similar themes, Franklin Roosevelt's "four freedoms." These texts would form focal points for the ceremony, which would also include a recitation of the names of those who died.

On the one hand, these prepared texts were broadly consonant with state discourse, representing inherited frameworks that played a crucial role in premediating the official response to 9/11. Observers would have no trouble connecting the readings with the consolation narratives that Bush, Giuliani, and others had so rapidly and so fervently articulated. On the other hand, this commemoration exhibited important differences from the dualistic mode. Speakers offered only brief introductions to these texts, otherwise leaving onlookers to interpret them—and their relevance to the events of September 11—privately. Moreover, these brief prefatory remarks evinced a slightly different orientation to interpreting and memorializing September 11.

The Gettysburg Address was the first text uttered during the ceremony. Bloomberg's introduction illuminated the subtle divergence in orientation: "One hundred thirty-nine years ago, President Abraham Lincoln looked out at his wounded nation, as he stood on a once beautiful field that had become its saddest and largest burying ground," Bloomberg said. "Then, it was Gettysburg. Today, it is the World Trade Center, where we gather on native soil to share our common grief."[45] In commemorations at the Pentagon and in Shanksville, Gettysburg is a *battlefield*. In Manhattan, Gettysburg is a *burying ground*. "Gettysburg," of course, may refer to either: to Gettysburg battlefield or to Gettysburg National Cemetery, where Lincoln spoke. But while speakers at the Pentagon and in Shanksville used Lincoln's words to explicitly transform the 9/11 deaths into sacrifices, onlookers at this first anniversary commemoration in New York were largely left to posit meaning privately.

Similarly, New Jersey Governor James McGreevey read an excerpt from the Declaration of Independence, invoking lines that have long played a role in the consolation genre:

> We hold these truths to be self-evident, that all men are created equal, that they are endowed by their Creator with certain unalienable rights, that among these are life, liberty and the pursuit of happiness. That to secure these rights, governments are instituted among men, deriving their just powers from the consent of the governed. [. . .]
>
> And for the support of this declaration, with a firm reliance on the protection of divine providence, we mutually pledge to each other our lives, our fortunes, and our sacred honor.[46]

Here, too, Bloomberg's introduction to the text was open-ended. The mayor referred to the Declaration not as a statement of values for which people died on 9/11, but as a more generic emblem of the symbolic commitments that had withstood the assault: "One year ago, the ground we are standing on shook, and the earth gave way. Although the buildings fell, the foundation on which all Americans stand will never fall, for it is the sacred principle of freedom and equality on which we build our lives."[47] Again, this commemorative text gestured toward an interpretation of the 9/11 deaths as sacrifices intended to preserve those "truths" that the Declaration proclaimed "self-evident." Yet Bloomberg never asserted this interpretation explicitly, and McGreevey recited the lines without comment.

The commemorative proceedings continued into the evening. At sunset, Bloomberg gathered with President Bush and heads of state from around the world in Battery Park. The assemblage took place at The

Sphere, a sculpture created by Fritz Koenig in 1971 that once stood in the plaza of the World Trade Center. Having survived the collapse of the Twin Towers—though not without scars—the sculpture was moved for a time to Battery Park, where it served as a temporary memorial to the 9/11 dead and a symbol of resilience amidst destruction. During the ceremony, Bloomberg offered one final piece of borrowed rhetoric—Roosevelt's "four freedoms"—and lit an eternal flame.

As I noted in chapter 2, the address now known as the "four freedoms" speech was Roosevelt's January 1941 State of the Union. In the speech, Roosevelt grappled with the turmoil unfolding across the globe and articulated his own vision for the future. He envisaged "a world founded upon four essential human freedoms"—"freedom of speech and expression," "freedom of every person to worship God in his own way," "freedom from want," and "freedom from fear," and argued that such a world was possible in his own day. At the time—as I suggested in chapter 2—Roosevelt's words offered a kind of anticipatory consolation, articulating an orienting set of ideals that the president argued were worth defending, even if it required blood sacrifice. The present generation's task, Roosevelt suggested, was to carry forth their ancestors' legacy by spreading democratic ideals across the globe. The excerpt Bloomberg read at Battery Park included the statement of the four freedoms as well as lines expressing faith that freedom's march was inexorable: "This nation has placed its destiny in the hands and heads and hearts of its millions of free men and women and its faith in freedom under the guidance of God. Freedom means the supremacy of human rights everywhere. . . . Our strength is in our unity of purpose. To that high concept, there can be no end, save victory."[48] Once again, the decision to read Roosevelt's words gestured toward an interpretation of the 9/11 deaths as part of a struggle between freedom and repression that continued to advance teleologically toward victory. And in this setting, at some remove from the sacred center, Bloomberg's words were a bit more freighted politically. Nonetheless, Bloomberg did not expound the comparison between past and present in specific terms; here, too, he largely left the task of interpretation to his audience.

The city's decision to rely on the political canon for the first anniversary—to reach to the past for words rather than to grapple explicitly with the moral and existential challenges of the present—generated both scholarly and popular criticism. I delve into popular responses, and their implications for our understanding of political consolation, below. For their part, scholars such as Bradford Vivian and Simon Stow pointed to the ways in which this landmark commemorative event encouraged an unquestioning patriotism: the values enshrined in the commemorative texts were presented as somehow neutral or beyond debate, thus stifling the possibility for critique.[49] However, it also set the stage for a commemorative mode that is far more amenable to critical perspectives than those that prevailed at the other sites, which resonated deeply with state discourse.

In 2003 and beyond, political leaders continued to rely on existing texts rather than original speechmaking—but the sources and contents of these texts shifted considerably. Between 2003 and 2011, politicians overwhelmingly relied on poetry and literature, turning far less frequently to the political canon for their words. Like the first anniversary ceremony, these commemorations declined to engage the particularities of September 11. Yet they exhibited a moral and existential searching that was less evident in 2002. The texts delivered were multivocal—they sustain a wide variety of interpretations—but in general, they sought to foster contemplation and a search for wisdom in suffering and loss. Without engaging in overt critique, they opened interpretive possibilities that departed substantially from state discourse and the moral binaries through which it apprehended the world.

SEPTEMBER 11 AND THE TRAGIC MODE

Consonant with a tragic orientation to collective suffering, in the years following the first anniversary, commemorative rituals in Manhattan drew together a heterogeneous audience through "an overt focus on points of ambiguity."[50] In general, the words uttered in these commemorations thematized grief, loss, and sorrow, facilitating reflection on the meaning of suffering, but leaving the task of interpretation to the individual. Perhaps most strikingly, the observances in Manhattan were virtually devoid of the moral oppositions that pervade dualistic discourse. They included no references to evil or its synonyms (e.g., barbarism or villainy). Speakers did not even mention "terrorism" or an "enemy." The texts delivered only occasionally invoked heroism or sacrifice or even underlined victims' innocence. Instead, speakers offered consolation through open-ended references to hope, resilience, and meaning. When describing how the living might honor the dead, they typically spoke of kindness, compassion, and service. Finally, in contrast to the nationalistic themes that permeated commemorative discourse at the Pentagon and in Shanksville, organizers reached outside the American political and literary canons in selecting texts. In the process, they defined the community of mourners in more encompassing terms, referring on numerous occasions to a broad human solidarity.[51]

This commemorative mode exhibited a subtle temporal structure. In the early years, speakers focused primarily on giving voice to suffering. Over time, the commemorations more frequently incorporated texts positing that suffering has meaning and encouraging hope or healing. Yet even these texts never fully defined what that meaning might be. Neither did the speakers who read them.

Consider first representative texts from early commemorations. These texts poignantly articulate grief and suffering, but do little to define their meaning in specific terms. In 2003, for example, Bloomberg read lines from former U.S. poet laureate Billy Collins lamenting the sheer scope of the losses:

> Names etched on the head of a pin.
> One name spanning a bridge, another undergoing a tunnel.
> A blue name needled into the skin.
> Names of citizens, workers, mothers and fathers,
> The bright-eyed daughter, the quick son.
> Alphabet of names in green rows in a field.
> Names in the small tracks of birds.
> Names lifted from a hat
> Or balanced on the tip of the tongue.
> Names wheeled into the dim warehouse of memory.
> So many names, there is barely room on the walls of the heart.[52]

Collins' words do not imbue the 9/11 deaths with any larger meaning. They simply give voice to loss, capturing both its overwhelming scale and its personal dimensions. The dead were many, but each was a specific individual—among them mothers, fathers, bright-eyed daughters, quick sons.

In 2004, Governor Pataki's reading reflected on the experience of losing a child, considering the particular depth of a bereaved parent's pain: "Even after the victories of World War II, Dwight Eisenhower, who saw too many young sons die, wrote: 'There's no tragedy in life like the death of a child; things never get back to the way they were.'"[53] Pataki's framing is especially striking: even as he referred to combat deaths associated with a celebrated victory, he invoked the language of tragedy—and the notion of indelible loss—rather than heroism or sacrifice. During these early years, even religious references generally stopped short of positing meaning. For instance, in 2004, Bloomberg read a lament from 2 Samuel, in which King David mourns the death of his son: "The king went up to the chamber over the gate, and wept; and as he went, thus he said: 'O my son Absalom, my son, my son Absalom! Would I have died for thee, O Absalom, my son, my son!'"[54] Again, these words simply and mournfully articulate a parent's grief and pain, offering a sense of empathy or understanding without intimating that loss and suffering hold purpose.

In later years, speakers engaged the question of meaning more overtly, but nonetheless through multivocal texts. For instance, in 2008, Secretary of Homeland Security Michael Chertoff read Rumi's poem "The Guest House":

> This being human is a guest house.
> Every morning a new arrival.
>
> A joy, a depression, a meanness,
> some momentary awareness comes
> as an unexpected visitor.
>
> Welcome and entertain them all!
> Even if they're a crowd of sorrows,
> who violently sweep your house
> empty of its furniture,
> still, treat each guest honorably.
> He may be clearing you out
> for some new delight.
>
> The dark thought, the shame, the malice,
> meet them at the door laughing,
> and invite them in.
>
> Be grateful for whoever comes,
> because each has been sent
> as a guide from beyond.[55]

Even painful occurrences have meaning and purpose, Rumi's words suggest: each "has been sent as a guide from beyond." Yet their specific meaning remains ambiguous, left for the listener to discern. Indeed, the text ostensibly leaves open the possibility that an event's meaning might never become apparent at all. Pataki articulated similar sentiments during this same 2008 commemoration, calling forth the memory of Robert Kennedy in Indianapolis. "At another moment of national grief—the death of Martin Luther King, Jr.—Robert Kennedy spoke these words of solace, written by the ancient Greek poet Aeschylus," Pataki said.

> He who learns must suffer.
> And even in our sleep, pain that cannot forget

falls drop by drop upon the heart,
and in our own despair, against our will,
comes wisdom by the awful grace of God.[56]

Like Rumi's poem, this text suggests that human sorrows have purpose without explicitly defining the purpose itself. Religious references, too, shifted toward themes of comfort and healing. In 2011, Giuliani read lines from Ecclesiastes: "To every thing there is a season, and a time for every purpose under heaven"—intimating, but not proclaiming, that the 10th anniversary might mark a shift in "seasons."[57]

When discussing how to honor the dead, speakers emphasized service and everyday acts of kindness. This theme was especially prominent in 2009, when the commemoration—taking a cue from Obama's decision to designate September 11 as the National Day of Service and Remembrance—took "service" as its orienting theme.[58] For instance, during this ceremony, New Jersey governor Jon Corzine read lines from Emily Dickinson:

If I can stop one Heart from breaking
I shall not live in vain
If I can ease one Life the Aching
Or cool one Pain
Or help one fainting Robin
Unto his Nest again
I shall not live in Vain.[59]

Giuliani articulated the value of service with lines from Martin Luther King: "This is the judgment. Life's most persistent and urgent question is, 'What are you doing for others?'"[60] The subtle ways in which such passages encouraged onlookers to honor the dead departed significantly from the pledge, common in state discourse, that the 9/11 losses will be rendered meaningful through victory in a "war on terror," or an encompassing struggle against "tyranny" that sought to "rid the world of evil."

In a similar vein, a number of texts delivered in these more recent commemorations evoked solidarity across a wide human community, even articulating the interconnectedness of humanity writ large. In 2008, the organizing theme for the commemoration was "the international family." Organizers recruited students who were attending local colleges and universities to represent each foreign nation that lost citizens on September 11. These students participated alongside family members in the ritual of reading the names. The words Bloomberg uttered as he introduced the year's theme are emblematic: "This morning we stand again as one family, one community of the world," he began.

> As in past years, the names of those who died will be read by their families. Joining them are the young faces of our future, students from around the world, attending our city's universities, who come on behalf of each country that lost someone that day.
>
> They help us remember that now, as then, the feelings of grief, sorrow, loss, and consolation are ones that we all share. As the proverb of the Sioux Indians reminds us: "With all beings and all things we shall be as relatives."[61]

Throughout the ceremony, politicians delivered readings from foreign authors whose diversity they highlighted explicitly: among them "[t]he great French writer Albert Camus," "the Polish poet Adam Zagajewski," and "the English poet Laurence Binyon."[62] Again, this encompassing vision of the community of sufferers, and the effort to evoke a generalized human solidarity, differed significantly from the nationalistic themes and sharp symbolic boundaries that pervaded the ceremonies at the Pentagon and in Shanksville. They also acknowledged overtly that not all the 9/11 dead were Americans—a clear departure from efforts to cast the dead as fallen soldiers who joined a storied national lineage in sacrificing their lives for freedom.

Throughout the years, the Manhattan commemorations gestured at times toward the dualistic mode, especially by continuing occasionally to incorporate texts from the political canon. Perhaps most significantly, Lincoln's Bixby letter has twice been featured in Manhattan: once in 2004, when Giuliani delivered the reading, and again on the 10th anniversary, when former president Bush read the text.[63] As I noted in chapter 1, the Bixby letter was sent from the Lincoln White House to a Massachusetts widow whom Lincoln believed to have lost five sons fighting in the Union cause. The letter echoes and extends themes Lincoln articulated in his address at Gettysburg, interpreting the young men's deaths as sacrifices for the Republic and expressing hope that its recipient would experience "the solemn pride that must be yours to have laid so costly a sacrifice upon the altar of freedom."

The brief introduction Bush offered before he read the letter in 2011 underscored the theme of sacrifice overtly: "President Lincoln not only understood the heartbreak of his country, he also understood the cost of sacrifice and reached out to console those in sorrow," Bush said.[64] Still operating within the broad constraints of the prevailing commemorative structure— relying on existing rhetorical material and offering only the briefest interpretation—Bush implied more emphatically than most speakers in

Manhattan that the 9/11 deaths were sacrifices for the nation, for "freedom." Similarly, Giuliani evoked the dualistic mode in 2003, when he quoted Winston Churchill: "We shall not fail or falter; we shall not weaken or tire. Neither the sudden shock of battle nor the long-drawn trials of vigilance and exertion will wear us down."[65] In this case, Giuliani gestured toward the claim—prevalent in commemorative discourse at the Pentagon and in Shanksville—that victory in the war on terror would honor the 9/11 dead and endow their loss with meaning. But in ceremonies that contained no explicit references to "evil" or an "enemy," to a war on terror or a struggle for civilization, this interpretation constituted only one option among many.

COMMEMORATION WITHOUT WORDS

In 2012, politicians were once again invited to provide a symbolic presence at the commemoration in lower Manhattan. This time, however, they would have no speaking role, not even as readers. Even Bloomberg, who remained the key organizer behind the ceremonies in Manhattan in the decade spanning 2002 to 2012—and who had offered the opening and closing remarks during each of the preceding years—was silent. Family members who participated in reading the names sometimes offered personal reflections when they spoke the name of the person they came to mourn. But these brief tributes were the only words uttered.[66]

The decision to eliminate the readings came amidst political struggles—pitting Bloomberg, who was serving as both New York City mayor and chairman of the National September 11 Memorial Foundation, against New York Governor Andrew Cuomo and New Jersey Governor Chris Christie—concerning the oversight of the site itself and the financing of the National September 11 Memorial Museum there.[67] In some sense, the decision—handed down from the 9/11 memorial and museum's president, Joseph C. Daniels—was continuous with the commitment Bloomberg had articulated from the first: holding a ceremony free from politics and focused on the families. Yet the absence of rhetoric took the event's ambiguity and multivocality to a new extreme.

Bloomberg's decision to steer the 2012 commemoration further from the "political" realm by focusing strictly on reading the names illuminates, in a particularly striking way, how Vietnam memory premediated the open-ended observances in Manhattan. In a certain sense, symbolic frameworks from Vietnam are pervasive in American commemorative culture, not just in this particular setting: lists of names have become virtually compulsory components of American public memorials, and they are frequently read aloud during commemorative rituals.[68] But the names have been especially central on 9/11 anniversaries in Manhattan, and perhaps for the same reason that they formed the basis for Maya Lin's memorial design: they offer a strategy for cultivating shared commemorative space amidst deep interpretive dissensus. After Lin's design was unveiled, for instance, the *New York Times* reflected that it "seems to capture all the feelings of ambiguity and anguish that the Vietnam War evoked [and] conveys the only point about the war on which people may agree: that those who died should be remembered."[69] The ritual of reading the names in Manhattan can be understood in a similar light—affirming the impulse to remember the dead within a polity that, 11 years later, could not agree on a narrative of why they died. As I show in the next chapter, the politics surrounding the World Trade Center site have remained heated in the years since September 11, and the issues at stake are far deeper than the debates over the memorial's financing that were so salient leading up to the 11th anniversary. Indeed, they concern the meaning of September 11 as an event, and, even more, the very meaning of the American project writ large.

Although the World Trade Center is the iconic site of memory for September 11, the anniversary observances in lower Manhattan have diverged steadily further from the dominant state interpretation over time: civil scriptures articulating a common American creed gave way to poetry and literature, which in turn gave way to silence. Elsewhere, I have examined the reasons for this divergence at length; it is also worth reflecting on them briefly here.[70] For one, differences in the events that transpired at each site influence commemoration in significant ways. As a military building, the Pentagon invites a war framing, and the dualistic mode of consolation, in a way that the World Trade Center does not—even though a majority of the Pentagon dead were civilians. In the case of Flight 93, the small measure of agency the passengers and crew possessed, and their decision to fight back against the hijackers, also supports a heroic interpretation, even if references to citizen-soldiers and national sacrifice eventually confront the reality that those aboard did not knowingly enter battle. Such a narrative would be more difficult to sustain in Manhattan, though perhaps not impossible—recall Giuliani's comparisons to Pearl Harbor, and his tendency to portray all the 9/11 dead, not only the rescue workers, as heroes.

The entrepreneurs, or, in Weberian terms, "carrier groups," who orchestrate the commemorations also play a substantial role.[71] As I have underscored throughout this chapter, Bloomberg's influence has been decisive in Manhattan, and, as mayor, he possessed interpretive liberties that a federal official would not. Had Giuliani's term extended longer, the Manhattan ceremonies might have taken shape quite differently, though it is impossible to know how his interactions with family members and other stakeholders would have influenced these events. The Pentagon observances, in contrast, are Department of Defense events dominated by state officials. In Shanksville, local officials and family members have come together with Pennsylvania state politicians and federal officials to produce commemorations in the dualistic mode. The Shanksville community has generally embraced its unwitting role as a national landmark and—in the aftermath of 9/11—portrayed its rural landscape as deeply patriotic, even quintessentially American. In 2003, for instance, Somerset County obtained the trademark for the slogan "America's County," claiming that they would "try to stress that the war on terrorism began here."[72] For their part, family members of those aboard Flight 93 frequently portrayed their loved ones in heroic terms in public settings—including television interviews, political events, and published memoirs—reinforcing state narratives with their own moral credibility. To take just one prominent example, on September 20, 2001, Lisa Beamer—whose husband, Todd Beamer, was a passenger—took to the public spotlight when she attended Bush's address to Joint Congress at the invitation of the White House. When the president hailed "the courage of passengers" such as her husband "who rushed terrorists to save others on the ground," Congress acknowledged Beamer with a standing ovation.[73]

Similarly, the audiences for these events—actual or imagined—matter, too. In particular, New York is a self-consciously cosmopolitan and global city. Here, the proportion of foreigners among the dead, and the breadth of backgrounds and nationalities represented among them, was too significant to be ignored. Together, these contextual features invite broad humanistic narratives instead of, or at least in addition to, nationalistic framings: it is *human* suffering, not only *American* suffering, memorialized in these events. As Bloomberg explained in reflections penned after the 10th anniversary, an awareness that the audience would be deeply pluralistic did much to shape the planning process: "our hope was to create a ceremony that was strong and simple and spoke across time, cultures, religions, and backgrounds."[74]

Finally, there is a temporal dimension to the commemorations. Commemorative discourse, as Olick argues, unfolds dialogically: each moment takes shape within a longer trajectory, responding—explicitly or implicitly—to what came before.[75] Throughout these pages, I have underscored how earlier moments in the consolation genre shape subsequent discourse. But this structuring influence is especially powerful in recurrent rituals such as the commemorations I have described here: once a particular mode is established at a commemorative site, it tends to solidify. Gettysburg references thus continually permeate the discourse in Shanksville; officials from the Obama administration echo familiar dualistic tropes from the Bush years at the Pentagon; and even the highest-level officials largely fall in line with the tragic mode in Manhattan.

Despite organizers' efforts to construct ceremonies that knit together diverse audiences by providing meaningful material for contemplation, the Manhattan commemorations have generated substantial public critique. In general, commentators have called precisely for a more robust effort at political consolation: for narratives that grapple with the specific event at hand and forge a place for it in national narratives. The expectation that contemporary political leaders will provide consolation, that they will offer moral and existential guidance in national rituals that call forth the memory of collective suffering, is now firmly entrenched, and it emanates from very different positions on the political spectrum.

CONSOLATION AND CONTEMPORARY GOVERNANCE

The critical commentary began even before the first anniversary ceremony took place. After Bloomberg's office revealed the plan for the 2002 observance, *New York Times* reporter Janny Scott reflected that the mayor's decision to rely on oratory from the American past "renders impossible precisely what was achieved at a moment he has chosen to hark back to, the dedication of the cemetery at Gettysburg, where Abraham Lincoln spoke: the courageous reaching for words to honor the fallen, to put their sacrifice in historical context, to find meaning in carnage and to inspire the people to carry on."[76] Garry Wills, author of the acclaimed *Lincoln at Gettysburg*, called upon political leaders to summon such courage: "There are people who can rise to the occasion, and it's cowardice not to try," he told the *Times*. Indeed, he suggested that it was "an insult to the dead at the towers, that you try to slap on the label from someone else's tragedy."[77] Similarly, Theodore C. Sorensen—the speechwriter best known for his work on John F. Kennedy's 1961 inaugural address—reflected: "I keep hearing that words cannot express our feelings about what happened. But it's not as though the American English vocabulary is limited. The imagination of our political leaders is limited, not the vocabulary."[78]

New York Times critic Michiko Kakutani's reflections, published the day after the first anniversary commemoration, gave voice to the cultural expectation for consolation narratives in detail. Kakutani acknowledged that "the initial impulse behind . . . Bloomberg's decision to exclude original speeches from ground zero observances was understandable," and conceded that "the task of articulating the country's grief and anger and defiance can easily result in simplistic pieties and blunt restatements of the obvious." Yet she argued that ultimately, Bloomberg and the other elected officials who relied on words from the past during the 2002 commemoration neglected a crucial duty incumbent upon elected officials in such moments—a duty central to their role as leaders. Kakutani wrote: "important moments throughout history have called upon leaders to articulate a vision, a mood, a direction, to give voice to shared feelings of grief or hope. On this occasion, politicians at the New York ceremonies recalling the attack abdicated that responsibility." In relying upon words from Lincoln, Jefferson, and Roosevelt, contemporary officials "chose not to articulate their own vision of America," and they "chose not to memorialize the meaning of the lives of the dead." Giving voice to collective identity and conferring meaning on suffering and loss are, according to this critique, crucial tasks of democratic leadership.

It seems clear that Kakutani was not calling for New York politicians to echo the dualistic mode that prevailed at the other sites. In fact, she gestured toward a critique of the Bush administration's approach to the anniversary as well, noting that the United States "has always been disinclined to view life through a tragic lens," that "uplift and patriotic avowals" pervaded many ceremonies, and that Bush's designation of the anniversary as "Patriot Day" seemed to have encouraged "creepily festive observances" in many locations across the country. She called, instead, for speechmaking that worked to make sense of "this particular and anomalous tragedy," an event that—she suggested—could not be adequately interpreted by reiterating texts penned in response to very different crises and challenges. Politicians, she implied, bore an obligation analogous to that of clergy, and they shirked that obligation on the first anniversary of September 11: "At the ground zero service yesterday, original oratory—which, as the scholar Kathleen Hall Jamieson once observed, comes from the Latin word 'orare,' meaning 'to pray'—was nowhere to be found."[79] The gesture toward prayer is telling: the matters that politicians neglected to address in this context were existential—the meaning of collective suffering, as well as its relation to a particular "vision of America."

Nearly a decade later, writing in the opinion pages of the *New York Daily News*, Robert Burke—whose firefighter brother died in the rescue effort at the World Trade Center—articulated a similar critique. In contrast to Kakutani, Burke—who criticized Bloomberg's decision to continue the tradition of delivering borrowed rhetoric during the milestone 10th anniversary ceremony—envisioned something closer to the dualistic mode. "American democracy and freedom were attacked on 9/11," he declared. "Thousands were murdered (not 'lost') simply for the crime of being American or associated with them." Despite apparent differences in his interpretation of 9/11, however, Burke called politicians to account in language that bore striking resemblance to Kakutani's own. Burke asked: "How did it become proper etiquette for leaders to remain silent at such times? Are not our elected representatives, at times of great crisis, supposed to rise to the occasion and define for us the situation at hand; explain its significance and magnitude and provide for us a path to follow? If not, what do we elect them for?" Providing symbolic orientation "in times of great crisis," Burke suggested, was not merely *a* task of democratic leadership, but *the* central one: "If not, what do we elect them for?" By relying on borrowed words during the 9/11 commemorations, Burke argued, elected officials committed an "abdication of responsibility."

Though Burke called all politicians—from Bloomberg to Obama—to account, he expressed particular concern with the president's special responsibility to offer an interpretation. "As other Presidents have done in their time, it is his [Obama's] burden to say something," Burke wrote. "He should risk offending some people in an attempt to give texture and meaning to the memory of that terrible day." The remarks Obama would deliver during a special ceremony at the Kennedy Center in Washington "[fell] short of his obligation to history and his office," for "Ground Zero holds a unique place in our national consciousness." It was this obligation that Lincoln fulfilled so memorably at Gettysburg: "Imagine," Burke wrote, if Lincoln "was handed a poem to read" at Gettysburg instead of delivering his enduring words.[80] The president, Burke suggested, is the nation's consoler-in-chief, and fulfilling this role requires a narrative specific to the events at hand, articulated at the sacred center of the crisis.

Inspired by Burke, Clyde Haberman reiterated and expanded this critique in the *New York Times*.[81] According to Haberman, Bloomberg's stated commitment to organizing commemorations free from politics "miscasts the duty of elected leaders," who face an obligation to do more than deliver poems or other readings.[82] "We expect something more meaningful from our officials. We count on them to explain where we are in an uncertain time, and to point us to the road ahead. That's not politics. It's leadership."[83] He took up the issue again in 2012, acknowledging the "risk that some bloviating politician will deliver remarks that are pablum or, worse, utterly self-serving," but arguing "that doesn't mean that leaders should be relieved of the opportunity—no, the obligation—to behave like, well, leaders."[84]

In Manhattan, then, the focus on points of ambiguity—on multivocal texts whose relevance to September 11 is left to the listener to discern—allowed for at least fleeting moments of unity among many in a heterogeneous population. The texts themselves invite moral and existential searching on the meaning of loss and the place of suffering in the human experience. Yet in adopting such an open-ended approach to commemoration, these ceremonies fall short of the expectations for political consolation. And as a result, the elected officials who participate are publicly called to account for failures of leadership, imagination, and vision.[85]

Looking beyond commemorative contexts to examine public debates over how best to rebuild and reconstruct the World Trade Center site reveals the powerful dissensus beneath the surface of these open-ended rituals. In the next chapter, I delve into such debates. And in the process, I return to the broadest theoretical questions outlined in the introduction, considering how the public struggle to define the meaning of New York's "ground zero" illuminates the conceptual relationships among consolation, trauma, and memory.

CHAPTER 7

Symbolic Politics on Sacred Ground

Though the events of September 11 spanned a number of physical spaces, none is more iconic than the World Trade Center. It was in lower Manhattan that the day's violence first became visible to the public, and it was there that the scope of the devastation and loss was most overwhelming. The World Trade Center site, treated with special reverence from the first, is thus the sacred center of the event now known as "9/11," and the location for the official national memorial commemorating this moment in history. And because this site—the piece of lower Manhattan that came to be known as "ground zero"—is so sacred within the American national imagination, it has also become a pivotal site of struggle, a centerpiece in interpretive battles over the meaning of September 11 and indeed a flash point in the American culture wars more generally. In this chapter, I conclude my analysis of September 11 by delving into conflicts and controversies that have erupted throughout the effort to reconstruct the 16-acre site on which the Twin Towers once stood. These conflicts, I argue, illuminate the continuing struggle to narrativize September 11 and, in the process, cut to the core of the broad theoretical questions at the heart of this study.

The effort to reconstruct the World Trade Center site has given way to a steady stream of public controversies covering a wide range of issues. Some of these debates have primarily been the product of local or regional power struggles, or questions of who, precisely, would bear responsibility for funding the massive undertaking of memorializing 9/11 and ensuring the site's upkeep.[1] Other debates—especially those surrounding the design of the national memorial—have pitted family members of the dead against one another or against elected officials. How should the names of the dead be arranged on the memorial?[2] Should they be located below ground, as architect Michael Arad originally envisioned, or at street level?[3] Should details such as age, affiliation, and tower location be included?[4] Should first responders receive special recognition?[5] How should unidentified human remains be treated?[6] Here, I focus on debates that have taken shape as struggles over the meaning of September 11 and the significance of its most iconic site: the debate over the International Freedom Center originally slated for a cultural center on the rebuilt site; the debate over Park51, the Islamic community center located two blocks from the World Trade Center; and the debate over the cross-shaped beam known as the "World Trade Center Cross" or the "Ground Zero Cross" and now included in the collection at the National September 11 Memorial Museum. In each of these cases, the struggle to define the meaning of September 11 ultimately gave way to a referendum on larger issues of collective identity, to a struggle over the meaning of the ambiguous and multivocal ideals at the core of the civil scriptures discussed in chapter 1. How should the American nation and the ideals for which it stands be represented at this sacred site of memory? Each debate, then, offers a compelling window onto the symbolic politics that have not only shaped the reconstruction of the World Trade Center site, but also have addressed the project of imagining the American nation in the post-9/11 era.

In examining these debates, I venture beyond official speechmaking and into the broader terrain of civil society.[7] Doing so reveals that—as I have suggested—September 11 remains "traumatic history" in Frank Ankersmit's sense: history "that is not yet fully owned," that presents "our faculty of historical and narrative association with a challenge that it is, as yet, unable to meet."[8] In line with the theoretical framework outlined in the introduction, the deep antipathies that have repeatedly emerged in these symbolic struggles suggest that the traumatic orientation to history indeed creates fertile ground for *ressentiment*: in the face of collective suffering whose meaning remains indeterminate, public expressions of antipathy, embodying deep divides over basic questions of interpretation, are the order of the day.[9]

THE MEMORIAL QUADRANT AND THE MEANING OF "FREEDOM"

As of spring 2005, an institution called the International Freedom Center (IFC) was slated for the World Trade Center site's memorial quadrant. The eight-acre portion of the site designated as the "memorial quadrant" included the footprints of the towers and was reserved primarily for the official memorial, but it also included space for a cultural center.[10] In the planned cultural center, the IFC would take its place alongside the Drawing Center, an established SoHo art museum that exhibited both historical and contemporary drawings and that intended to relocate to the site; the Signature Theater Company, an off-Broadway group; and the Joyce Theater, which presents dance.[11] The IFC's founders envisioned a museum that would situate September 11 within a global and historical context. Voicing their support for the World Trade Center Memorial's mission to "strengthen our resolve to preserve freedom, and inspire an end to hatred, ignorance, and intolerance," the founders explained that:

> the Center will celebrate freedom as a constantly-evolving world movement in which America has played a leading role. Visitors from around the globe will come to understand that the story of freedom is a narrative of hope, and that September 11 is an essential element of this story, powerfully illustrating that new challenges to freedom will always arise, that freedom's work remains unfinished, and that there is a place for all of us in this work.[12]

To bring their vision to life, the founders proposed exhibits that would "tell personal stories and explore crucial themes in the history of freedom," educational and cultural programs that would "stimulate a global conversation to advance freedom's cause," and a service and civic engagement network that would give visitors "the chance to act on behalf of freedom within their own communities and around the world."[13]

With a mission that pledged to "celebrate freedom" and to underscore America's "leading role" in advancing freedom's cause, on the surface the plans for the IFC ostensibly resonated with state narratives of 9/11. The proposal invoked Lincoln's Gettysburg Address, affirmed Bush's view that "freedom itself had been attacked at Ground Zero," and pledged to "ensure that in the distant future, when children with no direct knowledge of the tragedy come to Ground Zero, they will be able to learn about the infamy of September 11, 2001 and connect it to their own lives and times."[14] Yet more detailed reports on the founders' vision suggested that the institution might present a more multifaceted image of the United States than dualistic narratives allowed—an image that had the potential to challenge the sharp binary contrast between American freedom and the "tyranny" its leaders pledged to eradicate. For instance, the *New York Times* reported that the IFC would focus on the issue of human rights,[15] and would include exhibits that grappled with ongoing struggles against oppression as well as past atrocities.

> The center's galleries, or halls, are to be devoted to specific topics. In a Gallery of Nations, for example, each of the 82 countries that lost citizens on Sept. 11

will contribute one item for display. These could range from artifacts to national treasures to artistic tributes, center officials said.

The center also plans Freedom Sites evoking the cause of liberty, like a former gulag in Russia, which will be set up with other groups promoting freedom around the world. Freedom Hot Spots will focus on places around the world where people are campaigning against human rights abuses. The Challenge Galleries will emphasize what the planners view as current or historical challenges to freedom, like India's caste system. The center plans to feature the stories of ordinary people—slaves who resisted their masters, shopkeepers who risked all to fight the Nazis—as well as more prominent figures.[16]

Thus, while the center's founders deployed the familiar language of a quest for "freedom" and "liberty," here these terms were inflected with slightly different meanings than those they generally held in state discourse pertaining to 9/11. Some critics pointed out that these meanings might implicate the United States as well as celebrating it, and argued that critical views of American history—in the form of exhibits that portrayed American culpability in subverting human freedom as well as its laudability in enabling and expanding it—had no place on such sacred ground.

A June 7, 2005, op-ed in the *Wall Street Journal* by Debra Burlingame—a World Trade Center Memorial Foundation board member whose brother, Charles Burlingame III, was the pilot of the American Airlines flight that crashed into the Pentagon—ignited the controversy, referring to the plans for the IFC as "The Great Ground Zero Heist." Burlingame opened with the image of three Marines, wounded in the Iraq War, who had returned to "the empty pit of Ground Zero" on Memorial Day weekend. Noting that, at the time, the site contained "no faded flags or hand-painted signs of national unity," she asked: "So why do they come? What do they hope to see?" And, pointing out that the official memorial would break ground that year, Burlingame offered an answer: "no doubt they will expect to see the artifacts that bring those memories to life," a memorial that will "[allow] them to take in the sheer scope of the destruction, to see the footage and the photographs and hear the personal stories of unbearable heartbreak and unimaginable courage," and ultimately "take them back to who they were on that brutal September morning." Instead, Burlingame wrote, they would find exhibits that displayed America's own difficult pasts and grappled with the legacies of atrocities perpetrated by the United States: "Rather than a respectful tribute to our individual and collective loss, they will get a slanted history lesson, a didactic lecture on the meaning of liberty in a post-9/11 world. They will be served up a heaping foreign policy discussion over the greater meaning of Abu Ghraib and what it portends for the country and the rest of the world."

At heart, Burlingame's critique contested the meanings that the IFC organizers attributed to "freedom." The IFC founders, Burlingame asserted, "have stated that they intend to take us on 'a journey through the history of freedom'"—but, she cautioned, "do not be fooled into thinking that their idea of freedom is the same as that of those Marines." For the IFC organizers, "it is not only history's triumphs that illuminate, but also its failures."

> The public will have come to see 9/11 but will be given a high-tech, multimedia tutorial about man's inhumanity to man, from Native American genocide to the lynchings and cross-burnings of the Jim Crow South, from the Third Reich's Final Solution to the Soviet gulags and beyond. This is a history all should know and learn, but dispensing it over the ashes of Ground Zero is like creating a Museum of Tolerance over the sunken graves of the U.S.S. *Arizona*.

"Ground Zero," Burlingame argued, was no place for grappling with difficult history. Invoking the image of the U.S.S. *Arizona*—and thus calling forth the memory of a "good war" overwhelmingly understood through a stark dualistic narrative—she insisted on a similar orientation toward the sacred site in lower Manhattan. Arguing that the IFC "will not use the word 'patriot' the way our Founding Fathers did," Burlingame pointed to connections between the IFC organizers and organizations such as Human Rights First and the ACLU. She also noted that several of the organizers had publicly critiqued the Iraq War and called for investigations on the Bush administration's treatment of detainees. Burlingame suggested that the IFC would infuse the memorial site with these critiques. "The people who visit Ground Zero in five years will come because they want to pay their respects at the place where heroes died," Burlingame declared, calling for a site that featured images of courageous rescue workers rather than critiques of U.S. foreign policy.[17] Inspired by Burlingame, a group called Take Back the Memorial coalesced to expand the protest. They put forward a resolution titled "Campaign America," demanding that "ground zero" (i.e., the memorial quadrant) contain heroic representations of 9/11, and 9/11 only. Institutions "that house controversial debate, dialogue, artistic impressions, or exhibits referring to extraneous historical events," the resolution argued, should not be permitted at the site.[18]

The IFC's president and chief operating officer, Richard J. Tofel, responded to Burlingame in the opinion pages of the *Wall Street Journal*. Tofel acknowledged that the center "will host debates and note points of view with which you—and I—will disagree."[19] Its purpose, he suggested, would not be to present a particular image of freedom, but to facilitate contemplation on freedom's meaning: "It [the IFC] will not exist to precisely define 'freedom' or to tell people what to think, but to get them to think—and to act in the service of freedom as they see it."[20] The rancorous debate continued, however. The *New York Times* termed the "Campaign America" resolution "un-American."[21] The *New York Daily News*, in contrast, echoed Burlingame: "distinctly unwelcome at Ground Zero would be a forum dedicated to hashing over America's sins, alleged and real, at home and abroad."[22] An editorial in the *Washington Times* suggested that the memorial had been "hijacked," and conservative commentator Michelle Malkin termed it "The Ultimate Guilt Complex."[23]

Before long, Governor Pataki intervened. "I view that memorial site as sacred grounds, akin to the beaches of Normandy or Pearl Harbor," he said in June, echoing Burlingame's original analogy.[24] He added: "we will not tolerate anything on that site that denigrates America, denigrates New York or freedom, or denigrates the sacrifice or courage that the heroes showed on Sept. 11."[25] Pataki's ultimatum also applied to the Drawing Center, which attracted controversy of its own after the *New York Daily News* scrutinized its previous exhibitions and reported on material that took a critical stance toward the Bush administration.[26] The Drawing Center responded with a statement acknowledging the "inevitable tensions" between their mission and state interests; though they did not immediately bow out, they stated that they, "like any other cultural institution," had "a responsibility to adhere to its mission."[27] Ultimately, they withdrew with relatively little fanfare. In contrast, IFC organizers affirmed that their center would respect Pataki's parameters, suggesting that there was, in fact, no tension between their own goals and the imperatives associated with official commemoration. "Our programming must, and will, respect those lost on Sept. 11, and honor the country we all love," said Tom A. Bernstein, one of the center's founders.[28] In a letter to Stefan Pryor, the president of the Lower Manhattan Development Corporation, the IFC pledged: "We will not 'blame America' or attack champions of freedom. Any suggestion that we will feature anti-American programming is wrong. We are proud patriots."[29]

Burlingame and her allies in the Take Back the Memorial movement remained unsatisfied with these assurances, however. It was not enough to create a museum that pledged not to denigrate the nation; instead, the IFC's critics insisted that any cultural institution on the site tell *only* the story of 9/11.[30] In August, Burlingame told the *New York Times* that she would endorse plans for a cultural building only if it was "redesigned to be filled with the story of 9/11."[31] She explained: "We're not saying boycott the memorial; we're saying, fill it with the story of 9/11, or get it off the site."[32] On the fourth anniversary of September 11, several hundred people gathered for a rally on Church Street to protest the plans for the IFC. Protester Anthony Gardner, whose brother perished in the north tower, suggested that the center would undermine the site's function as a venue for commemoration: "The I.F.C. threatens to turn ground zero into a place of endless controversy rather than a place of honor."[33] Dissent, for Gardner, would represent an intrusion of the profane into a site he held sacrosanct. After the IFC released a report summarizing its plans in greater detail, New York Senator Hillary Clinton gave the protests against the museum additional political force from the left. In a statement released to the *New York Post*, Clinton relayed that she was "troubled by the serious concerns that family members and first responders have expressed to me," and said explicitly that she could not support the IFC.[34]

In contrast, the *New York Times* responded to the unfolding struggle with a series of editorials arguing that barring the IFC or monitoring the museum's content violated quintessential American values: in particular, the ideal of freedom enshrined in both the IFC's mission and the vigorous protest against it. In "bowing to some of the survivors' growing hostility to any version of 9/11 except their own," the *Times* opined in June, Pataki was "doing a disservice to history and to the very idea of freedom."[35] In July, the *Times* argued that Pataki in fact ran the risk of "turning ground zero into a place where we bury the freedoms that define this nation."[36] And in August, they wrote that the "core of the attack on the Freedom Center is the assumption that any debate or dissent near ground zero will dishonor the dead," arguing—in opposition—that "this attempt to stifle discussion at the site of the 9/11 attacks is utterly at odds with the spirit that should be embodied in this sacred place."[37]

In the end, Burlingame and her allies prevailed: on September 28, 2005, Pataki announced that there was "too much opposition, too much controversy" to move forward with the IFC, "and we must move forward with our first priority, the creation of an inspiring memorial."[38] The IFC immediately declared itself out of business.[39] For his part, Tofel voiced concern over the long-term implications of Pataki's decision. The IFC, he said, "helped give life to the original concept of what this place was about."[40] Without it, he claimed, the site would lack "a living memorial in any sense of the word"—an institution that would draw visitors with no personal connection to 9/11 back to the site as time passed.[41] Speaking collectively, the IFC's executives expressed disappointment at the "loss of a museum of freedom at the place where freedom was so brutally challenged."[42] Burlingame, in contrast, congratulated Pataki, suggesting that the IFC represented "an obstacle" not only for those directly affected by 9/11, "but for all Americans who will be coming to the World Trade Center memorial to hear the story of 9/11 and that story only."[43] The story of 9/11, she added, was not just about loss but was also "an uplifting story of decency triumphing over depravity."[44]

In the struggle over the IFC, the parties to the controversy agreed that the sacred value to be commemorated on hallowed ground in lower Manhattan was freedom. Both supporters and opponents of the museum understood themselves as patriotic, devoted to preserving and indeed further enshrining this archetypal American ideal. Yet—as Burlingame herself suggested in her original critique of the IFC—their understandings of freedom, and thus of how to construct a memorial that celebrated this ideal, diverged profoundly. Was September 11 to be understood as an event sui generis—interpreted as "an uplifting story of decency triumphing over depravity" that provided a window onto some fundamental American spirit—or as a moment in an ongoing global struggle for freedom, a struggle that remained incomplete, perhaps even a struggle in which the United States had fallen short of its own ideals? In this case, key stakeholders found themselves unable to establish a consensual interpretation of 9/11 and thus a common vision for its most sacred site of memory. While multivocal commemorations have brought many such stakeholders together to share in collective ritual amidst these deep disagreements—though punctuated by the kind of protest that arose over the IFC on the fourth anniversary—efforts to define the meaning of New York's "ground zero" in more concrete terms yield overt expressions of dissent, even resentment. As they grappled with the legacies of the collective suffering commemorated in lower Manhattan and struggled to establish a common account of 9/11 that could be embodied in a reconstructed World Trade Center site, these prominent moral entrepreneurs ultimately found themselves exchanging antipathies.

The debate over the meaning of "ground zero" did not end when Pataki banished the IFC from the memorial quadrant, however. Indeed, such debates were not even confined to the memorial quadrant—the patch of lower Manhattan that had become most inviolable among family members. Instead, public dissent became even more vociferous— and garnered far more attention on the national stage—when an Islamic community center selected a site two blocks from the World Trade Center.

The Muslim community center that generated bellicose debate across the nation in 2010 was originally called the Cordoba House. The *New York Times* reported that the Cordoba House was intended as "a monument to religious tolerance," and had been named for the Spanish city "where Muslims, Jews, and Christians lived together centuries ago in the midst of religious foment."[45] Slated for 45–51 Park Place, the center was eventually given the more generic name "Park51." But its founders understood the location as conveying a symbolic message: "We want to push back against the extremists," said Feisal Abdul Rauf, the imam who was slated to be the center's leading cleric, in 2009.[46] The center was to include a mosque, but it had a broader mission, modeled after the YMCA and the Jewish Community Center. Its founders also planned to include a swimming pool and a 500-seat auditorium, and to feature interfaith programming that would serve the general community. Despite its location (two blocks away from the epicenter of the destruction) and its encompassing mission (it would include prayer space, but its founders envisioned the center as much more than a place of worship), the center came to be known in much popular commentary as "the ground zero mosque." This misleading nomenclature fanned the flames of controversy.

Once again, parties to the debate overwhelmingly agreed that "ground zero"—in this instance conceived broadly as the World Trade Center site and the surrounding neighborhood—represented sacred ground, "hallowed," as commentators often put it, by the events that occurred there on September 11. But they disagreed as to whether the proposed Islamic community center would be a monument to religious freedom, tolerance, and democracy befitting this iconic American site, or an affront to those who perished at the site on 9/11 that would mar an inviolable place. The debate centered not so much on any legal issues at stake; indeed, a number of prominent commentators who argued against the community center acknowledged that the proposal violated no laws. It focused, instead, on emotional and symbolic matters: while opponents argued that there was a cultural and moral imperative for the center to pull out and find another location, supporters argued that the symbolic imperative ran in the other direction—that if built on sacred ground, the center would serve as an emblem of American pluralism and freedom.

The controversy unfolded as New York City's Landmarks Preservation Commission considered whether to designate the building located at 45–47 Park Place a protected landmark. The community center planned to tear down the building and replace it; granting the existing structure status as a landmark would halt the project.[47] Family members weighed in on both sides of the debate, making public statements that again brought to light a deep conflict over both the particular significance of New York's "ground zero" and the meaning of celebrated national values. Sally Regenhard, whose firefighter son, Christian, died in the rescue effort, said that the center would represent "sacrilege on sacred ground."[48] She added: "It's hard enough to go down to that pit of hell and death."[49] In contrast, Adele Welty—also the mother of a firefighter who perished at the World Trade Center—argued that Park51 would be a powerful testament to American pluralism, an emblem of religious freedom: "If we manage to get it built and can avoid violence in the process, the world can see that we are a towering nation, that we believe in and practice freedom of religion."[50] Valerie Lucznikowska, whose nephew, Adam Arias, died at the World Trade Center, echoed the sentiment: "I want tolerance, I want inclusion, and there is no better embodiment," she said.[51] The Anti-Defamation League (ADL) surprised many observers when it issued a public statement against the proposal. Abraham H. Foxman, the ADL's national director, argued that family members' emotional pain be afforded special consideration, citing similar attitudes toward Holocaust survivors: "Their anguish entitles them to positions that others would categorize as irrational or bigoted," he said, suggesting that a site "a mile away" from the epicenter of the 9/11 destruction might be more appropriate.[52]

This time, the local dispute took on the contours of a national referendum. Sarah Palin, the 2008 Republican vice presidential candidate, called the plan an "unnecessary provocation,"[53] while Giuliani invoked the familiar analogy to Pearl Harbor. "This is a desecration," he said over the radio on the Jeff Katz Show.

> Nobody would allow something like that at Pearl Harbor. Let's have some respect for who died there and why they died there. Let's not put this off on some kind of politically correct theory.

> I mean, they died there because of Islamic extremist terrorism. They are our enemy, we can say that, the world will not end when we say that. And the reality is, it will not and should not insult any decent Muslim because decent Muslims should be as opposed to Islamic extremism as you and I are.[54]

The boundaries Giuliani drew around the moral community in question— the community to whom New York's "ground zero" belonged—were revealing. In the us-and-them contrast he invoked—"You and I" versus "Islamic extremist terrorism," "our enemy"—"decent Muslims" occupied some liminal space. "Decent Muslims," according to Giuliani, are expected to respect the inviolability of "ground zero," but this hallowed place belongs to someone else; they cannot claim it as their own.

Mayor Bloomberg, however, argued precisely the opposite: the community center was not a desecration, but instead an emblem of the values most sacred in the American national tradition. After the Landmarks Preservation Commission voted against granting historic protection status to the building at 45–47 Park Place,[55] Bloomberg delivered an address on Governors Island off the tip of lower Manhattan. With the Statue of Liberty in the background, Bloomberg said that barring the center would "betray our values" and undermine "the best part of ourselves— and who we are as New Yorkers and Americans."[56] Indeed, he argued that doing so would violate the very freedoms that the first responders who participated in the rescue effort worked to defend. Bloomberg argued: "The attack was an act of war—and our first responders defended not only our City but also our country and our Constitution. We do not honor their lives by denying the very Constitutional rights they died protecting. We honor their lives by defending those rights—and the freedoms that the terrorists attacked."[57] In Bloomberg's narrative, 9/11 was an attack on the "spirit of openness and acceptance" that characterized both New York as a city and the United States as a nation, and thus it was imperative, morally and symbolically, to allow the plans for the center to go forward.[58] It is worth noting that Bloomberg never questioned whether Park51's proposed location—two blocks from the World Trade Center—was truly "hallowed ground," set apart from the rest of the city, reserved only for entities that honor the 9/11 dead and represent national values of the highest order. Instead, both Bloomberg and his opponents in the debate affirmed that this space, too, is sacred, even as they disagreed powerfully on what would represent a desecration: intervention that subverted the establishment of an Islamic center, or allowing the plans to move forward.

A few days later, the American Freedom Defense Initiative—organized by right-wing blogger Pamela Geller—gained approval for an advertisement on city buses protesting the plan for the center. The ad juxtaposed the image of the World Trade Center—with one tower in flames and a plane flying into the other—with a rendering of Park51, labeled "WTC MEGA MOSQUE," and asking: "WHY THERE?"[59] Eventually, Obama weighed in on the matter, indicating that the debate had indeed become a national referendum. The president's initial statement largely echoed Bloomberg's sentiments. Obama expressed understanding for "the emotions that this issue engenders," and said that "Ground Zero is, indeed, hallowed ground."[60] Yet, like Bloomberg, he argued that to allow the center would be to uphold "religious freedom," and thereby affirm a central tenet of American national identity.[61] Obama reflected: "The principle that people of all faiths are welcome in this country and that they will not be treated differently by their government is essential to who we are. The writ of the Founders must endure."[62] The next day, however, he backpedaled slightly, stating: "I was not commenting and I will not comment on the wisdom of making the decision to put a mosque there."[63] The remarks, Obama explained, were intended to address the legal aspect of the issue: "I was commenting very specifically on the right people have that dates back to our founding. That's what our country is about."[64]

Public opinion polling revealed significant opposition to the community center among New Yorkers even after the city gave the proposal the green light. Like a number of politicians, many New Yorkers apparently viewed the issue primarily through a moral and emotional rather than legal lens. In an August 27–31, 2010, *New York Times* poll among New Yorkers, 67 percent of respondents suggested that the center should *not* be built, agreeing that "while Muslims have the right to do it, they should find a less controversial location." Twenty-seven percent stated that the center *should* be built, agreeing that "moving it would compromise American values." When asked whether the organizers had a *right* to build it, 62 percent of respondents said yes, while 29 percent said no. Brooklyn resident Marilyn Fisher offered insight into this disjuncture in a follow-up interview: "My granddaughter and I were having this conversation and she said stopping them from building is going against the freedom of religion guaranteed by our Constitution," Fisher said. "I absolutely agree with her except in this case. I think everything in this world is not black and white; there is always a gray area and the gray area right now is sensitivity to those affected by 9/11, the survivors of the people lost." Opposition to the proposal was lower among Manhattan residents than their counterparts in the other boroughs, though still considerable: 51 percent of respondents from Manhattan said they favored the construction of the community center, while 41 percent were opposed.[65]

Plans for Park51 faltered in the wake of the furor. Tensions between Rauf and the site's developer, Sharif El-Gamal, head of Soho Properties, lead to a January 2011 announcement that Rauf's role would be significantly circumscribed.[66] Once the leading cleric and the public face for the project, Rauf would remain on the board but would no longer fundraise or speak on behalf of the center.[67] The imam who was tapped to take his place in leading Park51's Friday prayer services, Abdallah Adhami, stepped down merely three weeks later.[68] Later in the year, Soho Properties faced legal battles over back rent allegedly owed to Consolidated Edison.[69] In

August of 2011, following this series of setbacks, El-Gamal said that he was embracing a more deliberate and incremental approach to the project.[70] He retained his original vision for the community center, but said he would work to build relationships with donors and relevant constituencies in the surrounding community—neighborhood groups and Muslim organizations—before reconstructing the site.[71] Three years later, in April 2014, El-Gamal announced plans to implement a different vision: a three-story museum "dedicated to exploring the faith of Islam and its arts and culture" rather than the 15-story community center he had originally proposed.[72] The planned museum will still include prayer space.[73]

RELIGION IN THE RUBBLE: THE "WORLD TRADE CENTER CROSS"

Religious symbolism of a different sort took center stage in the conflict over the fate of an intersecting steel beam discovered in the rubble at the World Trade Center on September 13, 2001, and rapidly invested with profound, indeed transcendent, meaning. The object first garnered attention when construction worker Frank Silecchia encountered it in the course of the rescue and recovery effort, interpreting it as a Christian symbol—a cross—and pointing it out to fellow workers at the site.[74] Crucially, for Silecchia, the object was not just a cross-shaped beam—a piece of debris that he had invested with symbolic significance. It was instead a direct sign from God, a mode of divine communication. "Some people will say it's velocity or physics that put it there," Silecchia explained in October 2001. "To me, it's an act of God."[75] Silecchia expanded these reflections in the Christian magazine *Guideposts*: "the cross was a sign, a promise from God that he is with us even in the face of terrible evil and untold suffering. Especially then."[76] Vision, as Geneviève Zubrzycki points out, is "a cultural act," and indeed Silecchia's "way of seeing" the cross-shaped beam—quickly adopted by many others at the site—sacralized the object.[77]

Shortly after he stumbled on the cross-shaped beam, Silecchia brought it to the attention of Franciscan friar Brian Jordan, who worked as a chaplain at the World Trade Center site from September 2001 through June 2002. He, too, approached it as a religious symbol. Over the following decade, his energetic moral entrepreneurship transformed the beam into an object of veneration and a widely recognizable symbol among New Yorkers as well as the wider public. On October 4, 2001, Jordan presided over an initial ceremony at the World Trade Center site, where he conferred a blessing upon the beam and sprinkled it with holy water. "Behold the glory of the cross at Ground Zero," he said. "This is our symbol of hope, our symbol of faith, our symbol of healing."[78] On Sundays during the cleanup, Jordan celebrated mass in the presence of the cross-shaped beam.[79] More generally, many workers apparently used the "cross" as a site for respite, contemplation, and prayer throughout the recovery and cleanup effort. And as time went on, Jordan championed its preservation, advocating its inclusion in the eventual memorial.[80] When other artifacts from the World Trade Center site were transported to a hangar at John F. Kennedy International Airport, Jordan secured permission to store the cross outside St. Peter's Roman Catholic Church on Barclay Street nearby.[81] In October 2006, when it was moved, Jordan led a procession from the World Trade Center site to St. Peter's, where Kevin V. Madigan—the priest who had agreed to provide a temporary home for the cross—offered his own blessing.[82] The care and indeed reverence with which Jordan and others approached the object revealed that—for many—it was not just a notable artifact worthy of preservation. Instead, even five years after it was discovered and more than four years after the cleanup effort concluded, it remained a sacred object worthy of veneration in the present.

It was precisely the reverence with which this object was treated that fueled a conflict over its place within the National September 11 Memorial Museum: both its "form"—so easily interpreted as a cross—and "the stages on which [it was] displayed" augmented its force as a sacred symbol.[83] From the beginning, Jordan's efforts to preserve the cross for eventual inclusion in the museum attracted notable criticism. In 2003, Joshua Chadajo, the executive director of the Coalition for Jewish Concerns, said that the symbol "doesn't represent a number of the victims" and suggested that it be treated as a piece of the debris and "removed from the site."[84] Ellen Johnson, the president of the group American Atheists, sharply critiqued Jordan's interpretation of the object's transcendent meaning: "The idea that this is some kind of a message from a loving God is absolutely insane."[85] Jordan's critics also countered his claim that the cross was "an interfaith sign," challenging his assertion that if workers had "found a Star of David or a menorah or a crescent, we would have erected it and used it as a sign of God's presence."[86]

The debate intensified as the redevelopment of the World Trade Center site moved forward. In July 2011, the beam returned to the site; the museum was still under construction, but its curators had decided to give the object a permanent place in its collection. En route from St. Peter's to the World Trade Center, Jordan—along with about 200 family members and rescue workers—paused in Zuccotti Park to stand alongside the cross and offer another blessing. Former Mayor Giuliani was also in attendance. The artifact then traveled another block to the World Trade Center, where it was lowered by crane to the museum's underground location. "This is one of the most cathartic moments I have felt," Jordan reflected. "I feel a relief in the sense that I know it's found a permanent home, and for many of those who lost loved ones on that day, it is a relief for them, too."[87]

In a press release announcing the move and affirming that the museum would be the beam's "permanent setting," 9/11 Memorial officials referred to the artifact as the "World Trade Center Cross" and quoted Jordan: "I urge all those who believe in the consolation and power of the Cross to visit it in its future home in the Memorial Museum." To a certain extent, museum officials adopted more neutral language than Jordan. Museum Director Alice M. Greenwald said: "it will be our privilege to present the Cross in the Memorial Museum as a testament to the role of spirituality in providing comfort and strength to those who worked with courage and selfless devotion during the nine months of recovery at ground zero." But the language of the official statement also betrayed some commitment to sustaining the object's continued religious significance—the reverence it elicited from many—and revealed the tension between the museum's dual roles: preserving history and commemorating it. At a most basic level, the official press release referred to the object as a cross—not as a steel beam or an artifact—and indeed rendered it as a proper noun: "the World Trade Center Cross." Furthermore, the document explained that this piece of the rubble was "[i]mmediately recognized as a cross"—as though this was indeed its underlying objective identity. Memorial President Joseph Daniels reflected on the object's commemorative significance, and suggested that the commemorative mission ultimately predominated in the museum context: "The World Trade Center Cross is an important part of our commitment to bring back the authentic physical reminders that tell the history of 9/11 in a way nothing else could," he said. "Its return is a symbol of the progress on the Memorial and Museum that we feel rather than see, reminding us that commemoration is at the heart of our mission."[88]

Following the object's move from St. Peter's to the World Trade Center, American Atheists—a New Jersey–based nonprofit group—filed a lawsuit arguing that its inclusion in the 9/11 Memorial Museum violated the U.S. Constitution, the Constitutions of New York and New Jersey, and civil rights laws in both states. At issue was precisely the question of whether the beam was an artifact or a shrine, a piece of history or an object whose continued veneration was sanctioned or even encouraged by the state. Marc D. Stern, associate counsel of the American Jewish Committee, explained to the *New York Times* after the suit was filed that there was indeed ambiguity in the role that this object was to play at the site. On the one hand, he said: "It's a significant part of the story of the reaction to the attack, and that is a secular piece of history."[89] On the other hand, however, both "the repeated blessing of the cross" and "the way believers speak about the cross" reveal that "it has intense present religious meaning to many people."[90] The lawsuit invoked the July 23, 2011, blessing explicitly, arguing that the object was in fact venerated at the moment when it was incorporated into the museum, and that the state had thus endorsed its status as a sacred object.

> On July 23, 2011, Defendants placed a 20-foot cross ("the cross") on land owned by the Port Authority of New York and New Jersey and/or the City of New York. The cross, which has been altered to more closely resemble a Latin cross and, upon information and belief, inscribed with "Jesus" on its vertical beam, was placed in the planned September 11 Memorial and Museum in a televised ceremony that included its reconsecration and/or blessing by defendant Brian Jordan.[91]

According to American Atheists, the object's inclusion in the museum thus represented the "display of" a "religious icon on government land" and an "unlawful attempt to promote a specific religion" there.[92] The group requested that the beam be removed or that the museum allow for equal representation for all religious faiths, as well as nonbelievers, and offered to fund a memorial "for the atheists who died."[93] The lawsuit was dismissed: in March 2013, Judge Deborah A. Batts of the Federal District Court in Manhattan concluded that the beam—which was slated for an exhibit titled "Finding Meaning at Ground Zero"—was an artifact whose purpose in the museum was "historical and secular." "No reasonable observer would view the artifact as endorsing Christianity," Batts explained.[94]

Batts's ruling triggered fresh debate on how the sacred site of memory at the World Trade Center might best represent not only the events that transpired there, but also the American nation broadly conceived; it became an occasion for contesting national identity, for arguing over "how society should (or should not) be."[95] And again, the symbolic struggle featured competing understandings of the same fundamental values, values both sides ostensibly held sacred—in this case, religious freedom specifically. "The First Amendment, our most fundamental statement of rights, is clear that our government shall not show preference to one religion over any other belief system; it must remain neutral," wrote David Silverman, president of American Atheists. "Violating this most basic principle is not only against the law, it's un-American. . . . Atheists will have an equal place, or it [religious symbolism such as the cross] all must go. That's fair, that's legal, that's religious neutrality—that's the American way."[96] He announced that American Atheists would appeal the case.

Jordan Sekulow, executive director of the conservative American Center for Law and Justice (ACLJ), and Matthew Clark, an ACLJ attorney, argued precisely the opposite. Removing the artifact, they suggested, would represent an affront to historic American values, a denial of the ways in which religion—particularly Christianity—gave life to the nation: "The bottom line is that religion, and especially Christianity, is a part of our society, it's a part of our culture, and it's part of America's history. And no unending legal assault by secularists can change that fact."[97] Writing for Fox News, Sekulow posited more provocatively that—as a result of the lawsuit—"the Ground Zero Cross" was "at a different 'Ground Zero'— Ground Zero of an atheist attack on our religious past, and our religious future."[98] The "extraordinarily angry atheists," he argued, aim for "nothing less than the secularization of American culture, the shaming and mocking of faith right out of the American heart."[99] Invoking Jeffersonian language, he concluded: "Our Creator has endowed us with our liberty. It would be a deep and lasting shame if fear of lawsuits caused us to reject those God-given liberties and drive our Creator from the public square."[100]

Charles C. Haynes, a senior scholar at the Freedom Forum First Amendment Center and a director of the Religious Freedom Education Project at the Newseum in Washington, adopted less polemical language, but likewise presented an opposing interpretation of the American commitment to religious freedom and the protections it entails: "For James Madison, Thomas Jefferson and other early supporters of church-state separation, authentic religious liberty requires that government remain neutral toward religion while simultaneously upholding the right of religious people and institutions to participate fully in the public square."[101] The inclusion of the cross-shaped beam, he argued, protected and affirmed religious people's right to participate in public life, securing their inclusion in American civil society. Once again, then, the effort to narrativize and memorialize 9/11 became a window onto the profound tensions over "who Americans are," the question of collective self-definition at the heart of politics.[102]

As of spring 2014, American Atheists was appealing the case, while the cross-shaped beam stood inside the newly opened museum. Labeled "The Cross at Ground Zero," the display tells the story of Silecchia finding the "intersecting steel column and crossbeam" and bringing "the cross-shaped steel to the attention of other workers and members of the clergy"; it includes video footage of Jordan blessing the cross on October 4, 2001. A sign that announced "Catholic mass every Sunday under the cross at West Street" is displayed as well. The accompanying text, however, presents the cross as a symbol with significance to a population that far transcended Catholics or even Christians in general: "Individuals of many faiths and belief systems saw the cross as a symbol of hope, faith, and healing." In the same area are other pieces of what the museum calls "symbol steel," cut into shapes by ironworkers and given "as mementos and tokens of comfort to other workers and victims' relatives." They include a Maltese cross, a heart, a rendering of the Twin Towers, and a Star of David.

TRAUMA, *RESSENTIMENT*, AND THE MEANING OF SEPTEMBER 11

As I suggested in chapter 6, the annual commemorations in lower Manhattan recall the pain of 9/11—the wound it inflicted on individual lives as well as on the collective conscience—and provide symbolic material for introspection. Yet they do so without forging a clear place for it in a shared narrative. The debates I have traced in this chapter provide some indication of the challenges public officials might face if they addressed the call for consolation narratives more directly: if they worked, as Robert Burke put it on the pages of the *New York Daily News*, to "define for us the situation at hand; explain its significance and magnitude and provide a path for us to follow."[103]

Specifically, these debates reveal that beneath the open-ended commemorations I described in chapter 6 is an inability among key stakeholders to forge a consensual interpretation of 9/11, to settle upon its meaning such that it can be assimilated into larger collective narratives. Cultural trauma, it seems, is indeed the appropriate metaphor here: this injury, not—or not yet—fully incorporated into familiar American narratives, has left an enduring wound on the body politic. Who or what was attacked on September 11? The abstract values of "freedom" and "liberty," "tolerance" and "pluralism," and the cherished laws and policies they underwrite—freedom of religion, freedom of speech, the separation of church and state? What, precisely, do these abstract values represent? A commitment to a particularistic national tradition, to embracing the Christian commitments that inspired some of the nation's earliest visionaries? A commitment to tolerance and pluralism, to accommodating—or, even more, thematizing—cultural and religious heterogeneity within the nation's most sacred landscapes? Does upholding religious freedom necessitate religious neutrality, or does it instead require protections for explicit religious participation in public spaces? Is critical reflection on collective shortcomings—on difficult moments in the nation's past—a task befitting American ground held sacrosanct and inviolable?

Such questions remain a source of deep and abiding dissent. And without answers, Americans can neither forget September 11 nor fully move beyond it. Instead, its memory elicits powerful expressions of antipathy—toward the perpetrators; toward Islamic symbolism; toward interlocutors who disagree on the meaning of 9/11 and indeed the meaning of America itself. And these profound antipathies illuminate the insight that resentment is the outer-directed manifestation of trauma:[104] that it is a logical response to suffering that remains "most painfully present," but whose meaning remains elusive.[105]

The memorial and museum that now occupy the site embody this enduring sense of cultural trauma. Michael Arad's minimalist memorial design stands firmly within the Maya Lin genre. Two enormous voids mark the places where the Twin Towers once stood. Water plunges from street level into reflecting pools below; each pool contains a smaller void in its center that cuts still deeper into the earth. Bronze parapets surrounding the voids display the names of those who perished at all three of the 9/11 crash sites, as well as the six who died during the World Trade Center bombing in 1993. A forest of oak trees was added to Arad's original design in collaboration with landscape architect Peter Walker with the intention of augmenting the empty voids with subtle symbols of renewal and rebirth.[106] The memorial's focal point, however—like that of the Vietnam Veterans Memorial—is the names of the dead, and the indelible wound created by their loss, signified by the sheer enormity of the voids. Here, too, visitors regularly leave tokens on the memorial, marking particular names with small flags, flowers, photographs, and the like.

At some remove from the memorial stands 1 World Trade Center, a tower that stretches a symbolic 1,776 feet into the sky. Once known as the "Freedom Tower," it provides a more triumphalist—and, given its height, decidedly nationalistic—symbol alongside the voids that cut deep into the earth. The juxtaposition of minimalist memorial and triumphalist tower in some sense parallels the symbolic ambivalence of the Vietnam Memorial, vividly displaying the interpretive tensions that continue to characterize the struggle over the site, the event, and the place of both in American collective memory.[107]

The ongoing trauma of September 11 is perhaps most evident in the museum, which opened in May 2014. With its main exhibitions located 70 feet below ground level, in the footprints of the towers, the museum takes its visitors on a slow descent. On the ramp that leads down into the museum's dark, cavernous space, audio recordings quickly draw the visitor into the immediate experience of that day, as voices recall where they were when the news broke: Chicago; London; New Zealand; a coffee shop in

Knoxville, Tennessee; at the corner of Broadway and Rector Street in Manhattan. These voices narrate the shock of hearing the news on the radio, of turning on their televisions to see the violence and its effects, of watching the second plane crash into the south tower in real time, of struggling to reach loved ones, of feeling alone, lost, and afraid. Quotations from the recordings are projected in white print on columns in this dark space, with key phrases emboldened for emphasis. Descending further, visitors encounter two photographs of the Manhattan skyline—one taken at dusk, labeled August 2001, and the other from September 11, the skyline overtaken with rising clouds of smoke. At bedrock, a quotation from Virgil's *Aeneid* proclaims: "No day shall erase you from the memory of time."[108] Behind this wall is a repository for unidentified human remains, accessible only to family members, awaiting advancements in DNA technology.[109]

In the footprint of the south tower, an exhibit commemorates each life lost individually. The names are read continuously, spoken by those with personal connections to the dead: "my mother," "my husband," "my uncle," "my son," "my sister," "my best friend." Photographs and brief biographies are projected onto a wall, along with audio recordings of loved ones who give voice to memories of those they lost. In the footprint of the north tower, an extensive exhibit reconstructs the events of September 11, 2001, in painstaking, minute-by-minute detail. Visitors are confronted with the sound of sirens; with video footage of Katie Couric and Matt Lauer breaking the news live on NBC; with images of the burning towers and photographs of eyewitnesses whose shock and pain is palpable. In alcoves, set apart for the especially sensitive material they contain, audio recordings from survivors and rescue workers narrate the firsthand experience of the day; voicemails recount the final moments of some who perished; harrowing photographs show people leaping from the burning buildings. This is precisely the stuff of trauma: in the absence of an adequate narrative, the sufferer remains ensnared in the moment of injury, condemned to repeat the past.[110]

Even as the exhibit moves into the aftermath of September 11, the sense of enduring trauma is evident. Visitors encounter a massive array of images and artifacts—personal objects such as a watch, a wedding ring, and a pair of bloodstained shoes; images of candlelight vigils and makeshift memorials—that invite them to experience, or reexperience, the disparate reactions that the day's events generated. But they do so without placing these reactions or the event itself into a broader narrative context. Posters that featured photographs of Osama bin Laden and declared—as Bush had—"Wanted: Dead or Alive" appear on a wall just above images from a protest staged by artists near the military recruiting station in Times Square on September 25 and October 5, 2001. Their signs read: "Our Grief is Not a Cry for War." A single panel addresses the public debate over both the PATRIOT Act and the "Global War on Terror." In a film titled "Rebirth at Ground Zero"—in which images of the reconstruction surround the viewer, projected not only at the front of the room, but also on both sides—a woman expresses hope that she will one day be able to "integrate" the experience of September 11, 2001. If the museum—which bills itself as "the country's principal institution for examining the implications of the events of 9/11, documenting the impact of those events and exploring the continuing significance of September 11, 2001"—is any indication, such integration at the level of collective narratives has not yet become possible.[111]

Though political leaders have at times entered the fray in the interpretive struggles I have analyzed in this chapter, even the nation's highest officials have approached the sacred space known as "ground zero" with special care. As I noted in chapter 4, politicians were a silent presence during the first memorial service at the World Trade Center in October 2001, relying instead on clergy to provide words that would memorialize the dead and attempt to console the mourners. And even presidents have fallen in line with established commemorative practices during the anniversary observances, saving their speeches for other venues. When Bush traveled to New York on September 11, 2002, he delivered his soaring words describing the nation's expansive mission at Ellis Island—a site rich with symbolic meaning, but at some distance from lower Manhattan's "hallowed ground." Obama waded into the debate over Park51, then quickly worked to distance himself from its emotional dimensions: he was commenting on its legality, he said, not its "wisdom."

Indeed, even beyond the anniversary observances, political affairs held at the World Trade Center have generally featured polysemic expressions of respect and sorrow rather than efforts to articulate the meaning of September 11 in specific terms.[112] Obama's visit to lower Manhattan on May 5, 2011—on the heels of his announcement that a U.S. operation had killed Osama bin Laden—is illustrative. In his initial remarks from the White House on May 1—as I noted in chapter 5—Obama described the mission as a national triumph, an embodiment of who Americans are, and proclaimed: "Justice has been done."[113] He continued to articulate these themes in subsequent days. At a bipartisan Congressional dinner on May 2, he said: "We were reminded again that there is a pride in what this nation stands for, and what we can achieve, that runs far deeper than party, far deeper than politics."[114] Once again, the mission's success in killing bin Laden became an expression of national identity, a manifestation of essential and abiding American qualities. He reinforced this interpretation during his visit to New York, telling a group of police officers who worked at the World Trade Center site that the "reason" bin Laden's death was "important" was that "it sent a signal around the world that we have never forgotten the extraordinary sacrifices that were made on September 11th."[115] The mission, Obama suggested, honored police officers' fallen comrades, as well as their own contributions to the rescue and recovery effort. When he visited the World Trade Center, however, Obama made no remarks. Instead, he simply laid a wreath and bowed his head in silence.[116]

Such wordless gestures may indeed hold substantial symbolic power.[117] There are approaches to political consolation, and to symbolic expression more generally, other than spoken words. Consider, for instance, the iconic image of West German Chancellor Willy Brandt kneeling before the Warsaw Ghetto Memorial in 1970, communicating humility and regret for German atrocities in a manner that words perhaps could not have expressed.[118] Brandt later reflected: "I did what human beings do when speech fails them."[119] Obama's solemnity and silence no doubt communicated a respect for the dead, and for the site as a burial ground—no place for triumphant speechmaking or political point-scoring. Yet it is also worth considering the differences between such silent observances and narratives that maintain a place for—even thematize—moral and interpretive ambiguity while engaging an event in specific terms, grappling with the particular lessons it offers and even reconfiguring collective narratives accordingly. Moving beyond the painful memory of September 11, healing the seemingly indelible wound it left on the body politic, will almost certainly require more of the latter than Americans have witnessed in recent years.

Conclusion

CRISIS MOMENTS AND POLITICAL MEANINGS

Whatever else they may be, crisis moments are occasions for reflecting upon, rethinking, and—potentially—reorganizing political meanings.[1] Catastrophic events create moments of cultural and political liminality, when collectivities stand betwixt and between what they have been and what they will become, while the place of the disruptive event is negotiated.[2] The transformative potential of calamity and disaster resides not only in the disruptions to collective identity that such events inevitably create, disruptions that prompt political leaders and others to reconsider fundamental assumptions concerning who they are as a people. It resides also in the even more basic existential questions that arise in the process. What is the meaning of suffering? How do we make sense of loss and finitude?

Addressing these questions, and in the process providing a sense of continuity—even transcendence—in the face of human mortality, has long been a task of national narratives.[3] But it is an especially pressing one in our present moment, an age when politicians' symbolic, performative, and rhetorical tasks are defining rather than subsidiary elements of their leadership role.[4] In the United States, at least, politicians are comforters and consolers as much as they are policymakers and negotiators. Moreover, the interpretive frameworks that provide meaning and consolation in the immediate aftermath of crisis events infuse more pragmatic genres of political speechmaking, and thus figure centrally in the ongoing effect flow of these events. What actions, if any, are required to ensure that present suffering is rendered meaningful? How will the living ensure that the dead attain symbolic immortality in the ongoing life of their nation?

Political consolation is therefore not only a source of solace in the present, but a roadmap for the future, as social actors work to restore, reconstitute, or—perhaps—remake the collectivity, its institutions, and its common narratives.

The effort to articulate the meaning of present suffering is always, as Philip Abrams put it, "a struggle to create a future *out of* the past."[5] In the aftermath of September 11, politicians called on terms and tropes, ideas and images, from the past—sometimes the very distant past—to give shape to a disorienting series of events that initially confronted many observers as without precedent. Even as they evoked a sense of profound historical rupture, American leaders compared New York's "ground zero" to the U.S.S. *Arizona*, the field in bucolic Shanksville to Gettysburg, and the "war on terror" to the struggle against Nazism. Establishing such narrative associations between past and present was a crucial tool for political leaders as they addressed the existential questions at the core of political consolation; in the state discourse surrounding September 11, references to historical triumphs underwrote a progressive teleology, in which death and suffering became meaningful sacrifices that served a higher end. Attending to premediation—to the ways in which extant frameworks impinge upon new events even as they unfold—provides a crucial window onto the dynamics of culture and the sources of existential meaning.

At the same time, it also unsettles these very meanings, enabling what William Sewell calls "the de-reification of social life."[6] That is, it illuminates what is arguably *the* quintessential insight of the sociological tradition: the structures that confront us as ready-made and immutable, and that act back upon us, are in fact the result of vigorous "human activity."[7] The symbolic frameworks, the vocabularies of consolation, that often appear to speakers as incontestable answers to political and existential exigencies are, in the last analysis, contingent human products. And in this vein, it is worth reflecting on the role that interpretive and historical analysis might play in engaging the process of political meaning-making, especially with reference to liminal moments that feature heightened possibilities for its reorganization.

By "de-reifying" social life, historical approaches to interpretive analysis open the subjunctive. Exposing the processes through which even the most obdurate semiotic structures are actively constructed and carried forward, they offer space for the analyst and her readers to contemplate how such structures might be unmade or remade. The *Oxford English Dictionary* defines the subjunctive as "a verbal mood that refers to an action or state as conceived (rather than as a fact) and is therefore used chiefly to express a wish, command, exhortation, or a contingent, hypothetical, or prospective event." To enter the subjunctive mood, then, is to contemplate the world not as it is, but as it could be: to "[traffic] in human possibilities rather than in settled certainties" and thus to "render the world less fixed, less banal, more susceptible to recreation," as the psychologist Jerome Bruner puts it.[8]

The anthropologist Victor Turner identified the subjunctive with the liminal phase at the heart of the rites of passage he studied. Such rituals, he wrote, "move from the 'indicative' mood of cultural process through culture's 'subjunctive' mood back to the 'indicative' mood."[9] Even more, however, he suggested that the subjunctive liminal phase left an indelible mark on its participants: when the passage is complete, the "recovered [indicative] mood has now been tempered, even transformed, by immersion in subjunctivity."[10] Similarly, Wagner-Pacifici describes moments of contingency in social life—such as standoffs—as "action in the subjunctive mood," using the term to capture the "uncertainty" and "provisionality" that predominates in such circumstances, and drawing a parallel with Bernstein's conception of sideshadowing.[11] In lingering on liminal moments, highlighting the processes through which taken-for-granted narratives come to premediate unique and anomalous new realities, sideshadowing alternate possibilities, and attending to instances of discourse contamination or hybridization that illuminate gaps between events and codes, interpretive analysis raises questions in the subjunctive mood. What might have been, or what might still come to be? And this "immersion in subjunctivity" can leave its participants "transformed"—dereifying their sense of the world more permanently.[12]

None of this is to suggest that we can ever be free of cultural structures entirely, or that we should strive to be. As Clifford Geertz memorably argued, without "our ability to create, grasp, and use symbols," we would be utterly adrift—"more helpless . . . than the beavers."[13] This is perhaps especially true for the crisis moments that form the focus of this book. But the frameworks that premediate the unfolding present, that provide orientation and solace amidst liminality, can be more or less distorting. To bring my analysis to a close, then, I draw on the theoretical and historical material I have presented to consider how the alternate, tragic mode of political consolation might have constructed September 11 and diverted its effect flow, drawing on my empirical findings to enter the subjunctive mood and to "sideshadow" what might have been.

Here, I venture onto normative terrain, though with the hope that the careful historical account I have provided offers a foundation for evaluative judgment—that critique emerges as "the result of . . . historical description, not the reason for it."[14] Indeed, the current moment seems especially ripe for such reflections, offering some historical remove from events that nonetheless continue to grip and polarize the American public. Despite the powerful force of dualistic discourse in the wake of September 11, and its afterlife in various genres of political speechmaking, the meaning of this wound on the body politic is in many ways yet to be decided.

SIDESHADOWING AND SEPTEMBER 11

On November 7, 2001, former president Bill Clinton delivered remarks at Georgetown University in Washington, D.C., his own undergraduate alma mater. Addressed primarily to students—young adults who felt, perhaps, that they were experiencing the first grave national crisis of their lifetime—his speech reflected at length on the events of September 11, and their meaning for the nation and its future. He was careful to clarify that he spoke "in the context of my present job," as "a citizen," and that he supported "the efforts of President Bush, the national security team, and our allies in fighting the current terrorist threat."[15] Like Bush, he interpreted September 11 not as an isolated event, but as a signal of an oncoming struggle: "a struggle," he said, "for the soul of the 21st century and the world in which you students live and raise your own children and make your own way."[16] But he defined the contours of this struggle very differently from his successor.

At the moment when his nation was just beginning its "war on terror," Clinton reflected at some length upon the very meaning of the term "terror"—a term that had quickly become ubiquitous in state discourse yet was infrequently contemplated or interrogated in official speechmaking. In the process, Clinton simultaneously sought to provide reassurance to his youthful audience and to historicize the events they had witnessed two months prior:

> terror, the killing of noncombatants for economic, political, or religious reasons, has a very long history, as long as organized combat itself, and yet it has never succeeded as a military strategy standing on its own. . . . Those of us who come from various European lineages are not blameless. Indeed, in the first Crusade, when the Christian soldiers took Jerusalem, they first burned a synagogue with 300 Jews in it, and proceeded to kill every woman and child who was Muslim on the Temple Mount. . . . I can tell you that that story is still being told today in the Middle East and we are still paying for it.[17]

Terror, Clinton suggested, was not a new phenomenon or a source of historical rupture, but an old strategy, and an ineffectual one. His gesture toward collective guilt, especially for events that preceded the establishment of the American nation, would stir considerable controversy.[18] He continued, however, with reflections on the "terror" that punctuated the American story, portraying not an innocent nation but a fallible one. The America that Clinton depicted here had its own legacy as a perpetrator of violent atrocities:

> Here in the United States, we were founded as a nation that practiced slavery and slaves were, quite frequently, killed even though they were innocent. This country once looked the other way when significant numbers of Native Americans were dispossessed and killed to get their land or their mineral rights or because they were thought of as less than fully human and we are still paying the price today. Even in the 20th century in America people were terrorized or killed because of their race. And even today, though we have continued to walk, sometimes to stumble, in the right direction, we still have the occasional hate crime rooted in race, religion, or sexual orientation. So terror has a long history.[19]

Though guided by noble aspirations, American history was not an uninterrupted progressive march toward liberty and justice. It was, instead, a more complicated journey, punctuated with violence and injustice that emanated from within the nation. America, too, had played its part in the history of terror.

Unsettling the sharp moral binaries that permeated the dominant political discourse, Clinton narrated the events of September 11 in the tragic mode. He took seriously the task of consoling the young people to whom he spoke, reassuring them that "no terrorist campaign has ever succeeded, and this one won't if you don't give it permission."[20] Though he acknowledged that American society was "not a perfect society," he claimed that it was "stumbling in the right direction."[21] But in reflecting on the "long history" of terror, he also engaged in the self-examination that the tragic mode encourages. In the face of terrorism, Wagner-Pacifici notes, a tragic framing invites us to consider "[w]hat is 'terrorist' within ourselves or what could be terrorist within ourselves,"[22] and in the process, to contemplate the complex political and historical circumstances within which events unfold. Adequately addressing such matters requires deep historical knowledge and sustained consideration by a community of experts. The important point here is that Clinton's speech brought them to the surface, articulated them aloud, and in doing so, offered an alternate mode for contemplating the events of September 11 and their place within the American story. He condemned the violence perpetrated on 9/11 while calling for continued self-reflection: "You can have the most exciting time in human history," Clinton said as he closed his address, "but we have to defeat people who think they can find their redemption in our destruction. Then we have to be smart enough to get rid of our arrogant self-righteousness so that we don't claim for ourselves things that we deny for others."[23]

The preceding chapters illustrate in detail how the dualistic mode helped direct the American response to a profoundly ambiguous event in powerful ways. Clinton's words, in turn, provide a concrete basis for considering how the alternate, tragic mode of political consolation—this subtle but significant minor key in American political discourse—might have altered the effect flow of September 11. From the dualistic standpoint, the appropriate response to September 11 was to wage war—and, even more, to wage war not only against a particular and delimited enemy, a clear perpetrator, but also against "terror," even "evil," writ large. (In fact, Bush proclaimed that a "war on terror" had begun even before he was able to identify the 9/11 perpetrators in specific terms.) As I demonstrated in chapter 5, the claim that America's "mission" in the aftermath of September 11 was to eradicate evil itself—and thereby extend the reach of "civilization" beyond a new frontier—played a central role in legitimating not only war in Afghanistan, but also a preemptive strike in Iraq. The pervasive analogy between Pearl Harbor and September 11—invoked both implicitly and explicitly in political speechmaking—obscured profound differences between conflicts in disparate eras, with different "villains" and "victims," and within distinct global contexts. The same is true for the Gettysburg Address, whose language and themes were so frequently deployed in ways that conflated fallen soldiers and dead civilians in an effort to bring meaning to the unexpected and seemingly inexplicable loss of the latter. Such interpretations elide important cultural and moral distinctions.

This is not to dismiss entirely the value of the romantic sentiments associated with the dualistic mode. Certain romantic and collectivist tendencies—a sense of shared destiny, a sense of obligation to others, and an ability to maintain optimism for the future despite turmoil in the present—were no doubt crucial in fostering resilience, and indeed moral renewal, after 9/11.[24] As Durkheim observed long ago, collective effervescence—which was much in evidence in public rituals that affirmed sacred symbols (e.g., the American flag) and shared ideals (e.g., freedom and democracy) following September 11—has a profound moral and emotional impact and an exceptional power to repair tears in the social fabric.[25] Especially in the face of calamity, this sense of solidarity can inspire generosity and compassion toward those who suffer, as it undoubtedly did after 9/11.

Yet interpretations that conceive events in stark binary terms—leaving no room for moral ambiguity—tend to inhibit compromise, foster insularity, and as the 9/11 case so clearly demonstrates, prolong violence.[26] An "innocent" nation victimized by an unwarranted attack need not reflect on its own fallibility, or its potential to perpetrate injustice in response to injury.[27] As I have shown, this polarizing dualistic discourse carries forth the main thread of American political consolation—it is a symbolic framework toward which public officials habitually turn in the face of crisis. With roots in the Revolution and in the early images of the frontier that provided a vital foundation for American nationhood, this framework confronts many Americans as self-evident and unassailable amidst calamity.

However, as Clinton's words reveal, it was not the only interpretive possibility in the aftermath of 9/11, and it need not inevitably become the framework in which 9/11 is cast in American collective memory over the long haul. The tragic mode—an orientation that, though subterranean and subordinate, has its own considerable history in American political culture—represents an enduring alternative. There are landmark moments in American history—Lincoln accepting joint responsibility for national suffering on the eve of triumph; Robert Kennedy's call to "replace . . . violence . . . with an effort to understand"—that lay bare an underlying tragic sensibility, a capacity for grappling with moral ambiguity and for engaging in reflective self-examination, even self-criticism. While the multivocal commemorations in Manhattan gesture toward this tragic mode—and indeed have even remediated one of its defining moments, namely Kennedy's speech in Indianapolis—developing a full-fledged tragic interpretation of September 11 would require a narrative engagement with the particularities of the event and its historical context that the Manhattan commemorations leave aside. And, as Clinton's words suggest, the tragic orientation would likely reorient the effect flow of 9/11 in profound ways. While dualism divides the world unambiguously into good and evil—positing a blameless victim and an irredeemable perpetrator, leaving no room for neutrality or even uncertainty—tragedy thematizes ambiguity.[28] Tragedy, Northrop Frye explains, "eludes the antithesis of good and evil"[29]—the very antithesis that forms the backbone for dualism.

The dualistic interpretation of 9/11, however, sought precisely to subvert any effort to comprehend the perpetrators' motives. Giuliani's remarks before the United Nations on October 1, 2001—discussed in chapter 5—are emblematic: "Those who practice terrorism lose any right to have their cause understood by decent people and lawful nations."[30] Consolation was to be found in moral righteousness—America was attacked *because* it is a beacon for freedom—and the certainties it purportedly conferred: the battle might be lengthy, but good always triumphs over evil in the end.

With regard to September 11, then, the willingness to engage in critical introspection has been a long time coming; the dualistic themes Bush rapidly articulated continued to reverberate as the years wore on. The visibly effervescent response evident across the nation after Osama bin Laden's death, nearly a full decade after September 11, illustrates the enduring power of the anger, defiance, and desire for revenge that Bush's earliest speeches sought to evoke. As I noted in chapter 5, following Obama's May 1, 2011, announcement, spontaneous celebrations erupted in cities across America—in Lafayette Square, across from the White House; in Times Square; in college towns like Austin, Texas, and Morgantown, West Virginia; at the World Trade Center. Also illustrative is the resistance in the national political conversation to thoroughgoing self-examination after incidents such as Abu Ghraib—an American atrocity that was very much a part of the "event flow"[31] of September 11, a consequence comprehensible in terms of the binary framework that prevailed. Atrocities such as those committed at Abu Ghraib ostensibly require that their perpetrators perceive an enemy not only as malevolent, but also as less than human—a presumption that permeates dualistic discourse.[32]

However, there are also notable cultural and political pressures to reflect upon the meaning of September 11, as well as its darker and more insidious legacies in American policy. For one, the international context—an ever more powerful influence in our rapidly globalizing age—increasingly encourages collectivities to engage in self-examination, to reflect on their own misdeeds, and to acknowledge culpability through official public apologies and acts of atonement.[33] American political leaders have, in many ways, resisted the rise of this politics of regret. The exculpatory language that almost invariably seems to accompany references to Hiroshima in political discourse—references that are, themselves, exceedingly rare—is emblematic. The silence that prevails with regard to the subsequent bombing of Nagasaki reinforces the point.[34] But as I have shown, American political leaders have not evaded such imperatives altogether. Recall, for instance, that the elder Bush acknowledged the internment of Japanese Americans, and expressed regret for this injustice, in official addresses on the 50th anniversary of Pearl Harbor, complicating the heroic image of the victors and at least subtly unsettling the symbolic boundary distinguishing them from their erstwhile enemies. The effort to come to terms with the Vietnam War brought searching reflections, not only from political leaders in general, but also from some of its original architects. More recently, Obama's May 2013 speech at National Defense University seemed to signal a changing orientation to 9/11: a willingness to reflect on the ways in which "we compromised our basic values" in its aftermath; a call to "make decisions based not on fear, but hard-earned wisdom"; an exhortation to consider how that archetypal American value of freedom is bound up with another, that of justice.[35]

It is worth noting that a tragic orientation to collective suffering need not preclude any contemplation or condemnation of evil. The key here is precisely *contemplation*—deliberate and considered reflection on a historical event in all its complexity. As Richard Bernstein argues, in the philosophical tradition, to invoke evil was historically to foster contemplation. He explains: "When we survey historical attempts to comprehend evil"— from Augustine to Leibniz to Shakespeare to Dostoevsky to Arendt— "there is one characteristic that stands out. The confrontation with evil provokes *thinking*."[36] Susan Neiman's alternative history of philosophy illustrates this point magnificently, illuminating the effort to grapple with the problem of evil in all its intricacy as a driving force behind modern philosophical thought.[37] After 9/11, in contrast, "the world was divided in a simple (and simplistic) duality—the evil ones seeking to destroy us and those committed to the war against evil."[38] According to Bernstein, this rigid and polarizing discourse "represents an *abuse* of evil—a dangerous abuse" because "instead of inviting us to question and to *think*, this talk of evil is being used to stifle *thinking*."[39] The crux of the matter is the absolutist conception of evil that prevails in this discourse, a conception that reifies distinctions between allies and enemies and legitimates state violence while subverting "serious consideration of alternatives."[40] Raymond Williams stakes a similar claim in his work on tragedy, arguing that "[e]vil, as it is now widely used, is a deeply complacent idea"—but the history of tragedy demonstrates that it need not be.[41]

Adopting a tragic stance toward crisis requires a considerable tolerance for ambiguity—a willingness to grasp at, and struggle toward, narrativization and meaning without recourse to absolutes. And it is true that interpretive ambiguity in the face of profound suffering raises the possibility for anomie or *ressentiment*.[42] The unassimilated calamity can become an unresolved cultural trauma, an event that unsettles the foundations of collective identity and creates an enduring breach in familiar collective narratives.[43] Neither forgotten and left aside nor interpreted in a manner that elicits sufficient consensus, the wound in the body politic can become a source of profound animosity. Indeed, public debates surrounding the redevelopment of Manhattan's "ground zero" expose powerful fault lines that remain beneath the surface in the multivocal commemorations held annually at the site. But while trauma results from the lack of a narrative—an inability to assimilate suffering—the tragic mode enables actors to narrativize the past by reflecting on the complexity of human events and working to discern the wisdom they might hold for the future.

It is important, then, not to underestimate the human capacity for coming face-to-face with ambiguity, for coping with uncertainty, for engaging in the reflective self-examination that the tragic view of the world has the capacity to foster. Grappling with difficult history, working to forge a place for it in a common narrative, can ultimately lead to the rethinking and reconstruction of collective identities as actors work to adapt narratives to changing circumstances and new insights.[44] As a number of observers—discussed in chapter 6 —have suggested, coming to terms with a disruptive event such as 9/11 almost certainly requires a more robust effort to narrativize collective suffering than we have yet witnessed in Manhattan: public speechmaking that grapples with the event's (or, perhaps, events') meaning and its legacies in overt and specific terms. But such efforts need not take shape within a sharply divided symbolic universe that maintains an absolutist distinction between good and evil. Whether or not one considers them an exemplar, Clinton's words at Georgetown provide a sense for one alternate narrative possibility as the United States continues to grapple with the meaning of September 11 and its legacies. Because of the timing of his speech—November of 2001—his words also allow us to sideshadow, reminding us that different interpretations were possible, and that history could have unfolded otherwise.

PREMEDIATION AND SEPTEMBER 11

Like the national crises that preceded it, September 11 now has its own place in premediating new realities. On April 15, 2013, when two pressure cooker bombs exploded near the finish line of the Boston Marathon, the memory of September 11 loomed large. The intervening years, it is true, had brought a series of violent events that had shaken the citizenry and implicated political leaders in the work of consolation, including mass shootings at Virginia Tech in 2007, at Fort Hood in 2009, at a gathering with Representative Gabrielle Giffords in Arizona in 2011, and at Sandy Hook Elementary School in Connecticut in 2012. The violence at the U.S.

consulate in Benghazi, Libya, on September 11, 2012, also called forth searing memories of 9/11 in a powerful way. But the Boston Marathon bombing marked the first time since that fateful Tuesday in September of 2001 that violence unfolding on American soil was interpreted under the rubric of "terrorism." How did the specter of September 11 shape the meanings attributed to the events in Boston? And what might this suggest about the legacy of September 11 going forward?

Obama traveled to Boston three days after the bombing. He spoke during an interfaith memorial service, held at the Cathedral of the Holy Cross. The events were still new and shocking, and in many ways they remained in process even as he spoke. Yet the themes he articulated were familiar. Addressing the victims, the people of Boston, and the American nation writ large, Obama declared:

> Your resolve is the greatest rebuke to whoever committed this heinous act. If they sought to intimidate us, to terrorize us, to shake us from . . . the values that make us who we are as Americans, well, it should be pretty clear by now that they picked the wrong city to do it. . . .

> You showed us, Boston, that in the face of evil, Americans will lift up what's good. In the face of cruelty, we will choose compassion. In the face of those who would visit death upon innocents, we will choose to save and to comfort and to heal. We'll choose friendship. We'll choose love.

With these words, Obama reasserted American agency in the face of unexpected violence, and the chaos and uncertainty that ensued. Even before the suspects had been identified—it was not until a few hours after the memorial service that the FBI released video footage of the suspects—Obama adopted the language of "us" and "them." He contrasted American values—goodness, compassion, healing, friendship, comfort, and love—with the "evil" and "cruelty" of the perpetrators. They were, he said, "small, stunted individuals," and he called forth moral renewal that would overshadow their act of "senseless violence": "we don't cower in fear. We carry on. We race. We strive. We build and we work and we love and we raise our kids to do the same." This "heinous act" of violence, he implied, arose from outside the American moral community: it did not, Obama suggested, represent how "we" raise "our" children. And the suffering it wrought was but the harbinger of a brighter future: "this time next year," he said, "on the third Monday in April, the world will return to this great American city to run harder than ever and to cheer even louder for the 118th Boston Marathon."

In a certain sense, Obama's words embodied the basic moral contrasts that pervaded 9/11 discourse. His assumption that this act of violence emerged from outside the American body politic, not from American culture's own darker impulses, is striking. He concluded with a clear statement of American exceptionalism, describing "this country that we love" as a "special place," and indeed a "state of grace."[45] Yet the emotional valence of his words was different. Obama sought very clearly to cultivate resilience, even defiance, staking the familiar claim that present suffering would give way to a more hopeful future. But he did not evoke anger. On April 19, after suspect Dzhokhar Tsarnaev was arrested, Obama addressed the reality that this violence had, at least in some sense, emerged from within the nation, complicating the picture. There remained "many unanswered questions," he said. "Among them, why did young men who grew up and studied here, as part of our communities and our country, resort to such violence? How did they plan and carry out these attacks? And did they receive any help?"[46] While condemning "whatever hateful agenda drove these young men to such heinous acts," Obama suggested that this event would have to be understood in complex terms, and would require at least some measure of self-examination.[47]

CONSOLATION IN COMPARATIVE PERSPECTIVE

My hope is that this book simultaneously provides insights and invites further questions. The most obvious question it opens is that of comparison. How have other countries carried out their consolations? How does political structure influence consolation discourse, especially in cases where symbolic and bureaucratic leadership are divided rather than united, as they are in the U.S. presidency? To what extent do political leaders in other times and other places grapple with the existential matters that concern American leaders in the face of calamitous events?

Such questions are perhaps especially important in light of the challenges to the nation-state's legitimacy, or at least its primacy, as purveyor of collective meanings, an issue I discussed briefly in the introduction to this book. In this context, scholars have pointed to the growing salience of "transcultural" or "cosmopolitan" frameworks, suggesting that methodological nationalism is increasingly outmoded as an approach to memory and collective meaning.[48] The "national container," as Daniel Levy and Natan Sznaider put it, "is slowly showing fissures"[49]; memory, Astrid Erll suggests, takes shape "*across* and *beyond* cultures" rather than within "relatively clear-cut social formations" such as nation-states.[50]

These critiques, and the conceptual tools elaborated within them, offer innovative windows onto the sources of collective meaning and moral guidance in a complex and interconnected global environment. The questions they raise and the agendas they open will surely guide my own work on these issues going forward. My view remains, however, that there is still much work to be done to probe the ever-shifting, but still critically important, role of the nation and its leaders as a source and arbiter of meaning in our world. As Craig Calhoun puts it, for better or for worse, "[n]ationalism helps locate an experience of belonging in a world of global flows and fears."[51] Nations, national memories, and national cultures thus continue to require careful and sustained scholarly attention.

Given these concerns, it seems most fitting to devote the final pages of this book to a case that provides both a small start at a comparative approach to political consolation and, at the same time, sheds light on transcultural dimensions of collective meaning-making: namely, the July 7, 2005, suicide bombings in London. At a most basic level, the very nomenclature that was—not quite four years after September 11—already fairly well-established reflects transcultural dimensions of interpretation and remembrance: the event is often referred to by its date, "7/7," as were the 2004 train bombings in Madrid ("11-M"). That the nomenclature is a date perhaps reflects the challenges of classifying and interpreting these violent events, which are often signified according to when they occurred rather than what they were.

The events of 9/11 and 7/7 are connected by much more than their names, however. The U.K. had, from the first, been a staunch ally in the "war on terror," not only sending troops to Afghanistan, but also participating militarily in the 2003 invasion of Iraq. British Prime Minister Tony Blair had vigorously defended the decision to invade Iraq as well as the Bush administration's claims that this was a critical front in a struggle to preserve liberty itself.[52] In a July 2003 address before a joint session of the U.S. Congress, Blair spoke of his "most urgent sense of mission about today's world," and the need to preserve "the universal values of the human spirit"—namely: "Freedom not tyranny. Democracy not dictatorship. The rule of law not the . . . secret police."[53] The binary contrasts that formed the symbolic foundation for the "war on terror" permeated the prime minister's words. He, like Bush, warned of the danger "that terrorism and states developing weapons of mass destruction" would "come together," a risk that was not "fantasy," but "21st century reality."[54] And he affirmed messianic narratives that assigned the United States a special responsibility in this great struggle: "destiny," Blair said, "put you in this place in history, in this moment in time and the task is yours to do."[55] Bush and Blair were in fact together when the bombings occurred in London, gathered with other members of the G8 for a summit in Gleneagles, Scotland. How, then, did Blair and other British leaders give shape and meaning to this event?

Before making a brief return trip to London, Blair offered a short statement in Gleneagles. It was, he said, "particularly barbaric that this happened on a day when people are meeting to try to help the problems of poverty in Africa, and the long term problems of climate change and the environment."[56] Back in the capital, he expressed "sympathy" and "sorrow" for "those families who will be grieving, so unexpectedly and tragically, tonight."[57] Praising "the stoicism and resilience of the people of London," Blair called for strength and courage.[58]

> When they try to intimidate us, we will not be intimidated. When they seek to change our country or our way of life by these methods, we will not be changed. When they try to divide our people or weaken our resolve, we will not be divided and our resolve will hold firm. We will show, by our spirit and dignity, and by our quiet but true strength that there is in the British people, that our values will long outlast theirs.[59]

The transcultural dimensions of Blair's framing are clear. But so, too, is the appeal to a distinctively British sense of identity in Blair's call for dignity and quiet strength.

The day after the bombings, Queen Elizabeth II visited Royal London Hospital, which had received many of the victims.[60] In a statement, she expressed "admiration for the people of our capital city who . . . are calmly determined to resume their normal lives."[61] London, she recalled, had faced violence before, and she evoked the history of IRA attacks as well as the bombings the city endured during the Second World War: "Sadly we in Britain have been all too familiar with acts of terror and members of my generation . . . know that we have been here before. But those who perpetrate these brutal acts against innocent people should know that they will not change our way of life."[62] She reiterated this imagery during a World War II commemorative event two days later: "It does not surprise me that, during the present, difficult days for London, people turn to the example set by that generation—of resilience, humour, sustained courage, often under conditions of great deprivation."[63]

Four days after the bombings, on July 11, Blair delivered a more extensive address to Parliament. In his remarks, he echoed the Queen's effort to forge a parallel between past and present. Yet he also reflected on the differences between London of 1945 and London of 2005. "Yesterday we celebrated the heroism of WWII including the civilian heroes of London's blitz," he said. "Today what a different city London is—a city of many cultures, faiths and races, hardly recognisable from the London of 1945. So different and yet, in the face of this attack, there is something wonderfully familiar in the confident spirit which moves through the city, enabling it to take the blow but still not flinch from re-asserting its will to triumph over adversity." Despite the overwhelming demographic transformations that had turned London into a truly global city, Blair suggested, a distinctive collective spirit endured: "Britain may be different today but the coming together is the same."[64]

The self-conscious cosmopolitanism evident in Blair's address was even more pervasive in public mourning rituals, which evoked solidarity and a sense of shared suffering while at the same time acknowledging the diverse composition of both the victims and the city they inhabited.[65] One week after the bombings, the city—along with the entire European Union—observed two minutes of silence in memory of those killed on July 7.[66] The two minutes began with Last Post—the bugle call that signals the end of the day's activities in the British military, used also as a final farewell in military funerals and commemorative ceremonies—and ended with the national anthem.[67] The observance, London Mayor Ken Livingstone explained, was intended to demonstrate "that London will not be moved from our goal of building an open, tolerant, multiracial and multicultural society showing the world its future."[68] In the evening, thousands gathered in Trafalgar Square for a memorial, organized by the mayor.[69] The ritual began with the poet Ben Okri, born in Nigeria but based in London, reading "Lines in Potentis," a piece commissioned by Livingstone in 2002.[70] The poem begins:

> One of the magic centres of the world;
> One of the world's dreaming places.
> Ought to point the way to the world:
> For here lives the great music of humanity,
> The harmonisation of different
> Histories, cultures, geniuses, and dreams.
> Ought to shine to the world and tell
> Everyone that history, though unjust,
> Can yield wiser outcomes.
> And out of bloodiness can come love;
> And out of slave-trading

Can come a dance of souls;
Out of division, unity;
Out of chaos, fiestas.[71]

The image of London as a confluence of cultures, as a microcosm for humanity itself, provided a focal point for the event. The journalist Sir Trevor
McDonald described London as "a symbol of the universality of the
modern world."[72] And in this vein, Livingstone challenged the interpretation of the bombings as part of a "clash of civilizations." "Come to London
and see the world together in one city," he said. "Living in harmony as an
example to all."[73]

In November, families and friends of the deceased joined with the
Queen and Prince Philip as well as Tony Blair and his wife, Cherie Blair,
for an official memorial service at St. Paul's Cathedral. Neither the Queen
nor the prime minister spoke, though both met with family members
following the service; Mayor Livingstone delivered a reading from the
book of Isaiah. Rowan Williams, the Archbishop of Canterbury, gave the
sermon. He reflected on the arbitrary and indiscriminate nature of terrorist violence, and contrasted it with the notion of individualism—the
conviction that every person possesses specific and distinctive value:
"The shock of terrorist violence is just this sense of arbitrariness," Williams said. "It doesn't matter who you are, what you have done or not
done, what you think and believe, you are still a target just by being
where you are at a particular time. The terrorist is the enemy not just of
a system or a government but of the whole idea that we are each of us
unique and responsible and non-replaceable."[74] Terrorism was opposed
here not to freedom, but to the related yet distinct ideal of individualism, the modern conception of selfhood. Williams explained: "To those
who proclaim by their actions that it doesn't matter who suffers, who
dies, we say by our mourning, 'No. There are no generalities for us, no
anonymous and interchangeable people. We live by loving what is special, unique in each person. Everyone matters.'"[75]

Blair would go on to invoke the memory of 7/7 as he defended the Iraq
War before national and global audiences, describing it as one moment in
the broad Manichean narrative of the "war on terror."[76] But by the summer
of 2005, the Bush-Blair partnership, and the U.K.'s involvement in Iraq
and Afghanistan, had become the subject of considerable controversy
among the citizenry.[77] Indeed, a number of families had threatened to
boycott the memorial at St. Paul's, either in response to a perceived lack of
support from the government following the bombings or as a sign of

opposition to Blair's decision to go to war in Iraq.[78] In this heated political context, the first anniversary commemoration featured an elaborate series of rituals, but little in the way of official speechmaking. In the morning, dignitaries laid flowers outside King's Cross Station, where the four bombers arrived on the morning of July 7, 2005, and at Tavistock Square, where one of the bombs was detonated on a bus. At 11:30, memorial plaques were unveiled at Tavistock Square and at the tube stations where the bombs were detonated. And at noon, the nation once again observed two minutes of silence.

The highest-profile event took place in the early evening, at Regent's Park.[79] Culture Secretary Tessa Jowell delivered brief remarks, describing July 7 as "a day of infamy" and suggesting that, one year later, "it is right that we stop, as a city and as a nation, to remember . . . and to honour" those who died.[80] On the whole, however, the ceremony—in which the presence of dignitaries was intentionally limited[81]—bore a notable resemblance to the somber anniversary rituals in lower Manhattan. BBC Radio newsreader Peter Donaldson read the names of the dead, a ritual whose absence some family members lamented after the memorial service at St. Paul's.[82] The commemoration featured four poems, read not by political leaders or other dignitaries but by family members, interspersed with music by the London Community Gospel Choir. The texts gave voice to the private experience of grief and loss, and provided material for contemplation without placing the event in a clear narrative frame. Marie Fatayi-Williams, whose son perished in the bombings, read from Henry Scott Holland's "Death is Nothing at All":

> Death is nothing at all.
> I have only slipped away into the next room.
> I am I and you are you.
> Whatever we were to each other,
> That, we still are.[83]

Saba Mozakka, who lost her mother, read a poem titled "You Can't Have Departed" that conveyed grief and sorrow through a series of questions: "Where are you?" "Who says you are no more?" It concluded by simply giving voice to continuing pain: "Oh, our dearest, hold our hands, for we are so lonely."[84]

Even scratching the surface of the July 7 bombings and their memorialization points toward fresh questions and new terrain. Comparative investigations provide yet another form of sideshadowing, illuminating how different vocabularies encode similar events in disparate contexts. In the aftermath of September 11, cosmopolitan discourse certainly surfaced in New York, but not as rapidly or as overtly as it did in London, where it quickly became a central interpretive frame for the violence of 7/7. In a slightly different vein, Williams's reflections at St. Paul's Cathedral illuminated a conviction that perhaps implicitly animates many efforts to memorialize those killed in acts of terrorist violence in the United States, the U.K., and elsewhere: the lists of names that convey the scope of the event while also representing each unique life lost. They convey a sense that, as Williams put it, "[e]veryone matters"—a belief affronted by terrorist violence. There is an affinity between the discourse of individualism and that of freedom and liberty that is so common in U.S. commemorations, but these are distinct ideals, and invoking individualism as the value assaulted by terrorist violence casts the event in a somewhat different light. At best, such comparisons have the potential to foster both the reflection that sideshadowing encourages and the mutual understanding that our ever more interconnected world requires.

SOCIOLOGY IN THE SUBJUNCTIVE MOOD

Whether or not readers agree with the argument for rethinking September 11 through a tragic lens, then, there is a much larger theoretical point here. Namely, interpretive and historical analysis opens the subjunctive, enabling and in fact encouraging sideshadowing. It thus provides resources for contemplating what might have been or what might come to be. This is arguably a core element of the sociologist's vocation, at least as Weber envisioned it in his seminal statement on the subject. Quoting Tolstoy, Weber famously wrote: "Science is meaningless because it gives no answer to our question, the only question important for us: 'What shall we do and how shall we live?'" Yet Weber did not stop there: "if we are competent" in the pursuit of science as a vocation, he suggested, "we can force the individual, or at least we can help him, to give himself an *account of the ultimate meaning of his own conduct*." Social scientists, then, may not be able to answer that ultimate question of how we should live, but they can inspire a sense of moral and historical responsibility: "I am tempted to say of a teacher who succeeds in this: he stands in the service of 'moral' forces; he fulfils the duty of bringing about self-clarification and a sense of responsibility."

The historical analysis of political meaning-making can serve a similar purpose at the level of collective life. Exposing the contingency of seemingly incontestable symbolic structures and opening the subjunctive invites reflection and illuminates our responsibility for history in a particularly powerful way. Perhaps it even places us "in the service of 'moral' forces."[85] In this sense, Weber's vocation can do much to awaken the better angels of our nature. It ought to remain our own.

NOTES

PREFACE

1. George W. Bush, "Remarks on the Relief Efforts for Hurricane Katrina," August 31, 2005. Online by Gerhard Peters and John T. Woolley, *The American Presidency Project*, http://www.presidency.ucsb.edu/ws/?pid=73780.
2. Ibid.
3. "Waiting for a Leader," *New York Times*, August 31, 2005, A22.
4. Ibid.
5. Matthew Cooper, "Dipping His Toe into Disaster," *Time* 166, no. 11 (2005): 51.
6. For a detailed analysis of this address, see Simon Stow, "Do You Know What It Means to Miss New Orleans? George Bush, the Jazz Funeral, and the Politics of Memory," *Theory and Event* 11, no. 1 (2008).
7. George W. Bush, "Remarks on the Aftermath of Hurricane Katrina in Mobile, Alabama," September 2, 2005. Online by Gerhard Peters and John T. Woolley, *The American Presidency Project,* http://www.presidency.ucsb.edu/ws/?pid=64973.
8. Philip Abrams, *Historical Sociology* (Ithaca, NY: Cornell University Press, 1982), 8, emphasis in original.

INTRODUCTION

1. Sara Lukinson, ed., *September Morning: Ten Years of Poems and Readings from the 9/11 Ceremonies* (Brooklyn: powerHouse Books, 2012), "2002: Mayor Bloomberg, Introduction." The pages in *September Morning*—which contains the remarks and readings delivered during the first ten 9/11 anniversary com-memorations at the World Trade Center—are not numbered. They are instead labeled with the year of the commemoration, the name of the speaker, and a title. For clarity, I have provided this information in each reference to the volume.
2. Lukinson, *September Morning*, "2002: Mayor Bloomberg, Introduction."
3. Lukinson, *September Morning*, "2002: Governor Pataki, Lincoln's Gettysburg Address."
4. "Reading of 9/11 Victims' Names," National Broadcasting Company [NBC], September 11, 2002, LexisNexis Academic Broadcast Transcripts.
5. "Remarks by Secretary of Defense Donald Rumsfeld at a Defense Department Ceremony Marking the September 11th Terrorist Attack," September 11, 2002, *Federal News Service*, LexisNexis Academic.
6. Ibid.

7. Ibid.
8. "Remarks by President George W. Bush at Defense Department Ceremony Marking September 11th Terrorist Attack on the Pentagon," September 11, 2002, *Federal News Service*, LexisNexis Academic.
9. Ibid.
10. Ibid.
11. The passages behind this image are from the book of Matthew (5:14–16): "You are the light of the world. A city built on a hill cannot be hidden. No one after lighting a lamp puts it under the bushel basket, but on the lampstand, and it gives light to all in the house. In the same way, let your light shine before others, so that they may see your good works and give glory to your Father in heaven." As I explain in chapter 1, the "city upon a hill" trope can be traced to John Winthrop's seminal 1630 sermon, "A Model of Christian Charity." The trope has resurfaced in numerous high-profile political speeches in more recent years; notable examples include John F. Kennedy's January 9, 1961, address in Massachusetts, delivered just before he assumed the presidency, and Ronald Reagan's 1989 farewell address. More generally, the idea of the United States as a model for the world has been—and remains—pervasive in American political culture; see, e.g., Philip S. Gorski, "Civil Religion Today," ADRA Guiding Paper Series (State College: The Association of Religion Data Archives at The Pennsylvania State University, 2010): 11, and "Barack Obama and Civil Religion," *Political Power and Social Theory* 22 (2011): 183–184, 194, 198.
12. See, e.g., Astrid Erll, "Travelling Memory," *Parallax* 17, no. 4 (2011): 8; Eric J. Hobsbawm, *Nations and Nationalism since 1780: Programme, Myth, Reality* (New York: Cambridge University Press, 1992), 163–192; Daniel Levy and Natan Sznaider, *The Holocaust and Memory in the Global Age* (Philadelphia: Temple University Press, 2006), 35; Pierre Nora, "Between Memory and History: *Les Lieux de Mémoire*," *Representations* 26 (1989): 10–11.
13. See, e.g., Jeffrey C. Alexander, Ron Eyerman, Bernhard Giesen, Neil J. Smelser, and Pitor Sztompka, *Cultural Trauma and Collective Identity* (Berkeley: University of California Press, 2004).
14. See, e.g., Stanley Hauerwas, *Naming the Silences* (London: T&T Clark International, 2004); Alasdair MacIntyre, "Is Understanding Religion Compatible with Believing?," in *Rationality*, ed. Bryan R. Wilson (Oxford: Basil Blackwell, 1970); Odo Marquard, *In Defense of the Accidental: Philosophical Studies* (New York: Oxford University Press, 1991); Susan Neiman, *Evil in Modern Thought: An Alternative History of Philosophy* (Princeton, NJ: Princeton University Press, 2002); Kenneth Surin, *Theology and the Problem of Evil* (Eugene, OR: Wipf and Stock, 2004). See also recent works on the centrality of evil and suffering in classical sociologists' efforts to come to terms with modernity, especially W. S. F. Pickering and Massimo Rosati, eds., *Suffering and Evil: The Durkheimian Legacy* (New York: Berghahn Books, 2008); Iain Wilkinson, *Suffering: A Sociological Introduction* (Malden, MA: Polity Press, 2005).
15. Charles Taylor describes this historical transformation as "a move from a society where a belief in God is unchallenged and indeed, unproblematic, to one in which it is understood to be one option among others, and frequently not the easiest to embrace." Charles Taylor, *A Secular Age* (Cambridge, MA: Harvard University Press, 2007), 3.

16. David Hume, *Dialogues Concerning Natural Religion and Other Writings* (New York: Cambridge University Press, 2007), 74.
17. Gottfried Wilhelm Leibniz, *Theodicy: Essays on the Goodness of God, the Freedom of Man, and the Origin of Evil* (La Salle, IL: Open Court Press, 1985), 228.
18. Neiman, *Evil in Modern Thought*, xvi.
19. Voltaire, *Candide, or, Optimism* (New York: Modern Library, 2005).
20. As the philosopher Odo Marquard puts it, "the modern age is the age of distance: the first epoch in which impotence and suffering are not the taken-for-granted and normal state of affairs for human beings. Now, for the first time, want seems, in principle, masterable; pain avoidable; sickness conquerable; wickedness abolishable; and man's (finitude-induced) impotence outmaneuverable." Similarly, Hannah Arendt observed that "in the modern age and not before, men began to doubt that poverty is inherent in the human condition, to doubt that the distinction between the few, who through circumstances or strength or fraud had succeeded in liberating themselves from the shackles of poverty, and the labouring poverty-stricken multitude was inevitable and eternal." Arendt, in particular, locates this shift in the American colonial experiment. Odo Marquard, *In Defense of the Accidental*, 12; Hannah Arendt, *On Revolution* (New York: Penguin, 2006), 12.
21. Max Weber, *The Sociology of Religion* (Boston: Beacon Press, 1993), 112–115, 138–150; "The Social Psychology of the World Religions," and "Religious Rejections of the World and Their Directions," in *From Max Weber: Essays in Sociology*, ed. H. H. Gerth and C. Wright Mills (New York: Oxford University Press, 1946), 274–276, 358–359.
22. Although he famously reflected on the interplay between material deprivation and salvationist theodicy, Weber concluded that the human desire for "salvation and ethical religion" is ultimately rooted in "intellectualism as such, more particularly the metaphysical needs of the human mind as it is driven to reflect on ethical and religious questions, driven not by material need but by an inner compulsion to understand the world as a meaningful cosmos and to take up a position toward it." Weber, *The Sociology of Religion*, 116, 117. Indeed, Friedrich Tenbruck argues that the existential matters associated with theodicy formed the core of Weber's philosophical anthropology. See Friedrich Tenbruck, "The Problem of Thematic Unity in the Works of Max Weber," *British Journal of Sociology* 31, no. 3 (1980): 337–338.
23. Weber, "The Social Psychology of the World Religions," 275.
24. Ibid. See also the recent discussion of this point in Iain Wilkinson, "The Problem of Suffering as a Driving Force of Rationalization and Social Change," *British Journal of Sociology* 64, no. 1 (2013): 128.
25. Peter L. Berger, *The Sacred Canopy: Elements of a Sociological Theory of Religion* (Garden City, NY: Doubleday, 1967), 80; Colin Campbell, "A New Age Theodicy for a New Age," in *Peter Berger and the Study of Religion*, ed. Linda Woodhead, Paul Heelas, and David Martin (New York: Routledge, 2001), 73–77; Eva Illouz, *Oprah Winfrey and the Glamour of Misery: An Essay on Popular Culture* (New York: Columbia University Press, 2003), 4–5, 240. See also David Morgan, "Pain: The Unrelieved Condition of Modernity," *European Journal of Social Theory* 5, no. 3 (2002): 307–322; Bryan S. Turner, *For Weber: Essays on the Sociology of Fate*, 2nd ed. (London: Sage Publications, 1996), 142–176. Contemporary sociologists have extended Weber's work on theodicy in a number of

other directions. On how the education system provides theodicies that justify inequalities on intellectual grounds, see Pierre Bourdieu, *The Logic of Practice* (Stanford, CA: Stanford University Press, 1990), 27–28, 133. On how modern religions adapt traditional theodical frames to contemporary circumstances, see James Davison Hunter, "Subjectivization and the New Evangelical Theodicy," *Journal for the Scientific Study of Religion* 21, no. 1 (1982): 39–47. On the relationship between theodicy and life satisfaction, see Marc A. Musick, "Theodicy and Life Satisfaction among Black and White Americans," *Sociology of Religion* 61, no. 3 (2000): 267–287. On how social science itself addresses such questions in the form of "sociodicies," see Jon Elster, "Snobs," *London Review of Books* 20, no. 3 (1981): 10–12, and *Sour Grapes: Studies in the Subversion of Rationality* (New York: Cambridge University Press, 1983), 101–108; David Morgan and Iain Wilkinson, "The Problem of Suffering and the Sociological Task of Theodicy," *European Journal of Social Theory* 4, no. 2 (2001): 199–214; Arthur J. Vidich and Stanford M. Lyman, *American Sociology: Worldly Rejections of Religion and their Directions* (New Haven, CT: Yale University Press, 1985).

26. Peter L. Berger, Brigitte Berger, and Hansfried Kellner, *The Homeless Mind: Modernization and Consciousness* (New York: Vintage Books, 1974), 185.

27. As Susan Neiman puts it, "the great philosophers of the canon were concerned with nothing more or less gripping than the questions that move bright seventeen-year-olds to wonder, and worry, about sense and meaning." Neiman, *Evil in Modern Thought*, xviii.

28. Liah Greenfeld captures the meaning-conferring power of national identity in the modern context: "The least specialized identity, the one with the widest circumference, that is believed to define a person's very essence and guides his or her actions in many spheres of social existence is, of course, the most powerful. The image of social order is reflected in it most fully; it represents this image in a microcosm. In the course of history people's essence has been defined by different identities. . . . Such generalized identity in the modern world is the national identity." Liah Greenfeld, *Nationalism: Five Roads to Modernity* (Cambridge, MA: Harvard University Press, 1992), 20. There is a voluminous literature on the rise of nationalism, and scholars continue to debate its historical origins: Is nationalism a distinctively modern phenomenon, or does it have the deeper—even perennial—roots that its exponents often claim? For a strong modernist position, see John Breuilly, *Nationalism and the State*, 2nd ed. (Chicago: University of Chicago Press, 1994); Ernest Gellner, *Nations and Nationalism* (Ithaca, NY: Cornell University Press, 1983); Hobsbawm, *Nations and Nationalism since 1780*. For accounts that locate the emergence of nationalism in the early modern period, see Philip S. Gorski, "The Mosaic Moment: An Early Modernist Critique of Modernist Theories of Nationalism," *American Journal of Sociology* 105, no. 5 (2000): 1428–1468; Greenfeld, *Nationalism*. For a perennialist argument that underscores continuities between premodern communities and modern nationalism, see Anthony D. Smith, *The Ethnic Origins of Nations* (New York: Blackwell, 1986) and *Chosen Peoples: Sacred Sources of National Identity* (New York: Oxford University Press, 2003). My purpose here is not to intervene in this historical debate, but to affirm the point that national narratives became, in the modern world, a crucial source of collective meaning and identity, of the "symbolic order—culture—[that] is the human equivalent of animal instincts." Greenfeld, *Nationalism*, 18.

29. My intention is not to suggest a causal link between the rise of nationalism and the decline of religion, nor to posit a unilinear secularization narrative whereby religion disappears—or recedes to the private sphere—while nationalism provides a functional surrogate. As Benedict Anderson explains: "I am not claiming that the appearance of nationalism . . . was 'produced' by the erosion of religious certainties, or that this erosion does not itself require a complex explanation. Nor am I suggesting that somehow nationalism historically 'supersedes' religion. What I am proposing is that nationalism has to be understood by aligning it, not with self-consciously held political ideologies, but with the large cultural systems that preceded it, out of which—as well as against which—it came into being." Benedict Anderson, *Imagined Communities: Reflections on the Origin and Spread of Nationalism*, revised ed. (New York: Verso, 1991), 12. Today, it is abundantly clear that religion continues to play a tremendous role in the modern public sphere, and that the task facing scholars—as Geneviève Zubrzycki puts it—is to "identify the conditions under which religion and nationalism are fused, split, or juxtaposed." Geneviève Zubrzycki, *The Crosses of Auschwitz: Nationalism and Religion in Post-Communist Poland* (Chicago: University of Chicago Press, 2006), 21. In the U.S. context, religion and nationalism were often juxtaposed and indeed fused from the start; see, e.g., Robert N. Bellah, *The Broken Covenant: American Civil Religion in a Time of Trial*, 2nd ed. (Chicago: University of Chicago Press, 1992), 12–13; Gorski, "Barack Obama and Civil Religion," 186–187. For a comparative perspective on the role of religion in public life, see José Casanova, *Public Religions in the Modern World* (Chicago: University of Chicago Press, 1994).
30. Anderson, *Imagined Communities*, 11.
31. In this vein, scholars have long noted the binding power of hardships and trials in forging solidarity, common identity, and commitment to the collective good. As Ernest Renan put it in his classic statement on nationhood: "suffering in common unifies more than joy does. Where national memories are concerned, griefs are of more value than triumphs, for they impose duties, and require a common effort." Ernest Renan, "What Is a Nation?," in *The Collective Memory Reader*, ed. Jeffrey K. Olick, Vered Vinitzky-Seroussi, and Daniel Levy (New York: Oxford University Press, 2011), 83. See also Frank R. Ankersmit, "Trauma and Suffering: A Forgotten Source of Western Historical Consciousness," in *Western Historical Thinking: An Intercultural Debate*, ed. Jörn Rüsen (New York: Berghahn, 2002), 76; Wolfgang Schivelbusch, *The Culture of Defeat: On National Trauma, Mourning, and Recovery* (New York: Metropolitan Books, 2003), 10–11, 17, 19–20, 29–30.
32. Anderson, *Imagined Communities*, 11. Again, whether or not these bonds are indeed perennial or merely invented in the present to serve present purposes is a matter of enduring scholarly debate. Several leading scholars of collective memory have suggested a *via media* between perennialist positions such as Anthony Smith's and more presentist accounts of invented traditions (e.g., Eric Hobsbawm and Terence Ranger, eds., *The Invention of Tradition* [New York: Cambridge University Press, 1983]). Focusing on the complex interplay between past and present, these perspectives examine agents' efforts to reconstruct the past while also capturing how events—and their earliest interpretations—set limits on subsequent representations. See, e.g., Gary Alan Fine, "Reputational Entrepreneurs and the Memory of Incompetence: Melting Supporters, Partisan Warriors, and Images of President Harding,"

American Journal of Sociology 101, no. 5 (1996): 1159–1193; Jeffrey K. Olick and Daniel Levy, "Collective Memory and Cultural Constraint: Holocaust Myth and Rationality in German Politics," American Sociological Review 62, no. 6 (1997): 921–936; Michael Schudson, Watergate in American Memory: How We Remember, Forget, and Reconstruct the Past (New York: Basic Books, 1992); Barry Schwartz, "Social Change and Collective Memory: The Democratization of George Washington," American Sociological Review 56, no. 2 (1991): 221–236; Robin Wagner-Pacifici, "Memories in the Making: The Shapes of Things that Went," Qualitative Sociology 19, no. 3 (1996): 301–321. I draw heavily on these insights as I examine the interplay between past and present in the pages that follow.

33. Robert N. Bellah, Richard Madsen, William M. Sullivan, Ann Swidler, and Steven M. Tipton, Habits of the Heart: Individualism and Commitment in American Life, updated ed. (Berkeley: University of California Press, 1996), 153. On nations as "communities of memory" in Bellah et al.'s sense of the term, see Jeffrey K. Olick, The Sins of the Fathers: Germany, Memory, Method (Chicago: University of Chicago Press, forthcoming).

34. "Memory studies" is a vibrant, interdisciplinary field with deep roots in the sociological tradition. Émile Durkheim's student, Maurice Halbwachs, is widely understood as the field's founding figure; see Maurice Halbwachs, On Collective Memory (Chicago: University of Chicago Press, 1992). Though I draw on numerous insights from this field and its leading scholars in the pages that follow, space considerations preclude a more detailed overview of its development. For an orientation to memory studies more broadly, see Astrid Erll, Memory in Culture (New York: Palgrave Macmillan, 2011); Barbara A. Misztal, Theories of Social Remembering (Philadelphia: Open University Press, 2003); Jeffrey K. Olick and Joyce Robbins, "Social Memory Studies: From 'Collective Memory' to the Historical Sociology of Mnemonic Practices," Annual Review of Sociology 24 (1998): 105–140; Jeffrey K. Olick, Vered Vinitzky-Seroussi, and Daniel Levy, eds., The Collective Memory Reader (New York: Oxford University Press, 2011).

35. Astrid Erll, "Remembering Across Time, Space, and Cultures: Premediation, Remediation and the 'Indian Mutiny,'" in Mediation, Remediation, and the Dynamics of Cultural Memory, ed. Astrid Erll and Ann Rigney (Berlin: Walter de Gruyter, 2009), 111. As Erll elaborates: "What is known about an event which has turned into a site of memory . . . seems to refer not so much to what one might cautiously call the 'actual event,' but instead to a canon of existent medial constructions, to the narratives, images and myths circulating in a memory culture."

36. Ibid.

37. Ibid., 114. Barry Schwartz's twin concepts of "keying" and "framing" capture similar dynamics. See, e.g., Barry Schwartz, Abraham Lincoln in the Post-Heroic Era: History and Memory in Late Twentieth-Century America (Chicago: University of Chicago Press, 2008), xi. I adopt Erll's terminology because I found that her concept of "premediation," in particular, was an especially powerful tool in illuminating how the past implicitly structures efforts to interpret the present, sensitizing me to continuities and resonances that I likely would not have grasped otherwise.

38. Erll, "Travelling Memory," 8; Hobsbawm, Nations and Nationalism since 1780, 163–192; Levy and Sznaider, The Holocaust and Memory in the Global Age, 35;

Nora, "Between Memory and History," 10–11. On the enduring significance of the nation-state as an organizing frame, however, see, e.g., Rogers Brubaker, *Nationalism Reframed: Nationhood and the National Question in the New Europe* (New York: Cambridge University Press, 1996); Craig Calhoun, *Nations Matter: Culture, History, and the Cosmopolitan Dream* (New York: Routledge, 2007); Jeffrey K. Olick, ed., *States of Memory: Continuities, Conflicts, and Transformations in National Retrospection* (Durham, NC: Duke University Press, 2003) and *The Sins of the Fathers*; Zubrzycki, *The Crosses of Auschwitz*.

39. For a detailed treatment of these debates, see Olick, *The Sins of the Fathers*.
40. Jean-François Lyotard, *The Postmodern Condition: A Report on Knowledge* (Minneapolis: University of Minnesota Press, 1984), xxiv.
41. Emmanuel Levinas, "Useless Suffering," in *The Problem of Evil: A Reader*, ed. Mark Larrimore (Malden, MA: Blackwell, 2001), 376–377.
42. Neiman, *Evil in Modern Thought*, 2.
43. Robert Bellah, *The Broken Covenant*, 1.
44. James Davison Hunter, *Culture Wars: The Struggle to Define America* (New York: Basic Books, 1991). The "culture wars" argument generated substantial controversy and critique; see, e.g., Paul DiMaggio, John Evans, and Bethany Bryson, "Have Americans' Social Attitudes Become More Polarized?," *American Journal of Sociology* 102, no. 3 (1996): 690–755; Morris P. Fiorina, Samuel J. Abrams, and Jeremy Pope, *Culture War?: The Myth of a Polarized America* (New York: Pearson Longman, 2005); Alan Wolfe, *One Nation, after All* (New York: Viking, 1998). Such critiques, however, often focused on individual attitudes rather than the collective narratives that were the subject of Hunter's analysis.
45. See, e.g., Alan I. Abramowitz, *The Disappearing Center: Engaged Citizens, Polarization, and American Democracy* (New Haven, CT: Yale University Press, 2010); Naomi R. Cahn and June Carbone, *Red Families v. Blue Families: Legal Polarization and the Creation of Culture* (New York: Oxford University Press, 2010); Michael Dimock, Jocelyn Kiley, Scott Keeter, and Carol Doherty, *Political Polarization in the American Public* (Washington, DC: Pew Research Center, 2014); William A. Galston, *Can a Polarized Political System Be "Healthy"?* (Washington, DC: Brookings Institution, 2010); Andrew Gelman, *Red State, Blue State, Rich State, Poor State: Why Americans Vote the Way They Do* (Princeton, NJ: Princeton University Press, 2009); Marc J. Hetherington and Jonathan D. Weiler, *Authoritarianism and Polarization in American Politics* (New York: Cambridge University Press, 2009).
46. Ian Hacking, *Rewriting the Soul: Multiple Personality and the Sciences of Memory* (Princeton, NJ: Princeton University Press, 1995), 184–186; Wolfgang Schivelbusch, *The Railway Journey: The Industrialization of Time and Space in the 19th Century* (Berkeley: University of California Press, 1987), 135–136.
47. For detailed conceptual histories, see Hacking, *Rewriting the Soul*; Ruth Leys, *Trauma: A Genealogy* (Chicago: University of Chicago Press, 2000); Allan Young, *The Harmony of Illusions: Inventing Post-Traumatic Stress Disorder* (Princeton, NJ: Princeton University Press, 1995), 13–142.
48. Cathy Caruth, ed., *Trauma: Explorations in Memory* (Baltimore: Johns Hopkins University Press, 1995), 4–5.
49. Didier Fassin and Richard Rechtman, *The Empire of Trauma: An Inquiry into the Condition of Victimhood* (Princeton, NJ: Princeton University Press, 2009), 22. On trauma as a moral and cultural category, see also Joseph E. Davis, *Accounts of Innocence: Sexual Abuse, Trauma, and the Self* (Chicago: University of Chicago

Press, 2005), 134–136; Kirby Farrell, *Post-Traumatic Culture: Injury and Inter-pretation in the Nineties* (Baltimore: Johns Hopkins University Press, 1998), 12; Eva Illouz, *Cold Intimacies: The Making of Emotional Capitalism* (Malden, MA: Polity Press, 2007), 52; Marita Sturken, "Narratives of Recovery: Re-pressed Memory as Cultural Memory," in *Acts of Memory: Cultural Recall in the Present*, ed. Mieke Bal, Jonathan B. Crewe, and Leo Spitzer (Hanover, NH: University Press of New England), 231–232.

50. Alexander et al., *Cultural Trauma and Collective Identity*.
51. Kai T. Erikson, *Everything in Its Path: Destruction of Community in the Buffalo Creek Flood* (New York: Simon and Schuster, 1976), 186–245.
52. Arthur Neal, *National Trauma and Collective Memory: Major Events in the American Century* (Armonk, NY: M. E. Sharpe, 1998).
53. Core texts include Jeffrey C. Alexander, *Trauma: A Social Theory* (Malden, MA: Polity Press, 2012); Alexander et al., *Cultural Trauma and Collective Identity*; Ron Eyerman, *Cultural Trauma: Slavery and the Formation of African-American Identity* (New York: Cambridge University Press, 2001), *The Assassination of Theo van Gogh: From Social Drama to Cultural Trauma* (Durham, NC: Duke University Press, 2008), and *The Cultural Sociology of Political Assassination: From MLK and RFK to Fortuyn and van Gogh* (New York: Palgrave Macmillan, 2011); Ron Eyerman, Jeffrey C. Alexander, and Elizabeth Butler Breese, eds., *Narrating Trauma: On the Impact of Collective Suffering* (Boulder, CO: Paradigm Publishers, 2011); Hiro Saito, "Reiterated Commemoration: Hiroshima as National Trauma," *Sociological Theory* 24, no. 4 (2006): 353–376.
54. Alexander, *Trauma*, 2.
55. Eyerman, *The Cultural Sociology of Political Assassination*, xv. It is worth noting that the collectivity in question need not be a nation-state. Alexander traces how the Holocaust "has come over the last sixty years to be redefined as a traumatic event for all of humankind"; see *Trauma*, 31. Eyerman examines how the cultural trauma of slavery became a touchstone for African-American identity; see *Cultural Trauma*. Because the nation-state remains a predominant organizing principle for collective life, however, cultural traumas often take the form of *national* traumas. See, for instance, Hiro Saito, "Reiterated Com-memoration," on Hiroshima as a cultural trauma in Japan; Eyerman, *The Assassination of Theo van Gogh* and *The Cultural Sociology of Political Assassination*, on political assassinations and their ramifications for national identity.
56. Alexander et al., *Cultural Trauma and Collective Identity*, 1.
57. See, for instance, Alon Confino, "Remembering the Second World War, 1945–1965: Narratives of Victimhood and Genocide," *Cultural Analysis* 4 (2005): 46–75; Bernhard Giesen, *Triumph and Trauma* (Boulder, CO: Paradigm Publishers, 2004); Jeffrey K. Olick, *The Politics of Regret: On Collective Memory and Historical Responsibility* (New York: Routledge, 2007); Lauren Rivera, "Managing 'Spoiled' National Identity: War, Tourism, and Memory in Croatia," *American Sociological Review* 73, no. 4 (2008): 613–634; Barry Schwartz, *Abraham Lincoln in the Post-Heroic Era*; Vered Vinitzky-Seroussi, "Commemorating a Difficult Past: Yitzhak Rabin's Memorials," *American Sociological Review* 67, no. 1 (2002): 30–51; Robin Wagner-Pacifici and Barry Schwartz, "The Vietnam Veterans Memorial: Commemorating a Difficult Past," *American Journal of Sociology* 97, no. 2 (1991): 376–420.
58. Bellah et al., *Habits of the Heart*, 153; Renan, "What Is a Nation?," 83; Schivelbusch, *The Culture of Defeat*, 10–11, 17, 19–20, 29–30.

59. Giesen, *Triumph and Trauma*, 3, 9–10.
60. Ibid., 3.
61. See, e.g., Barry Schwartz, *Abraham Lincoln and the Forge of National Memory* (Chicago: University of Chicago Press, 2000), 10, and *Abraham Lincoln in the Post-Heroic Era*, 8–9.
62. Olick, *The Politics of Regret*, 121–122. On the rise of political apologies, see also Danielle Celermajer, *The Sins of the Nation and the Ritual of Apologies* (New York: Cambridge University Press, 2009), 14–42; Melissa Nobles, *The Politics of Official Apologies* (New York: Cambridge University Press, 2008), 4–13.
63. Ankersmit, "Trauma and Suffering," 76.
64. Ibid., 79. Ankersmit locates the origins of this traumatic orientation "somewhere in the sixteenth and seventeenth centuries" (p. 79). At this point, he argues, the "socio-political reality" was no longer understood as a "God-willed order" but instead perceived as amenable to human intervention (p. 80). This coincides with the history outlined above—the Enlightenment shift away from theistic understandings of evil and suffering. Subsequent crises of meaning in the latter half of the twentieth century, it seems, only reinforced and augmented this phenomenon, and indeed coincided with the rise of trauma discourse in popular, psychiatric, and intellectual arenas.
65. Ankersmit, "Trauma and Suffering," 79.
66. Jean Améry, *At the Mind's Limits: Contemplations by a Survivor on Auschwitz and Its Realities* (Bloomington: Indiana University Press, 1980), 68–69; Olick, *The Politics of Regret*, 163–164. Traumatic events, Olick argues, represent interruptions in modern linear temporality. If an experience is disruptive yet inexplicable and therefore unassimilable, it interrupts time's normal progression. On the emergence of modern linear temporality, see Reinhart Koselleck, *Futures Past: On the Semantics of Historical Time* (New York: Columbia University Press, 2004).
67. Olick, *The Politics of Regret*, 32. As Olick argues, any effort to diagnose cultural or collective traumas must be cognizant of the ontological shift it entails: that is, such diagnoses must be "articulated in terms of collective"—not individual—"narratives." For a critique of the cultural trauma literature that contains important cautionary notes on the moral and historical pitfalls of conceptual imprecision, see Wulf Kansteiner, "Genealogy of a Category Mistake: A Critical Intellectual History of the Cultural Trauma Metaphor," *Rethinking History* 8, no. 2 (2004): 193–221.
68. Alexander et al., *Cultural Trauma and Collective Identity*, 37; Alexander, *Trauma*, 15. Alexander and his colleagues advance this constructivist view of trauma against what they call the "naturalistic fallacy"—the assumption that trauma inheres in events rather than their subsequent representation.
69. Jeffrey K. Olick, "From Usable Pasts to the Return of the Repressed," *The Hedgehog Review* 9, no. 2 (2007): 21, emphasis in original.
70. In this vein, it is again worth highlighting studies of collective memory that illuminate how the particularities of events set limits on their representation, even far into the future. See sources in note 32 above.
71. Émile Durkheim, *The Division of Labor in Society* (New York: Free Press, 1984), 304, and *Suicide: A Study in Sociology* (New York: Free Press, 1951), 258.
72. Eyerman, *The Cultural Sociology of Political Assassination*, 12–13.
73. Olick, *The Politics of Regret*, 154–155, 167. See also Friedrich Wilhelm Nietzsche, *On the Genealogy of Morals: A Polemic* (New York: Oxford University Press, 1999), 22 and passim; Max Scheler, *Ressentiment* (Milwaukee, WI:

Marquette University Press, 1994), 20–21 and passim. Scheler took special care to underscore the importance of subjective perception in generating *ressentiment*: "this psychological dynamite [*ressentiment*] will spread with the discrepancy between the political, constitutional, or traditional status of a group and its factual power. It is the difference between these two factors that is decisive, not one of them alone" (p. 28).

74. Weber, "The Social Psychology of the World Religions," 270–271. Although classical treatments generally portray *ressentiment* as a pathological condition, Olick suggests that its relationship to trauma—which generally evokes sympathy for victims—complicates this assumption. He points to Holocaust survivor Jean Améry's reflections on his own *ressentiment*, which suggest that a refusal to move forward in time may be the only morally adequate response to the most reprehensible atrocities: when suffering is inexplicable, *ressentiment* may be our "only recourse." Olick, *The Politics of Regret*, 166. As Améry puts it: "I hope that my resentment—which is my personal protest against the antimoral natural process of healing that time brings about, and by which I make the genuinely humane and absurd demand that time be turned back—will also perform a historical function." Améry, *At the Mind's Limits*, 77.

75. Olick, *The Politics of Regret*, 154.

76. In more general terms, other observers have argued that a discourse of *ressentiment* is an increasingly salient thread of American political culture and a concomitant of growing polarization. See, e.g., James Davison Hunter, *To Change the World: The Irony, Tragedy, and Possibility of Christianity in the Late Modern World* (New York: Oxford University Press, 2010), 107–109; Bryan S. Turner, "Max Weber and the Spirit of Resentment: The Nietzsche Legacy," *Journal of Classical Sociology* 11, no. 1 (2011): 86–89.

77. On genre, see Mikhail Bakhtin, *Speech Genres and Other Late Essays* (Austin: University of Texas Press, 1986), 60–102; Karlyn Kohrs Campbell and Kathleen Hall Jamieson, *Presidents Creating the Presidency: Deeds Done in Words* (Chicago: University of Chicago Press, 2008), 9–16; Olick, *The Politics of Regret*, 57–60.

78. Olick, *The Politics of Regret*, 59. Olick appropriates Bakhtin's conception of genre for the sociology of memory. *Pace* structuralism, Olick explains, Bakhtin understood genres as "the results of long developmental processes . . . rather than formally defined features of an atemporal system." As Bakhtin put it: "Each individual utterance is a link in the chain of speech communion. Any utterance, in addition to its own theme, always responds (in the broad sense of the word) in one form or another to others' utterances that precede it." Bakhtin, *Speech Genres and Other Late Essays*, 93–94.

79. Eyerman, *The Cultural Sociology of Political Assassination*, 6.

80. Luc Boltanski powerfully describes the position of the "spectator" who witnesses human suffering through the media: "In relation to the media, the spectator occupies the position . . . of someone to whom a *proposal of commitment* is made. A different spectator, who recounts a story to him . . . conveys statements and images to a spectator who may take them up and, through his words, pass on in turn what he has taken from these statements and images and the emotions they aroused in him." Luc Boltanski, *Distant Suffering: Morality, Media and Politics* (Cambridge, UK: Cambridge University Press, 1999), 149, emphasis in original.

81. Campbell and Jamieson, *Presidents Creating the Presidency*, 76.

82. Jeffrey C. Alexander, *The Performance of Politics: Obama's Victory and the Democratic Struggle for Power* (New York: Oxford University Press, 2010), 9 and passim; James W. Ceaser, Glen E. Thurow, Jeffrey K. Tulis, and Joseph M. Bessette, "The Rise of the Rhetorical Presidency," *Presidential Studies Quarterly* 11, no. 2 (1981): 158–171; Roderick P. Hart, *The Sound of Leadership: Presidential Communication in the Modern Age* (Chicago: University of Chicago Press, 1987), 14–21, 83–85; Jason L. Mast, *The Performative Presidency: Crisis and Resurrection During the Clinton Years* (New York: Cambridge University Press, 2013), 7–8, 25, 27–29; Bruce Miroff, "The Presidency and the Public: Leadership as Spectacle," in *The Presidency and the Political System*, 9th ed., ed. Michael Nelson (Washington, DC: CQ Press, 2010), 211–216; Jeffrey K. Tulis, *The Rhetorical Presidency* (Princeton, NJ: Princeton University Press, 1987), 4–6 and passim.

83. Gorski, "Barack Obama and Civil Religion," 203.

84. Robert N. Bellah, "Civil Religion in America," *Daedalus* 96, no. 1 (1967): 1–21; Campbell and Jamieson, *Presidents Creating the Presidency*, 12; Roderick P. Hart, *The Political Pulpit* (West Lafayette, IN: Purdue University Press, 1977), 9; Roderick P. Hart and John L. Pauley, *The Political Pulpit Revisited* (West Lafayette, IN: Purdue University Press, 2005), 16; Michael Novak, *Choosing Our King: Powerful Symbols in Presidential Politics* (New York: Macmillan, 1974), 127.

85. Tulis, *The Rhetorical Presidency*, 4. The concept of the "rhetorical presidency" describes a shift in presidential strategy that Tulis traces to Theodore Roosevelt and, even more, Woodrow Wilson: modern presidents, Tulis and his colleagues argue, sustain and augment their political authority through rhetorical leadership, appealing directly to the American public to promote their legislative or policy agendas. The rise of the rhetorical presidency marked a substantial transformation in the very meaning of governance, as twentieth-century presidents were expected to be popular leaders in a way that their predecessors were not. Important versions of this argument include Ceaser et al., "The Rise of the Rhetorical Presidency"; Tulis, *The Rhetorical Presidency*; Jeffrey K. Tulis, "Reflections on the Rhetorical Presidency in American Political Development," in *Speaking to the People: The Rhetorical Presidency in Historical Perspective*, ed. Richard J. Ellis (Amherst: University of Massachusetts Press, 1998). Subsequently, scholars of communication and rhetoric have argued that rhetorical leadership is not only "about" promoting "specific legislative or policy measures," but also fostering a coherent collective identity, "'form[ing]' a mass' out of an increasingly diversifying American people." Vanessa Beasley, *You, the People: American National Identity in Presidential Rhetoric* (College Station: Texas A&M University Press, 2004), 7. In a similar vein, see also Mary E. Stuckey, *Defining Americans: The Presidency and National Identity* (Lawrence: University of Kansas Press, 2004).

86. Mary E. Stuckey, *The President as Interpreter-in-Chief* (Chatham, NJ: Chatham House Publishers, 1991), 1.

87. Hart, *The Sound of Leadership*, 28, 38.

88. Robin Wagner-Pacifici, "Theorizing the Restlessness of Events," *American Journal of Sociology* 115, no. 5 (2010): 1354. See also Alexander, *The Performance of Politics*; Mabel Berezin, "Cultural Form and Political Meaning: State-subsidized Theater, Ideology, and the Language of Style in Fascist Italy," *American Journal of Sociology* 99, no. 5 (1994): 1237–1286; William H. Sewell, "Historical Events as Transformations of Structures: Inventing Revolution at the Bastille," *Theory and Society* 25, no. 6 (1996): 841–881; Philip Smith, *Why War?*:

The Cultural Logic of Iraq, the Gulf War, and Suez (Chicago: University of Chicago Press, 2005).

89. Lynn Hunt, *Politics, Culture, and Class in the French Revolution* (Berkeley: University of California Press, 1984), 54; see also Olick, *The Politics of Regret*, 39.

90. Here, I take particular inspiration from Clifford Geertz's essay on ideology: "Whatever else ideologies may be—projections of unacknowledged fears, disguises of ulterior motives, phatic expressions of group solidarity—they are, most distinctively, maps of problematic social reality and matrices for the creation of collective conscience." Clifford Geertz, *The Interpretation of Cultures: Selected Essays* (New York: Basic Books, 1973), 220. For a different perspective on the American context—a conception of "moral and religious argumentation . . . as a strategic political tool"—see Colleen J. Shogan, *The Moral Rhetoric of American Presidents* (College Station: Texas A&M University Press, 2006), 4.

91. Bellah, "Civil Religion in America," 10. I discuss the concept of "civil religion" in greater detail in chapter 1.

92. Archival sources included the *Federal News Service*, *CQ Transcriptions*, *The American Presidency Project*, *FDCH Political Transcripts*, the C-SPAN Video Library, and the Office of the Mayor of New York City's news archive. I also consulted television news transcripts, newspapers, and news magazines for coverage of speeches related to September 11 and its commemoration that were not archived elsewhere.

93. Wagner-Pacifici and Schwartz, "The Vietnam Veterans Memorial," 383.

94. On civil society, see Jeffrey C. Alexander and Philip Smith, "The Discourse of American Civil Society: A New Proposal for Cultural Studies," *Theory and Society* 22, no. 2 (1993): 160–167; Jeffrey C. Alexander, *The Civil Sphere* (New York: Oxford University Press, 2006), 4–9.

95. Reception theory has a long and cross-disciplinary history, with roots in literary theory (e.g., Wolfgang Iser, *The Act of Reading: A Theory of Aesthetic Response* [Baltimore: Johns Hopkins University Press, 1978]; Hans-Robert Jauss, *Toward an Aesthetic of Reception* [Minneapolis: University of Minnesota Press, 1982]) and in communication studies (e.g., Stuart Hall, "Encoding, Decoding," in *The Cultural Studies Reader*, ed. Simon During [New York: Routledge, 1993]; Janice A. Radway, *Reading the Romance: Women, Patriarchy, and Popular Literature* [Chapel Hill: University of North Carolina Press, 1991]). Influential sociological statements include Wendy Griswold, "The Fabrication of Meaning: Literary Interpretation in the United States, Great Britain, and the West Indies," *American Journal of Sociology* 92, no. 5 (1987): 1077–1117; JoEllen Shively, "Cowboys and Indians: Perceptions of Western Films among American Indians and Anglos," *American Sociological Review* 57, no. 6 (1992): 725–734. In memory studies, there are vibrant traditions of research on oral history and "popular" or "vernacular" memory; on the interplay between official and vernacular memory, and the ways that ordinary citizens have transformed official symbols in the U.S. context, see especially John Bodnar, *Remaking America: Public Memory, Commemoration, and Patriotism in the Twentieth Century* (Princeton, NJ: Princeton University Press, 1992).

96. Official politics, as Olick argues, is a "field" in the sociological sense—a specific site of struggle whose rules, structure, and boundaries are the subject of ongoing contestation. Olick, *The Politics of Regret*, 92–97. The concept of "field" is itself a source of wide-ranging theoretical debate; Olick's adaptation draws primarily from Pierre Bourdieu. For a definition, see Pierre Bourdieu and

Loïc J. D. Wacquant, *An Invitation to Reflexive Sociology* (Chicago: University of Chicago Press, 1992), 97.

97. As I explain in chapter 2, I borrow the term "dualistic" from Weber's discussion of theodicy; see Weber, *The Sociology of Religion*, 144–145, and "Religious Rejections of the World and Their Directions," 358–359.

98. Wagner-Pacifici, "Theorizing the Restlessness of Events," 1354.

99. Ankersmit, "Trauma and Suffering," 79.

100. On this point, see especially Jeffrey C. Alexander, *The Meanings of Social Life: A Cultural Sociology* (New York: Oxford University Press, 2003); Isaac Ariail Reed, *Interpretation and Social Knowledge: On the Use of Theory in the Human Sciences* (Chicago: University of Chicago Press, 2011).

101. William H. Sewell, *Logics of History: Social Theory and Social Transformation* (Chicago: University of Chicago Press, 2005), 369.

102. Peter L. Berger and Thomas Luckmann, *The Social Construction of Reality: A Treatise in the Sociology of Knowledge* (Garden City, NY: Anchor Books, 1967).

CHAPTER 1

1. Bellah, *The Broken Covenant*, 11–12, 24–25, 36–60; Conrad Cherry, *God's New Israel: Religious Interpretations of American Destiny* (Chapel Hill: University of North Carolina Press, 1998); Michael Walzer, *Exodus and Revolution* (New York: Basic Books, 1986), 6, 106.

2. Anderson, *Imagined Communities*, 11.

3. Bellah, *The Broken Covenant*, 27. See also Gorski, "Civil Religion Today," 4, and "Barack Obama and Civil Religion," 178.

4. Bellah, "Civil Religion in America," 18.

5. Ibid. The term "civil religion" originated with Rousseau; Bellah's adaptation—first articulated in his 1967 *Daedalus* essay, then expanded in *The Broken Covenant*—brought the term into the sociological lexicon. For reviews drawing together the approaches to "civil religion" that developed in the years after Bellah's original essay, see Philip Hammond, "The Sociology of American Civil Religion: A Bibliographical Essay," *Sociological Analysis* 37, no. 2 (1976): 169–182; James Mathisen, "Twenty Years after Bellah: Whatever Happened to American Civil Religion?," *Sociology of Religion* 50, no. 2 (1989): 129–146. Similar terms abound: Sidney Mead refers to "the theology of the Republic"; Winthrop Hudson to "culture-religion"; Martin Marty to "religion-in-general"; Robin Williams and Will Herberg to the "common religion"; Roderick Hart to "civic piety"; Conrad Cherry to a "national religious faith." My intention is not to equate these terms and authors—indeed, there are important tensions and disagreements among them—but to point out that a wide range of scholars have underscored the powerful role of religious symbolism in American political culture. Sidney E. Mead, *The Nation with the Soul of a Church* (New York: Harper and Row, 1975), 18; Winthrop S. Hudson, *American Protestantism* (Chicago: University of Chicago Press, 1961), vi; Martin E. Marty, *The New Shape of American Religion* (New York: Harper, 1959), 31; Robin Murphy Williams, *American Society: A Sociological Interpretation* (New York: Knopf, 1956), 312; Will Herberg, *Protestant, Catholic, Jew: An Essay in American Religious Sociology* (Garden City, NY: Doubleday, 1960), 75; Hart, *The Political Pulpit*, 5; Cherry, *God's New Israel*, 1.

6. But see Philip Gorski's work reviving this line of theorizing, especially "Barack Obama and Civil Religion."

7. An important strand of critique suggested that Bellah's neo-Durkheimian view of civil religion posited an overly integrative portrait of American political culture, obscuring multiplicity and conflict. As Philip Gorski notes, Bellah's subsequent work more fully captured the multiplicity of American political culture; in *Habits of the Heart*, for instance, Bellah and his colleagues wrote of "American traditions" in the plural, and traced the interplay and tensions among biblical, republican, utilitarian, and expressive vocabularies. See Gorski, "Civil Religion Today," 1, and "Barack Obama and Civil Religion," 180; Bellah et al., *Habits of the Heart*, 27–51. In borrowing Bellah's language of "civil religion" and "civil scriptures," my intention is not to suggest a monolithic view of American political culture, past or present, but to point to a core of texts, ideas, and images—a political canon—that continue to have a tremendous influence on the meanings attributed to collective suffering at the level of official discourse. Like any canon, these texts provide a particular and limited view of the historical moments within which they were written, and they achieved canonical status retrospectively, through struggles among actors with different visions of the American nation, its history, and the prospects for its future. And like any canonical texts, the civil scriptures continue to generate profound interpretive conflicts. Indeed, I argue at the end of this chapter that they have endured at least in part *because* they are ambiguous and multivocal; they are thus able to be appropriated by actors who otherwise speak out of very different traditions or philosophies, and who indeed may pursue opposing, even irreconcilable, agendas. The civil scriptures, in other words, are the canon around whose interpretation many contemporary political-cultural debates, informed by disparate traditions and philosophies, take shape. In the pages that follow, I trace how the civil scriptures have informed different modes of political consolation, and how they have been deployed to support opposing views in conflicts surrounding the effort to rebuild the World Trade Center site in lower Manhattan.

8. On the influence of the Puritans, see Bellah, *The Broken Covenant*, 13–21; Bellah et al., *Habits of the Heart* 28–30; Sacvan Bercovitch, *The American Jeremiad* (Madison: University of Wisconsin Press, 1980) and *The Puritan Origins of the American Self* (New Haven, CT: Yale University Press, 1975); Perry Miller, *Errand into the Wilderness* (Cambridge, MA: Harvard University Press, 1956) and *Nature's Nation* (Cambridge, MA: Harvard University Press, 1967); Alexis de Tocqueville, *Democracy in America* (New York: Penguin, 2004), 322.

9. All quotations in this and the preceding paragraph are from John Winthrop, "A Model of Christian Charity," in *The Puritans in America: A Narrative Anthology*, ed. Alan Heimert and Andrew Delbanco (Cambridge, MA: Harvard University Press, 1985), 91–92.

10. Bellah, *The Broken Covenant*, 15. See also Cherry, *God's New Israel*, 27.

11. Bercovitch, *The American Jeremiad*, 3–4; Miller, *Errand Into the Wilderness*, 8–9.

12. Bercovitch, *The Puritan Origins of the American Self*, 225.

13. Bercovitch, *The American Jeremiad*, 6.

14. Ibid., 6–7. In interpreting the Puritan jeremiad as a fundamentally optimistic genre, Bercovitch breaks with Perry Miller's foundational analysis, which—according to Bercovitch—"excludes (or denigrates)" the "pervasive theme of affirmation and exultation." Certainly my own more contemporary research suggests that the optimism Bercovitch identified in the Puritan variant of the jeremiad has been a vital interpretive resource for American political

consolation. See also Kevin Rozario, *The Culture of Calamity: Disaster and the Making of Modern America* (Chicago: University of Chicago Press, 2007), 63–65.

15. Bercovitch, *The American Jeremiad*, 8.
16. Ibid., emphasis in original.
17. Rozario, *The Culture of Calamity*, 20.
18. Bellah, "Civil Religion in America," 9. As Michael Walzer documents: "In 1776, Benjamin Franklin proposed that the Great Seal of the United States should show Moses with his rod lifted and the Egyptian army drowning in the sea; while Jefferson urged a more pacific design: the column of Israelites marching through the wilderness led by God's pillars of clouds and fire." Walzer, *Exodus and Revolution*, 6.
19. Eviatar Zerubavel, *Hidden Rhythms: Schedules and Calendars in Social Life* (Berkeley: University of California Press, 1985), 86.
20. Ibid. See also Pitrim Sorokin and Robert K. Merton, "Social Time: A Methodological and Functional Analysis," *American Journal of Sociology* 42, no. 5 (1937): 623.
21. Bellah, *The Broken Covenant*, 3–4; Barry Schwartz, "The Social Context of Commemoration: A Study in Collective Memory," *Social Forces* 61, no. 2 (1982): 380–384, 389, 396; Lyn Spillman, *Nation and Commemoration: Creating National Identities in the United States and Australia* (New York: Cambridge University Press, 1997), 69–73, 112–113, 115, 119, and "When Do Collective Memories Last?: Founding Moments in the United States and Australia," in *States of Memory*, 161–162, 174–176.
22. Bellah, *The Broken Covenant*, 4.
23. The National Archives and Records Administration's transcription of the Declaration is available at http://www.archives.gov/exhibits/charters/declaration_transcript.html.
24. Ibid.
25. Ibid.
26. Bellah, *The Broken Covenant*, 3–4; Walzer, *Exodus and Revolution*, 106.
27. Carolyn Marvin and David Ingle argue that "violent blood sacrifice makes enduring groups cohere," and thus that "the nation is the shared memory of blood sacrifice, periodically renewed." Holding the nation together, renewing its members' sense of solidarity, "requires the willing deaths of a significant portion of its members." Carolyn Marvin and David W. Ingle, *Blood Sacrifice and the Nation: Totem Rituals and the American Flag* (New York: Cambridge University Press, 1999), 1, 4, 5. Whether or not periodic violence is *the* core of the nation or essential to its endurance, blood sacrifice has certainly figured centrally in constituting American national identity. The text of the Declaration reveals the importance assigned to blood sacrifice from the outset.
28. Bercovitch, *The American Jeremiad*, 127.
29. John Adams, "Letter from John Adams to Abigail Adams, 'Your Favour of June 17 . . . ,'" and "'Had a Declaration . . . ,'" *Adams Family Papers, An Electronic Archive*, Massachusetts Historical Society, http://www.masshist.org/digitaladams/archive. Though the Revolution certainly took on augmented significance in memory, in this context, it is worth noting Charles Royster's observation that many of the revolutionaries believed that their moment held special significance: "The revolutionaries," Royster writes, "got much pleasure and inspiration from imagining their children's gratitude for their service in the decisive years." While they recognized that "each generation had to defend

self-government anew," they also "knew that they would stand above all their descendants." Charles Royster, *A Revolutionary People at War* (Chapel Hill: University of North Carolina Press, 1979), 8.

30. Sarah J. Purcell, *Sealed with Blood: War, Sacrifice, and Memory in Revolutionary America* (Philadelphia: University of Pennsylvania Press, 2002), 3.

31. Ibid., 21.

32. Quoted in Purcell, *Sealed with Blood*, 42.

33. Quoted in Purcell, *Sealed with Blood*, 41.

34. Thomas Paine, *The American Crisis* (London: R. Carlile, 1819), 11.

35. Ibid., 12.

36. Ibid., 15.

37. Bellah, "Civil Religion in America," 9.

38. Michael Kammen, *A Season of Youth: The American Revolution and the Historical Imagination* (New York: Oxford University Press, 1980), 189, 16; see also Bercovitch, *The American Jeremiad*, 133–134. Kammen draws on anthropologist Victor Turner's sense of a "rite of passage," explaining: "Certain political transitions retrospectively acquire new symbolic meaning, so that the fate of an individual may become a metaphor for the destiny of a tribe, a community, or even a nation" (p. 190). See Victor Turner, *Dramas, Fields, and Metaphors: Symbolic Action in Human Society* (Ithaca, NY: Cornell University Press, 1974), 13–14, and *The Ritual Process: Structure and Anti-Structure* (New York: Aldine de Gruyter, 1995), 94–95. In a similar vein, Catherine Albanese interprets the Revolution as a hierophany—that is, a manifestation of the sacred—that "provided the fundamental basis for American civil religion as we know it," a "new mythic center" for the patriots and their descendants. Catherine L. Albanese, *Sons of the Fathers: The Civil Religion of the American Revolution* (Philadelphia: Temple University Press, 1976), 6, 9. On hierophany, see Mircea Eliade, *The Myth of the Eternal Return: Cosmos and History* (New York: Harper, 1959), 4. Finally, W. Lloyd Warner also documented the importance of the Revolutionary era, suggesting that it was the most significant source of collective symbolism in "Yankee City's" tercentenary ritual. W. Lloyd Warner, *The Living and the Dead: A Study of the Symbolic Life of Americans* (Westport, CT: Greenwood Press, 1975), 133–134.

39. Bellah, "Civil Religion in America," 9; see also Barry Schwartz, *George Washington: The Making of an American Symbol* (New York: Free Press, 1987), 29, 89, 116, 176–177.

40. This and the preceding three quotations are all from Edward T. Linenthal, *Sacred Ground: Americans and Their Battlefields* (Urbana: University of Illinois Press, 1991), 11–18. It is worth noting that during the Revolution itself, officers were the quintessential martyrs; the image of the Revolutionary martyr became more democratic in collective memory. See the discussion in Purcell, *Sealed with Blood*, 144–149, 173.

41. Linenthal, *Sacred Ground*, 21.

42. Ibid. As Purcell argues, this imagery of martial sacrifice and national birth originated in the rhetoric of the Revolutionary era itself; see Purcell, *Sealed with Blood*. But as I discuss below, it certainly became a more prominent theme in American civil religion as the nation sought to come to terms with massive carnage during the Civil War and in its aftermath. And the struggle to come to terms with the Civil War remained central during the centennial commemorations that Linenthal describes, revealing the dynamic and ongoing interplay

between past and present. For a detailed analysis of the centennial commemorations, see Spillman, *Nation and Commemoration*, 57–93.

43. Schwartz, *Abraham Lincoln in the Post-Heroic Era*, 77; see also Neal, *National Trauma and Collective Memory*, 22–23.

44. Catherine L. Albanese, *America: Religions and Religion* (Belmont, CA: Wadsworth, 1992), 446. As Bellah points out, John Adams articulated this sense of mission a decade before the American Revolution, when he wrote: "I always consider the settlement of America with Reverence and Wonder—as the Opening of a grand scene and Design in Providence for the Illumination of the Ignorant and the Emancipation of the slavish Part of Mankind all over the earth." John Adams, "John Adams dairy 10, includes legal notes, 24 January–25 February 1765, August 1765," *Adams Family Papers: An Electronic Archive*, Massachusetts Historical Society, http://www.masshist.org/digitaladams/archive. See the discussion in Bellah, *The Broken Covenant*, 33. Ernest Tuveson offers important historical context here: "The use of the word 'scene' hints that it is part of a drama, and it is not unreasonable to assign such an idea to an eschatological source, for no other philosophy of history in the Western World saw the historical process as one dramatic action. . . . To give the colonies, now advanced to their grander title, such a crucial part would seem a presumption indeed. For, however noble their origins, they were, as Adams certainly knew, a very small and, even to well informed Europeans, very obscure part of the world; they had not yet even effectively asserted their constitutional position within the British system. The notion of their climactic importance, occurring to so sensible a man as Adams, must have come from an ideology; and Adams' references to providential purpose betray the background of that ideology, now intermingled with Whiggism." Ernest Lee Tuveson, *Redeemer Nation: The Idea of America's Millennial Role* (Chicago: University of Chicago Press, 1968), 102–103.

45. Bellah, *The Broken Covenant*, 33–34.

46. George Washington, "Inaugural Address," April 30, 1789. Online by Gerhard Peters and John T. Woolley, *The American Presidency Project*, http://www.presidency.ucsb.edu/ws/?pid=25800, emphasis added.

47. Tuveson, *Redeemer Nation*.

48. For extensive discussions of "American exceptionalism" and its history, see Seymour Martin Lipset, *American Exceptionalism: A Double-Edged Sword* (New York: W. W. Norton and Company, 1997); Deborah L. Madsen, *American Exceptionalism* (Jackson: University Press of Mississippi, 1998). See also the influential passages in Tocqueville, *Democracy in America*, 517–518.

49. Examples include Walter Russell Mead, *Special Providence: American Foreign Policy and How It Changed the World* (New York: Knopf, 2001); Tuveson, *Redeemer Nation*.

50. Bercovitch, *The American Jeremiad*, 163–164; Janice Hocker Rushing, "The Mythic Evolution of 'The New Frontier' in Mass Mediated Rhetoric," *Critical Studies in Mass Communication* 3, no. 3 (1986): 265; Schwartz, "The Social Context of Commemoration," 389; Richard Slotkin, *Regeneration through Violence: The Mythology of the American Frontier, 1600–1860* (Middletown, CT: Wesleyan University Press, 1973), *The Fatal Environment: The Mythology of the American Frontier in the Age of Industrialization, 1800–1890* (New York: Atheneum, 1985), and *Gunfighter Nation: The Myth of the Frontier in Twentieth-Century America* (New York: Atheneum, 1992); Henry Nash Smith, *Virgin Land: The American West as Symbol and Myth* (Cambridge, MA: Harvard University Press, 1950).

51. Slotkin, *Regeneration through Violence*, 5.
52. Ibid.
53. Ibid., 57.
54. Schwartz, "The Social Context of Commemoration," 389.
55. Ibid.
56. The literature on the frontier and its significance in American history is vast, and it is worth underscoring that my concern here is more limited: namely, to articulate the role that frontier mythology has played in imbuing crises and calamities with meaning.
57. See, e.g., Janice Hocker Rushing, "The Rhetoric of the American Western Myth," *Communication Monographs* 50, no. 1 (1983): 14–32; Smith, *Virgin Land*, 110–111.
58. Leroy G. Dorsey, "The Frontier Myth in Presidential Rhetoric: Theodore Roosevelt's Campaign for Conservation," *Western Journal of Communication* 59, no. 1 (1995): 3.
59. Ryan Malphurs, "The Media's Frontier Construction of President George W. Bush," *The Journal of American Culture* 31, no. 2 (2008): 187.
60. Rushing, "Mythic Evolution," 270.
61. Ronald H. Carpenter, "America's Tragic Metaphor: Our Twentieth-Century Combatants as Frontiersmen," *Quarterly Journal of Speech* 76, no. 1 (1990): 3.
62. Rushing, "Mythic Evolution," 272.
63. Richard Maxwell Brown, *Strain of Violence: Historical Studies of American Violence and Vigilantism* (New York: Oxford University Press, 1975), 36.
64. Rushing, "Mythic Evolution," 272.
65. Richard R. Flores, "The Alamo: Myth, Public History, and the Politics of Inclusion," *Radical History Review* 77 (2000): 94. See also Holly Beachley Brear, *Inherit the Alamo: Myth and Ritual at an American Shrine* (Austin: University of Texas Press, 1995), 4, 22.
66. Bercovitch, *The American Jeremiad*, 163.
67. Ibid., 163–164, emphasis in original.
68. Quoted in Julius W. Pratt, "The Origin of 'Manifest Destiny,'" *American Historical Review* 32, no. 4 (1927): 796. According to Pratt, the term "manifest destiny" originated in an 1845 issue of the *Democratic Review* that addressed lingering opposition to the annexation of Texas, but gained wider currency a few months later when it was invoked in the New York *Morning News*. Almost certainly inspired by this editorial, U.S. Representative Robert C. Winthrop of Massachusetts introduced the term in political discourse, invoking "that new revelation of right which has been designated as *the right of our manifest destiny to spread over this whole continent*" during a January 1846 speech on the House floor (p. 795), emphasis in original. On the precursors and afterlife of "manifest destiny," see Anders Stephanson, *Manifest Destiny: American Expansion and the Empire of Right* (New York: Hill and Wang, 1995).
69. Frederick Jackson Turner, *The Significance of the Frontier in American History* (Madison: State Historical Society of Wisconsin, 1894). The Turner thesis generated substantial debate and critique among generations of historians; see, e.g., Richard W. Etulain, ed., *Does the Frontier Experience Make America Exceptional?* (New York: Bedford/St. Martin's, 1999); Patricia Nelson Limerick, *The Legacy of Conquest: The Unbroken Past of the American West* (New York: W. W. Norton and Company, 1987); Clyde A. Milner, ed., *A New Significance: Reenvisioning the History of the American West* (New York: Oxford University Press,

1996); George Rogers Taylor, ed., *The Turner Thesis: Concerning the Role of the Frontier in American History*, 3rd ed. (Lexington, MA: Heath, 1972). As Ronald Carpenter explains, however, Turner's intention was not only to make a statement about historiography or even provide a foundation for future research. Instead, his thesis also contained "another thematic element . . . one which in its ultimate effect became the rhetorical source of a mythic, national self-image among a mass readership." Ronald H. Carpenter, *The Eloquence of Frederick Jackson Turner* (San Marino, CA: Huntington Library, 1983), 52. In this vein, some historians have categorized Turner as a "Jeremiah" for his day; see, e.g., Smith, *Virgin Land*, 4.

70. Carpenter, *The Eloquence of Frederick Jackson Turner*, 50.

71. "[T]o the frontier the American intellect owes its striking characteristics," Turner wrote, and described them as follows: "That coarseness and strength combined with acuteness and inquisitiveness; that practical, inventive turn of mind, quick to find expedients; that masterful grasp of material things, lacking in the artistic but powerful to effect great ends; that restless, nervous energy; that dominant individualism, working for good and for evil, and withal that buoyancy and exuberance which comes with freedom—these are traits of the frontier, or traits called out elsewhere because of the existence of the frontier." Turner, *The Significance of the Frontier in American History*, 33.

72. Janice Hocker Rushing, "Ronald Reagan's 'Star Wars' Address: Mythic Containment of Technical Reasoning," *Quarterly Journal of Speech* 72, no. 4 (1986): 415–433.

73. Carpenter, "America's Tragic Metaphor"; J. Justin Gustainis, "John F. Kennedy and the Green Berets: The Rhetorical Use of the Hero Myth," *Communication Studies* 40, no. 1 (1989): 41–53.

74. Leroy G. Dorsey, "The Myth of War and Peace in Presidential Discourse: John Kennedy's 'New Frontier' Myth and the Peace Corps," *Southern Communication Journal* 62, no. 1 (1996): 42–55.

75. An estimated 620,000 soldiers lost their lives, a figure approximately equal to the number of Americans who perished in the Revolution, the War of 1812, the Mexican War, the Spanish-American War, World War I, World War II, and the Korean War combined. A comparable proportion of the contemporary American population—two percent—would be six million. Drew Gilpin Faust, *This Republic of Suffering: Death and the American Civil War* (New York: Vintage Books, 2008), xi.

76. Bellah, "Civil Religion in America," 10, 11.

77. Ibid., 10.

78. Barry Schwartz, "Rereading the Gettysburg Address: Social Change and Collective Memory," *Qualitative Sociology* 19, no. 3 (1996): 398.

79. Abraham Lincoln, "Address at the Dedication of the National Cemetery at Gettysburg, Pennsylvania," November 19, 1863. Online by Gerhard Peters and John T. Woolley, *The American Presidency Project*, http://www.presidency.ucsb.edu/ws/?pid=73959.

80. Edwin Black, "Gettysburg and Silence," *Quarterly Journal of Speech* 80, no. 1 (1994): 22.

81. Lincoln, "Address at the Dedication of the National Cemetery."

82. Ibid. On Lincoln's interpretation of the bloodshed at Gettysburg as "a form of regeneration," see John Channing Briggs, *Lincoln's Speeches Reconsidered* (Baltimore: Johns Hopkins University Press, 2005), 312.

83. On Lincoln's sources of inspiration, see Gabor Boritt, *The Gettysburg Gospel: The Lincoln Speech that Nobody Knows* (New York: Simon and Schuster, 2006), 120–122; Faust, *This Republic of Suffering*, 189; Simon Stow, "Pericles at Gettysburg and Ground Zero: Tragedy, Patriotism, and Public Mourning," *American Political Science Review* 101, no. 2 (2007): 201–204; Garry Wills, *Lincoln at Gettysburg: The Words that Remade America* (New York: Simon and Schuster, 1992).

84. Schwartz, "Rereading the Gettysburg Address," 401–403, and "The New Gettysburg Address: Fusing History and Memory," *Poetics* 33, no. 1 (2005): 65–66.

85. Schwartz, "Rereading the Gettysburg Address," 401.

86. The influence of the Gettysburg Address on American political speechmaking transcends the consolation genre. Barry Schwartz's body of work on Lincoln in American memory traces these influences in detail; see especially "Rereading the Gettysburg Address." In brief, Schwartz identifies three distinct "readings" of the Gettysburg Address. The first interprets the address as an affirmation of "[n]ational integrity" and a justification for continuing the fight (p. 402). The second, which emerged during the Progressive era, interprets the address through a populist lens, as a cry for equality that "affirm[ed] the power of democracy to raise the common man above the man of privilege, learning, and refinement" (pp. 404–405). Finally, the third reading, which took shape during the civil rights movement, interprets the address as an appeal for racial integration. For more detail, see also Barry Schwartz, "Memory as a Cultural System: Abraham Lincoln in World War II," *American Sociological Review* 61, no. 5 (1996): 916, 919, "The New Gettysburg Address," and *Abraham Lincoln in the Post-Heroic Era*, 79–81, 126.

87. Faust, *This Republic of Suffering*, 189.

88. On the Bixby letter's role in consolation discourse during the Second World War, see Schwartz, *Abraham Lincoln in the Post-Heroic Era*, 79–82. According to Schwartz, the Gettysburg Address and the letter to Lydia Bixby were the core texts in Lincoln's "secular theodicy," at least as it was remediated during World War II.

89. Subsequent investigations revealed that Bixby lost two sons. The letter's authorship has also been a source of considerable controversy; some analysts have attributed it to Lincoln's secretary, John Hay. For an argument that Hay was the true author, see Michael Burlingame, "The Trouble with the Bixby Letter," *American Heritage* 50, no. 4 (1999): 64–67. For an argument that Lincoln in fact penned the letter, see Joe Nickell, *Unsolved History: Investigating Mysteries of the Past* (Lexington: University Press of Kentucky, 2005), 90–105.

90. Abraham Lincoln, "The Celebrated 'Bixby' Letter," November 21, 1864, The Alfred Whital Stern Collection of Lincolniana, Rare Book and Special Collections Division, Library of Congress, http://hdl.loc.gov/loc.rbc/lprbscsm.scsm0360.

91. On this point, see Briggs, *Lincoln's Speeches Reconsidered*, 334.

92. Ibid., 329.

93. Ibid., 334.

94. Julia Ward Howe, "Battle Hymn of the Republic," *Atlantic Monthly* 9, no. 52 (1862): 10.

95. Bellah, "Civil Religion in America," 10–11; Eyal Naveh, *Crown of Thorns: Political Martyrdom in America from Abraham Lincoln to Martin Luther King, Jr.* (New York: New York University Press, 1990), 50–82.

96. Eric Foner, *The Fiery Trial: Abraham Lincoln and American Slavery* (New York: W. W. Norton and Company, 2010), 333.

97. Phineas D. Gurley, *Faith in God; Dr. Gurley's Sermon at the Funeral of Abraham Lincoln* (Philadelphia: Department of History of the Office of the General Assembly of the Presbyterian Church in the U.S.A., 1940), 17, 18.

98. Ibid., 20.

99. Ibid., 23, emphasis in original.

100. Ibid.

101. All quotations in this paragraph are from Matthew Simpson, *Funeral Address Delivered at the Burial of Abraham Lincoln* (New York: Carlton and Power, 1865), 9–21.

102. On the theme of covenant and judgment, see Bellah, *The Broken Covenant*, 53–54. On the parallels between Lincoln's second inaugural and the Puritan jeremiad, see Ronald C. White, Jr., *Lincoln's Greatest Speech: The Second Inaugural* (New York: Simon and Schuster, 2002), 151–153.

103. Faust, *This Republic of Suffering*, 54, 189.

104. On the tragic themes in Lincoln's second inaugural, see Edwin Black, "The Ultimate Voice of Lincoln," *Rhetoric and Public Affairs* 3, no. 1 (2000): 56; John Burt, *Lincoln's Tragic Pragmatism* (Cambridge, MA: Harvard University Press, 2013), 684–707.

105. Abraham Lincoln, "Inaugural Address," March 4, 1865, Online by Gerhard Peters and John T. Woolley, *The American Presidency Project*, http://www. presidency.ucsb.edu/ws/?pid=25819, emphasis in original.

106. Ibid.

107. See, e.g., the discussions of this point in Briggs, *Lincoln's Speeches Reconsidered*, 315–316; Foner, *The Fiery Trial*, 323–326; Garry Wills, "Lincoln's Greatest Speech?," *Atlantic Monthly* 284, no. 3 (1999): 63–64; White, *Lincoln's Greatest Speech*, 23, 150–151.

108. Lincoln, "Inaugural Address," emphasis in original.

109. Ibid.

110. Ibid.

111. Burt, *Lincoln's Tragic Pragmatism*, 693, 697.

112. Burt, *Lincoln's Tragic Pragmatism*, 698; Wills, "Lincoln's Greatest Speech?," 69; White, *Lincoln's Greatest Speech*, 144–145.

113. Reinhold Niebuhr, "The Religion of Abraham Lincoln," *The Christian Century* 82, no. 6 (1965): 172.

114. Ibid., 173.

115. Faust, *This Republic of Suffering*, 54, 189.

116. For a detailed analysis of the complex understanding of agency espoused in Lincoln's second inaugural, see Andrew C. Hansen, "Dimensions of Agency in Lincoln's Second Inaugural," *Philosophy and Rhetoric* 37, no. 3 (2004): 223–254.

117. Lincoln, "Inaugural Address."

118. Of course, Lincoln himself did not survive to oversee this reconciliation, and it is impossible to know what Reconstruction would have looked like had he remained president. For reflections on how Lincoln's second inaugural might have guided his approach to Reconstruction, see Wills, "Lincoln's Greatest Speech?," 67–68. On the triumph of a "reconciliationist" narrative that privileged regional reunification over racial justice and "emancipationist" vision, see David W. Blight, *Race and Reunion: The Civil War in American Memory* (Cambridge, MA: Harvard University Press, 2001), 2 and passim.

119. Burt, *Lincoln's Tragic Pragmatism*, 680.

120. Ibid., 25; see also 699.

121. Earl Warren, "Eulogy to John F. Kennedy," *Vital Speeches of the Day* 30, no. 4 (1963): 99.

122. Richard Cardinal Cushing, "Eulogy to John F. Kennedy," *Vital Speeches of the Day* 30, no. 4 (1963): 100. Barry Schwartz details the parallels between the funeral rituals arranged for the two fallen presidents: Kennedy's "coffin was carried by horse-drawn caisson to the Capitol and placed on the same catafalque that had borne Abraham Lincoln's remains. Common ritual paraphernalia revealed continuity and common fate: two presidents, two martyrs. Ritual symbols constituted the link, transformed external parallels involving bullets, fleeing assailants, and hurried oath-takings into mystical bonds that unite generations." Schwartz, "Memory as a Cultural System," 921.

123. Lyndon B. Johnson, "Remarks at a Candlelight Memorial Service for President Kennedy," December 22, 1963. Online by Gerhard Peters and John T. Woolley, *The American Presidency Project*, http://www.presidency.ucsb.edu/ws/?pid= 26576.

124. Ibid.

125. For a sociologically informed account of the event, see Diane Vaughan, *The Challenger Launch Decision: Risky Technology, Culture, and Deviance at NASA* (Chicago: University of Chicago Press, 1996).

126. All quotations in this and the preceding paragraph are from Ronald Reagan, "Address to the Nation on the Explosion of the Space Shuttle Challenger," January 28, 1986. Online by Gerhard Peters and John T. Woolley, *The American Presidency Project*, http://www.presidency.ucsb.edu/ws/?pid=37646.

127. Reagan also—and perhaps more memorably—invoked lines from John Gillespie Magee's sonnet "High Flight" as he concluded his remarks: "The crew of the space shuttle Challenger honored us by the manner in which they lived their lives. We will never forget them, nor the last time we saw them, this morning, as they prepared for their journey and waved goodbye and 'slipped the surly bonds of earth' to 'touch the face of God.'" Reagan, "Address to the Nation on the Explosion of the Space Shuttle Challenger." For a detailed analysis of Reagan's address, see Mary E. Stuckey, *Slipping the Surly Bonds: Reagan's Challenger Address* (College Station: Texas A&M University Press, 2006).

128. For a comprehensive analysis of how various constituencies interpreted, memorialized, and otherwise sought to come to terms with the bombing, see Edward T. Linenthal, *The Unfinished Bombing: Oklahoma City in American Memory* (New York: Oxford University Press, 2001).

129. Al Gore, "Oklahoma City National Memorial Dedication," October 25, 1998, National Archives and Records Administration, http://clinton4.nara.gov/WH/EOP/OVP/speeches/okcity.html, emphasis in original.

130. "Oklahoma City National Memorial Dedication," C-SPAN Video Library, April 19, 2000, http://www.c-spanvideo.org/program/156664-1.

131. William J. Clinton, "Remarks at the Oklahoma City National Memorial Dedication Ceremony in Oklahoma City, Oklahoma," April 19, 2000. Online by Gerhard Peters and John T. Woolley, *The American Presidency Project*, http://www.presidency.ucsb.edu/ws/?pid=58391.

132. Karen Cerulo, *Identity Designs: The Sights and Sounds of a Nation* (New Brunswick, NJ: Rutgers University Press, 2005), 163.

133. Spillman, "When Do Collective Memories Last?," 163. See also Spillman, *Nation and Commemoration*, 69–72, 116, 119. Schwartz makes a similar point; see "The Social Context of Commemoration," 396.

134. See, e.g., Hunter, *Culture Wars*.

135. All quotations in this paragraph are from Stuart A. Wright, *Patriots, Politics, and the Oklahoma City Bombing* (New York: Cambridge University Press, 2007), 4–19.

136. There is now a substantial literature in sociology documenting how multivalent symbols enable diverse constituencies to come together in memorializing "difficult pasts"; a crucial impetus for this literature was Wagner-Pacifici and Schwartz, "The Vietnam Veterans Memorial." See also the agenda-setting discussion in Vinitzky-Seroussi, "Commemorating a Difficult Past." Differentiating between "multivocal" commemorations and "fragmented" commemorations—in which distinct discourses about the past are aimed at disparate audiences in separate spaces—Vinitzky-Seroussi argues that such multivocal commemorations are more likely to occur in relatively consensual political cultures, when the past is perceived as less relevant to the present, and when nonstate agents of memory have sufficient power and resources to pursue their commemorative agendas even if conflicts persist. I take up this literature in more detail in chapter 6, when I discuss September 11 commemorations.

CHAPTER 2

1. Quoted in Patrick J. Maney, *The Roosevelt Presence: The Life and Legacy of FDR* (Berkeley: University of California Press, 1992), 55–56.

2. Quoted in Maney, *The Roosevelt Presence*, 56.

3. Quoted in Maney, *The Roosevelt Presence*, 55. See also Betty Houchin Winfield, *FDR and the News Media* (New York: Columbia University Press, 1994), 4.

4. Stuckey, *The President as Interpreter-in-Chief*, 1. See also Hart, *The Sound of Leadership*, 3, 58.

5. Stuckey, *The President as Interpreter-in-Chief*, 33.

6. Franklin D. Roosevelt, "Radio Address to the Democratic National Convention Accepting the Nomination," July 19, 1940. Online by Gerhard Peters and John T. Woolley, *The American Presidency Project*, http://www.presidency.ucsb.edu/ws/?pid=15980.

7. All quotations in this paragraph are from Franklin D. Roosevelt, "Annual Message to Congress on the State of the Union," January 6, 1941. Online by Gerhard Peters and John T. Woolley, *The American Presidency Project*, http://www.presidency.ucsb.edu/ws/?pid=16092.

8. Franklin D. Roosevelt, "Third Inaugural Address," January 20, 1941. Online by Gerhard Peters and John T. Woolley, *The American Presidency Project*, http://www.presidency.ucsb.edu/ws/?pid=16022.

9. Franklin D. Roosevelt, "Address at Hyde Park, New York," July 4, 1941. Online by Gerhard Peters and John T. Woolley, *The American Presidency Project*, http://www.presidency.ucsb.edu/ws/?pid=16139.

10. Ibid.

11. Weber, *The Sociology of Religion*, 144–145. The dualistic worldview long predates the particular American variant I describe here. One of the foundational sources of the dualistic worldview was Manichaeism; reflecting these historical origins, the term "Manichean" is now often used as a synonym for dualism. For rhetorical variety, I occasionally follow this practice.

12. As Tom Engelhardt argues: "The Japanese attack on Pearl Harbor fit the lineaments of this story [the frontier narrative] well. At the country's periphery, a savage, nonwhite enemy had launched a barbaric attack on Americans going about their lives early one Sunday morning, and that enemy would be repaid in brutal combat on distant jungle islands in a modern version of 'Indian fighting.'" Tom Engelhardt, *The End of Victory Culture: Cold War America and the Disillusioning of a Generation*, revised ed. (Amherst: University of Massachusetts Press, 2007), 5.

13. Alexander and Smith, "The Discourse of American Civil Society," 160–165. See also Alexander, *The Civil Sphere*, 53–67, and *The Performance of Politics*, 10.

14. Michèle Lamont and Marcel Fournier, eds., *Cultivating Differences: Symbolic Boundaries and the Making of Inequality* (Chicago: University of Chicago Press, 1992), 1–7; Michèle Lamont, *Money, Morals, and Manners: The Culture of the French and the American Upper-Middle Class* (Chicago: University of Chicago Press, 1992), xvii, 1–2.

15. Franklin D. Roosevelt, "Address to Congress Requesting a Declaration of War with Japan," December 8, 1941. Online by Gerhard Peters and John T. Woolley, *The American Presidency Project*, http://www.presidency.ucsb.edu/ws/?pid=16053.

16. Ibid.

17. Ibid.

18. Franklin D. Roosevelt, "Message to Congress Requesting War Declarations with Germany and Italy," December 11, 1941. Online by Gerhard Peters and John T. Woolley, *The American Presidency Project*, http://www.presidency.ucsb.edu/ws/?pid=16058.

19. All quotations in this paragraph are from Franklin D. Roosevelt, "Christmas Eve Message to the Nation," December 24, 1941. Online by Gerhard Peters and John T. Woolley, *The American Presidency Project*, http://www.presidency.ucsb.edu/ws/?pid=16073.

20. All quotations in this paragraph are from Winston Churchill, "Address to Joint Session of U.S. Congress, 1941," December 26, 1941, National Churchill Museum, http://www.nationalchurchillmuseum.org/churchill-address-to-congress.html.

21. Franklin D. Roosevelt, "State of the Union Address," January 6, 1942. Online by Gerhard Peters and John T. Woolley, *The American Presidency Project*, http://www.presidency.ucsb.edu/ws/?pid=16253.

22. Ibid.

23. Franklin D. Roosevelt, "Fireside Chat," February 23, 1942. Online by Gerhard Peters and John T. Woolley, *The American Presidency Project*, http://www.presidency.ucsb.edu/ws/?pid=16224.

24. Ibid.

25. Ibid.

26. Franklin D. Roosevelt, "Address at Shibe Park, Philadelphia, Pennsylvania," October 27, 1944. Online by Gerhard Peters and John T. Woolley, *The American Presidency Project*, http://www.presidency.ucsb.edu/ws/?pid=16458.

27. Schwartz, *Abraham Lincoln in the Post-Heroic Era*, 81.

28. Dwight D. Eisenhower, "D-Day Statement to Soldiers, Sailors, and Airmen of the Allied Expeditionary Force, 6/44," June 6, 1944, National Archives and Records Administration, http://research.archives.gov/description/186473.

29. Ibid.
30. Franklin D. Roosevelt, "Prayer on D-Day," June 6, 1944. Online by Gerhard Peters and John T. Woolley, *The American Presidency Project*, http://www.presidency.ucsb.edu/ws/?pid=16515.
31. Ibid.
32. Harry S. Truman, "Broadcast to the American People Announcing the Surrender of Germany," May 8, 1945. Online by Gerhard Peters and John T. Woolley, *The American Presidency Project*, http://www.presidency.ucsb.edu/ws/?pid=12241.
33. Ibid.
34. Harry S. Truman, "Radio Report to the American People on the Potsdam Conference," August 9, 1945. Online by Gerhard Peters and John T. Woolley, *The American Presidency Project*, http://www.presidency.ucsb.edu/ws/?pid=12165.
35. Ibid.
36. Harry S. Truman, "Radio Address to the American People After the Signing of the Terms of Unconditional Surrender by Japan," September 1, 1945. Online by Gerhard Peters and John T. Woolley, *The American Presidency Project*, http://www.presidency.ucsb.edu/ws/?pid=12366.
37. Ibid.
38. Ibid.
39. John Bodnar, *The "Good War" in American Memory* (Baltimore: Johns Hopkins University Press, 2010), 2.
40. Renan, "What Is a Nation?," 80.
41. Bodnar, *The "Good War" in American Memory*. See also Studs Terkel, *"The Good War": An Oral History of World War II* (New York: Pantheon, 1984).
42. Ronald Reagan, "Remarks at the Annual Convention of the National Association of Evangelicals in Orlando, Florida," March 8, 1983. Online by Gerhard Peters and John T. Woolley, *The American Presidency Project*, http://www.presidency.ucsb.edu/ws/?pid=41023. It is worth noting that, in this speech primarily known for the phrase "evil empire," Reagan discussed the American capacity for evil as well. But he placed it in the context of a progressive teleology in which the United States had overcome its dark impulses: "Our nation, too, has a legacy of evil with which it must deal," he said. "The glory of this land has been its capacity for transcending the moral evils of our past. For example, the long struggle of minority citizens for equal rights, once a source of disunity and civil war, is now a point of pride for all Americans. We must never go back."
43. Ronald Reagan, "Address to Members of the British Parliament," June 8, 1982. Online by Gerhard Peters and John T. Woolley, *The American Presidency Project*, http://www.presidency.ucsb.edu/ws/?pid=42614. Michael Paul Rogin (*Ronald Reagan, the Movie and Other Episodes in Political Demonology* [Berkeley: University of California Press, 1987]) places this "political replacement of Nazism by Communism" (p. 3) that emerged in the 1940s and was revivified especially powerfully in Reagan's rhetoric during the 1980s within a "countersubversive tradition" of "political demonology"—that is, "the creation of monsters as a continuing feature of American politics by the inflation, stigmatization, and dehumanization of political foes" (p. xiii). Demonization, Rogin argues, "allows the countersubversive, in the name of battling the subversive, to imitate his enemy" (p. xiii). Reagan, however, represents a unique moment in the tradition of American political demonology in that he—"[u]nlike any other

president since the end of World War II"—split "the good within the country from the bad without" while maintaining the presumption that evil "is not (any longer) in us or in me" (p. xvii).

44. In 1961, John F. Kennedy noted the 20th anniversary in an address at an AFL-CIO convention in Miami, yet he downplayed its significance for the present: it was "an important anniversary," he said, but "[w]e face entirely different challenges on this Pearl Harbor." John F. Kennedy, "Address in Miami at the Opening of the AFL-CIO Convention," December 7, 1961. Online by Gerhard Peters and John T. Woolley, *The American Presidency Project*, http://www.presidency.ucsb.edu/ws/?pid=8476. On the contextual factors that prompted both the United States and Japan to downplay the 20th anniversary in the interest of shoring up their relationship, see Roger Dingman, "Reflections on Pearl Harbor Anniversaries Past," *Journal of American-East Asian Relations* 3, no. 3 (1994): 283–284. Lyndon Johnson mentioned the anniversary at a state dinner with British Prime Minister Harold Wilson three years later, on December 7, 1964, praising Britain's continued readiness to act "whenever liberty is threatened, whenever the choice is between freedom and slavery." Lyndon B. Johnson, "Toasts of the President and Prime Minister Harold Wilson," December 7, 1964. Online by Gerhard Peters and John T. Woolley, *The American Presidency Project*, http://www.presidency.ucsb.edu/ws/?pid=26749. And on the 34th anniversary, in 1975, Gerald Ford stopped at the U.S.S. *Arizona* Memorial en route to Washington from a trip to Asia. Ford's address reflected overtly on the meaning of the war's losses: "In all the history of war there is a recurrent question, why do young men have to die? Why not save, instead of spend, our bravest and our best?" Ford expressed hope that "we can and will build a safer and saner world" while also maintaining that "vigilance, the price of liberty, must be paid and repaid by every generation." Gerald Ford, "Remarks at Pearl Harbor Memorial Ceremonies in Honolulu, Hawaii," December 7, 1975. Online by Gerhard Peters and John T. Woolley, *The American Presidency Project*, http://www.presidency.ucsb.edu/ws/?pid=5422. Milestone anniversaries—the 10th, 25th, 30th, and 40th—passed without acknowledgment in presidential speechmaking.

45. Emily S. Rosenberg, *A Date Which Will Live: Pearl Harbor in American Memory* (Durham, NC: Duke University Press, 2003), 80–81. Edward Linenthal's account suggests that the speeches delivered during the 1962 dedication remained consonant with established official narratives. U.S. Representative Olin E. Teague, the chairman of the House Committee on Veterans' Affairs, reflected: "upon this sacred spot we honor the specific heroes who surrendered their lives . . . while they were in full bloom, so that we could have our full share of tomorrows. They remain imprisoned within this shattered hulk [the U.S.S. *Arizona*] so that we could be free." Quoted in Linenthal, *Sacred Ground*, 181–182.

46. Dingman, "Reflections on Pearl Harbor Anniversaries Past," 288.

47. Geoffrey M. White, "Mythic History and National Memory: The Pearl Harbor Anniversary," *Culture and Psychology* 3, no. 1 (1997): 80.

48. Ibid., 81.

49. Ibid., 80–81.

50. Dingman, "Reflections on Pearl Harbor Anniversaries Past," 291.

51. Ibid.

52. "This Week with David Brinkley," American Broadcasting Company [ABC], December 1, 1991, LexisNexis Academic Broadcast Transcripts.
53. Ibid.
54. Secretary of War Henry Stimson's 1947 account in *Harper's* provided an explication of the administration's position for a national audience. Henry L. Stimson, "The Decision to Use the Atomic Bomb," *Harper's* 194, no. 1161 (1947): 97–107. The issue of how many American lives were saved, as well as the issue of whether the bombings were the proximate cause of Japan's surrender, has been the subject of intense historical debate. For an overview of historians' debates on Truman's decision, see J. Samuel Walker, "Recent Literature on Truman's Atomic Bomb Decision: A Search for Middle Ground," *Diplomatic History* 29, no. 2 (2005): 311–334.
55. George Bush, "Remarks to the Pearl Harbor Survivors Association in Honolulu, Hawaii," December 7, 1991. Online by Gerhard Peters and John T. Woolley, *The American Presidency Project*, http://www.presidency.ucsb.edu/ws/?pid=20314.
56. Ibid.
57. Ibid.
58. Jeffrey K. Olick, *In the House of the Hangman: The Agonies of German Defeat, 1943–1949* (Chicago: University of Chicago Press, 2005), 212.
59. Bush, "Remarks to the Pearl Harbor Survivors Association in Honolulu, Hawaii."
60. Ibid.
61. Ibid.
62. White, "Mythic History and National Memory," 82.
63. George Bush, "Remarks at a Ceremony Commemorating the 50th Anniversary of Pearl Harbor," December 7, 1991. Online by Gerhard Peters and John T. Woolley, *The American Presidency Project*, http://www.presidency.ucsb.edu/ws/?pid=20315.
64. Ibid.
65. Ibid.
66. All quotations in this and the preceding paragraph are from George Bush, "Remarks to World War II Veterans and Families in Honolulu, Hawaii," December 7, 1991. Online by Gerhard Peters and John T. Woolley, *The American Presidency Project*, http://www.presidency.ucsb.edu/ws/?pid=20316.
67. Bodnar, *The "Good War" in American Memory*, 203.
68. All quotations in this paragraph are from Ronald Reagan, "Remarks at a Ceremony Commemorating the 40th Anniversary of the Normandy Invasion, D-Day," June 6, 1984. Online by Gerhard Peters and John T. Woolley, *The American Presidency Project*, http://www.presidency.ucsb.edu/ws/?pid=40018.
69. Bodnar also argues that Reagan's "highly emotional and sentimental address" helped his bid for reelection in 1984 "immeasurably." Bodnar, *The "Good War" in American Memory*, 205.
70. See also Bodnar, *The "Good War" in American Memory*, 205–208.
71. Wagner-Pacifici and Schwartz, "The Vietnam Veterans Memorial," 382.
72. Bodnar, *The "Good War" in American Memory*, 201.
73. Tom Brokaw, *The Greatest Generation* (New York: Random House, 1998).
74. Stephen E. Ambrose, *Band of Brothers* (New York: Simon and Schuster, 1992). In 2001, HBO aired a TV miniseries based on Ambrose's book; Steven Spielberg and Tom Hanks served as executive producers.

75. William J. Clinton, "Remarks Commemorating the United States Navy Role in the Normandy Invasion," June 6, 1994. Online by Gerhard Peters and John T. Woolley, *The American Presidency Project*, http://www.presidency.ucsb.edu/ws/?pid=50296.

76. Ibid.

77. "Remarks by Secretary of Defense William Perry at Utah Beach Ceremony," June 6, 1994, *Federal News Service*, LexisNexis Academic.

78. William J. Clinton, "Remarks on the 50th Anniversary of D-Day at Utah Beach in Normandy," June 6, 1994. Online by Gerhard Peters and John T. Woolley, *The American Presidency Project*, http://www.presidency.ucsb.edu/ws/?pid=50299.

79. Ibid.

80. William J. Clinton, "Remarks on the Anniversary of D-Day at Pointe du Hoc in Normandy, France," June 6, 1994. Online by Gerhard Peters and John T. Woolley, *The American Presidency Project*, http://www.presidency.ucsb.edu/ws/?pid=50297.

81. Ibid.

82. William J. Clinton, "Remarks on the 50th Anniversary of V-E Day in Arlington, Virginia," May 8, 1995. Online by Gerhard Peters and John T. Woolley, *The American Presidency Project*, http://www.presidency.ucsb.edu/ws/?pid=51328.

83. Ibid.

84. William J. Clinton, "Remarks at the National Cemetery of the Pacific in Honolulu," September 2, 1995. Online by Gerhard Peters and John T. Woolley, *The American Presidency Project*, http://www.presidency.ucsb.edu/ws/?pid=51790.

85. Bodnar, *The "Good War" in American Memory*, 200–208.

86. George L. Mosse, *Fallen Soldiers: Reshaping the Memory of the World Wars* (New York: Oxford University Press, 1990), 211. Mosse's analysis focuses predominantly on Europe, but he generalizes his claims to the United States as well. Indeed, he suggests that the Vietnam Veterans Memorial on the national mall in Washington, D.C., constitutes the most compelling evidence of the myth's demise. Although U.S. officials succumbed to pressure from veterans' groups and added a traditional war memorial next to Maya Lin's minimalist wall of names—as I detail in chapter 3—Mosse asserts: "the visitors, including veterans of the Vietnam War, seem to prefer the new way of commemorating the fallen to the old and traditional monument" (p. 224). On the Vietnam Veterans Memorial's divergence from traditional war monuments, see also Marita Sturken, *Tangled Memories: The Vietnam War, the AIDS Epidemic, and the Politics of Remembering* (Berkeley: University of California Press, 1997), 44–84; Wagner-Pacifici and Schwartz, "The Vietnam Veterans Memorial," 392–400.

87. Engelhardt, *The End of Victory Culture*, 6. He also notes the resurgence of victory culture after September 11, especially in the buildup to the Iraq War.

88. Schwartz, *Abraham Lincoln in the Post-Heroic Era*, 187. Schwartz is careful not to overstate the contrast between past and present, however. Older, heroic narratives and beliefs also persist alongside, and coexist with, this newer "post-heroic culture" (p. 263).

89. Olick, *The Politics of Regret*, 121–122.

90. Kai Erikson reflects on the relative inattention to the bombing of Nagasaki. Nagasaki, he writes, "does not seem to have been the subject of any thought at all. The orders of the bomber command were to attack Japan as soon as the bombs were ready. One was ready on August 9, three days after the leveling of

Hiroshima. Boom. . . . There is no law of nature that compels a winning side to press its superiority, but it is hard to slow down, hard to relinquish an advantage, hard to rein in the fury. . . . Many a casual slaughter can emerge from such moods." Kai T. Erikson, *A New Species of Trouble: The Human Experience of Modern Disasters* (New York: W. W. Norton and Company, 1994), 200. On the suppression of Hiroshima in American memory, see Robert Jay Lifton and Greg Mitchell, *Hiroshima in America: Fifty Years of Denial* (New York: Putnam, 1995).

91. Ronald Reagan, "Statement on the 40th Anniversary of the Bombing of Hiroshima," August 6, 1985. Online by Gerhard Peters and John T. Woolley, *The American Presidency Project*, http://www.presidency.ucsb.edu/ws/?pid=38975. This is not merely a partisan strategy. In his 1981 farewell address, President Jimmy Carter spoke in the passive voice even as he warned of the dangers of nuclear warfare: "It's now been 35 years since the first atomic bomb fell on Hiroshima," he said. Jimmy Carter, "Farewell Address to the Nation," January 14, 1981. Online by Gerhard Peters and John T. Woolley, *The American Presidency Project*, http://www.presidency.ucsb.edu/ws/?pid=44516.

92. For detailed analyses of the controversy, see Edward T. Linenthal and Tom Engelhardt, eds., *History Wars: The Enola Gay and Other Battles for the American Past* (New York: Henry Holt, 1996); Vera L. Zolberg, "Contested Remembrance: The Hiroshima Exhibit Controversy," *Theory and Society* 27, no. 4 (1998): 565–590. For the details of the original proposal, see Philip Nobile, ed., *Judgment at the Smithsonian: The Bombing of Hiroshima and Nagasaki* (New York: Marlowe and Company, 1995), 1–126.

93. Zolberg, "Contested Remembrance," 577. For the proposed text, see Nobile, *Judgment at the Smithsonian*, 96–116.

94. William J. Clinton, "The President's News Conference," April 18, 1995. Online by Gerhard Peters and John T. Woolley, *The American Presidency Project*, http://www.presidency.ucsb.edu/ws/?pid=51237.

95. This resistance to self-examination in the face of difficult legacies is not, of course, unique to the United States. For instance, Lisa Yoneyama argues that Japan's memory of Hiroshima—and the portrayal of Japan as a fundamentally peace-loving nation—rests on a repression of Japan's militaristic past. As she puts it: "Whether within mainstream national historiography, which remembers Hiroshima's atomic bombing as victimization experienced by the Japanese collectivity, or in the equally pervasive, more universalistic narrative on the bombing that records it as having been an unprecedented event in the history of humanity, Hiroshima memories have been predicated on the grave obfuscation of the prewar Japanese Empire, its colonial practices, and their consequences." Lisa Yoneyama, *Hiroshima Traces: Time, Space, and the Dialectics of Memory* (Berkeley: University of California Press, 1999), 3. See also R. J. B. Bosworth's discussion of debates over the past in postwar Japanese historiography, especially the extent to which the Ministry of Education continued to assert censorship rights over history textbooks. R. J. B. Bosworth, *Explaining Auschwitz and Hiroshima: History Writing and the Second World War, 1945–1990* (New York: Routledge, 1993), 167–190.

96. As I illustrate in chapter 7, the term "ground zero" has now become an emblem for a sacred site with the highest significance for the American nation. Recognizing the term's history, I have chosen not to render it as a proper noun. When it appears as a proper noun in quoted material, however, I have rendered it as such.

CHAPTER 3

1. See, e.g., John Patrick Diggins, *Max Weber: Politics and the Spirit of Tragedy* (New York: Basic Books, 1996), 11; Robert C. Pirro, *The Politics of Tragedy and Democratic Citizenship* (New York: Continuum International Publishing Group, 2011), 4; Simon Schama, "The Unloved American," *The New Yorker* 79, no. 3 (2003): 35; David Simpson, "It's Not About Cheering Us Up," *London Review of Books*, 25, no. 7 (2003): 17–19.

2. Burt, *Lincoln's Tragic Pragmatism*, 4–5 and passim. It is also worth noting that, as the United States entered the First World War, President Woodrow Wilson reflected aloud on the tragic dimensions of the circumstances at hand and the decision he felt bound to make. "With a profound sense of the solemn and even tragical character of the step I am taking and of the grave responsibilities which it involves . . . I advise that the Congress declare the recent course of the Imperial German Government to be in fact nothing less than war against the government and people of the United States," Wilson said in an April 2, 1917, address to Joint Congress. Woodrow Wilson, "Address to a Joint Session of Congress Requesting a Declaration of War Against Germany," April 2, 1917. Online by Gerhard Peters and John T. Woolley, *The American Presidency Project*, http://www.presidency.ucsb.edu/ws/?pid= 65366. John Bodnar notes that it was quite some time before "virtuous" accounts of World War I predominated over "critical" or "humanitarian" narratives. In the decades immediately following World War I, literature and film tended to take a tragic stance toward the war: "It was not until nearly 1940 that Hollywood and others began to reinvigorate the more reverential look at the 'Great War' in order to push public opinion toward supporting another American intervention into a European struggle." Bodnar, *The "Good War" in American Memory*, 237.

3. Terry Eagleton, *Sweet Violence: The Idea of the Tragic* (Malden, MA: Blackwell, 2003); Rita Felski, ed., *Rethinking Tragedy* (Baltimore: Johns Hopkins University Press, 2008), 2–3; Raymond Williams, *Modern Tragedy* (London: Chatto and Windus, 1966), 15–16.

4. Felski, *Rethinking Tragedy*, 3.

5. T. R. Henn, *The Harvest of Tragedy* (New York: Routledge, 2011), 65.

6. George Steiner, *The Death of Tragedy* (New York: Knopf, 1961). Among those who have excavated the concept's rich and varied history while also working to illuminate continuities in its myriad uses, an early example is Williams, *Modern Tragedy*. Here, I rely heavily upon several more recent efforts in a similar direction, especially Eagleton, *Sweet Violence*; Felski, *Rethinking Tragedy*; David Scott, *Conscripts of Modernity: The Tragedy of Colonial Enlightenment* (Durham, NC: Duke University Press, 2004).

7. Felski, *Rethinking Tragedy*, 14.

8. Ibid. In summarizing the colloquial definition of tragedy as "very sad," Felski invokes Eagleton, *Sweet Violence*, 3.

9. See, e.g., Eagleton, *Sweet Violence*; Felski, *Rethinking Tragedy*.

10. See, e.g., J. Peter Euben, *The Tragedy of Political Theory: The Road Not Taken* (Princeton, NJ: Princeton University Press, 1990); Pirro, *The Politics of Tragedy*; Christopher Rocco, *Tragedy and Enlightenment: Athenian Political Thought and the Dilemmas of Modernity* (Berkeley: University of California Press, 1997); Stow, "Pericles at Gettysburg and Ground Zero."

11. See, e.g., Scott, *Conscripts of Modernity*.

12. See, e.g., Jeffrey C. Alexander, "On the Social Construction of Moral Univer-sals: The 'Holocaust' from War Crime to Trauma Drama," *European Journal of Social Theory* 5, no. 1 (2002): 5–85; Ronald N. Jacobs, *Race, Media, and the Crisis of Civil Society: From Watts to Rodney King* (New York: Cambridge University Press, 2000) and "The Problem with Tragic Narratives: Lessons from the Los Angeles Uprising," *Qualitative Sociology* 24, no. 2 (2001): 221–243; Robin Wagner-Pacifici, *The Moro Morality Play: Terrorism as Social Drama* (Chicago: University of Chicago Press, 1986). In general, sociological adaptations have taken inspiration from genre theory, examining how actors draw upon the ar-chetypal tragic plot structure to emplot social dramas, rather than from ac-counts that highlight tragedy's role as a kind of secular theodicy. Especially important sources of guidance for existing sociological work on tragedy include Northrop Frye, *Anatomy of Criticism: Four Essays* (Princeton, NJ: Princeton Uni-versity Press, 1957); Hayden White, *Metahistory: The Historical Imagination in Nineteenth-Century Europe* (Baltimore: Johns Hopkins University Press, 1973).
13. Eagleton, *Sweet Violence*, 3.
14. David Scott, "Tragedy's Time: Postemancipation Futures Past and Present," in *Rethinking Tragedy*, 201.
15. See, e.g., Simon Goldhill, *Love, Sex and Tragedy: How the Ancient World Shapes Our Lives* (London: John Murray, 2004), 229; Wagner-Pacifici, *The Moro Mo-rality Play*, 283.
16. Felski, *Rethinking Tragedy*, 11.
17. Scott, "Tragedy's Time," 210.
18. Eagleton, *Sweet Violence*, 21. On the relationship between tragedy and theol-ogy, see Paul Ricoeur, *The Symbolism of Evil* (New York: Harper and Row, 1967), 211–231; Wendy Farley, *Tragic Vision and Divine Compassion: A Contemporary Theodicy* (Louisville, KY: Westminster/John Knox Press, 1990).
19. Recall Jeffrey Alexander and Philip Smith's account of the distinction be-tween liberty and repression at the heart of American civil society discourse. Alexander and Smith, "The Discourse of American Civil Society," 161–162.
20. See Goldhill, *Love, Sex and Tragedy*, 229–231; Pirro, *The Politics of Tragedy*, 17–20; Rocco, *Tragedy and Enlightenment*, 16–17, 27–28; Stow, "Pericles at Gettysburg and Ground Zero," 198–199; Wagner-Pacifici, *The Moro Morality Play*, 283.
21. Goldhill, *Love, Sex and Tragedy*, 231.
22. Simon Goldhill, "The Great Dionysia and Civic Ideology," in *Nothing to Do with Dionysos? Athenian Drama in Its Social Context*, ed. John J. Winkler and Froma I. Zeitlin (Princeton, NJ: Princeton University Press, 1990), 126.
23. Eyerman, *The Cultural Sociology of Political Assassination*, 34–35; Rick Perlstein, *Nixonland: The Rise of a President and the Fracturing of America* (New York: Scrib-ner, 2008), 254–261. On the meanings of "the sixties," see, e.g., David Farber, ed., *The Sixties: From Memory to History* (Chapel Hill: University of North Caro-lina Press, 1994); Todd Gitlin, *The Sixties: Years of Hope, Days of Rage* (New York: Bantam Books, 1987); Eleanor Townsley, "'The Sixties' Trope," *Theory, Culture and Society* 18, no. 6 (2001): 99–123.
24. Cushing, "Eulogy to John F. Kennedy," 100. See also Eyerman, *The Cultural Sociology of Political Assassination*, 6; Schwartz, "Memory as a Cultural System," 921.
25. Eyerman, *The Cultural Sociology of Political Assassination*, 34–35, 72–73.
26. Ibid., 36–42, 47–55.

27. Perlstein, *Nixonland*, 246–247, 257.
28. Ibid., 257.
29. Robert F. Kennedy, "Remarks on the Assassination of Martin Luther King, Jr.," April 4, 1968, American Rhetoric Online Speech Bank, http://www.americanrhetoric.com/speeches/rfkonmlkdeath.html.
30. Ibid.
31. On the evening of April 3, 1968, King said: "Well, I don't know what will happen now; we've got some difficult days ahead. But it really doesn't matter with me now, because I've been to the mountaintop. And I don't mind. Like anybody, I would like to live a long life—longevity has its place. But I'm not concerned about that now. I just want to do God's will. And He's allowed me to go up to the mountain. And I've looked over, and I've seen the Promised Land. . . . And so I'm happy tonight; I'm not worried about anything; I'm not fearing any man. Mine eyes have seen the glory of the coming of the Lord." Martin Luther King, Jr., "I've Been to the Mountaintop," April 3, 1968, Martin Luther King, Jr. Papers Project, http://mlk-kpp01.stanford.edu/kingweb/publications/speeches/I%27ve_been_to_the_mountaintop.pdf.
32. All quotations in this paragraph are from Kennedy, "Remarks on the Assassination of Martin Luther King, Jr."
33. Arthur M. Schlesinger, Jr., *Robert Kennedy and His Times* (Boston: Houghton Mifflin, 1978), 617.
34. Pirro, *The Politics of Tragedy*, 2; Schlesinger, *Robert Kennedy and His Times*, 618–620. According to Schlesinger, Robert Kennedy originally engaged with Greek tragedy at Jacqueline Kennedy's suggestion. She herself had found consolation in Edith Hamilton's book for non-specialists, *The Greek Way* (New York: W. W. Norton and Company, 1930), which she introduced to her brother-in-law during a trip to Antigua during the Easter holiday in 1964.
35. Kennedy, "Remarks on the Assassination of Martin Luther King, Jr." Christopher S. Morrissey points out that Kennedy's words were a slight misquotation of Edith Hamilton's translation of *Agamemnon*. Most importantly, Kennedy substituted "despair" for Hamilton's "despite." It is not clear whether the misquotation was deliberate or accidental. Christopher S. Morrissey, "'In Our Own Despair': Robert Kennedy, Richard Nixon, and Aeschylus' *Agamemnon*," Annual Meeting of the Classical Association of Canada, May 12, 2002. For an overview of Morrissey's account, see http://www.morec.com/rfk.htm. For Hamilton's translation, see Edith Hamilton, *Three Greek Plays: Prometheus Bound, Agamemnon, The Trojan Women* (New York: W. W. Norton and Company, 1937), 170.
36. Kennedy, "Remarks on the Assassination of Martin Luther King, Jr."
37. Ibid.
38. Ibid. Here, Kennedy drew from Edith Hamilton, who wrote: "An old Greek inscription states that the aim of mankind should be 'to tame the savageness of man and make gentle the life of the world.'" Edith Hamilton, *The Ever-Present Past* (New York: W. W. Norton and Company, 1964), 34.
39. As a result, Perlstein argues, "the legend of RFK as a pol with magic powers grew." Perlstein, *Nixonland*, 257; see also Pirro, *The Politics of Tragedy*, 3.
40. Pirro, *The Politics of Tragedy*, 3–4.
41. Cornel West, "Prophetic Christian as Organic Intellectual: Martin Luther King, Jr.," in *The Cornel West Reader* (New York: Basic Civitas Books, 1999), 426.
42. Ibid., 427.

43. On hybridization in King's speech, see Jonathan Rieder, *The Word of the Lord is Upon Me: The Righteous Performance of Martin Luther King, Jr.* (Cambridge, MA: Harvard University Press, 2008). On King's adaptation of American civil religion, see West, "Prophetic Christian as Organic Intellectual," 432–433.

44. Rieder, *The Word of the Lord is Upon Me*, 5.

45. Robert F. Kennedy, "Remarks to the Cleveland City Club," April 5, 1968, John F. Kennedy Presidential Library and Museum, http://www.jfklibrary.org/Research/Research-Aids/Ready-Reference/RFK-Speeches/Remarks-of-Senator-Robert-F-Kennedy-to-the-Cleveland-City-Club-Cleveland-Ohio-April-5-1968.aspx.

46. Ibid.

47. Ibid. The source for this quotation is Lincoln's letter to his friend, James C. Conkling, intended to be read at a September 3, 1863, rally in Springfield, Illinois. Abraham Lincoln, "To James C. Conkling," in *Collected Works of Abraham Lincoln*, vol. 6, ed. Roy P. Basler (New Brunswick, NJ: Rutgers University Press, 1953), 410.

48. Kennedy, "Remarks to the Cleveland City Club."

49. Ibid.

50. Ibid.

51. Lyndon B. Johnson, "Statement by the President on the Assassination of Dr. Martin Luther King, Jr.," April 4, 1968. Online by Gerhard Peters and John T. Woolley, *The American Presidency Project*, http://www.presidency.ucsb.edu/ws/?pid=28781.

52. Lyndon B. Johnson, "Address to the Nation Upon Proclaiming a Day of Mourning Following the Death of Dr. King," April 5, 1968. Online by Gerhard Peters and John T. Woolley, *The American Presidency Project*, http://www.presidency.ucsb.edu/ws/?pid=28783.

53. Ibid.

54. Ibid.

55. Perlstein, *Nixonland*, 272.

56. Quoted in Perlstein, *Nixonland*, 272.

57. Thurston Clarke, *The Last Campaign: Robert F. Kennedy and 82 Days that Inspired America* (New York: Henry Holt and Company, 2008), 7.

58. Eyerman, *The Cultural Sociology of Political Assassination*, 63–73.

59. Lyndon B. Johnson, "Statement by the President Following the Shooting of Senator Robert F. Kennedy," June 5, 1968. Online by Gerhard Peters and John T. Woolley, *The American Presidency Project*, http://www.presidency.ucsb.edu/ws/?pid=28907.

60. Lyndon B. Johnson, "Address to the Nation Following the Attack on Senator Kennedy," June 5, 1968. Online by Gerhard Peters and John T. Woolley, *The American Presidency Project*, http://www.presidency.ucsb.edu/ws/?pid=28908.

61. Ibid. On media narratives, see Eyerman, *The Cultural Sociology of Political Assassination*, 63–69.

62. Johnson, "Address to the Nation Following the Attack on Senator Kennedy."

63. Ibid.

64. Edward Kennedy, "A Tribute to His Brother," *Vital Speeches of the Day* 34, no. 18 (1968): 546, quoting Robert Kennedy.

65. John Hellman, *American Myth and the Legacy of Vietnam* (New York: Columbia University Press, 1986), 15.

66. Engelhardt, *The End of Victory Culture*, 14.

67. Hellman, *American Myth and the Legacy of Vietnam*, 36, 37–38.
68. Lyndon B. Johnson, "Christmas Message to the Americans in Viet-Nam," December 23, 1964. Online by Gerhard Peters and John T. Woolley, *The American Presidency Project*, http://www.presidency.ucsb.edu/ws/?pid=26769.
69. Ibid.
70. Lyndon B. Johnson, "Annual Message to Congress on the State of the Union," January 12, 1966. Online by Gerhard Peters and John T. Woolley, *The American Presidency Project*, http://www.presidency.ucsb.edu/ws/?pid=28015.
71. Ibid.
72. Ibid.
73. Lyndon B. Johnson, "Prayer for Peace, Memorial Day, 1966," May 26, 1966. Online by Gerhard Peters and John T. Woolley, *The American Presidency Project*, http://www.presidency.ucsb.edu/ws/?pid=27618.
74. Lyndon B. Johnson, "Annual Message to Congress on the State of the Union," January 10, 1967. Online by Gerhard Peters and John T. Woolley, *The American Presidency Project*, http://www.presidency.ucsb.edu/ws/?pid=28338.
75. Lyndon B. Johnson, "Remarks at the Presidential Prayer Breakfast," February 1, 1968. Online by Gerhard Peters and John T. Woolley, *The American Presidency Project*, http://www.presidency.ucsb.edu/ws/?pid=29060. For Roosevelt's original address, see Franklin D. Roosevelt, "Radio Address on United Flag Day," June 14, 1942. Online by Gerhard Peters and John T. Woolley, *The American Presidency Project*, http://www.presidency.ucsb.edu/ws/?pid=16276.
76. Johnson, "Remarks at the Presidential Prayer Breakfast."
77. In performances during the late 1980s, Dylan incorporated a new verse on the Vietnam War. Mike Marqusee, *Wicked Messenger: Bob Dylan and the 1960s* (New York: Seven Stories Press, 2005), 268. On Dylan's position vis-à-vis 1960s social movements, see also Ron Eyerman and Andrew Jamison, *Music and Social Movements: Mobilizing Traditions in the Twentieth Century* (New York: Cambridge University Press, 1998), 24, 116.
78. On the role of music in social protest during the Vietnam era, see, e.g., Eyerman and Jamison, *Music and Social Movements*; Sarah Hill, "'This Is My Country': American Popular Music and Political Engagement in '1968,'" in *Music and Protest in 1968*, ed. Beate Kutschke and Barley Norton (New York: Cambridge University Press, 2013); Charles Shaar Murray, *Crosstown Traffic: Jimi Hendrix and Post-War Pop* (London: Faber and Faber, 1989); John Street, *Music and Politics* (Malden, MA: Polity Press, 2012).
79. Philip Smith, *Why War?*, 90.
80. All quotations in this paragraph are from Martin Luther King, Jr., "Beyond Vietnam," April 4, 1967, Martin Luther King, Jr. Papers Project, http://mlk-kpp01.stanford.edu/kingweb/publications/speeches/Beyond_Vietnam.pdf.
81. Robert F. Kennedy, "Conflict at Vietnam and at Home," March 18, 1968, Landon Lectures, Kansas State University, http://ome.ksu.edu/lectures/landon/trans/Kennedy68.html.
82. Ibid. For a more detailed discussion of the event, see Clarke, *The Last Campaign*, 42–48.
83. Kennedy, "Conflict at Vietnam and at Home."
84. Ibid.
85. In this vein, Ronald Jacobs has pointed to the pitfalls of tragic narratives in the face of social crises. According to Jacobs, the archetypal tragic plot culminates in catastrophe, and thus tragic narratives have a tendency to subvert agency and invite fatalism. "Because the reader expects catastrophe as its

inevitable end," he writes, "tragedy is a particularly dangerous form of discourse if one values civic engagement." Jacobs, *Race, Media, and the Crisis of Civil Society*, 11. In contrast, Wagner-Pacifici suggests that tragic social dramas "ought to tend in the direction of intermittent existential ambiguity and turmoil (recognition of opposing imperatives) and gains in this-worldly consciousness," which in turn have the potential to underwrite meaningful social change. Kennedy's address identified precisely the tension between these two possibilities of tragic narratives, and worked to affect the latter. Wagner-Pacifici traces this tension to an apparent contradiction in Aristotle's *Poetics*: in chapter 13, Aristotle identifies the ideal tragic plot as "that in which a rather (but not superbly) good man comes to a bad end"; in the next chapter, "Aristotle then identifies as best those plays containing a plot in which a tragic action is intended but prevented by the truth being discovered in time." Wagner Pacifici, *The Moro Morality Play*, 238, 13.

86. All quotations in this paragraph are from Kennedy, "Conflict at Vietnam and at Home."

87. Richard Nixon, "Inaugural Address," January 20, 1969. Online by Gerhard Peters and John T. Woolley, *The American Presidency Project*, http://www. presidency.ucsb.edu/ws/?pid=1941.

88. Ibid.

89. Engelhardt, *The End of Victory Culture*, 14.

90. Richard Nixon, "Address to the Nation Announcing Conclusion of an Agreement on Ending the War and Restoring Peace in Vietnam," January 23, 1973. Online by Gerhard Peters and John T. Woolley, *The American Presidency Project*, http://www.presidency.ucsb.edu/ws/?pid=3808.

91. Ibid.

92. Gerald Ford, "Statement Following Evacuation of United States Personnel from the Republic of Vietnam," April 29, 1975. Online by Gerhard Peters and John T. Woolley, *The American Presidency Project*, http://www.presidency.ucsb. edu/ws/?pid=4874.

93. Loren Baritz, *Backfire: A History of How American Culture Led Us into Vietnam and Made Us Fight the Way We Did* (Baltimore: Johns Hopkins University Press, 1998), 15; Patrick Hagopian, *The Vietnam War in American Memory: Veterans, Memorials, and the Politics of Healing* (Amherst: University of Massachusetts Press, 2009), 8; Hellman, *American Myth and the Legacy of Vietnam*, 100, 211.

94. Slotkin, *Regeneration through Violence*, 5. On the challenges that Vietnam posed to this mythology, and the ways in which a new image of a paramilitary warrior emerged to fill the void, see James William Gibson, *Warrior Dreams: Paramilitary Culture in Post-Vietnam America* (New York: Hill and Wang, 1994).

95. Hagopian, *The Vietnam War in American Memory*, 79–92; Wagner-Pacfici and Schwartz, "The Vietnam Veterans Memorial," 388–392. For Scruggs's own account, see Jan C. Scruggs and Joel L. Swerdlow, *To Heal a Nation: The Vietnam Veterans Memorial* (New York: Harper and Row, 1985).

96. Scruggs and Swerdlow, *To Heal a Nation*, 53.

97. Hagopian, *The Vietnam War in American Memory*, 149. Compare this designation, for instance, to that of the "United States Marine Corps War Memorial," dedicated in 1954, or the "National World War II Memorial," dedicated in 2004. On the Vietnam Veterans Memorial's divergence from the standard war memorial genre, see Wagner-Pacifici and Schwartz, "The Vietnam Veterans Memorial," 392–396.

98. Wagner-Pacifici and Schwartz, "The Vietnam Veterans Memorial," 389.

99. Ibid., 381–382.
100. Quoted in Wagner-Pacifici and Schwartz, "The Vietnam Veterans Memorial," 393. Both scholarly interpretations and the public response suggest that the memorial largely actualizes this intention. As one *Washington Post* editorial, published on the day of the dedication, put it: "Every individual will bring his own special feelings to this scene and find his own special message in it." "The Vietnam Memorial," *Washington Post*, November 13, 1982, A18. For scholarly interpretations, see also Peter Ehrenhaus, "Silence and Symbolic Expression," *Communication Monographs* 55, no. 1 (1988): 41–57; Kristin Ann Hass, *Carried to the Wall: American Memory and the Vietnam Veterans Memorial* (Berkeley: University of California Press, 1998); Kirk Savage, *Monument Wars: Washington, D.C., the National Mall, and the Transformation of the Memorial Landscape* (Berkeley: University of California Press, 2009), 20–21, 261–279; Marita Sturken, *Tangled Memories*, 44–84.
101. Ehrenhaus, "Silence and Symbolic Expression," 55.
102. Kenneth Bredemeier, "Preparations for Salute to Vietnam Vets Nearly Done: Nation Ready to Salute Vietnam Veterans," *Washington Post*, November 9, 1982, B1, and "Diverse Crowd is Unanimous in Homage to Vietnam Veterans," *Washington Post*, November 14, 1982, A18; Ed Bruske and Kenneth Bredemeier, "Vietnam War Dead's Names Read, Remembered: A Vigil of Love for the Vietnam War Dead," *Washington Post*, November 11, 1982, B1.
103. "Dedication of the Vietnam War Memorial," C-SPAN Video Library, November 13, 1982, http://www.c-spanvideo.org/program/88364-1.
104. Ibid.
105. Ibid.
106. It is noteworthy that Warner himself referred to the memorial as a "monument." Marita Sturken clarifies the distinction: "Whereas a monument most often signifies victory, a memorial refers to the life or lives sacrificed for a particular set of values. Whatever triumph a memorial may refer to, its depiction of victory is always tempered by a foregrounding of the lives lost." Sturken, *Tangled Memories*, 47–48.
107. "Dedication of the Vietnam War Memorial."
108. All quotations in this and the preceding two paragraphs are from Theodore H. Evans, "Remembering the Sacrifice," in *The Vietnam Reader*, ed. Walter Capps (New York: Routledge, 1991), 249–252.
109. Savage, *Monument Wars*, 276–279; Sturken, *Tangled Memories*, 51–58; Wagner-Pacifici and Schwartz, "The Vietnam Veterans Memorial," 394–396.
110. Subsequently, the Vietnam Women's Memorial, dedicated in 1993, was also added.
111. Wagner-Pacifici and Schwartz, "The Vietnam Veterans Memorial," 392.
112. Ronald Reagan, "Remarks at Dedication Ceremonies for the Vietnam Veterans Memorial Statue," November 11, 1984. Online by Gerhard Peters and John T. Woolley, *The American Presidency Project*, http://www.presidency.ucsb.edu/ws/?pid=39414.
113. Ibid.
114. Hass, *Carried to the Wall*, 87–102; Sturken, *Tangled Memories*, 74–81; Wagner-Pacifici and Schwartz, "The Vietnam Veterans Memorial," 403–404.
115. Robert S. McNamara, *In Retrospect: The Tragedy and Lessons of Vietnam* (New York: Times Books, 1995), 207.
116. Ibid., xxi.

117. Ibid.

118. Ibid., 333.

119. Ibid.

120. Ibid. For McNamara's continued efforts to reinterpret Vietnam in the tragic mode, see Robert S. McNamara, James Blight, Robert Brigham, Thomas Bierstecker, and Herbert Schandler, *Argument Without End: In Search of Answers to the Vietnam Tragedy* (New York: Public Affairs, 1999). As Pirro points out, McNamara describes the source of the nation's tragic downfall in somewhat different terms than Kennedy before him. Where Kennedy emphasized pride—a failure of character and ego—McNamara focuses instead on failures of information and knowledge. According to Pirro, this approach can be seen as having something of "an exculpatory effect, as relieving him of his just portion of personal responsibility for the needless suffering and death brought about by U.S. policies in Vietnam." Pirro, *The Politics of Tragedy*, 7. Indeed, these are important differences. In both cases, however, meaning emerges through self-examination and a willingness to acknowledge and learn from the errors of the past, even if those errors spring from different sources.

121. A full list of the quotations included in the King memorial is available on the National Park Service website, http://www.nps.gov/mlkm/photosmultimedia/quotations.htm.

CHAPTER 4

1. "Plane Crashes into World Trade Center," NBC, September 11, 2001, Lexis-Nexis Academic Broadcast Transcripts. As Barbie Zelizer explains, "in the absence of clear information about the present, journalism is easily able to import information from the past" as a way of providing orientation amidst uncertainty. Both media outlets and political officials would continue to reach to the past for guidance on September 11, 2001, though the reference points quickly shifted after the second hijacked plane—United Airlines Flight 175—hit the south tower. Barbie Zelizer, "Cannibalizing Memory in the Global Flow of News," in *On Media Memory: Collective Memory in a New Media Age*, ed. Motti Neiger, Oren Meyers, and Eyal Zandberg (New York: Palgrave Macmillan, 2011), 34–35.

2. "Remarks by President Bush at Emma Booker Elementary School," September 11, 2001, *Federal News Service*, LexisNexis Academic.

3. Ibid.

4. Craig Calhoun, Paul Price, and Ashley Timmer, eds., *Understanding September 11* (New York: The New Press, 2002), 2; Wagner-Pacifici, "Theorizing the Restlessness of Events," 1352. In the aftermath, other definitions of the event would emerge, especially among family members who suggested that September 11 was in part a failure of intelligence or preparedness. These critiques resulted most notably in the establishment of the 9/11 Commission, an independent, bipartisan entity that was to "make a full and complete accounting of the circumstances surrounding the attacks, and the extent of the United States' preparedness for, and immediate response to, the attacks" (Public Law 107–306, 107th Congress). Was September 11 primarily an intelligence failure, a "breakdown . . . in our nation's defense capabilities," as Mindy Kleinberg, whose husband died in the World Trade Center, put it? Was it an event that "should have been predictable," as Mary Fetchet, who lost her son at the World Trade Center, asserted? Was September 11 in part a technological

disaster, in which "failures in evacuation procedures, building code issues and emergency communications" added substantially to the death toll, as Sally Regenhard, whose son died at the World Trade Center, argued? For the statements by Kleinberg and Fetchet, see the March 31, 2003, Public Hearing of the National Commission on Terrorist Attacks upon the United States, http://govinfo.library.unt.edu/911/archive/hearing1/9-11Commission_Hearing_2003-03-31.pdf, 188, 181. For the statement by Regenhard, see the November 19, 2003, Public Hearing of the National Commission on Terrorist Attacks upon the United States, http://govinfo.library.unt.edu/911/archive/hearing5/9-11Commission_Hearing_2003-11-19.pdf, 33; see also Scott Gabriel Knowles, *The Disaster Experts: Mastering Risk in Modern America* (Philadelphia: University of Pennsylvania Press, 2011).

5. "Remarks by President George W. Bush," September 11, 2001, *Federal News Service*, LexisNexis Academic.

6. "Address to the Nation by President George W. Bush Regarding Terrorist Attacks on the World Trade Centers and the Pentagon," September 11, 2001, *Federal News Service*, LexisNexis Academic.

7. Ibid.

8. Ibid.

9. William J. Clinton, "The President's Radio Address," August 8, 1998. Online by Gerhard Peters and John T. Woolley, *The American Presidency Project*, http://www.presidency.ucsb.edu/ws/?pid=54763.

10. Ibid.

11. "New York's Governor and Mayor of New York City Address Concerns of the Damage," Cable News Network [CNN], September 11, 2001, LexisNexis Academic Broadcast Transcripts.

12. Ibid.

13. "Press Conference with Mayor Rudolph Giuliani (R-New York City); Governor George Pataki (R-NY)," September 11, 2001, *Federal News Service*, LexisNexis Academic. Not all prominent observers were as circumspect, however. Shortly after the north tower collapsed—the north tower was the first to be hit, but the second to come down—Tom Brokaw, reporting live on NBC, said: "There's been a declaration of war by terrorists against the United States." He elaborated: "This is war. This is a declaration and an execution of an attack on the United States. Two of the most conspicuous symbols of the American system of capitalism, the Pentagon, which of course is the headquarters of the most mighty military in the world[,] was attacked today as well." "Attack on America: 10:00 AM," NBC, September 11, 2001, LexisNexis Academic Broadcast Transcripts. Zelizer provides context for the striking certainty with which Brokaw spoke: "when memory moves into the global flow of news, it by definition loses some of its locality, internal variation, nuance, and particularity. It also loses the starting point so central to memory-work—and its adjacent local pauses, hesitations, and tentativeness—already at the beginning of its shaping. Instead, news works by playing to mnemonic certainty." This "cannibalization" of local memory "in the global flow of news" is especially pronounced "following crisis, trauma, and catastrophe." Zelizer, "Cannibalizing Memory," 28, 29. Though some hesitation and tentativeness played out on screen on the morning of September 11, it was short-lived, as Brokaw's authoritative and unambiguous interpretation of the hijackings and crashes as acts of war reveals. On media framings of September 11 more generally, see,

e.g., Elisabeth Anker, "Villains, Victims and Heroes: Melodrama, Media, and September 11," *Journal of Communication* 55, no. 1 (2005): 22–37; Brian A. Monahan, *The Shock of the News: Media Coverage and the Making of 9/11* (New York: New York University Press, 2010). On the ways in which media outlets echoed Bush's discourse, see Kevin Coe, David Domke, Erica S. Graham, Sue Lockett John, and Victor W. Pickard, "No Shades of Gray: The Binary Discourse of George W. Bush and an Echoing Press," *Journal of Communication* 54, no. 2 (2004): 234–252.

14. "Press Conference with Mayor Rudolph Giuliani (R-New York City); Governor George Pataki (R-NY)."

15. Ibid.

16. Ibid.

17. See the discussion in Eric Pooley, "Mayor of the World," *Time* 158/159, no. 28/1 (2001/2002): 42, 44.

18. On this point, see Alyson M. Cole, *The Cult of True Victimhood: From the War on Welfare to the War on Terror* (Stanford, CA: Stanford University Press, 2007), 150–154; James W. Messerschmidt, *Hegemonic Masculinities and Camouflaged Politics: Unmasking the Bush Dynasty and its War Against Iraq* (Boulder, CO: Paradigm Publishers, 2010), 95–111.

19. "Statement by President Bush After National Security Team Meeting," September 12, 2001, *Federal News Service*, LexisNexis Academic.

20. Ibid.

21. Ibid.

22. On "occasions," see Campbell and Jamieson, *Presidents Creating the Presidency*, 48, 53, 58, 68, 72, 149, 164; Olick, *The Sins of the Fathers*.

23. The speech Bush delivered during this service can, more than any other, be properly understood as his official "national eulogy." See the discussion of national eulogies in Campbell and Jamieson, *Presidents Creating the Presidency*, 73–103.

24. All quotations in this and the preceding three paragraphs are from "America Mourns, 11:45 AM," NBC, September 14, 2001, LexisNexis Academic Broadcast Transcripts.

25. All quotations in this and the preceding paragraph are from "Remarks by President George W. Bush at National Prayer Service," September 14, 2001, *Federal News Service*, LexisNexis Academic.

26. Ibid. The phrase "the warm courage of national unity" comes from Franklin Roosevelt's first inaugural address, in March 1933. Roosevelt said: "We face the arduous days that lie before us in the warm courage of national unity." Franklin D. Roosevelt, "Inaugural Address," March 4, 1933. Online by Gerhard Peters and John T. Woolley, *The American Presidency Project*, http://www.presidency.ucsb.edu/ws/?pid=14473.

27. "America Mourns, 11:45 AM."

28. Howe, "Battle Hymn of the Republic," 10.

29. "Remarks by President Bush to Rescue Workers at the World Trade Center," September 14, 2001, *Federal News Service*, LexisNexis Academic.

30. Ibid.

31. Video footage is available through the American Rhetoric Online Speech Bank, http://www.americanrhetoric.com/speeches/gwbush911ground zerobullhorn.htm.

32. The Clinton and Schumer quotations are from "Democratic Response to President Bush's Weekly Radio Address by Senator Charles Schumer (D-NY) and

Senator Hillary Clinton (D-NY)," September 15, 2001, *Federal News Service*, LexisNexis Academic.

33. "Remarks by President George W. Bush upon Returning to the White House from Camp David," September 16, 2001, *Federal News Service*, LexisNexis Academic.

34. Pooley, "Mayor of the World," 51–52.

35. "New York City Mayor Rudolph Giuliani (R), New York Governor George Pataki (R) and Others Briefing on the World Trade Center Recovery Operation," September 15, 2001, *Federal News Service*, LexisNexis Academic, and "Mayor Giuliani and Fire Commissioner Von Essen Address New York," CNN, September 15, 2001, LexisNexis Academic Broadcast Transcripts. Giuliani attended numerous funerals following September 11. The eulogies he delivered are largely unrecorded, since he did not reveal to the media which funerals he would attend. But his chief speechwriter, John Avlon, has publicly recounted some of their overriding themes. "There are lines I remember we were using at the time," he told the *Village Voice* in 2011. "'We met the worst of humanity with the best of humanity' . . . 'We're the land of the free because we're the home of the brave.'" The fallen rescue workers, Avlon said, were "the actual physical contemporary embodiment of those Biblical passages that say, 'Greater love hath no man than this, that a man lay down his life for his friends.'" Harry Siegel, "The 9/11 Eulogies," *Village Voice* Blogs, September 9, 2011, http://blogs.villagevoice.com/runninscared/2011/09/the_911_ eulogies.php.

36. "News Conference with New York City Mayor Rudolph Giuliani and New York Police Commissioner Bernard Kerik," September 16, 2001, *Federal News Service*, LexisNexis Academic.

37. Ibid.

38. Ibid.

39. "Press Conference with New York Stock Exchange Chairman Richard Grasso, New York Mayor Rudy Giuliani, New York Governor George Pataki and Others," September 17, 2001, *Federal News Service*, LexisNexis Academic.

40. Ibid.

41. "President Bush Address to a Joint Session of Congress," September 20, 2001, *Federal News Service*, LexisNexis Academic.

42. Ibid. The 9/11 Commission subsequently concluded that the intended target was likely the U.S. Capitol or the White House. National Commission on Terrorist Attacks Upon the United States, *The 9/11 Commission Report: Final Report of the National Commission on Terrorist Attacks Upon the United States* (New York: W. W. Norton and Company, 2004), 14.

43. "President Bush Address to a Joint Session of Congress."

44. Ibid.

45. Ibid. Once again, violence is understood as the source of this regeneration.

46. Ibid.

47. Donileen R. Loseke, "Examining Emotion as Discourse: Emotion Codes and Presidential Speeches Justifying War," *The Sociological Quarterly* 50, no. 3 (2009): 498–499. As William Sewell argues, "the emotional tone of action can be an important sign of structural dislocation and rearticulation," and "the resolution of structural dislocation—whether by restoring the ruptured articulation or by forging new ones—results in powerful emotional release that consolidates the rearticulation." Sewell, "Historical Events as Transformations of Structures," 865. In this highly visible address, Bush sought to evoke

such an emotional release, to complete the transformation from grief to anger to resolve. Moving forward with resolve, Bush suggested, would reconsolidate an American nation that maintained certain quintessential characteristics—an encompassing sense of mission, for instance, and an abiding commitment to freedom—yet reoriented itself structurally and symbolically toward a war on terrorism.

48. This and all remaining quotations in "Defining the Mission" are from "President Bush Address to a Joint Session of Congress."
49. All quotations in this and the preceding five paragraphs are from "Prayer Service at Yankee Stadium," CNN, September 23, 2001, LexisNexis Academic Broadcast Transcripts.
50. Details on the October 28, 2001, memorial service and the quotations in this paragraph are all from "World Trade Center Family Memorial Service," CNN, October 28, 2001, LexisNexis Academic Broadcast Transcripts.
51. "Text of Mayor Giuliani's Farewell Address," *New York Times*, December 27, 2001, www.nytimes.com/2001/12/27/nyregion/27CND-GIUL-TEXT.html.
52. Ibid.
53. Ibid. With these lines, he unambiguously reinforced an interpretation of 9/11 as an act of war.
54. Ibid.
55. Ibid.
56. "Prayer Service at Yankee Stadium."
57. Pooley, "Mayor of the World," 42, 44.
58. On relationships among various genres of political speech, see Campbell and Jamieson, *Presidents Creating the Presidency*; Olick, *The Sins of the Fathers*. There is evidence that politicians' efforts to console and inspire the nation immediately after 9/11 had a significant impact on public opinion. In a *Washington Post*/ABC News poll on September 20, 2001, 80 percent of respondents who watched Bush's address to Joint Congress said his speech made them "more confident in this country's ability to deal with this crisis." Only 4 percent said it made them less confident, with 14 percent reporting that it had not made a difference. For the polling results, see http://www.washingtonpost.com/wp-srv/politics/polls/vault/stories/data092001.htm. More generally, Americans reported remarkably high levels of confidence in government officials and institutions. See, e.g., Kimberly Gross, Paul R. Brewer, and Sean Aday, "Confidence in Government and Emotional Responses to Terrorism after September 11, 2001," *American Politics Research* 37, no. 1 (2009): 107–128; Marc J. Hetherington and Michael Nelson, "Anatomy of a Rally Effect: George W. Bush and the War on Terrorism," *Political Science and Politics* 36, no. 1 (2003): 37–42; Andrew J. Perrin and Sondra J. Smolek, "Who Trusts? Race, Gender, and the September 11 Rally Effect among Young Adults," *Social Science Research* 38, no. 1 (2009): 134–145. Analyzing the response to 9/11 in civil society, Jeffrey Alexander documents a "moral revivification," suggesting that the resilience the United States exhibited was precisely the opposite of the response that bin Laden had hoped to elicit when he orchestrated the attacks. Jeffrey C. Alexander, "From the Depths of Despair: Performance, Counterperformance, and 'September 11,'" *Sociological Theory* 22, no. 1 (2004): 103.
59. Wagner-Pacifici, "Theorizing the Restlessness of Events," 1354.
60. "Remarks by President George W. Bush at the National Prayer Service."

CHAPTER 5

1. Anderson, *Imagined Communities*, 11.
2. On the relationship between symbolic meanings and the struggle for power and resources, see especially Alexander, *The Performance of Politics*; Hunt, *Politics, Culture, and Class in the French Revolution*; Olick, *The Politics of Regret*; Wagner-Pacifici, "Theorizing the Restlessness of Events."
3. Olick, *The Sins of the Fathers*.
4. See the discussion in Malphurs, "The Media's Frontier Construction of President George W. Bush," 188–190.
5. "Remarks by President Bush at Meeting with Military Leadership," September 17, 2001, *Federal News Service*, LexisNexis Academic.
6. Ibid.
7. Ibid.
8. Malphurs, "The Media's Frontier Construction of President George W. Bush," 193; Debra Merskin, "The Construction of Arabs as Enemies: Post–September 11 Discourse of George W. Bush," *Mass Communication and Society* 7, no. 2 (2004): 169.
9. "Remarks by President Bush at Meeting with Military Leadership." On the analogy with a hunt, see also Malphurs, "The Media's Frontier Construction of President George W. Bush," 191.
10. "Remarks by President Bush at Meeting with Military Leadership."
11. Ibid.
12. Ibid.
13. This and all preceding quotations in this paragraph are from "Text: Giuliani at the United Nations," *Washington Post*, October 1, 2001, www.washingtonpost.com/wp-srv/nation/specials/attacked/transcripts/giulianitext_100101.html.
14. See, e.g., the discussions of the cosmopolitanization and globalization of Holocaust memory, and the process through which it became a symbolic representation of evil, in Alexander, "On the Social Construction of Moral Universals"; Daniel Levy and Natan Sznaider, "Memory Unbound: The Holocaust and the Formation of Cosmopolitan Memory," *European Journal of Social Theory* 5, no. 1 (2002): 87–106.
15. "Text: Giuliani at the United Nations."
16. "Statement by President Bush Announcing Military Action Against the Taliban," October 7, 2001, *Federal News Service*, LexisNexis Academic.
17. Ibid.
18. All quotations in this paragraph are from "State of the Union Address by President George W. Bush," January 29, 2002, *Federal News Service*, LexisNexis Academic.
19. According to speechwriter David Frum, who coined the phrase "axis of hatred"—which was later changed to "axis of evil" in keeping with "the theological language that Bush had made his own since September 11"—this was indeed the analogy that had inspired the term. "No country on earth more closely resembled one of the old Axis powers than present-day Iraq," Frum wrote in a 2003 memoir about his experience working within the Bush administration. David Frum, *The Right Man: The Surprise Presidency of George W. Bush* (New York: Random House, 2003), 234.
20. "State of the Union Address by President George W. Bush," January 29, 2002.
21. Cole, *The Cult of True Victimhood*, 159.

22. All quotations in this paragraph are from "President George W. Bush Remarks at 2002 Graduation Exercise of the United States Military Academy," June 1, 2002, *Federal News Service*, LexisNexis Academic.
23. On vigilante justice, see Brown, *Strain of Violence*, 95–133.
24. "President George W. Bush Remarks at 2002 Graduation Exercise of the United States Military Academy."
25. Ibid.
26. Ibid.
27. For a discussion of the relationship between Bush's decision-making and the moral values he espoused, see Peter Singer, *The President of Good and Evil: Questioning the Ethics of George W. Bush* (New York: Plume, 2004).
28. White House Chief of Staff Andrew Card revealed that the administration had timed these public statements carefully: "From a marketing point of view," he said, "you don't introduce new products in August." Elisabeth Bumiller, "Bush Aides Set Strategy to Sell Policy on Iraq," *New York Times*, September 7, 2002, A6.
29. "Vice President Dick Cheney Discusses 9/11's Anniversary, Iraq, Nation's Economy and Politics," NBC, September 8, 2002, LexisNexis Academic Broadcast Transcripts.
30. "White House Presses Case Against Iraq," CNN, September 8, 2002, LexisNexis Academic Broadcast Transcripts. On the same day, the phrase appeared in a front-page *New York Times* article, which explained: "Hard liners are alarmed that American intelligence underestimated the pace and scale of Iraq's nuclear program before Baghdad's defeat in the [G]ulf [W]ar. Conscious of this lapse in the past, they argue that Washington dare not wait until analysts have found hard evidence that Mr. Hussein has acquired a nuclear weapon. The first sign of a 'smoking gun,' they argue, may be a mushroom cloud." Michael R. Gordon and Judith Miller, "U.S. Says Hussein Intensifies Quest for A-Bomb Parts," *New York Times*, September 8, 2002, A1.
31. "Remarks of President George W. Bush," October 7, 2002, *Federal News Service*, LexisNexis Academic.
32. Bush administration officials had considered both Governors Island and Ellis Island as settings for the speech; they ultimately selected Ellis Island for its "more spectacular" camera angles. Administration officials told reporters that the speech was intended, in part, to generate support for taking military action against Iraq. Bumiller, "Bush Aides Set Strategy to Sell Policy on Iraq."
33. "President George W. Bush Address to the Nation," September 11, 2002, *Federal News Service*, LexisNexis Academic.
34. "Remarks by President George W. Bush to the United Nations General Assembly," September 12, 2002, *Federal News Service*, LexisNexis Academic.
35. Ibid.
36. "State of the Union Address by President George W. Bush," January 28, 2003, *Federal News Service*, LexisNexis Academic.
37. Ibid. He thus framed Iraq as a new frontier for the "redeemer nation."
38. Ibid. Again, note the frontier imagery here.
39. Ibid.
40. Ibid.
41. "Remarks by Secretary of State Colin Powell to the U.N. Security Council Re: Iraq's Weapons of Mass Destruction," February 5, 2003, *Federal News Service*, LexisNexis Academic.

42. Ibid.
43. Ibid. On Powell's reputation, see "The Case Against Iraq," *New York Times*, February 6, 2003, A38.
44. "Remarks by Secretary of State Colin Powell to the U.N. Security Council."
45. Ibid.
46. Steven R. Weisman, "Powell Calls His U.N. Speech a Lasting Blot on His Record," *New York Times*, September 9, 2005, A10.
47. "President Bush Address to the Nation," March 19, 2003, *Federal News Service*, LexisNexis Academic.
48. Ibid.
49. See, e.g., Richard Clarke, *Against All Enemies: Inside America's War on Terror* (New York: Free Press, 2004); Frum, *The Right Man*; Ron Suskind, *The Price of Loyalty: George W. Bush, the White House, and the Education of Paul O'Neill* (New York: Simon and Schuster, 2004); George Tenet, *At the Center of the Storm: My Years at the CIA* (New York: HarperCollins, 2007).
50. Smith, *Why War?*, 156.
51. Ibid., 157. More broadly, Smith argues for "think[ing] of culture as a contributory if not sufficient cause for war," suggesting that apocalyptic narratives—which posit a stark contrast between good and evil and contend that present events have world-historical significance—"are the most effective at generating and legitimating massive society-wide sacrifice" (pp. 11, 27). Indeed, the dualistic narrative I have identified has clear apocalyptic themes, evoking an unbridgeable chasm between the forces of good and the forces of evil, and presenting the conflict at hand as a struggle for civilization itself. On the millenialist themes in Bush's speechmaking and their place within a much longer lineage of apocalyptic thinking, see also John R. Hall, *Apocalypse: From Antiquity to the Empire of Modernity* (Malden, MA: Polity Press, 2009), 186–188.
52. The concept of legitimacy has a long history in sociology, beginning with Weber's classic typology distinguishing traditional, charismatic, and legal-rational forms of authority. Following Weber, Seymour Martin Lipset defined legitimacy as "the capacity" of a given political system "to engender and maintain the belief that the existing political institutions are the most appropriate ones for the society." Seymour Martin Lipset, *Political Man: The Social Bases of Politics* (Garden City, NY: Doubleday, 1960), 77; see also Max Weber, *Economy and Society* (Berkeley: University of California Press, 1978), 212–301, 941–955. Legitimation claims, then, aim to establish legitimacy among the citizenry. My primary intention is to analyze the symbolic content of legitimation claims—the justifications politicians have deployed for particular policy decisions and their relationship to the political consolation discourse I analyzed in chapter 4. Here, however, I also attend briefly to data that sheds light on their resonance among the citizenry, venturing into the issue of legitimacy.
53. ABC News/*Washington Post* Terrorist Attack Poll #3, September 2001. ICPSR03294-v1. Ann Arbor, MI: Inter-university Consortium for Political and Social Research [distributor], 2001. http://doi.org/10.3886/ICPSR03294.v1.
54. Ibid. Among these respondents, nearly 72 percent voiced strong support, while nearly 12 percent said they supported it "somewhat."
55. Ibid.
56. Gallup Poll, November 8–11, 2001, and January 7–9, 2002, http://www.gallup.com/poll/116233/afghanistan.aspx.

57. Gallup Poll, July 19–21, 2004, and March 7–10, 2013, http://www.gallup.com/poll/116233/afghanistan.aspx.
58. Smith, *Why War?*, 175.
59. Rogin, *Ronald Reagan, the Movie and Other Episodes in Political Demonology*, xiii. See also the discussion of Reagan in chapter 2, note 54, of the present work. While Reagan largely "escaped contamination," Rogin notes that most American leaders who have engaged in political demonology have ultimately "failed to separate themselves from the demons that plagued them," as was the case with Bush (p. xvii).
60. "Public Struggles with Possible War in Iraq," Pew Research Center, January 30, 2003, http://www.people-press.org/2003/01/30/public-struggles-with-possible-war-in-iraq/.
61. Gallup Poll, March 24–25, 2003, http://www.gallup.com/poll/1633/iraq.aspx.
62. The House passed the resolution 297–133; in the Senate, the vote was 77–23.
63. "President Bush Address to the Nation," May 1, 2003, *Federal News Service*, LexisNexis Academic.
64. Ibid.
65. Elisabeth Bumiller, "Keepers of Bush Image Lift Stagecraft to New Heights," *New York Times*, May 16, 2003, A1. See also the discussions in Engelhardt, *The End of Victory Culture*, 310–312; Smith, *Why War?*, 171–172.
66. For the cover image, see http://www.time.com/time/covers/0,16641,2003 1006,00.html.
67. "President George W. Bush Address to the Nation," September 7, 2003, *Federal News Service*, LexisNexis Academic.
68. Ibid.
69. Gallup Poll, October 6–8, 2003, http://www.gallup.com/poll/1633/iraq.aspx.
70. "Remarks by President George W. Bush," December 14, 2005, *Federal News Service*, LexisNexis Academic.
71. Ibid.
72. Ibid.
73. Gallup Poll, December 16–18, 2005, http://www.gallup.com/poll/1633/iraq.aspx.
74. "Remarks by President George W. Bush," March 19, 2008, *Federal News Service*, LexisNexis Academic.
75. Steven Kull, Clay Ramsay, Stefan Subias, Evan Lewis, and Phillip Warf, "Misperceptions, the Media and the Iraq War," Program on International Policy Attitudes/Knowledge Networks, October 2, 2003, http://www.pipa.org/OnlineReports/Iraq/IraqMedia_Oct03/IraqMedia_Oct03_rpt.pdf.
76. Ibid. For a summary of polling data across a wider range of sources, see Scott L. Althaus and Devon M. Largio, "When Osama Became Saddam: Origins and Consequences of the Change in America's Public Enemy #1," *Political Science and Politics* 37, no. 4 (2004): 795–799; Philip Everts and Pierangelo Isernia, "The War in Iraq," *Public Opinion Quarterly* 69, no. 2 (2005): 264–323.
77. Monica Prasad, Andrew J. Perrin, Kieran Bezila, Steve G. Hoffman, Kate Kindleberger, Kim Manturuk, and Ashleigh Smith Powers, "'There Must Be a Reason': Osama, Saddam, and Inferred Justification," *Sociological Inquiry* 79, no. 2 (2009): 142–162.
78. For instance, while it is easy to assume that popular beliefs followed from the Bush administration's decision to juxtapose references to September 11 and

Saddam Hussein, there is some evidence that Americans viewed Hussein as a suspect from the outset. Althaus and Largio, "When Osama Became Saddam," 797–799. Nevertheless, whether the Bush administration was constructing or reinforcing public perceptions of a symbolic link between 9/11—or the possibility of "another 9/11"—this discourse clearly helped to constitute the effect flow of September 11 and to underwrite an expansive view of the war on terror.

79. Geertz, *The Interpretation of Cultures*, 220.

80. Alexander, *The Performance of Politics*, 4; Jeffrey C. Goldfarb, *Reinventing Political Culture: The Power of Culture versus the Culture of Power* (Malden, MA: Polity Press, 2012), 5.

81. Eric Lewis, "Torture's Future," *New York Times* Campaign Stops Blog, November 21, 2011, http://campaignstops.blogs.nytimes.com/2011/11/21/tortures-future/.

82. David Brooks, "Obama, Gospel and Verse," *New York Times*, April 26, 2007, A25. See also Reinhold Niebuhr, *The Irony of American History* (Chicago: University of Chicago Press, 2008).

83. Goldfarb, *Reinventing Political Culture*, 5.

84. On the transition from the campaign to the presidency, see Alexander, *The Performance of Politics*. More generally, see also Weber on the routinization of charisma. Max Weber, *The Theory of Social and Economic Organization* (New York: Free Press, 1947), 363–372.

85. David Johnston and Charlie Savage, "Obama Signals His Reluctance to Investigate Bush Programs," *New York Times*, January 12, 2009, A1.

86. Olick, *The Politics of Regret*, 57–60.

87. "Remarks by President Barack Obama," December 1, 2009, *Federal News Service*, LexisNexis Academic.

88. Ibid.

89. Ibid.

90. "Remarks by President Barack Obama to Coalition Forces in Afghanistan," December 3, 2010, *Federal News Service*, LexisNexis Academic.

91. Obama's public criticism of the Iraq War was especially important in his efforts to distinguish himself from his main opponent in the Democratic primary, Hillary Clinton. In 2002, while representing New York in the U.S. Senate, Clinton had voted for the Iraq War Resolution.

92. "Transcript: Obama's Speech Against the Iraq War," National Public Radio [NPR], January 20, 2009, http://www.npr.org/templates/story/story.php?storyId=99591469.

93. Ibid.

94. All quotations in this paragraph are from "Remarks by United States President Barack Obama to Military Personnel at Camp Lejeune," February 27, 2009, *Federal News Service*, LexisNexis Academic.

95. All quotations in this paragraph are from "Address to the Nation by President Barack Obama," August 31, 2010, *Federal News Service*, LexisNexis Academic.

96. In a certain sense, Bush adopted this position after acknowledging that Hussein had not possessed WMD. Yet he continued to invoke connections to September 11 in a way that his successor generally did not.

97. "Remarks by President Barack Obama on the Death of Osama bin Laden," May 1, 2011, *Federal News Service*, LexisNexis Academic.

98. Ibid.

99. Ibid.
100. All quotations in this and the preceding paragraph are from "Prepared Remarks by President Barack Obama at a September 11th Commemoration," September 11, 2011, *Federal News Service*, LexisNexis Academic.
101. This quotation, along with all quotations in the preceding paragraph, is from "Remarks by President Barack Obama," May 23, 2013, *Federal News Service*, LexisNexis Academic.
102. "Remarks by President George W. Bush at the National Prayer Service."
103. All quotations in this and the preceding two paragraphs are from "Remarks by President Barack Obama," May 23, 2013.
104. Stow, "Do You Know What It Means to Miss New Orleans?"
105. Ankersmit, "Trauma and Suffering," 79. See also Améry, *At the Mind's Limits*, 68–69; Olick, *The Politics of Regret*, 163–164.
106. "Address by President Bush to the United Nations General Assembly," November 10, 2001, *Federal News Service*, LexisNexis Academic.
107. "Remarks by President Barack Obama at the Graduation Ceremony for the United States Military Academy at West Point," May 28, 2014, *Federal News Service*, LexisNexis Academic.
108. Ibid.
109. Barack Obama, "Address to the Nation on United States Strategy to Combat the Islamic State of Iraq and the Levant Terrorist Organization," September 10, 2014. Online by Gerhard Peters and John T. Woolley, *The American Presidency Project*, http://www.presidency.ucsb.edu/ws/?pid=107266.

CHAPTER 6

1. Robin Wagner-Pacifici, *Discourse and Destruction: The City of Philadelphia versus MOVE* (Chicago: University of Chicago Press, 1994), 145–147.
2. Michael André Bernstein, *Foregone Conclusions: Against Apocalyptic History* (Berkeley: University of California Press, 1994), 3.
3. Ibid., 3–4.
4. "Pennsylvania—9/11/02," Public Broadcasting Service [PBS], September 11, 2002, http://www.pbs.org/newshour/bb/terrorism/july-dec02/pennsylvania_9-11.html.
5. "Remarks by General Colin Powell, Former Secretary of State, Former Chairman of the Joint Chiefs of Staff, at a Memorial Ceremony for United Airlines Flight 93," September 11, 2009, *Federal News Service*, LexisNexis Academic.
6. "Remarks by Defense Secretary Donald Rumsfeld and Chairman of the Joint Chiefs of Staff General Richard Myers at Memorial Ceremony for Victims of the September 11, 2001 Terrorist Attack on the Pentagon," September 11, 2003, *Federal News Service*, LexisNexis Academic.
7. "Remarks by President George W. Bush at the Pentagon 9/11 Memorial Dedication Ceremony," September 11, 2008, *Federal News Service*, LexisNexis Academic.
8. "Remarks by Tom Ridge, Director, Office of Homeland Security at a Ceremony Marking September 11th Anniversary," September 11, 2002, *Federal News Service*, LexisNexis Academic.
9. "Homeland Security's Tom Ridge Pledges Resolve at Sept. 11 Memorial Service," September 11, 2004, U.S. Department of State, http://iipdigital.usembassy.gov/st/english/texttrans/2004/09/20040911173759cpata

ruk0.3871271.html#axzz2RCSlNmw6. Ridge—who was the governor of Pennsylvania until shortly after 9/11, when Bush appointed him to head the newly created Department of Homeland Security—has spoken at Shanksville frequently, and has repeated this formulation in subsequent commemorations.

10. "Remarks by Defense Secretary Donald Rumsfeld and Chairman of the Joint Chiefs of Staff General Richard Myers at Memorial Ceremony."

11. Ibid.

12. "Remarks by Defense Secretary Donald Rumsfeld at Memorial Service for Unidentified Pentagon Victims of 9/11 Attack," September 12, 2002, *Federal News Service*, LexisNexis Academic.

13. Ibid.

14. Anderson, *Imagined Communities*, 9.

15. Ibid., 11.

16. It is perhaps worth providing brief biographical detail on the five individuals given special recognition in this ceremony: Ronald F. Golinski, a 60-year-old retired colonel who was working for the Army; Ronald Hemenway, a 37-year-old Navy electronics technician first class; James T. Lynch, a 55-year-old civilian television and video technician who worked for the Navy; Rhonda Rasmussen, a 44-year-old civilian budget analyst who worked for the Army; and Dana Falkenberg, a three-year-old who perished along with her parents and sister aboard Flight 77. For the list of individuals honored, see Jim Garamone, "Remains of Pentagon Attack Victims Buried at Arlington," September 12, 2002, U.S. Department of Defense, www.defense.gov/news/newsarticle/aspx?id=43465. For biographical details, see the profiles compiled by the *Washington Post*, http://projects.washingtonpost.com/911victims.

17. "Flight 93 Fifth Anniversary Commemoration," C-SPAN Video Library, September 11, 2006, http://www.c-span.org/Events/Flight-93-Fifth-Anniversary-Commemoration/5219/.

18. "Remarks by General Colin Powell, Former Secretary of State, Former Chairman of the Joint Chiefs of Staff, at a Memorial Ceremony for United Airlines Flight 93."

19. Ibid.

20. Ibid.

21. "Remarks by President George W. Bush at Defense Department Ceremony Marking September 11th Terrorist Attack on the Pentagon," September 11, 2002, *Federal News Service*, LexisNexis Academic.

22. Ibid.

23. "Remarks by General Peter Pace, Chairman, Joint Chiefs of Staff, and Secretary of Defense Robert Gates," September 11, 2007, *Federal News Service*, LexisNexis Academic.

24. "Remarks by Defense Secretary Donald Rumsfeld and Chairman of the Joint Chiefs of Staff General Richard Myers at Memorial Ceremony."

25. Wagner-Pacifici, "Memories in the Making," 304.

26. Ibid. On moral and cultural entrepreneurship, see also Paul DiMaggio, "Cultural Entrepreneurship in Nineteenth-Century Boston," *Media, Culture and Society* 4, no. 1 (1982): 35; Fine, "Reputational Entrepreneurs and the Memory of Incompetence," 1162; Wagner-Pacifici and Schwartz, "The Vietnam Veterans Memorial," 382.

27. Wagner-Pacifici, "Memories in the Making," 304.

28. Wagner-Pacifici, *Discourse and Destruction*, 8.

29. Ibid.
30. "Remarks by Admiral Michael Mullen, Chairman of the Joint Chiefs of Staff, at the Pentagon 9/11 Memorial Dedication Ceremony," September 11, 2008, *Federal News Service*, LexisNexis Academic.
31. "Remarks by Secretary of Defense Donald Rumsfeld and General Richard Myers, Chairman, Joint Chiefs of Staff at Ceremony Marking Three Months Since the Terrorist Attack on the Pentagon," December 11, 2001, *Federal News Service*, LexisNexis Academic, emphasis added.
32. "Remarks by Defense Secretary Donald Rumsfeld and Chairman of the Joint Chiefs of Staff General Richard Myers at Memorial Ceremony," emphasis added.
33. "Prepared Remarks of Attorney General Alberto Gonzales at the Flight 93 Memorial Ceremony," September 11, 2005, *Federal News Service*, LexisNexis Academic, emphasis added.
34. Ibid., emphasis added.
35. All quotations in this paragraph are from Wagner-Pacifici, *Discourse and Destruction*, 146.
36. "Former President William J. Clinton Delivers Remarks at Flight 93 Memorial Dedication," September 10, 2011, *CQ Transcriptions*, LexisNexis Academic.
37. Ibid., emphasis added.
38. Wagner-Pacifici, *Discourse and Destruction*, 146.
39. "Former President William J. Clinton Delivers Remarks at Flight 93 Memorial Dedication."
40. In this vein, it is interesting to compare this speech with Clinton's response to the Oklahoma City bombing, discussed in chapter 1. His remarks in Oklahoma City drew analogies—both implicit and explicit—between the dead and fallen soldiers, gesturing subtly toward the differences but never reflecting on the distortions of such analogies as he did in this more recent address in Shanksville.
41. "Former President George W. Bush Delivers Remarks at Flight 93 Memorial Dedication," September 10, 2011, *CQ Transcriptions*, LexisNexis Academic.
42. There is a substantial literature addressing when and why such multivocal commemorations—which bring pluralistic audiences together at the same place and time—are likely to occur. As Vered Vinitzky-Seroussi demonstrates, divisive events may also be memorialized through *fragmented* commemorations, in which diverse audiences gather in disparate spaces where they memorialize the past in their own particularistic (and conflicting) discourses. Vinitzky-Seroussi, "Commemorating a Difficult Past," 31–32; on multivocal commemorations, see also Wagner-Pacifici and Schwartz, "The Vietnam Veterans Memorial," 392–394, 404–407. While the Manhattan ceremonies have clearly assumed a multivocal form, September 11 commemorations are in a certain sense fragmented; as I show in this chapter, distinct discourses have taken shape at each of the three crash sites. Yet this fragmentation is primarily a product of the events themselves, unfolding as they did at multiple sites, rather than explicit conflicts that drove key agents or entrepreneurs to commemorate 9/11 in separate spaces. The conflicts I examine in the next chapter shed light on the challenges of bringing diverse constituencies together in reconstructing the World Trade Center, which—despite the multi-sited nature of the event—is unquestionably the sacred center for September 11 memory, and the location for the national memorial and museum devoted to

the event. As Christina Steidl points out, the commemorative field—that is, "the collection of spaces and narratives that accumulate in the commemoration of an event over time"—is a complex one. Christina R. Steidl, "Remembering May 4, 1970: Integrating the Commemorative Field at Kent State," *American Sociological Review* 78, no. 5 (2013): 753. In the next chapter, I argue that September 11 remains a cultural trauma; collective actors still struggle to assimilate the event into the broad collective narratives that might integrate this field.

43. "Mayor Michael R. Bloomberg: 'We Owe It to Those That We Lost to Expand Our Quest,'" *New York Times*, September 11, 2002, A15.

44. Ibid.

45. Lukinson, *September Morning*, "2002: Mayor Bloomberg, Introduction."

46. Lukinson, *September Morning*, "2002: Governor McGreevey, The Declaration of Independence (excerpt)."

47. Lukinson, *September Morning*, "2002: Mayor Bloomberg, The Ground We Stand On."

48. "Michael Bloomberg Delivers Remarks at Dedication of Temporary Memorial," September 11, 2002, *FDCH Political Transcripts*, LexisNexis Academic.

49. Stow, "Pericles at Gettysburg and Ground Zero," 204–206; Bradford Vivian, "Neoliberal Epideictic: Rhetorical Form and Commemorative Politics on September 11, 2002," *Quarterly Journal of Speech* 92, no. 1 (2006): 18–21.

50. Wagner-Pacifici, *The Moro Morality Play*, 283.

51. Between the first and 10th anniversaries, each commemoration featured a general theme that oriented the readings. Though the themes varied slightly, these texts exhibited broad continuities to form a generally coherent—though avowedly multivocal—commemorative mode. For a listing of these themes, see Lukinson, *September Morning*.

52. Lukinson, *September Morning*, "2003: Mayor Bloomberg, Reading of the Names." "The Names" was subsequently published in Billy Collins, *Aimless Love: New and Selected Poems* (New York: Random House, 2013), 254–256.

53. Lukinson, *September Morning*, "2004: Governor Pataki, If Tears Could Bring You Back."

54. Lukinson, *September Morning*, "2004: Mayor Bloomberg, Reading of the Names."

55. Lukinson, *September Morning*, "2008: Secretary Chertoff, The Guest House." For the original source, see Rumi, "The Guest House," in *The Essential Rumi*, translated by Coleman Barks (San Francisco: Harper San Francisco, 1995), 109.

56. Lukinson, *September Morning*, "2008: Governor Pataki, Drop by Drop Upon the Heart."

57. Lukinson, *September Morning*, "2011: Mayor Giuliani, Ecclesiastes."

58. See the table of contents in Lukinson, *September Morning*. Bush had originally designated the September 11 anniversary as "Patriot Day."

59. Lukinson, *September Morning*, "2009: Governor Corzine, If I Can Stop One Heart from Breaking." For the original source, see Emily Dickinson, *The Complete Poems of Emily Dickinson*, vol. 2, ed. Thomas H. Johnson (Cambridge, MA: Harvard University Press, 1963), 672.

60. Lukinson, *September Morning*, "2009: Mayor Giuliani, Everybody Can Be Great."

61. Lukinson, *September Morning*, "2008: Mayor Bloomberg, Reading of the Names."

62. Lukinson, *September Morning*, "2008: Governor Paterson, Losing a Loved One (excerpt)"; "2008: Governor Corzine, Try to Praise the Mutilated World (excerpt)"; "2008: Mayor Giuliani, For the Fallen."

63. Lukinson, *September Morning*, "2004: Mayor Giuliani, Letter from Abraham Lincoln"; "2011: President Bush, Letter from Abraham Lincoln." In 2004, the text fit broadly with the commemoration's focus on parents who had lost children.

64. Lukinson, *September Morning*, "2011: President Bush, Letter from Abraham Lincoln."

65. Lukinson, *September Morning*, "2003: Mayor Giuliani, Go Forward Together."

66. Vivian Yee, "At Ground Zero, Readers Offer Plain-Spoken Tributes to Those Lost," *New York Times*, September 12, 2012, A26.

67. Michael M. Grynbaum, "9/11 Memorial Bars Elected Officials from Speaking at Ceremony," *New York Times*, July 12, 2012, A17.

68. As George Mosse notes, lists of names were an important component of national memory well before the Vietnam Veterans Memorial was conceived or constructed. Mosse, *Fallen Soldiers*, 49, 99. But Maya Lin's memorial design undoubtedly made them far more central, perhaps even compulsory, in commemorating loss. Among the "five physical program elements" listed in the guidelines for the competition to design the National September 11 Memorial was the stipulation that the memorial "[r]ecognize each individual who was a victim of the attacks," including those killed in New York, Pennsylvania, and Virginia in 2001 and those killed in the World Trade Center bombing in 1993. "World Trade Center Site Memorial Competition Guidelines," Lower Manhattan Development Corporation, https://www.911memorial.org/sites/all/files/LMDC%20Memorial%20Guidelines.pdf, 19. See also the discussion in James E. Young, "The Stages of Memory at Ground Zero," in *Religion, Violence, Memory, and Place*, ed. Oren Baruch Stier and J. Shawn Landres (Bloomington: Indiana University Press, 2006), 218–221.

69. Wagner-Pacifici and Schwartz, "The Vietnam Veterans Memorial," 394.

70. Christina Simko, "Rhetorics of Suffering: September 11 Commemorations as Theodicy," *American Sociological Review* 77, no. 6 (2012): 892–897.

71. For an adaptation of Weber's notion of "carrier groups," see Alexander et al., *Cultural Trauma and Collective Identity*, 11.

72. Cindi Lash, "Somerset Dubs Itself America's County," *Pittsburgh Post-Gazette*, August 3, 2003, C1.

73. "President Bush Addresses a Joint Session of Congress." Beamer subsequently penned a memoir that extended this narrative. See Lisa Beamer (with Ken Abraham), *Let's Roll!: Ordinary People, Extraordinary Courage* (Wheaton, IL: Tyndale House Publishers, 2002).

74. See the foreword by Michael Bloomberg in Lukinson, *September Morning*.

75. Olick, *The Politics of Regret*, 57–60.

76. Janny Scott, "The Silence of the Historic Present," *New York Times*, August 11, 2002, 29.

77. Ibid.

78. Clyde Haberman, "Speechless in the Face of History," *New York Times*, August 30, 2002, B1.

79. All quotations in this and the preceding paragraph are from Michiko Kakutani, "Vigilance and Memory: Critic's Notebook; Rituals, Improvised or Traditional," *New York Times*, September 12, 2002, B14.

80. All quotations in this and the preceding paragraph are from Robert Burke, "Why Obama Should Speak Here," *New York Daily News*, September 4, 2011, http://www.nydailynews.com/opinion/obama-speak-9-11-family-member-urges-president-speak-ground-zero-9-11-article-1.951815.
81. Haberman, "Speechless in the Face of History." From the time the plans for the first anniversary were unveiled, Haberman had publicly criticized Bloomberg's approach to the ceremonies. Following the sixth anniversary, he complained that politicians "flew rhetorically on borrowed wings," and sardonically quoted Herman Melville: "It is better to fail in originality than to succeed in imitation." Clyde Haberman, "For 9/11, the Eloquence is Borrowed," *New York Times*, September 14, 2007, B1.
82. Clyde Haberman, "Shrinking from History," *New York Times* City Room Blog, September 7, 2011, http://cityroom.blogs.nytimes.com/2011/09/07/shrinking-from-history/.
83. Ibid.
84. Clyde Haberman, "At 9/11 Event, Leadership Isn't Invited," *New York Times*, July 18, 2012, A21.
85. Memory scholars, too, have pointed to the pitfalls of such open-ended commemorations. As Vered Vinitzky-Seroussi and Chana Teeger argue, such an approach "[widens] the audience that can share the moment," but it does so "at the expense of a certain depth"—the reflections on "this particular and anomalous tragedy" that, according to Kakutani, were missing in 2002. Vered Vinitzky-Seroussi and Chana Teeger, "Unpacking the Unspoken: Silence in Collective Memory and Forgetting," *Social Forces* 88, no. 3 (2010): 1112; Kakutani, "Vigilance and Memory."

CHAPTER 7

1. Charles V. Bagli, "In Latest Phase of Ground Zero Building Dispute, a New Call for Oversight," *New York Times*, June 9, 2012, A17; Patricia Cohen, "Dispute Over Money Delays 9/11 Museum," *New York Times*, November 22, 2011, C3, and "Construction Frozen in a Fight Over Financing," *New York Times*, June 3, 2012, A21; Patrick McGeehan, "For Museum and Memorial, Issues of Money and Fence-Mending Lie Ahead," *New York Times*, September 10, 2011, A19; Michael Schwirtz, "Cuomo and Christie Request Federal Financing for Sept. 11 Museum," *New York Times* City Room Blog, June 16, 2012, http://cityroom. blogs.nytimes.com/2012/06/16/cuomo-and-christie-request-federal-financing-for-sept-11-museum/?ref=memorials&_r=0. On the struggles among architects, public officials, and commercial interests, see Paul Goldberger, *Up From Zero: Politics, Architecture, and the Rebuilding of New York* (New York: Random House, 2004); Philip Nobel, *Sixteen Acres: Architecture and the Outrageous Struggle for the Future of Ground Zero* (New York: Henry Holt and Company, 2005).
2. David W. Dunlap, "Display of Names at Trade Center Memorial Is a Painstaking Process," *New York Times*, March 24, 2009, A25.
3. Glenn Collins, "Protesters Step Up Calls for 9/11 Memorial Above Ground," *New York Times*, February 28, 2006, B3; David W. Dunlap, "The Effect of Moving 9/11 Names to Street Level," *New York Times*, June 22, 2006, B4; David W. Dunlap and Charles V. Bagli, "New Look at Memorial Lowers Cost," *New York Times*, June 21, 2006, B1.

4. David W. Dunlap, "9/11 Memorial Faces Setback over Names," *New York Times*, June 27, 2006, B1, "Deciding How to Arrange the Names of the 9/11 Fallen," *New York Times*, August 17, 2006, B2, "Plan Is Changed for Arranging Names on Trade Center Memorial," *New York Times*, December 14, 2006, B3, "Still, the Question of Displaying the Names of 9/11," *New York Times*, January 11, 2007, B2, and "Relatives' Groups Use TV and Internet to Call for More Details with Names on 9/11 Memorial," *New York Times*, January 25, 2007, B2.

5. Collins, "Protesters Step Up Calls for 9/11 Memorial Above Ground"; Dunlap, "Display of Names at Trade Center Memorial Is a Painstaking Process," "9/11 Memorial Faces Setback over Names," and "Plan Is Changed for Arranging Names on Trade Center Memorial."

6. Stephen Farrell, "Remains of 9/11 Victims Will Be Moved," *New York Times*, May 6, 2014, A20, and "In 'Ceremonial Transfer,' Remains of 9/11 Victims Are Moved to Memorial," *New York Times*, May 11, 2014, A20; Anemona Hartocollis, "Mayor Is Urged to Ask 9/11 Victims' Relatives Where to Put Remains," *New York Times*, April 4, 2011, A16, and "Poll of 9/11 Families Is Sought Over Unidentified Remains," *New York Times* City Room Blog, June 2, 2011, http://cityroom.blogs.nytimes.com/ 2011/06/02/poll-of-911-families-is-sought-over-unidentified-remains/?ref = memorials.

7. Alexander, *The Civil Sphere*, 4–9; Alexander and Smith, "The Discourse of American Civil Society," 160–167.

8. Ankersmit, "Trauma and Suffering," 78, 79. See also Neil J. Smelser, "Epilogue: September 11, 2001, as Cultural Trauma," in Jeffrey C. Alexander et al., *Cultural Trauma and Collective Identity* (Berkeley: University of California Press, 2004), 265. Smelser argued that although it remained too early to tell, September 11 had all the makings of a cultural trauma. In particular, he documented a perception that "the country will never be the same, and that both the reverberation of tragic events and the aggressive 'war on terrorism'—as it has come to be called—would be without end."

9. On the conceptual connection between trauma and *ressentiment*, see Olick, *The Politics of Regret*, 153–173. On *ressentiment* generally, see Améry, *At the Mind's Limits*, 62–81; Nietzsche, *On the Genealogy of Morals*, 22 and passim; Scheler, *Ressentiment*, 20–21 and passim; Turner, "Max Weber and the Spirit of Resentment."

10. Philip Nobel suggests that the footprints were sanctified in June 2002, when Governor Pataki pledged that there would be no commercial development on the site where the Twin Towers once stood. "Where the towers stood is hallowed ground," Pataki said before an audience of about 400 family members. Jacob H. Fries, "No Buildings Where Towers Once Stood, Pataki Vows," *New York Times*, June 30, 2002, 23. See the discussion in Nobel, *Sixteen Acres*, 177.

11. Robin Pogrebin, "Galleries Devoted to Liberty and Art," *New York Times*, May 20, 2005, E27.

12. "Content and Governance Report," International Freedom Center, September 23, 2005, http://www.renewnyc.com/content/pdfs/IFC_submission.pdf, 1, 16.

13. Ibid., 16.

14. Ibid., 3, 4.

15. Robin Pogrebin, "Gehry Is Selected as Architect of Ground Zero Theater Center," *New York Times*, October 13, 2004, A1.

16. Pogrebin, "Galleries Devoted to Liberty and Art."

17. The Burlingame quotations in this and the preceding paragraph are from Debra Burlingame, "The Great Ground Zero Heist," *Wall Street Journal*, June 7, 2005, A14.

18. "A Sense of Proportion at Ground Zero," *New York Times*, July 29, 2005, A22.

19. Richard J. Tofel, "A Fitting Place at Ground Zero," *Wall Street Journal*, June 9, 2005, A16.

20. Ibid.

21. "A Sense of Proportion at Ground Zero."

22. "Getting to the Heart of the Freedom Center," *New York Daily News*, June 21, 2005, 34.

23. Frank Gaffney, "A Memorial Hijacked?," *Washington Times*, July 6, 2005, A15; Michelle Malkin, "The Desecration of Ground Zero," Jewish World Review, June 8, 2005, http://www.jewishworldreview.com/michelle/malkin060805.php3.

24. Patrick D. Healy, "Pataki Warns Cultural Groups for Museum at Ground Zero," *New York Times*, June 25, 2005, B1.

25. Ibid.

26. Douglas Feiden, "'Violated . . . Again.' Kin Slap Art Center's 9/11 Pieces," *New York Daily News*, June 24, 2005, 7. One exhibit depicted the U.S. atrocities at Abu Ghraib; another drew connections between the Bush family and bin Laden. The next day, the *New York Times* reported that a current exhibit at the Drawing Center appeared "to make light of President Bush's description of Iraq, Iran and North Korea as the Axis of Evil." Healy, "Pataki Warns Cultural Groups for Museum at Ground Zero."

27. Healy, "Pataki Warns Cultural Groups for Museum at Ground Zero."

28. Ibid.

29. David W. Dunlap, "Drawing Center May Drop Plan to Move to Ground Zero," *New York Times*, July 23, 2005, B3.

30. As Wagner-Pacifici argues, any effort to draw boundaries around 9/11 as an event encounters difficulties; she points out, for instance, that "social and political agents have alternately incorporated within September 11 the wars in Afghanistan and Iraq, the legitimization of the torture of 'enemy combatants,' and the militarization of public health structures and activities." Wagner-Pacifici, "Theorizing the Restlessness of Events," 1353–1354. In this case, however, it seems clear that the Take Back the Memorial movement referred to the events that took place on September 11 and the ensuing rescue and recovery effort, explicitly excluding any of the larger policy challenges that 9/11 occasioned.

31. David W. Dunlap, "Freedom Center's Place at 9/11 Site Is in Question," *New York Times*, August 12, 2005, B2.

32. Robin Finn, "Fighting for the Underlying Meaning of Ground Zero," *New York Times*, August 12, 2005, B2.

33. Anthony Ramirez, "At Ground Zero Rally, Anger over a Planned Museum," *New York Times*, September 11, 2005, 36.

34. "Hillary's Home Run," *New York Post*, September 24, 2005, 20. See also Manny Fernandez, "Clinton Says She Opposes Freedom Center," *New York Times*, September 25, 2005, 39.

35. "Freedom and Ground Zero," *New York Times*, June 27, 2005, A14.

36. "Keeping Ground Zero Free," *New York Times*, July 12, 2005, A20.

37. "The Governor's Proxy," *New York Times*, August 16, 2005, A14.
38. David W. Dunlap, "Governor Bars Freedom Center at Ground Zero," *New York Times*, September 29, 2005, A1.
39. Ibid.
40. Robin Finn, "Out of a Job, and Out of Patience with Politicians," *New York Times*, October 7, 2005, B2.
41. Ibid.
42. Dunlap, "Governor Bars Freedom Center at Ground Zero."
43. Ibid.
44. Ibid.
45. Javier C. Hernández, "Planned Sign of Tolerance Bringing Division Instead," *New York Times*, July 14, 2010, A22.
46. Ralph Blumenthal and Sharaf Mowjood, "Muslim Prayers and Renewal Near Ground Zero," *New York Times*, December 9, 2009, A1.
47. Hernández, "Planned Sign of Tolerance Bringing Division Instead."
48. Ibid.
49. Ibid.
50. Lisa Miller, "War Over Ground Zero," *Newsweek* 156, no. 7, August 16, 2010, http://www.newsweek.com/war-over-ground-zero-71469. Regenhard, also interviewed for the article, disagreed.
51. Hernández, "Planned Sign of Tolerance Bringing Division Instead."
52. Michael Barbaro, "Debate Heating Up on Plans for Mosque Near Ground Zero," *New York Times*, July 31, 2010, A1.
53. Ibid.
54. Maggie Haberman, "Rudy: GZ Mosque Is a 'Desecration,' 'Decent Muslims' Won't Be Offended," *Politico*, August 2, 2010, http://www.politico.com/blogs/maggiehaberman/0810/Rudy_Mosque_is_a_desecration_.html?showall.
55. Javier C. Hernández, "Mosque Near Ground Zero Clears Key Hurdle," *New York Times* City Room Blog, August 3, 2010, http://cityroom.blogs.nytimes.com/2010/08/03/mosque-near-ground-zero-clears-key-hurdle/.
56. "Mayor Bloomberg Discusses the Landmarks Preservation Commission Vote on 45–47 Park Place," News from the Blue Room, August 3, 2010, http://www.nyc.gov/portal/site/nycgov/menuitem.c0935b9a57bb4ef3daf2f1c701c789a0/index.jsp?pageID=mayor_press_release&catID=1194&doc_name=http://www.nyc.gov/html/om/html/2010b/pr337-10.html&cc=unused1978&rc=1194&ndi=1.
57. Ibid.
58. Ibid.
59. Michael M. Grynbaum, "City Buses to Get Ads Opposing Islam Center," *New York Times*, August 10, 2010, A18, and "Dispute over Ad Opposing Islamic Center Highlights Limits of the M.T.A.'s Powers," *New York Times*, August 12, 2010, A22.
60. "Remarks by President Obama at the White House Iftar Dinner," August 13, 2010, *Federal News Service*, LexisNexis Academic.
61. Ibid.
62. Ibid.
63. Samuel Goldsmith, "I Never Said Where to Build Mosque," *New York Daily News*, August 15, 2010, 5.
64. Ibid.

65. All polling data and quotations in this paragraph are from Michael Barbaro and Marjorie Connelly, "New York Poll Finds Wariness for Muslim Site," *New York Times*, September 3, 2010, A1.

66. Paul Vitello, "Amid Rift, Imam's Role in Islam Center Is Sharply Cut," *New York Times*, January 15, 2011, A17.

67. Ibid.

68. The announcement followed controversy over a comment Adhami made to an NY1 News reporter asserting a link between homosexual behavior and childhood sexual abuse, though Adhami stated that he was relinquishing the role in order to spend more time completing a book. Paul Vitello, "Imam Steps Down from Project Near Ground Zero," *New York Times* City Room Blog, February 4, 2011, http://cityroom.blogs.nytimes.com/2011/02/04/imam-steps-down-from-project-near-ground-zero/?_php=true&_type=blogs&_r=0.

69. Matt Flegenheimer, "Judge Says Islamic Center Can Stay, But Owes Rent," *New York Times* City Room Blog, November 29, 2011, http://cityroom.blogsnytimes.com/2011/11/29/judge-rules-that-islamic-center-can-stay-but-owes-rent/.

70. Anne Barnard, "After Uproar, a New Tack to Build Islamic Center," *New York Times*, August 2, 2011, A21.

71. Ibid.

72. Sharon Otterman, "Developer Shrinks Plans for Muslim Center," *New York Times*, April 30, 2014, A21.

73. Ibid. Controversy over perceived Islamic symbolism in the design for the Flight 93 memorial near Shanksville, Pennsylvania, yielded a different outcome. In 2005, the memorial's design was altered so that a crescent-shaped cluster of trees that framed the crash site—interpreted by critics as a religious symbol that would honor the perpetrators—was filled in to form a circle. The memorial's architect, Paul Murdoch, explained that the design emerged out of the existing topography at the site, but critics gained traction when Tom Burnett, Sr.—whose son died aboard Flight 93—joined the fray. Sean D. Hammill, "Critics See Symbols of Islam in Flight 93 Memorial Design," *New York Times*, May 5, 2008, A15; Jennifer C. Yates, "Crescent Design for Sept. 11 Memorial Replaced," Associated Press, November 30, 2005.

74. Greg Gittrich and Corky Siemaszko, "In Rubble, a Sacred Find," *New York Daily News*, October 5, 2001, 18.

75. Ibid.

76. Frank Silecchia, "The Cross at Ground Zero," *Guideposts*, http://www.guideposts.org/faith-and-hope/faith-renewed-cross-ground-zero.

77. Geneviève Zubrzycki, "Aesthetic Revolt and the Remaking of National Identity in Québec, 1960–1969," *Theory and Society* 42, no. 5 (2013): 425. Here, Zubrzycki adapts David Morgan's concept of the "sacred gaze"; see David Morgan, *The Sacred Gaze: Religious Visual Culture in Theory and Practice* (Berkeley: University of California Press, 2005).

78. Gittrich and Siemaszko, "In Rubble, a Sacred Find."

79. Brian Jordan, "The Meaning of the Cross at Ground Zero," *National Catholic Register*, September 6, 2011, http://www.ncregister.com/site/article/the-meaning-of-the-cross-at-ground-zero/; Eric Konigsberg, "Brief Journey for an Icon of the Attack on New York," *New York Times*, October 6, 2006, B1.

80. Stephen McKinley, "Priest Wants WTC Cross Memorial Preserved," *Gotham Gazette*, September 2002, http://www.gothamgazette.com/citizen/sep02/irish-wtc.shtml.

81. Konigsberg, "Brief Journey for an Icon of the Attack on New York."
82. Ibid.
83. Zubrzycki, "Aesthetic Revolt," 465. As Zubrzycki argues, studies of iconic images or objects must take into account their "semiotic potential," their "actual material attributes" (p. 427); the shape and proportion of these steel beams enabled, though of course did not determine, their sacralization.
84. Julia Levy, "WTC Cross: Sign from God or Debris?," *New York Sun*, May 14, 2003, 11.
85. Ibid.
86. Ibid.
87. Colleen Long, "World Trade Center Cross Moved to Permanent Home," Associated Press, July 24, 2011.
88. All quotations in this paragraph are from "World Trade Center Cross Is Installed in 9/11 Memorial Museum," National September 11 Memorial and Museum Press Release, July 23, 2011, http://www.911memorial.org/sites/all/files/WTCCrossNewsReleaseFINAL.pdf.
89. Elissa Gootman, "Atheists Sue to Block Display of Cross-Shaped Trade Center Beam in 9/11 Museum," *New York Times*, July 29, 2011, A20.
90. Ibid.
91. American Atheists et al. v. Port Authority et al., New York Southern District Court, Case 1:2011cv06026, filed August 26, 2011.
92. Ibid.
93. David Silverman, "Of Course the 9/11 Cross Is a Religious Symbol," *Washington Post* On Faith Blog, May 2, 2013, http://www.washingtonpost.com/blogs/on-faith/wp/2013/05/02/of-course-the-911-cross-is-a-religious-symbol/.
94. Larry Neumeister, "NY Judge Tosses Lawsuit over Sept. 11 Steel Cross," Associated Press, March 29, 2013.
95. Zubrzycki, "Aesthetic Revolt," 464; see also Zubrzycki, *The Crosses of Auschwitz*, especially chapter 5.
96. Silverman, "Of Course the 9/11 Cross Is a Religious Symbol."
97. Jordan Sekulow and Matthew Clark, "Why the 'Ground Zero Cross' Should Remain," *Washington Post* On Faith Blog, April 4, 2013, http://articles.washingtonpost.com/2013-04-04/national/38268407_1_ground-zero-cross-american-atheists-federal-court.
98. Jay Sekulow, "Angry Atheists, History, and America's Future," Fox News Opinion, April 8, 2013, http://www.foxnews.com/opinion/2013/04/08/angry-atheists-history-and-america-future/.
99. Ibid.
100. Ibid.
101. Charles C. Haynes, "Judge: Atheist Group Takes Separation of Church and State Too Far on 'Ground Zero Cross,'" *Washington Post* On Faith Blog, April 7, 2013, http://www.faithstreet.com/onfaith/2013/04/07/judge-atheist-group-takes-separation-of-church-and-state-too-far-on-ground-zero-cross/21915.
102. See especially Alexander, *The Performance of Politics*; Hunt, *Politics, Culture, and Class in the French Revolution*; Olick, *The Politics of Regret*.
103. Burke, "Why Obama Should Speak Here."
104. Olick, *The Politics of Regret*, 154–155.
105. Ankersmit, "Trauma and Suffering," 79.

106. For a discussion of the competition and the memorial design, see Young, "The Stages of Memory at Ground Zero."
107. On the "Freedom Tower"—now known as 1 World Trade Center—and the struggle for September 11 memory, see David Simpson, *9/11: The Culture of Commemoration* (Chicago: University of Chicago Press, 2006), 63–64.
108. The context for this quotation—which described two lovers, Nisus and Euryalus, who fell together in battle—has generated its own controversy, as classicists and other observers have questioned its appropriateness in this disparate context. Caroline Alexander, "Out of Context," *New York Times*, April 7, 2011, A27; David W. Dunlap, "A Memorial Inscription's Grim Origins," *New York Times*, April 3, 2014, A20.
109. Some family members have protested the way in which this arrangement incorporates the unidentified remains into the paid museum experience. Though the public cannot access the repository, on the wall that is emblazoned with Virgil's words, there is a plaque explaining that the unidentified remains are housed on the site. Stephen Farrell, "In 'Ceremonial Transfer,' Remains of 9/11 Victims Are Moved to Memorial"; Kevin Fasick, "Don't Bury Them!: 9/11 Kin Protest City Putting Remains at Memorial," *New York Post*, May 11, 2014, 2; Joseph Stepansky, Erik Badia, and Larry McShane, "Many WTC Kin Rip Basement Burial; Others Call it 'Respectful,'" *New York Daily News*, May 11, 2014, 4.
110. Améry, *At the Mind's Limits*, 68–69; Caruth, *Trauma*, 4–5; Olick, *The Politics of Regret*, 163–164.
111. This statement is available on the museum's official website, http://www.911memorial.org/about-museum.
112. An exception is Governor Pataki's speech on July 4, 2004, when he laid the cornerstone for 1 World Trade Center; the building was then known as the "Freedom Tower." Pataki evoked the American founding moment, explaining that the building's 1,776-foot height was intended to recall the year of the "nation's birth." "Today," he said, "we, the heirs of that revolutionary spirit of defiance, lay this cornerstone and unmistakably signal to the world the unwavering strength of this nation, and our resolve to fight for freedom." George Pataki, "Laying of the Cornerstone for Freedom Tower," July 4, 2004, http://www.renewnyc.org/content/speeches/Gov_speech_Freedom_Tower.pdf.
113. "Remarks by President Barack Obama on the Death of Osama bin Laden."
114. "Remarks by President Barack Obama at a Congressional Bipartisan Dinner," May 2, 2011, *Federal News Service*, LexisNexis Academic.
115. "Remarks by President Barack Obama to Police Officers," May 5, 2011, *Federal News Service*, LexisNexis Academic.
116. Mark Landler, "President, at Ground Zero, Pays Tribute to Victims of Bin Laden," *New York Times*, May 6, 2011, A13.
117. For instance, the day after Obama's visit to the World Trade Center, the *New York Times* opined: "His silence was the best way to honor the victims of the Sept. 11, 2001, terrorist attacks. No words were needed to remind Americans of our continuing pain." "The Quiet at Ground Zero," *New York Times*, May 6, 2011, A26.
118. For sociological interpretations of this event, see Alexander et al., *Cultural Trauma and Collective Identity*, 131–132; Olick, *The Politics of Regret*, 100–101, 110–112.
119. Quoted in Olick, *The Politics of Regret*, 101.

CONCLUSION

1. For discussions of the transformative power of historical events, see especially Sewell, "Historical Events as Transformations of Structures," 841–844; Wagner-Pacifici, "Theorizing the Restlessness of Events," 1356.
2. Wagner-Pacifici, *The Moro Morality Play*, 9–10. On liminality more generally, see Victor Turner, "Social Dramas and Stories about Them," *Critical Inquiry* 7, no. 1 (1980): 160–166, and *The Ritual Process*, 94–130.
3. Anderson, *Imagined Communities*, 10–12.
4. Alexander, *The Performance of Politics*, 9 and passim; Hart, *The Sound of Leadership*, 14–21, 83–85; Mast, *The Performative Presidency*, 7–8, 25, 27–29; Miroff, "The Presidency and the Public," 211–216; Stuckey, *The President as Interpreter-in-Chief*, 1 and passim; Tulis, *The Rhetorical Presidency*, 4–6 and passim.
5. Abrams, *Historical Sociology*, 8, emphasis in original.
6. Sewell, *Logics of History*, 369.
7. Berger and Luckmann, *The Social Construction of Reality*, 18.
8. Jerome Bruner, *Actual Minds, Possible Worlds* (Cambridge, MA: Harvard University Press, 1986), 26, 159. It is worth noting that, while the subjunctive mood is rarely used in English, it is highly developed and much more commonly employed in other languages (e.g., the Romance languages). This raises interesting questions about the ways in which languages themselves facilitate and constrain our very ability to imagine and articulate alternate histories, our capacity to envision our worlds differently.
9. Turner, "Social Dramas and Stories about Them," 163.
10. Ibid.
11. Robin Wagner-Pacifici, *Theorizing the Standoff: Contingency in Action* (New York: Cambridge University Press, 2000), 3.
12. Turner, "Social Dramas and Stories about Them," 163.
13. Geertz, *The Interpretation of Cultures*, 99.
14. Olick, *The Sins of the Fathers*.
15. Bill Clinton, "'A Struggle for the Soul of the 21st Century': A Speech Given by Bill Clinton at Georgetown University on Nov. 7," *Salon*, November 10, 2001, http://www.salon.com/2001/11/10/speech_9/.
16. Ibid.
17. Ibid.
18. See, e.g., Frum, *The Right Man*, 145–146.
19. Clinton, "A Struggle for the Soul of the 21st Century."
20. Ibid.
21. Ibid.
22. Wagner-Pacifici, *The Moro Morality Play*, 286.
23. Clinton, "A Struggle for the Soul of the 21st Century." Such reflections, as I noted in chapter 6, are sociologically more likely to emanate from outside the highest echelons of power. Clinton's response to the terrorist violence that unfolded during his own administration, which I discussed briefly in chapter 4, generally lacked the vengeful and apocalyptic fervor of his successor's rhetoric. But it espoused an American exceptionalism that was considerably less prominent in this 2001 address, and it asserted a much stronger symbolic boundary between the United States and its enemies.
24. Alexander, "From the Depths of Despair," 103. See also Ronald Jacobs and Philip Smith's argument that romantic narratives which envision a shared utopian future engender "maximal participation, solidarity, and trust in a

common political culture." Ronald N. Jacobs and Philip Smith, "Romance, Irony, and Solidarity," *Sociological Theory* 15, no. 1 (1997): 68.

25. Émile Durkheim, *The Elementary Forms of Religious Life* (New York: Free Press, 1995), 424. On the special significance of the American flag, see Marvin and Ingle, *Blood Sacrifice and the Nation*, 1, 11, and passim.

26. See especially the discussions in Richard J. Bernstein, *The Abuse of Evil: The Corruption of Politics and Religion since 9/11* (Malden, MA: Polity Press, 2005), 22–23; Jacobs and Smith, "Romance, Irony, and Solidarity," 68–69; Wagner-Pacifici, *The Moro Morality Play*, 279–282.

27. Marita Sturken makes this point powerfully in her study of the consumer culture surrounding sites of terrorist violence, especially Oklahoma City and the World Trade Center. The comfort objects such as teddy bears and snow globes through which so many tourists experience these sites of memory, she argues, reinforce the widespread presumption of American innocence and undermine engagement with the profound historical and political questions that surround such events. Marita Sturken, *Tourists of History: Memory, Kitsch, and Consumerism from Oklahoma City to Ground Zero* (Durham, NC: Duke University Press, 2007), 3–32 and passim.

28. Felski, *Rethinking Tragedy*, 11; Wagner-Pacifici, *The Moro Morality Play*, 283.

29. Frye, *Anatomy of Criticism*, 211.

30. "Text: Giuliani at the United Nations."

31. Wagner-Pacifici, "Theorizing the Restlessness of Events," 1381.

32. See Michael Rogin's argument, which I discussed chapter 5, that demonology—a strategy that involves the "dehumanization of political foes"—provides justification "in the name of battling the subversive, to imitate [one's] enemy." Rogin, *Ronald Reagan, the Movie and Other Episodes in Political Demonology*, xiii.

33. Olick, *The Politics of Regret*, 121–138. See also Celermajer, *The Sins of the Nation and the Ritual of Apologies*, 14–42; Nobles, *The Politics of Official Apologies*, 4–13.

34. Erikson, *A New Species of Trouble*, 200.

35. "Remarks by President Barack Obama," May 23, 2013, *Federal News Service*, LexisNexis Academic.

36. Bernstein, *The Abuse of Evil*, 9, emphasis in original.

37. Neiman, *Evil in Modern Thought*.

38. Bernstein, *The Abuse of Evil*, 10.

39. Ibid., 10–11, emphasis in original.

40. Ibid., 83. Similarly, Neiman seeks to preserve the term "evil" while expressing dismay at contemporary abuses. The Bush administration, she argues, demonstrated that "some ways of abusing the word evil can lead to evil themselves." Neiman, *Evil in Modern Thought*, xiv. Again, the atrocities committed at Abu Ghraib illustrate this point powerfully.

41. Williams, *Modern Tragedy*, 59.

42. On anomie, see Eyerman, *The Cultural Sociology of Political Assassination*, 12–13. On *ressentiment*, see Olick, *The Politics of Regret*, 153–173.

43. Alexander et al., *Cultural Trauma and Collective Identity*, 1.

44. Alexander, *Trauma*, 26–27.

45. This quotation, along with all quotations in the preceding paragraph, is from "Remarks by President Barack Obama," April 18, 2013, *Federal News Service*, LexisNexis Academic.

46. Barack Obama, "Remarks on the Arrest of Terrorist Attack Suspect Dzhokhar Tsarnaev," April 19, 2013. Online by Gerhard Peters and John T. Woolley, *The American Presidency Project*, http://www.presidency.ucsb.edu/ws/?pid=103501.
47. Ibid.
48. On "transcultural" frameworks, see Erll, "Travelling Memory," 4–18. On "cosmopolitan" frameworks, see Levy and Sznaider, *The Holocaust and Memory in a Global Age*, 2–4 and passim.
49. Daniel Levy and Natan Sznaider, *Human Rights and Memory* (University Park, PA: The Pennsylvania State University Press, 2010), 56.
50. Erll, "Travelling Memory," 9, 7, emphasis in original.
51. Calhoun, *Nations Matter*, 1.
52. Jeffrey Alexander offers valuable reflections on the symbolic role of the British prime minister in comparison with that of the U.S. president. "British history unrolls a sacred scroll of prime ministers who became triumphant heroes and casts down others as profane," he argues. "This process of democratic collective representation unfolds alongside a powerful monarchy that would seem, in principle, to separate the expressive from the instrumental functions of government but in practice has not. Indeed, as leaders not only of party but also government, prime ministers often assume a symbolic superiority over rank-and-file party members more exaggerated than the distance between presidents and powerful, longer-serving senators in the United States." Prime ministers, he points out, "rule in a more sovereign manner than American presidents, who face divided power, and they can serve longer terms and be voted into office time after time." There are thus powerful symbolic dimensions to the office of prime minister, and its occupants "have extraordinary performative opportunity to become legendary (or not) in their own times." Alexander, *The Performance of Politics*, 295–296.
53. Tony Blair, "Prime Minister's Speech to the U.S. Congress," July 18, 2003, The U.K. Government Web Archive, http://collections.europarchive.org/tna/20060726063803/http://pm.gov.uk/output/Page4220.asp.
54. Ibid.
55. Ibid.
56. "Statement by Prime Minister Blair on the London Bomb Blasts," July 7, 2007, G8 Information Centre, University of Toronto, http://www.g8.utoronto.ca/summit/2005gleneagles/blair_blasts050707.html.
57. Tony Blair, "Downing Street Statement Following Terror Attacks in London," July 7, 2005, The U.K. Government Web Archive, http://collections.europarchive.org/tna/20060726063803/http://pm.gov.uk/output/Page7858.asp.
58. Ibid.
59. Ibid.
60. Alan Hamilton, "Terrorists Will Not Change Our Way of Life, Says Queen," *The Times*, July 9, 2005, 7.
61. "Royal London Hospital, Following Terrorist Bombs in London," July 8, 2005, Official Website of the British Monarchy, Speeches and Articles, http://www.royal.gov.uk/LatestNewsandDiary/Speechesandarticles/2005/TheQueenthanksmedicalandemergencyworkersfortheirre.aspx.
62. Ibid.
63. "World War II Commemorative Event, Horse Guards Parade," July 10, 2005, Official Website of the British Monarchy, Speeches and Articles, http://www.

royal.gov.uk/LatestNewsandDiary/Speechesandarticles/2005/TheQueenmark
sthe60thanniversaryoftheendofWorldWarI.aspx.

64. All quotations in this paragraph are from Tony Blair, "Statement to Parliament on the London Bombings," July 11, 2005, The U.K. Government Web Archive, http://collections.europarchive.org/tna/20060726063803/http:// pm.gov.uk/output/Page7903.asp.

65. Of the 52 people who died in the bombings, 36 were British citizens. Sandra Laville, "Angry Families Threaten to Boycott Remembrance Service at St. Paul's," The Guardian, November 1, 2005, 11.

66. Matthew Beard, "Europe Will Fall Silent to Mourn the Victims of Suicide Attacks," The Independent, July 14, 2005, 11; Neil Tweedie and Sally Pook, "A Solemn Silence Speaks Volumes in the Capital," The Daily Telegraph, July 15, 2005, 3. As Vinitzky-Seroussi and Teeger note, moments of silence— "intentional, purposive and planned in advance"—"can become the ultimate mechanism through which to promote memory." Interrupting "the usual flow of time, of gestures and bodily movements, of speech, and of thoughts," ritualized moments of silence may come "to be internalized without external surveillance, creating 'docile bodies' disciplined in the act of memory." Vinitzky-Seroussi and Teeger, "Unpacking the Unspoken," 1108–1109.

67. Tweedie and Pook, "A Solemn Silence Speaks Volumes."

68. Beard, "Europe Will Fall Silent."

69. Joan Smith, "So What is the Way to Express Public Grief?," The Independent, July 15, 2005, 33; Tweedie and Pook, "A Solemn Silence Speaks Volumes."

70. Alan Hamilton, "Cities Stand Still and Silent to Send Defiant Message," The Times, July 15, 2005, 9.

71. Ben Okri, "Lines in Potentis," in Wild (London: Rider, 2012), 26.

72. Johann Hari, "Vigil for the Dead in the Universal City," The Independent, July 15, 2005, 6.

73. Tweedie and Pook, "A Solemn Silence Speaks Volumes."

74. Neil Tweedie, "Grieving Parents Take Tube to July 7 Service," The Daily Telegraph, November 2, 2005, 3.

75. Sean O'Neill, "All Faiths Stand United as London Remembers the Victims of July 7," The Times, November 2, 2005, 14.

76. See, e.g., Blair's series of foreign policy speeches in the spring of 2006, delivered in London, Australia, and the United States, respectively. Tony Blair, "'Clash about Civilisations' Speech," March 21, 2006, The U.K. Government Web Archive, http://collections.europarchive.org/tna/20060726063803/ http://pm.gov.uk/output/Page9224.asp; "'Global Alliance for Global Values' Speech," March 27, 2006, The U.K. Government Web Archive, http:// collections.europarchive.org/tna/20060726063803/http://pm.gov.uk/ output/Page9245.asp; "PM's Foreign Policy Speech—Third in a Series of Three," May 26, 2006, The U.K. Government Web Archive, http://collections. europarchive.org/tna/20060726063803/http://pm.gov.uk/output/ Page9549.asp.

77. On the controversies over the Iraq War in the years preceding the bombings, see Smith, Why War?, 185–195.

78. Laville, "Angry Families Threaten to Boycott."

79. This and the descriptions in the preceding paragraph are from Alan Hamilton, "At Noon, Nation Keeps Two Minutes' Silence," The Times, July 7, 2006, 3.

80. Sally Pook, "Regent's Park," The Daily Telegraph, July 8, 2006, 5.

81. Sally Pook, "Names to be Read Out on Day of Mourning," *The Daily Telegraph*, July 7, 2006, 14.

82. Sandra Laville, "July 7 Memorial Service: Prime Minister Faces Families of the Dead," *The Guardian*, November 2, 2005, 7; Pook, "Names to be Read Out on Day of Mourning."

83. Pook, "Regent's Park"; "London Bombings Remembered," CBS News, July 7, 2006, http://www.cbsnews.com/videos/london-bombings-remembered/. The poem "Death is Nothing at All" is drawn from Holland's 1910 sermon "King of Terrors," in Henry Scott Holland, *Facts of the Faith; Being a Collection of Sermons Not Hitherto Published in Book Form* (London: Longman, Greens and Co., 1919).

84. Shadab Vajdi, "You Can't Have Departed," translated by Lotfali Khonji. Unpublished poem. For media coverage, see Pook, "Regent's Park"; "London Bombings Remembered."

85. All quotations in this and the preceding paragraph are from Weber, "Science as a Vocation," in *From Max Weber*, 143, 152, emphasis in original.

INDEX

Note: The letter 'n' following locators refers to notes

"The Great Ground Zero Heist," 177–178
Greenfeld, Liah, 218 n. 28
Ground zero, 66, 174
  debate over meaning of, 174–195
  lower Manhattan as, 66, 118, 128, 158
  meaning of term, 243 n. 96
  reconstruction of, debates on, 174–175, 205
  for World War II atomic bombings, 66
"Ground Zero Cross," 175, 186–191. *See also* "World Trade Center Cross"
"Ground zero mosque," 175, 182–186. *See also* Park51, "ground zero mosque"
"Ground Zero Spirit" photograph, 115–116
Gurley, Phineas D., 33

Haberman, Clyde, 172, 266 n. 81
Hagopian, Patrick, 86
Hamilton, Edith, 246 n. 35, n. 38
Haynes, Charles C., 190
Hellman, John, 78
Hendrix, Jimi, 81
Henn, T. R., 69
Hierophany, American Revolution as, 230 n. 38
Hiroshima atomic bombing
  Bush, G. H. W., refusal to apologize for, 57–58
  Japan's memory of, 243 n. 95
  political discourse on, 65–66, 203, 243 n. 91
  presidential addresses on, 53, 65–66, 243 n. 91
  Reagan on anniversary of, 66
  Stimson on, 241 n. 54
  Truman on, 53
Historical accretions, genres as, 11
History, traumatic, 9–10, 175
Hitler, Adolph, comparison with September 11 perpetrators, 125
Holland, Henry Scott, 212
Holocaust, 222 n. 55
  postmodern condition and, 7–8
  as symbolic representation of evil, 256 n. 14
Howe, Julia Ward, 32–33, 107
Hume, David, on evil, 5

Hunter, James Davison, on culture wars, 8
Hybridization, 148, 156–158

Ideology, Geertz on, 226 n. 90
Imagined community, 6
Ingle, David, 229 n. 27
Innocent victims, September 11 dead as, 153
International family theme, in September 11 commemorations, 165–166
International Freedom Center, 175–181
  Burlingame and allies' response to assurances on, 179–180
  Burlingame's initial critique of, 177–178
  founding and vision for, 175–177
  New York Times editorials on, 180
  Pataki's abandonment of, 180–181
  Pataki's initial response to Burlingame on, 179
  Take Back the Memorial and "Campaign America" against, 178
  Tofel's response to Burlingame on, 178–179
Inversion, 81
Iraq invasion, 131, 133, 257 n. 30, n. 32. *See also* Legitimation, consolation and
Iraq War
  Bush on (*See under* Bush, George W.)
  Obama on, 139–141, 260 n. 91

Jacobs, Ronald, 248–249 n. 85, 273–274 n. 24
Jeremiad, 22–23
  American, 23, 228–229 n. 14
Johnson, Lyndon
  on John F. Kennedy's assassination, 38
  on Martin Luther King, Jr.'s assassination, 76
  on Pearl Harbor anniversary, 240 n. 44
  on Robert Kennedy's assassination, 77
  on Vietnam War, 79–81
Jordan, Brian, 186–188, 190
Jowell, Tessa, 212

Obama, Barack (*continued*)
  2011, May 1, death of Osama bin
    Laden, 141–142
  2013, May, National Defense
    University, 144–146, 204
  2014, on ISIS, 147
  2014, May, West Point
    commencement, 146
  on Boston Marathon bombing,
    206–207
  at Iraq War close, 140–141
  on Iraq War, during campaign,
    139–140, 260 n. 91
  on Iraq War, during presidency,
    140–141
Official politics, as "field," 226 n. 96
Oklahoma City bombing, 39–42,
  263 n. 40, 274 n. 27
Okri, Ben, 210–211
Olick, Jeffrey, 9, 11, 59, 65, 122–123,
  169, 223 n. 66–67, 224 n. 74, n. 78
1 World Trade Center, 192, 272 n. 112

Paine, Thomas, 25–26, 51, 80
Park51, "ground zero mosque," 175,
  182–186
  American Freedom Defense
    Initiative and Geller on, 184
  Anti-Defamation League on, 183
  beginning of controversy over,
    182–183
  Bloomberg on, 184
  Giuliani on, 183–184
  Palin on, 183
  public opinion on, 185
  revision of plans for, 185–186
Pasha, Izak-El Mu'eed, 119
Pataki, George
  Freedom Tower dedication speech of,
    272 n. 112
  on International Freedom Center
    debate, 179, 180–181
  on September 11 anniversaries, 1–2,
    163, 164–165
Pearl Harbor
  anniversaries of, 55–62, 240 n. 44
  Bush, G. H. W., on 50th anniversary
    of, 58–62
  dedication speeches for U. S. S.
    Arizona Memorial, 240 n. 45

Engelhardt on, 238 n. 12
Ford on, 240 n. 44
initial interpretation of, 48–51
Johnson on, 240 n. 44
Kennedy on, John F., 240 n. 44
September 11 comparisons to, 108,
  109, 111–112, 179, 183, 201
Pentagon September 11 dead
  as fallen soldiers, 149–152
  memorial ceremony for, 150–152,
    262 n. 16
Periodization, 23
Perry, William, on D-Day 50th
  anniversary, 63
Pirro, Robert, 74, 251 n. 120
Political assassination, 37–38, 71–78.
  See also Assassination, political
Political consolation, 3–5, 11–13,
  196–197
Political demonology, 133,
  239–240 n. 43, 274 n. 32
Politicians. *See also specific politicians*
  rhetorical tasks of, 11–13, 196–197
  speechmaking genres of, 11–13, 120,
    137
  wordless gestures of, 195
Politics
  of legitimation, 122–123
  meaning-making practices in, 13
  official, 226 n. 96
  of regret, 9, 65, 203
  religion and, 12
Postmodern condition, 7–8
Postwar era, 7–8
Powell, Colin
  February 5, 2003, UN speech of,
    130–131
  on Shanksville as modern
    Gettysburg, 152
Pratt, Julius W., 232 n. 68
Premediation, 7, 11–12, 197
  September 11 and, 205–207
  World War II commemoration as,
    55–64
Presidency, rhetorical, 13, 196,
  225 n. 85
Puritans, 21–23

Queen Elizabeth II, on July 7, 2005,
  London suicide bombings, 209